FIRST
THINGS

FIRST THINGS

AN INQUIRY INTO THE FIRST PRINCIPLES OF MORALS AND JUSTICE

Hadley Arkes

PRINCETON UNIVERSITY PRESS • PRINCETON, NEW JERSEY

Copyright © 1986 by Princeton University Press

Published by Princeton University Press, 41 William Street,
Princeton, New Jersey 08540
In the United Kingdom: Princeton University Press,
Guildford, Surrey

All Rights Reserved

Library of Congress Cataloging in Publication Data will
be found on the last printed page of this book

ISBN 0-691-07702-9 (cloth)   02247-X (pbk)

This book has been composed in Linotron Sabon

Cloth bound editions of Princeton University Press books
are printed on acid-free paper, and binding materials are
chosen for strength and durability. Paperbacks, although
satisfactory for personal collections, are not usually
suitable for library rebinding.

Printed in the United States of America by Princeton
University Press, Princeton, New Jersey

For Daniel Nicholas Robinson

Every man is a good judge of what he understands: in special subjects the specialist, over the whole field of knowledge the man of general culture. This is the reason why political science is not a proper study for the young. The young man is not versed in the practical business of life from which politics draws its premises and its data. He is, besides, swayed by his feelings, with the result that he will make no headway and derive no benefit from a study the end of which is not *knowing* but *doing*. It makes no difference whether the immaturity is in age or in character. The defect is not due to lack of years but to living the kind of life which is a succession of unrelated emotional experiences. To one who is like that, knowledge is as unprofitable as it is to the morally unstable. On the other hand, for those whose desires and actions have a rational basis, a knowledge of these principles of morals must be of great advantage.

—Aristotle, *Nicomachean Ethics*, bk. I, ch. 3

CONTENTS

PREFACE

In his redoubtable comedy *Jumpers*, Tom Stoppard gave us a picture of the true skeptics of our age, the people who will not even concede the possibility of "knowing" that the train for Bristol left yesterday from Paddington Station. After all, the report on the departure of the train could have been a "malicious report or a collective trick of memory." Nor could it be known that the same train will leave the station tomorrow, for "nothing is certain." The skeptics will agree that the train for Bristol leaves Paddington Station only when they themselves are there to see it leave—and even then they will agree "only on the understanding that all the observable phenomena associated with the train leaving Paddington could equally well be accounted for by Paddington leaving the train." These earnest people, who tenaciously deny their capacity to know anything, let alone anything of moral consequence, may nevertheless show an inclination to vote, to raise children, and even to run for office. They get on, that is, with the business of life, in offering judgments for the raising of their children and the better ordering of their communities, even while they insist that there are no grounds on which any of these judgments can be regarded as true and justified.

Those who spend their lives in academic enclaves, or in professions occupied with the products of those enclaves, will know that Stoppard's portrait is a caricature of a type who is very real, and who walks among us. That type could be found in the eighteenth century, in the restricted circles of those who were read in "skeptical philosophy," but it did not command the same credulity among the educated as it commands today, and it did not claim the same presence in the ranks of serious lawyers and jurists. In 1793, in the first case that brought forth a substantial opinion from our Supreme Court, Justice James Wilson recognized that the Court could not appeal to any precedents built up from its own cases, and so he found it necessary to speak first about "the principles of general jurisprudence." But before he and his colleagues would begin setting forth the principles of legal judgment, he found it necessary to acknowledge something of the laws of reason and the grounds of our moral understanding. Before Wilson would invoke the authority of any case at law or any writer on matters legal, he would invoke the authority of "Dr. [Thomas] Reid, in his excellent enquiry into the human mind, on the principles of *common sense*, speaking of the sceptical and illiberal philosophy, which under bold, but false pretentions to liberality, prevailed in many parts of Europe before he wrote."

In other words, the Court would ascend to the task of judgment only after it insisted, in the first instance, that it was indeed possible to judge: the Court would reject that "skepticism" in philosophy which denied the possibility of "knowing" moral truths, just as it denied the possibility of "knowing" almost anything else. To put it another way, the Court would insist on the possibility of moral understanding and the existence of moral truths as the only intelligible ground on which men, anywhere, could claim the authority of office and presume to render judgments that were justified and binding. As it turned out, the judgment that the Court rendered that day in the case of *Chisholm* v. *Georgia* was soon swept away by a constitutional amendment (the Eleventh). As a consequence, the case is rarely read these days, for it built no lasting precedent in the groundwork of our law. And yet, even though the judgment of the Court was overturned, nothing in that constitutional amendment could sweep away the impressive reasoning that was put forth, with clarity and elegance, by Wilson and Chief Justice Jay. But the amendment that dissolved the authority of *Chisholm* v. *Georgia* swept away from our recollection the opinions of Wilson and Jay. It helped, then, to remove even further from our own generation the memory of a time when jurists of the first rank were familiar with the writings of Reid and other serious works of philosophy—a time when the learned men of the age recognized that skepticism in morals was a false ally of "liberality" and no tenable foundation for those who would preserve constitutional government.

I shall have occasion, in the opening chapters of this book, to cite again the writings of Thomas Reid, and part of my purpose here is to restore that tradition of understanding in which Reid held such an evident, important place. That tradition of moral reflection took seriously the notion of "first principles" in morals and law, as well as in physics and mathematics, because it recognized that our knowledge, in all its branches, found its common philosophic origin in the laws of reason or the "principles of understanding." That tradition helped to make the statesmen and jurists of James Wilson's day conspicuously better than the statesmen and jurists of our own. It freed them from the curious infirmity of imposing judgments with the force of law, or of seeking to preserve republican government in the face of dangers from abroad, while at the same time professing no ground of surety that any of these judgments were true, or that the moral preference for constitutional government over despotism represented anything more than the tentative beliefs that happened to be shared within this particular community. This book finds its place in a body of writing which has emerged in recent years and which seeks to take seriously again the tradition of political philosophy and the truths that it once took, as its mission, to impart. A project of this kind would seek to detach the urbane from the need to affect the current styles of moral skepticism. It would try to remind them of a tradition of understanding in which the worldly and the educated need not be embarrassed to acknowledge, in public, their awareness of moral truths, even while they may decorously tremble at the responsibility that comes with "knowing."

THIS BOOK was written during a year of sabbatic leave that was furnished, and in large part supported, by Amherst College, and for that generous provision I am grateful to the president and trustees of Amherst. But it was possible to have the benefit of a full year of work on this project as a result of the substantial support that was offered, also, by the Institute of Educational Affairs. I would especially thank Philip Marcus, the executive director of the IEA, and two members of his board, Diane Ravitch and Leslie Lenkowsky, for the encouragement that long preceded the grants from the Institute. Several friends and colleagues read the manuscript in its entirety; at times they read sections again in later drafts, and they often gave me, in writing, the benefit of their comments and suggestions. For these acts of devoted service and supererogation I wish to thank Daniel Robinson, Werner Dannhauser, John de Gioia, Anne Marks, and Marvin Olasky. Other friends were kind enough to review sections of the manuscript, and among them I would express my thanks to George Kateb, William Kennick, and my faithful editor over three books, Sanford Thatcher.

Almost every section of this book has been molded by an effort to make the arguments accessible—and disarming—to the students in my course on "Political Obligations." Their engagement in "the argument" has moved well beyond the classroom and conventional hours; it has brought to my door students I had never met, but who had evidently listened for hours to students bearing my arguments, and who now wished to carry on the dispute more directly. I hope that my character has been improved by these exertions. I am sure that I have come to understand my own project better as a result of the need to explain it to the resistant, and to deal with the criticisms raised by my most thoughtful students. I could not do justice in offering a list of their names or contributions; I will simply record a special thanks to three former students who worked closely with me and absorbed themselves deeply in these arguments: Bruce Shortt, Peter Weidman, and Peter Ezersky are now applying their arts of philosophy, to the benefit of the republic, in the practice of law.

Since the time I began to teach on the questions in this book, almost every section of the project has been the topic of an extended discussion with Daniel Robinson, over coffee at night, on the long-distance wire, or during rambling walks through the streets of Georgetown. He continues in that rare office of friend and tutor. He has ever been my most eager audience and my most pointed—and benign—critic. It may be strange to confess that almost every conversation we have had over the past fifteen years has touched, in one way or another, on the enduring arguments, reflected in these pages, over contingent and necessary truths and the ground of our moral understanding. That curious fact may stand as the measure of this friendship. He has preserved an interest in this book in all its phases; and apart from my own gifted teachers, no one has contributed so broadly and persistently to the understanding that informs these pages. For these reasons—and more—this book is dedicated to him.

Amherst, Massachusetts   H.A.
March 1985

FIRST
THINGS

I

INTRODUCTION

In the opening passage of the *Politics*, as Aristotle begins to explain the nature and ends of a polity, he takes care to make the elementary point that "men do all their acts with a view to achieving something which is, in their view, a good." Whether we seek to change any state of affairs or to resist change, whether we decide to spend our days writing books or repairing cars, all of our actions imply at least a rough understanding of the things that are, in general, good or bad, better or worse. When we contemplate those things that stand, universally, as good or bad, justified or unjustified, we are in the domain of morals (or ethics); and as Aristotle understood, the matter of ethics is, irreducibly, a *practical* concern: ethics involves an understanding of the standards that ultimately guide our practice or the activities of our daily lives. Those standards, of necessity, are abstract; if they were not, they could not be universal in their application. There is nothing "empirical" about them, and yet no practical action may be taken in our daily lives, no decision may be made between one course of action or another, without looking outward to these general understandings about the things that are right and wrong, just and unjust.

Of course, as we shall see, not every decision we make has moral significance. Whether we decide to eat *coq au vin* rather than spaghetti, whether we travel by bus or by train, our choice may not be affected with large moral meanings. But choices of this kind are properly available to us only when we have assured ourselves that we are choosing among legitimate things. If the choice were between the eating of spaghetti or human flesh, if we stepped on a bus in order to get to work saving lives in a hospital or to travel on a mission for the Mafia, then the act of eating or traveling would not be so barren of moral significance. Eating and traveling, we might say, are instrumental "goods"; they are means to larger ends. Whether they are ultimately justified or not will depend on the grounds on which we can know that the ends to which they are directed are themselves ultimately justified or unjustified. And the principles that establish our understanding of these things form the subject of morals or ethics.

But as Aristotle recognized, they also constitute the foundation of politics and political understanding. It was the mark of Aristotle's own understanding that his work on the *Ethics* immediately preceded and formed the groundwork for his treatise on politics. At the end of the *Ethics*, Aristotle derided those Sophists who sought to teach what was desirable in politics simply by making a compilation of all existing laws and constitutions and affecting to choose "the best"—as though the choice of the best would well up from the list, without any need to reflect on the principles of judgment.[1] For it was only from the principles or standards of judgment that the distinction between the good and the bad could finally be drawn. In politics we are faced with the task of legislating, of making laws that are binding on whole communities. The act of legislating would stand out as a massive act of presumption unless it were understood that there are in fact propositions with a universal reach, which can define what is good or bad, just or unjust, for people in general. If that were not the case, if those principles of justice did not exist, it would be impossible to show why it should ever be justified to restrict the freedom of individuals and displace their private choice with the imposition of a common law.

The central questions in politics are questions about the nature of justice, and the people who spend their lives talking about political events—whether they are historians, economists, citizens, or philosophers—all find themselves casting judgments. They will offer judgments about the kinds of public policies that are right and wrong, about the revolutions in this world that are good or bad, and about the kinds of political regimes that are just and unjust. And yet, to place one set of laws or one political order above another, to arrange things in a hierarchy of preference or desirability, is to render a judgment that is distinctly *moral*. A judgment, in turn, can issue only from a proposition—i.e., only from a statement which affirms or denies that something is true. It is hardly comprehensible to make a judgment (to say that one line is longer than another, or that one public law is better than another) unless there are grounds on which to think that the judgment is *true*. Still less would it make sense to commend a judgment to other people—to suggest that any reasonable person should favor a certain law, say, on civil rights—unless the grounds on which the law would be "good" were thought to be true for others as well as for oneself.

In short, the judgments on politics that seem to be offered so widely and emphatically today would have to imply the existence of *moral principles*, the principles on which moral judgments would have to be founded if they are to be regarded as valid or comprehensible. But historians, economists, journalists, taxi drivers—in brief, most people who offer judgments on the politics of the day—have not taken as

[1] Aristotle, *Nicomachean Ethics*, bk. X, ch. 9.

4

their mission, or their dominant professional concern, the task of getting clear about the nature of those principles on which their judgments rest. In fact, the paradox of our own day is that these political judgments are offered most intensely at a time when more and more literate people have become convinced that there are no principles of morals and justice in the strictest sense. They have become convinced, that is, that there are no propositions about the nature of right and wrong which are both universal and true, and which therefore hold their truth across cultures. Anyone with experience in the academy will recognize that moral "relativism" has become the secular religion these days among those with a college education. In this persuasion, moral understandings are replaced by "values," which are regarded as "good" and valid only because they are "valued" by the person or the culture that holds them. Even among those who recoil from moral "relativism," there is a disposition to think that moral understanding depends on certain religious beliefs, which must be accepted on faith, and which cannot be verified ultimately by reason. And so the most that can be said, in the perspective dominant today, is that "moral beliefs" may be widely shared; but whether those "beliefs" are also true—whether they are more than mere beliefs—is a question, for the most part, that is put beyond serious reckoning.

But these dispositions, we know, are part of our modern condition; they were not the understandings of the men who founded this republic or of the philosophers who shaped the minds of our political men. John Locke had no doubt that "morality [stood] amongst the sciences capable of demonstration: wherein I doubt not but from self-evident propositions by necessary consequences, as incontestible as those in mathematics, the measures of right and wrong might be made out to anyone that will apply himself with the same indifference and attention to the one as he does to the other of these sciences."[2] Our most influential pamphleteer, Thomas Paine, had no embarrassment in offering a "Dissertation on First Principles of Government." "Every art and science," he wrote, "has some point or alphabet at which the study of that art or science begins and by the assistance of which the progress is facilitated. The same method ought to be observed with respect to the science of government."[3] In this manner both Locke and Paine were elaborating upon the sign that stood above the door of Plato's Academy: "Let no man enter here who does not know geometry." The best preparation for philosophy and the moral sciences

[2] John Locke, *An Essay Concerning Human Understanding* [1690], ed. A.S. Pringle-Pattison (Oxford: Clarendon Press, 1924), p. 277.

[3] Thomas Paine, "Dissertation on First Principles of Government," in *Common Sense and Other Political Writings* (Indianapolis: Bobbs-Merrill, 1953), p. 155.

lay in that discipline which began with axioms or necessary truths, and which proceeded to extend its body of knowledge through the most rigorous application of reason and logic.

IN THE CIRCLES of those who discuss high-minded things, the most widely traveled fallacy these days seems to be the notion that the presence of disagreement on matters of morals must indicate the absence of universal truths. Yet, it is not uncommon for mathematicians to disagree over proofs and conclusions, and nothing in their disagreement seems to inspire anyone to challenge the foundations of mathematics or to call into question the possibility of knowing mathematical truths. The challenge is not offered, the doubts are not registered, because it is understood that mathematics rests on a body of axioms that guarantee the existence of *some* right answers. It seems to be merely assumed, without critical reflection, that mathematics is somehow different in that way from moral understanding. In that respect, our modern outlook depends on a critical act of forgetting what Locke and Plato, Madison and Lincoln, once knew: that there are axioms or first principles in the domain of morals as well as in mathematics; that those principles are virtually indifferent to variations in culture and geography, in the same way that the law of contradiction is indifferent to the distinction between London and Istanbul; and that in morals, as well as in mathematics, the presence of axioms or necessary truths makes it possible to have *some* right answers.

Several years ago, in beginning one of my courses at Amherst, I remarked to my students, partly in jest, that we ought to stop wasting our time with arguments that are "refutable." By that I simply meant that we spend so much of our time, in the humanities and the social sciences, lingering with the problematic and the baffling, that it is probably worth taking a brief moment to consider those truths in the domain of morals and law that we not only know, but that *cannot be otherwise.* This book is an attempt to take up that mandate by "reminding" us of the things that philosophers and statesmen once knew. I use "reminding" here in the spirit of Plato's *Meno*, in the gentle fiction that all knowledge is a recollection of things we once knew, or of things locked away inside us that may spring forth, out of our natural recognitions, if only they are unlocked. And so my responsibilities here may be satisfied mainly by recalling, in sequences aptly arranged, the recognitions that were put in place long ago by the gifted writers who have formed our tradition of moral philosophy. I will claim only a modest liberty to "improve" upon the things that were left us. I will try to fill in ellipses and make certain connections more explicit. On occasion I may even presume to read certain teachings in a different light, which may be more consistent with their own premises, and which may make them, altogether, slightly clearer and more defensible. In any event, it will be my pleasure to point out that what I am offering here is not entirely novel: most of the ingredients have been furnished already by a tradition of writing and reflection on politics, and the only exertion of genius that the modern commentator need supply is that of presenting more artfully what writers in the past have sought to uncover for us.

THE CENTRAL PROBLEM, of course, involves the ground on which we can claim to "know" the existence of morals or any truth of moral standing. That question is posed to us in the most dramatic and consequential way in politics, because in politics people are being committed through the exercise of authority: they are being *obligated* to obey, to respect as law, policies with which they may deeply disagree. That state of affairs presents the sternest test of the question of whether those who make law for others are acting merely on the basis of their own self-interest, or whether they are legislating on the basis of propositions that are indeed valid and binding for everyone. As we advance in this book, we will be moving through a series of cases that have been the source of intense controversy over the years, as the law has sought to commit citizens to policies that have not always been popular or congenial: the obligation to participate in a war; the obligation to go to the rescue of those in danger (including the obligation to intervene abroad and go to the rescue of people in another country); and the obligation not to destroy a fetus in the womb.

But there is always the possibility of a tension between self-interest and morality, between the things that may give us pleasure and the things that we are obliged to do out of a respect for the commands of moral reason. In fact, there would be no real meaning for morality in our language and our lives if morals were reduced simply to those things which accorded with our own self-interest. In that sense there is nothing unique about the policies or tensions I have mentioned here. Any moral principle will come into conflict, at one point or another, with someone's self-interest. And that is the perennial problem for the polity as it faces the need to legislate on *any* matter, not merely on questions of war and abortion. I have chosen these questions because they happen to inspire a more vigorous challenge, which will take us back, persistently, to "first principles." It is important to bear in mind, then, that the cases I have selected here become important only because they offer instances which test out the principles I am putting forth. They may help to draw out the implications that arise from "first principles," and they will perform their proper function if they keep directing our attention back—if they keep raising questions about the adequacy of the groundwork I have established, in the earlier sections of the book, as the foundation for my judgments.

My own reflection has finally brought me to conclude that Kant was precisely accurate in his observation that anything valid in the domain of morals and law must arise as an inference either from the idea of law (or the very concept of morals) or from the notion of a "rational being"—a being who is free to form his own acts, and who has access, through his reason, to the understandings that must govern his choice. I will try, in the pages that follow, to show how moral judgments may—indeed, *must*—be extracted from this core of understanding. The best place to begin is where the two parts come together: as Kant remarked, "the idea of law . . . is present only in a rational being."[4] That is to say, only a being possessed of reason would be able to conceive, in the first place, the notion of a "law" or moral rule which may be in conflict with his own self-interest. But that is simply to recall the connection between morals and law that was made at the very beginning of political philosophy: In the first pages of the *Politics*, where Aristotle set out to explain why a polity is necessary, he explicitly rejected the rationales that were to become familiar and dominant in our own day. He rejected the contention that a polity can be justified by the need to provide security against assaults and to promote commercial intercourse. What he argued instead was that the case for polity arose decisively, preeminently, from the existence of morals itself—and from the nature of a being who had the capacity for morals.

It is a measure of the erosion in our own intellectual tradition that this original understanding of the foundations of law and polity may come as a surprise to most of our educated classes today, even though it was firmly settled among the literate in the middle of the last century. What is even more sobering is that this ancient teaching is likely to be quite as unfamiliar to most of the men and women who fill out the judiciary. It would be no small step toward the restoration of our own, best tradition—and no mean entry into the "first principles" of morals and justice—if we recalled, in the first instance, this original case for polity and the classic understanding of the connection between morals and law.

[4] Immanuel Kant, *Groundwork of the Metaphysics of Morals* [1785], trans. H.J. Paton (New York: Harper & Row, 1964), p. 69 [chapter 1].

PART ONE
THE GROUNDWORK OF MORAL JUDGMENT

II

ON THE CAPACITY FOR MORALS
AND THE ORIGINS OF LAW

Aristotle assumed, without saying, what modern political science would raise to the point of a more explicit recognition: that it is the presence of "law" or authority which marks the character of a polity. In the modern vernacular, the "political system" is that association which has the authority to make and enforce decisions regarded as *binding* for a society.[1] It is the attribute of law, of course, that it binds; it states a rule that will be regarded as compulsory for all who come within its jurisdiction. Some commentators have suggested that the connection between law and "obligation" traces back to a common root in the Latin *ligare* (to bind). That is why the notion of "obligation" conveys the sense of the moral stakes—and the sources of bitter divisiveness—that are bound up with the nature of law. It is the peculiarity of law that it may bind, may create an obligation to obey, even on the part of people who had no agency in making the law and who may be hostile to its maxims. For that reason, the obligation to the law must have a different source from the obligation that arises, say, out of a promise tendered personally in a contract or agreement. As we shall see, the obligation to the law may properly arise only from a moral principle that underlies the law and that compels respect or obedience, quite apart from the feelings anyone may bear.

But the essential logic of law is widely understood, even if its moral properties and requirements are not commonly recognized. Almost everyone understands that when we pass a law which forbids discrimination on the basis of race in places of public accommodation, we are not saying, "This measure reflects the moral understandings held by a majority of people in this country, and everyone who is struck by its moral force ought to join us in obeying it." We are saying, rather, that people are *obliged* to obey the law, even if it runs counter to what they may regard as their "moral" convictions. The logic of the law, then, is a logic of commitment, and as I hope to make clear in a moment, the law draws its properties here from the logic of morals. The law displaces private notions of good and bad in favor of moral understandings that are held to be universally valid—and therefore binding on everyone within the society. That connection was under-

[1] See David Easton, *The Political System* (New York: Knopf, 1953), ch. 5.

11

stood at the beginning by Aristotle: the defining feature of a polity was the presence of an authority that could lawfully govern the whole of society, and that state of affairs could be justified *only* if one could get clear on the necessary connection between the logic of law and the logic of morals.

Aristotle observed in the opening section of the *Politics* that the polity is a "natural" association for human beings ("it is evident," he wrote, "that the polis [or polity] belongs to the class of things that exist by nature, and that man is by nature an animal intended to live in a polis"[2]). Like the family, the polity was an outgrowth or an emanation of human nature, and so the question was, From what part of our nature did the polity arise? Aristotle remarked that the polity was "prior in the order of nature to the family and the individual" and that, among all other associations, such as the family, the polis was the most "sovereign and inclusive association," the "completion of associations existing by nature."[3] With that, Aristotle seemed to suggest that the polity was not only a reflection of human nature, but that it was a reflection of the highest parts of human nature, the parts that deserved to be "sovereign" over the rest.

Aristotle was also careful to mention that the condition of living in a polity was not possible or necessary for all kinds of beings. For animals it was not possible, and for gods it was not necessary. It was both possible *and* necessary for human beings—which meant that the polity was an emanation not only from the things that were highest in human nature, but from the things that were most *distinctively* human. Aristotle sought to mark off the things that were distinctively human by distinguishing human things from the things that were subhuman or superhuman. He began with the separation between the human and the subhuman—with the distinction between men and animals.

In drawing the distinction, Aristotle took as the decisive point that "man alone of the animals is furnished with the faculty of language." But Aristotle's meaning here may easily be deflected as "language" is taken to mean "speech," and as speech is converted into "communication." Very soon it will be suggested by an aspiring analyst that animals, too, are capable of "communicating": they may indicate their likes or dislikes, their desire to be fed and comforted. In the same vein it has been suggested that inanimate things, such as clouds, may have

[2] Aristotle, *Politics*, 1253a.
[3] *Ibid.*, 1252a.

12

"language": when clouds darken, they may "communicate" their "intention" to rain.

And yet, as Aristotle made clear, this was not the kind of language or speech he had in mind, and it may even be argued that it is not really speech that is truly decisive here after all, but the capacity marked by the kind of language that is distinctively human. As Aristotle put it, animals may emit sounds to indicate pleasure or pain, but human beings may do far more than that. Humans can make use of their language "to declare what is advantageous and what is the reverse, and . . . to declare what is just and what is unjust."[4] What Aristotle had in mind, then, was not really language itself, but language as a necessary means of giving reasons over matters of right and wrong. The same point was made in a telling way by the redoubtable Thomas Reid, the eighteenth-century philosopher: "A fox is said to use stratagems, but he cannot lie; because he cannot give his testimony, or plight his veracity. A dog is said to be faithful to his master; but no more is meant but that he is affectionate, for he never came under any engagement. I see no evidence that any brute animal is capable of either giving testimony or making a promise."[5]

It was argued to me recently by a sociobiologist that animals do indeed lie or deceive. A case was recalled in which a mother fox made sounds to simulate the noise of enemies; in that way, she managed to scare off her own offspring and keep them from grabbing away the food she had captured. But although the mother fox emitted sounds for the sake of deceiving, she did not "lie," and the point may be made more precisely in this way: when animals deceive and they are confronted with their own acts of deception, we do not expect them to *give excuses*. It is inconceivable, in other words, that they could give reasons to justify what they have done, and that capacity to offer justifications is really at the heart of what Aristotle understood, in this case, by the faculty of "speech." It will become evident later that, in any strict meaning, the notion of acting morally is bound up with the exercise of *giving reasons*. And by "giving reasons," of course, we would not mean merely reporting on one's motives ("I hit him because I felt the need for excitement"), but offering *justifications*. To say that human beings alone among animals have the capacity to give reasons over matters of right and wrong is virtually to say that human beings

---

[4] *Ibid.*, 1253a.

[5] Thomas Reid, *Essays on the Active Powers of the Human Mind* (Cambridge: MIT Press, 1969 [1788]), p. 442.

alone have the capacity for morals. Therefore, if the very nature of human beings makes it necessary and fitting that humans live in an association governed by law, this is not because we are the only creatures capable of generating lyrics or playful epigrams. The necessity of law and polity arise out of the unique capacity of human beings for moral judgment.

Aristotle was not fully explicit on the connection between the two—between the capacity for morals and the existence of polity—but his writing left little doubt that this connection was indeed established in his own understanding. "It is the peculiarity of man," he wrote, "in comparison with the rest of the animal world, that he alone possesses a perception of good and evil, of the just and the unjust; . . . and it is association in [a common perception] of these things which makes a family and a polis."[6] Hence the classic understanding that the polity is, most essentially, an ethical association: it is an association of people who are joined together by a sense of common ends; who found their lives together on procedures they regard, by and large, as just; and whose highest end is to cultivate an understanding of justice and morals among their own members. The task of the polity is not strictly to prevent pain or encourage the accumulation of wealth, because the polity would default on its commitments here every time it would visit punishment on wrongdoers or frustrate the projects of criminals. The responsibility of the political order is to preserve people, as much as possible, from suffering harm *unjustly*—which is to say that the mission of the polity is to render justice. And as it does that, it teaches something to its members in a public way about the principles on which it acts, the principles that define what is right and wrong, just and unjust.

In the classic understanding, the polity engages in moral teaching through the law. Just why that kind of teaching should be implicit in law becomes clear only when we understand the way in which the logic of morals meshes with the logic of law. At that point it will become clear, also, that it is the existence of morals itself which virtually *entails* the existence of law or polity. But before we explain that connection between the logic of morals and the logic of law, it is worth lingering for a moment with Aristotle's own elaboration of the problem. For one thing, it makes his own intention unmistakable; but it also manages to bring out, from a number of different angles, the

---

[6] Aristotle, *Politics*, 1253a.

implications that arise when the polity is understood, most essentially, as a moral association.

WHEN THE QUESTION is raised in our own time about the origins of polity, something absorbed from our current public philosophy manages to produce answers that are remarkably uniform. Whether the account is offered by the young or the old, by students or jurists, the reasons for having a political order are usually cast along two lines of justification: (1) to provide security against assaults on our lives or property, and (2) to establish the conditions that permit commerce to go forward and advance the material condition of our lives. This construction of the ends of political life would fit rather comfortably with the understanding held by Thomas Hobbes, and the coincidence is not accidental. These answers to the question are proffered by the "children" of a modern liberal political order, and Hobbes was one of the principal figures in the revolution in political philosophy that eventually shaped the modern political order. He was one of the leaders, that is, in the effort to scale down the ends of politics, to remove from political life those questions about the highest moral ends which proved so enduringly contentious, and which were so often productive of civil war. When the understanding of the age has been supplied by Hobbes, we may expect to have blocked from our view the understandings that came before Hobbes. And so it usually comes as a surprise to discover that Aristotle had anticipated, about two thousand years earlier, the kinds of arguments that would be made by Hobbes, and that he also managed to refute them.

Aristotle insisted that the polity could not be conceived merely as an "alliance" to provide for "mutual defense against all injury, or to ease exchange and promote economic intercourse." If those ends were sufficient, then "the Etruscans and the Carthaginians [who are united by such bonds] would be in the position of belonging to a single state; and the same would be true of all peoples who have commercial treaties with one another." That is to say, these rather modest ends could be achieved without the presence of law; they could be achieved quite often through the "treaties" that were contracted by two sovereign political orders, which made no pretense of sharing the same principles and subscribing to the same understandings of justice. In fact, these ends may be sought, in part, by enemies in a war. During the Second World War, the United States and Germany honored an informal agreement not to use poison gas on one another. More recently, the United States and the Soviet Union have entered into a series of treaties to reduce the risk of assault on one another (through the limitation of strategic arms), and for the purpose of encouraging commercial exchange. If the modern understanding were adequate, and those limited ends were sufficient to define the purposes of a polity, one would have to conclude that the United States and the Soviet Union had become, in effect, incorporated in the same polity. In that event, citizens of the United States would stand on no different plane, in relation to one another, from that on which they stand in relation to subjects of the Soviet Union. For if there are no other ends in politics apart from reducing the risk of assault and promoting commercial exchange, there would be no purpose contained in the political association of Americans that is not essentially contained in their association (through treaties) with the subjects of the Soviet state.

At the same time it would be evident that there would be no need for "law" in governing relations among individuals within the same society. The agreements fashioned between the United States and Germany (or between the United States and the Soviet Union) arose out of the self-interest of each party, and it was clear that the agreements would be preserved only so long as they were thought to serve the interests of the parties. In a similar way, the ends of providing "mutual defense against all injury" and promoting "economic intercourse" could be pursued within a society through the domestic equivalent of treaties: i.e., through a series of "contracts" that were entered into by individuals and corporations. People may be free, as they are now, to form mutual protective associations and hire their own police forces; they may be free to make contracts for the purpose of promoting trade. Neither of these purposes strictly requires the presence of law. The agreements arise out of self-interest, and like the treaties between sovereign states, their validity may be understood to rest on the enduring self-interest of the parties in preserving these relations of reciprocity.

The fact that contracts are enforced by law in our society does not mean that there is anything in the notion of a contract itself that requires the presence of law. If we have added the force of law to support contracts, that is because we recognize an "obligation" to respect certain promises even when that commitment no longer serves the self-interest of the person who made the original promise. In other words, the law enters for the sake of enforcing a rule of right and wrong whose validity no longer depends entirely on the self-interest of the parties. But to speak of rules of that kind is to recognize, again, the logic of "morals." And if morals exist, then people may be committed on many other matters that run counter to their self-interest, even when they have not personally "contracted" for those commitments. But if the only purpose of the polity were to offer protection against assaults and to promote commercial exchange, there would be nothing in those ends that contained any necessary moral significance. An association committed solely to those ends may still not be disposed to recognize any rule of action that transcends self-interest. Therefore, it could never have any cause or justification for annexing to itself the authority of law. That is in fact the understanding that must govern the "association" of countries like the United States and the Soviet Union, which are divided in the most radical way in their understanding of the principles of justice. But the relations between citizens within the United States cannot be likened to the relations arising by treaty between the United States and the Soviet Union without removing from those relations the commitments which reflect the distinctly moral understandings that bind Americans to one another and invest their relations with moral significance.

WHEN THE POLITY is conceived, then, merely as a system of contracts or treaties, the problem, as Aristotle said, is that in arrangements of this kind none of the contracting parties "concerns itself to ensure a proper quality or character among the members." That is to say, the members manifest no responsibility to cultivate a sense of morals or justice in one another. If I place an order or make a "contract" to purchase a new car, the relation of buying and selling does not confer any warrant on the buyer or the seller to concern himself with the moral character of the other party. We would have reason to be concerned about the basic honesty of one another, but that concern arises out of our self-interest in completing the transaction without being injured. And yet nothing in my contractual relations with the car dealer would entitle me to ask whether he abuses his wife or his children or whether he discriminates against other customers on the basis of their race. If it turns out that the car dealer batters his children, he may lose custody of them, but the polity that acts as our agent in punishing the father and removing his children from danger cannot be acting merely as the agent of my self-interest as his customer. The polity, in that case, would be exercising a mandate that cannot arise merely from the requirements of making and enforcing contracts.

The actions of the polity here would be comprehensible only from the standpoint of an association whose main responsibility—and whose primary reason for being—is to vindicate moral rights and wrongs. As Aristotle wrote, "any polis which is truly so called, and is not merely one in name, must devote itself to the end of encouraging

17

goodness." And when a polity does not devote itself to that end, when it fails to take seriously its commitments as a moral association, then it "sinks into a mere alliance, which only differs in space [i.e., in the proximity of the members] from other forms of alliance where the members live at a distance from one another." In that event, also, "law becomes a mere covenant [or contract] . . . instead of being, as it should be, a rule of life such as will make the members of a polis good and just."[7]

None of this is to say, of course, that there is anything fundamentally suspect or illegitimate about "contracts." For many parts of our lives, contracts may be the only appropriate device for arranging our relations. They are especially apt when the matter at hand must be regulated by the preferences and interests of the parties, and when no larger principle comes into play to command one decision rather than another. There is no principle, for example, that makes it necessary or desirable that everyone buy a Chevrolet. We would not be warranted then in *compelling* people to buy Chevrolets, and by the same reasoning, we would not be justified in compelling General Motors to deliver a Chevrolet to every adult in the country. That matter is properly left to the preferences and interests of individuals and the contracts they make with one another. But the question of whether a parent shall be free to batter a helpless child cannot be left simply to the preferences of the participants (whether those preferences encompass the pleasures of the villain or the consent of a masochistic victim). Nor would an adult be permitted to contract himself into slavery or peonage, even if he were quite happy overall with the arrangement. If we object in these instances, if we refuse to permit these matters to be governed solely by the consent of the parties, it is because we think there is a rule or principle involved that does not depend for its validity on the self-interest or the preferences of the participants. But when we say that, we have backed, once again, into the logic of a moral principle. And once we discover that logic, we discover that the only proper response is a law that compels all parties to respect the principle—in these instances, to refrain from battering children or from contracting oneself into slavery. Conversely, if we insist that there should be no law, that *all* matters should be regulated by a series of contracts, then we would be saying, in effect, that there are no principles which are valid and binding for an individual unless they accord with his own preferences. But that would be to say, with literal strictness, that there are no morals.

[7] *Ibid.*, 1280b.

18

Aristotle, therefore, was exactly correct: if the polity ceased to concern itself with the conditions of justice or the moral character of its citizens, there would have to be a recession of law and its replacement with a system of covenants made by consenting parties. That trend could only mark a state of affairs in which a people and its leaders had ceased to recognize the points at which moral principles are engaged in their lives; and that dimness of recognition is likely to set in when people no longer understand the real meaning and implication of "morals." But where that understanding is preserved, where there is a recognition of the "logic of morals," there would be a recognition, with Aristotle, that it is the existence of morals itself—and of creatures with the capacity for morals—that makes law and polity necessary.

I SUGGESTED earlier that this connection would be established without strain as soon as one became clear on the strict meaning or logic of morals. The awareness of that logic has been part of our natural understanding, in the recognitions that are already locked within us about the way in which we use words. Of course, those recognitions have been partly obscured in recent years by the conventions that have taken hold in our public discourse. The tendency in that discourse is to confound questions of morals with matters of the most mystic religious belief or the most subjective personal taste. In either event it is assumed that the exercise of moral judgment is cut off from the prospect of giving reasons, citing evidence, and establishing the truth or falsity of propositions. It is often assumed, also, that "morals" are mainly about matters of sex, gambling, and fraud, rather than about the grounds on which any action may be said to be "justified." But even when there is a recognition that morals address the gravest questions about the way in which human beings ought to conduct their lives, it is largely taken for granted that moral perspectives arise from "beliefs" of the most personal nature, which cannot be used to judge (much less prescribe) the conduct of others.

The problem here was reflected rather well in the college students I came to know in the late sixties and early seventies. It was important for many of them to insist that the war in Vietnam could not be regarded merely as an enterprise plagued by poor management and bad luck, but as a thoroughly *immoral* venture. They were disposed to argue, in a more classic vein, that politics could not be ruled by some internal logic of its own, separated from questions of morals. But when the same students were faced with other problems that arose in public policy—problems of drugs, prostitution, pornography, abortion—they became liberals in a rather old sense they usually disdained.

19

Their tendency then was to argue that the law should have nothing to do with questions of "morals," because morals were matters of the most personal taste or the most private, religious belief.

The most curious thing about this understanding of morals is that it would have reduced the indictment of the Vietnam war to the level of the utterly trivial. If someone said that the war in Vietnam was wrong or immoral, what he was really saying was, "The Vietnam war is not to my *taste*; I don't happen to like it—but feel free to pursue it if you like that sort of thing." Whatever else may be said of the antiwar position in this country, it must be recognized at least that this was not the logic of its argument: it did not assimilate the question of the war to propositions on the order of, "I don't like spinach"—statements of the most personal feeling or sensation, which bear no relevance to the things that are right or wrong for others as well as for oneself. The opponents of the war meant to say that the war should be closed down for *everyone*, that *no one* should be allowed to pursue the war even if he happened to take pleasure in it.

But with this form of argument, opponents of the war were recognizing the essential logic of morals (even if they were not all aware of the properties and implications of the language they were using). They recognized, in other words, the difference between two kinds of propositions, which can be expressed with propositions of this type:

(1) I like spinach.
(2) It is wrong to inflict pain without justification.

In the first statement, we speak of personal feelings or sensations, and we imply that we are speaking only about our own preferences. We would not think less of anyone who did not share our preference for spinach—certainly we would not *condemn* anyone for manifesting a different taste, and we would not regard our preference as binding on others. In the second kind of proposition, however, we recognize that we are in fact speaking of things that would be right or wrong for people, regardless of whether they enjoyed what they were doing. For that reason, the judgment "It is wrong to do X without justification" would be regarded as binding on other people, even if those people happened to disagree with it.

It is not very important how we label these propositions—whether we call the second type "moral" or simply use the heading Propositions of the X Form. The critical point is that the two kinds of propositions here bear different logics, and the enterprise of moral inquiry involves the task of drawing out the properties or implications that emerge from this second type. In that vein, it is the purpose of this book to

20

draw out some of those implications as the analysis unfolds. What we recognize, though, in the first place is that moral propositions are in fact distinguished quite sharply from statements of subjective, personal feelings or private, religious belief. Moral statements purport to speak about the things that are *universally* good or bad, right or wrong, just or unjust—which is to say, good or bad, right or wrong, *for others as well as for oneself.*

The differences we recognize in the conventions of our ordinary language reflect an awareness of a real difference between speaking in a manner that is wholly personal and speaking, in a *universal* voice, about rights and wrongs that do not depend for their validity on personal feelings. If we try to account for why we have the special vocabulary of moral terms, quite distinct from expressions of merely personal feeling, we recognize that the subject of ethics would not have its distinctness or special dignity if it did not involve, in its plainest purpose, the task of articulating the things that are universally right or wrong. As G.E. Moore put it, with a directness that could hardly have been plainer, the term "ethics" is used "to cover an enquiry for which, at all events, there is no other word: the general enquiry into what is good. . . . [It is necessary, then] for Ethics to enumerate all true universal judgments, asserting that such and such a thing was good, whenever it occurred."[8] It is hard to imagine why so much uncertainty and dimness has now covered over, in our common discourse, what has been settled in the literature of ethics for more than two thousand years. The study of ethics, as Aristotle said, is the task of "examining the problem raised by the concept of a universal good."[9]

Nor is it clear why a distinction should be made between morals and ethics. Etymologically, they both have the same root: "Ethics" is drawn from the Greek *ethos*, meaning "custom," and "moral" traces back to the Latin *mos, mores*, meaning "custom(s)," "manner(s)." The origin of both words reflected an understanding that rooted them in the habits or customs of a people; but as the study of ethics and morals matured, the meaning of both terms had to be enlarged in accord with a more rigorous understanding of the properties that attach to these concepts. Most notable among these properties was the universal quality of moral judgments. No one would suggest, I take it, that *either* "morals" *or* "ethics" should refer, as Moore said, to "all true universal judgments" about the nature of good and bad, while the other term

[8] G.E. Moore, *Principia Ethica* (Cambridge: Cambridge University Press, 1971 [1903]), pp. 2, 21.

[9] Aristotle, *Nicomachean Ethics*, bk. I, ch. 6.

should be reserved for those notions of good or bad that do not claim to be either "true" or "universal." At any rate, we recognize again in our ordinary language that, when we invoke these terms, we are purporting to speak in the gravest way about matters of right and wrong, with standards that may be used in judging others as well as ourselves.[10]

When we invoke the language of morals, we praise and we blame, we commend and condemn, we applaud and deride, we approve and disapprove. It would make no sense, however, to cast these judgments on other people unless it were assumed that there are standards of judgment, accessible to others as well as ourselves, which allow these people to know that what they are doing is right or wrong. As the philosophers would say, the standards of judgment must be knowable in a "trans-subjective" way;[11] they must be accessible, in principle, to us all, and only standards of that kind may be used, properly, in judging the acts of others. It would be incoherent, then, to show outrage over the acts of other people if one held, at the same time, that the standards of moral judgment were irreducibly personal and subjective. If they were, we would have no grounds for saying that the person who commits genocide does not in fact do what he regards as just or good *in his own perspective*; and if there is nothing other than a "personal" perspective on these matters, why should we think that our own "personal" view should be any more accurate or authoritative than his? Outrage and indignation would be thoroughly out of place, because in the strictest sense there could be no ground for a *judgment*. Almost two hundred years ago, Thomas Reid was quite luminous in explaining just why subjective feelings could not furnish the ground of a judgment:

> Feeling, or sensation, seems to be the lowest degree of animation we can conceive. . . . We commonly distinguish *feeling* from *thinking*. . . . A feeling must be agreeable, or uneasy, or indifferent. It may be weak or strong. It is expressed in language either by a single word, or by such a contexture of words as may be the subject or predicate of a proposition, but such as cannot by themselves make a proposition. For it implies neither affirmation nor negation; and therefore cannot have the qualities of true or false, which distinguish propositions from all other forms of speech, and judgments from all other acts of the mind. . . . The *tooth*

[10] According to the *Oxford English Dictionary*, the Latin expression for morals was formed by Cicero as a rendering of the Greek ἠθικός (*ethikos*). The *OED* defines ethics as "The science of morals; the department of study concerned with the principles of human duty. . . ."

[11] See Richard Flathman, *The Public Interest* (New York: John Wiley, 1966), p. 89.

ache, the *head ache*, are words which express uneasy feelings; but to say that they express a judgment would be ridiculous.[12]

A judgment can be justified only when there is a standard of judging which can be *known*, and which can support the truth of the judgment. For that reason a judgment must be underlain by a *proposition*, which can affirm or deny the truth of any matter. And as Reid observed, by a "moral sense" we mean "the power of judging in morals":

> Suppose that, in a case well known to both [my friend and me], my friend says, *Such and such a man did well and worthily; his conduct is highly approvable*. This speech ... expresses my friend's judgment of the man's conduct. This judgment may be true or false, and I may agree in opinion with him, or I may dissent from him without offence, as we may differ in other matters of judgment.
> Suppose again, that, in relation to the same case, my friend says, *The man's conduct gave me a very agreeable feeling*.
> This speech, if approbation be nothing but an agreeable feeling, must have the very same meaning with the first. . . . But this cannot be. . . . The first expresses plainly an opinion or judgment of the conduct of the man, but says nothing of the speaker; to wit, that he had such a feeling.[13]

In the latter case, the only "judgment" that can be rendered is a judgment on the question of whether the speaker is indeed affected by the feeling he reports. But as Reid correctly remarks, the question of his feeling has no bearing on the matter raised in the first instance, which was whether the action of the man was *justified* and worthy of approval. Was his action governed by a principle that could be honored as a proper ground of action, and would we be compelled to approve the same action, done in the same circumstances and for the same reason, by *anyone* else? If acts were governed by nothing more than subjective feelings, these questions would fail to be comprehensible; nor would there be any sense behind the notion of "morals" or any need for the function of a "judge." As Reid wryly observed, the person who filled that office would bear the title absurdly: "he ought to be called a feeler."[14]

WHEN WE INVOKE the language of morals, then, we move away from statements of personal taste and private belief; we offer a judgment

[12] Reid, *supra*, note 5, p. 459. Emphasis in original.
[13] *Ibid.*, pp. 464-65. Emphasis in original.
[14] *Ibid.*, p. 474.

about the things that are universally right or wrong, just or unjust. And once we are clear that the logic of morals must incorporate the sense of a true judgment that is universal in its reach, the connection between the logic of morals and the logic of law virtually establishes itself. For it should be clear now that when we say, "X is wrong," we are saying that it is wrong for *anyone* to do X, that X is universally undesirable, that it is wrong to do X even if a person finds pleasure in doing it, and that *everyone* ought to refrain from doing X. We might put the matter to ourselves in another way, by considering our judgment of a person who offered the following argument. What if he said, "I think it is wrong to torture small children for one's own pleasure," but then went on to say, "*Therefore* each person should consult his own conscience—he should make his own decision as to whether or not he will torture children—according to his own sense of right and wrong and of the things that give him pleasure."

Whatever we might say of this person, we would have to say that he does not understand the import of the words he is using. The most dramatic form in which this same fallacy appeared in our politics came over a hundred years ago, in the celebrated debate between Stephen Douglas and Abraham Lincoln. Douglas declared that he was personally opposed to slavery, but he wished to leave the matter to "popular sovereignty" (i.e., to the preferences of the local majority) in the several territories of the United States. Lincoln quickly pointed out that one could profess, with Douglas, not to "care" whether slavery were voted up or down only if a decision in favor of slavery was no better or worse, in principle, than a decision in favor of freedom. Lincoln put it this way in the debate at Quincy, Illinois:

> [W]hen Judge Douglas says he "don't care whether slavery is voted up or down," . . . he cannot thus argue logically if he sees anything wrong in it; . . . He cannot say that he would as soon see a wrong voted up as voted down. When Judge Douglas says that whoever, or whatever community, wants slaves, they have a right to have them, he is perfectly logical if there is nothing wrong in the institution; but if you admit that it is wrong, he cannot logically say that anybody has a right to do a wrong.[15]

If a man were to be restrained from injuring another person when he was not justified in inflicting that harm, he would not suffer any restraint of his rightful freedom; for as Lincoln explains, there cannot

---

[15] *The Collected Works of Abraham Lincoln*, ed. Roy P. Basler (New Brunswick: Rutgers University Press, 1953), vol. III, pp. 256-57.

be a "right" to do a wrong. What Lincoln expressed in the passage above was the connection between the logic of morals and the logic of law. It is hard to find many places in the canons of political philosophy where this connection—which is so critical to our understanding of political life—is made with the same explicitness. There is a passage in which Thomas Aquinas makes, in essence, the same point,[16] but John Stuart Mill came closer to the understanding set forth by Lincoln when he observed that

> we do not call anything wrong unless we mean to imply that a person ought to be punished in some way or other for doing it. ... [Mill goes on to say that the notion of deserving or not deserving punishment] lies at the bottom of the notions of right and wrong; that we call any conduct wrong, or employ, instead, some other term of dislike or disparagement, according as we think that the person ought, or ought not, to be punished for it; and we say it would be right to do so and so, or merely that it would be desirable or laudable, according as we would wish to see the person whom it concerns compelled, or only persuaded and exhorted, to act in that manner.[17]

Both Lincoln and Mill have recognized, in these passages, the precise connection between morals and law that Aristotle suggested, but never fully explained. The matter may be put, finally, in this way: once we come to the recognition that any act stands in the class of a wrong—once we come to the recognition, say, that it is wrong to kill without justification—the logic of that recognition forbids us from treating that act any longer as a matter merely of personal taste or private choice. The logic of the recognition that we are dealing with a "wrong" compels us to forbid that act to people generally or universally—which is to say, we forbid it with the force of law.

LET ME PAUSE here to rephrase the set of connections that Aristotle suggested to us. Polity arises from the capacity of human beings for moral judgment. The mark of a polity is the presence of law, and law (as we can see now) arises directly from the logic of morals. We may say that the logic of morals (or the existence of moral propositions) virtually entails the existence of law and, with that, the existence of polity. We have law *only* because we have morals—only because it is possible to speak of things that are right and wrong. Hence the natural

---

[16] Aquinas, *Summa Theologiae*, 2a2ae, 57, 3.
[17] John Stuart Mill, *Utilitarianism* (Indianapolis: Bobbs-Merrill, 1957 [1861]), p. 61.

understanding that seems to be accessible to most people: when it is commonly said that "there ought to be a law," that phrase is typically employed after people have already come to a judgment that something happens to be *wrong*. It took a systematic dose of arcane philosophy in order to instruct lawyers and judges over the years that there are no moral ends intrinsic to the definition of law, that law is simply whatever is promulgated by the sovereign and enforced as law, and that, in the words of Justice Holmes, "every word of moral significance [ought to] be banished from the law altogether."[18] In the interests of a new analytic clarity, the philosophers of legal "positivism" schooled generations of lawyers to an understanding of law that was analytically truncated. For they detached from the very definition of law that which had been understood from the earliest times to be incorporated in its character: not merely that law was binding, but that it was binding precisely because it sought to embody principles about the nature of right and wrong. It required a teaching that was distinctly modern in order to make a whole profession of jurists forget professionally what Blackstone taught: that the law represents "a rule of civil conduct prescribed by the supreme power in a state, commanding what is right and prohibiting what is wrong."[19]

In the traditional understanding, law exists only because rights and wrongs exist, and the function of law—the purpose of the polity—is to do justice: it is to vindicate wrongs and cultivate a sense of morals and justice in the population. And when the question was asked, "How does the polity engage in moral teaching?," the traditional answer was that the polity taught through the laws. When the law expressed the recognition, for example, that it was wrong to batter children, it taught in a dramatic, public way that the battering of children could not be regarded any longer as a matter of personal taste or private choice. The act of battering children would be removed from the domain of

[18] Oliver Wendell Holmes, "The Path of the Law," in *Collected Legal Papers* (New York: Harcourt Brace & Co., 1920), p. 179.

[19] William Blackstone, *Commentaries on the Laws of England* (Philadelphia: Rees Welsh & Co., 1897 [1765-69]), sec. II, p. 44. Blackstone was referring to "municipal" or "civil" law, as opposed to religious law or natural law, which did not have to be set down and tailored to the circumstances of particular communities. It is a reflection of the modern mind in jurisprudence that the editor of this version of the *Commentaries*, Professor William Draper Lewis of the law school at the University of Pennsylvania, felt obliged to point out that the definition of law was sufficiently expressed by Blackstone's phrase, "a rule of civil conduct prescribed by the supreme power in a state." The remaining words—viz., "commanding what is right and prohibiting what is wrong"—offered an appendage, in Lewis's judgment, that "must either be superfluous or convey a defective idea of municipal law" (p. 44n).

private choice and lifted to the plane of public obligation, where it would be forbidden with the force of law. What that change conveyed, in its essential logic, was that we were dealing now with a matter of morals rather than with a matter of merely personal taste.[20]

The understanding that emerges here would tend to reverse the cliché, gleaned so widely these days from sociology texts and fortune cookies, that we must never "legislate morality." When the matter is understood in its proper strictness, we would have to say that we may "legislate *only* morality." It is a presumptuous thing we may do when we legislate for other people—when we restrict their personal freedom and displace their private choice with the commands of public law. The argument in this book is that we are justified in imposing such measures only when we can establish, as the foundation of the law, propositions that can claim the true properties of a moral proposition. That is to say, we are justified in legislating only when the law is governed by an understanding of right and wrong that can tenably claim to be valid, in principle, for everyone. As I will try to show very soon, true moral propositions have that quality because they express "principles" in the hardest sense: i.e., propositions that are true *as a matter of necessity*. In that event, it is possible to show that moral propositions are not only universal but *categorical*: they are true under all conditions and contingencies. They could not furnish a ground for legislation if the "truths" they conveyed were merely contingent or statistical—if they were merely true for most people most of the time. Nor would they claim the standing of law if their truths varied with alterations in local culture or with the vagaries of what majorities, in one place or another, are pleased to regard as right and wrong. As Kant put it, "a law has to carry with it absolute necessity if it is to

---

[20] Surveys of public opinion in the mid-1960's indicated that in the years 1963-66 there was a decisive shift of opinion in the United States in regard to racial segregation. By 1966 a majority of whites in the South as well as in the North had agreed that it was wrong to discriminate on the basis of race in places of public accommodation, even when those establishments were privately owned. The conviction had also settled in the country that there had been a justification for striking at this kind of discrimination through the federal government, with the Civil Rights Act of 1964. It is hard to imagine that the culture of the South had changed so dramatically between 1963 and 1966. The change would seem to bear a relation to the fact that some rather different understandings were being held forth in public by the men at the top of the state. Public men were teaching new lessons through the things they were saying in public and, even more important, through the things they were willing to make binding on the country with the force of public law. As the ancients knew, and the moderns confirmed, the laws may reshape the attitudes of the public, and they may instruct people in new understandings of the duties they owe one another.

be valid morally—vaild, that is, as a ground of obligation."[21] For that reason, laws had to be categorical; "otherwise they would not be laws."[22]

That understanding would establish, to put it mildly, a very strict standard. If we apply it, as I think we can, one result would be far fewer laws on the books than we have today. But it would follow, also, that what government may legitimately do—what it may do with the sanction of a moral principle—it may do with the full reach of the principle itself, with a sweep that need not honor the distinction between the public and the private. Once we establish, for example, that it is wrong to kill without justification, we recognize that private murders are quite as wrong as public murders, or that the battering of children may be reached by the law regardless of whether it takes place in the street or in the bedroom.[23]

We are likely, of course, to encounter skepticism from many quarters, from conservatives as well as liberals, as soon as we begin speaking about principles that define categorical and "necessary" truths in morals. Yet, as I will try to show, we typically recognize the logic of the distinction between things that are only contingently good and things that are categorically good, even if people are not always familiar with the labels. It could never be said, for example, that it is always harmful to drink alcohol, even if the liquor is taken rarely and in very small quantities. But it could never be warranted to say that genocide may be harmless or inoffensive if it is practiced in moderation. In that kind of distinction, which is made quite commonly, we show a recognition of the difference between things that are only contingently good or bad—whose goodness or badness may depend on conditions or circumstances—and things that are wrong under all conditions. Quite apart from the distinctions that have become familiar to us, however, I think we can satisfy ourselves that, if moral propositions are to make

[21] Immanuel Kant, *Groundwork of the Metaphysics of Morals* [1785], trans. H.J. Paton (New York: Harper & Row, 1964), p. 57; p. 389 of the standard edition of the Royal Prussian Academy (hereafter RPA ed.).

[22] Immanuel Kant, *Critique of Practical Reason* [1788], trans. Lewis White Beck (Indianapolis: Bobbs-Merrill, 1956), p. 18; p. 20 of the RPA ed.

[23] I do not mean to ignore the obvious argument that there are acts we would consider "wrong" but which we may be reluctant, nevertheless, to bring within the reach of the law. A child may be punished unjustly and sent to bed without his supper, and yet the police do not intervene and lawsuits are not typically filed. But this matter of the boundaries of law is far more problematic than it has been thought to be, and I shall have more to say on it later, when I deal with the "limits" of the law. I have taken up this question in part already in *The Philosopher in the City: The Moral Dimensions of Urban Politics* (Princeton: Princeton University Press, 1981), pp. 355-60.

sense to us as moral propositions, they must have the property of being necessary and, therefore, categorical.

As to the source of these categorical judgments, I think we will see that Kant was precisely accurate after all in the understanding he offered on this issue. The rudiments of that understanding I mentioned briefly earlier, and I will take the occasion later to show how categorical judgments may be drawn from the core he suggested to us. But it is worth recalling, very quickly, the steps Kant took in marking off that core. Kant once said that "nothing but the idea of the law in itself . . . can constitute that preeminent good which we call moral," and as he pointed out, the idea of law is "present only in a rational being."[24] That is, only a being with reason can conceive the notion of a "good," or a principle of justice, that may override his own self-interest. Kant went on to say, in addition, that "since moral laws have to hold for every rational being as such, we ought . . . to derive our principles from the general concept of a rational being as such. . . ."[25]

Kant suggested here that the principles of right and wrong could be drawn as implications that flowed from the concept of morals itself (the "idea of law") or from the very notion of a rational creature—a creature with the capacity to reason over moral things, and with the freedom to choose between right and wrong. I will try to show, in the chapters to come, just how those inferences may be drawn. When they are drawn accurately, the propositions that emerge from this core will have the force of necessity; for the concept of morals itself and the notion of a rational creature rest, in turn, on propositions that Kant would have called "apodictic," or necessary, truths. At the same time, the propositions extracted in this way are hardly trivial. They provide nothing less than the "first principles" of morals and justice, and they reach matters of political consequence.

During a debate on the Bill of Rights in the First Congress, James Madison recalled the "self-evident" truth which had been mentioned in the Declaration of Independence—the proposition "All men are created equal." That was the premise on which the American republic had been founded, and Madison referred to that central truth of the Declaration as an "absolute truth."[26] That kind of language would

---

[24] Kant, *supra*, note 21, p. 69; p. 401 of the RPA ed.

[25] *Ibid.*, p. 79; p. 412 of the RPA ed.

[26] See Madison's speech (June 8, 1789), reprinted in Bernard Schwartz, *The Bill of Rights: A Documentary History* (New York: Chelsea House and McGraw-Hill, 1971), vol. II, p. 1029. In his speech at Peoria on the Kansas-Nebraska Act (September 1854), Lincoln remarked that "the doctrine of self-government is right—absolutely and eter-

stir unease in the circles of the educated today, and yet Madison understood the Declaration to be stating a truth that had the properties of an apodictic truth. For that reason, the case in principle for republican government—and the case in principle against slavery—would hold true in all places and at all times, which meant that it would hold true across cultures. And this case for government by consent, as *the only lawful government* over men, would be drawn from precisely the same ground that Aristotle established, in the very beginning, as the foundation for law and polity.

---

nally right," and he spoke here with no touch of hyperbole. Lincoln, *supra*, note 15, vol. II, p. 265.

III

THE "ONE AND ONLY LEGITIMATE CONSTITUTION": GOVERNMENT BY LAW AND GOVERNMENT BY CONSENT

With a spark of liberal conviction, but with measured philosophic sobriety, Kant would write in 1797 that there is "one and only legitimate constitution, namely, that of a pure republic."[1] In our own day, there seems to have been a collective forgetting of the grounds on which "lawful" government may be said to be, in principle, the best form of government for countries everywhere, regardless of local traditions and customs. Anyone who might fail to accord a proper legitimacy to a local barbarism invested with the authority of its own "traditional culture" would probably be accused of seeking to "impose the 'values' of his own society on the rest of the world." But when Kant spoke of the moral superiority of republican government, he spoke for other literate men of his age, and he spoke with an understanding that could trace its threads back to the classics.

Kant conceded that forms of government would vary from place to place as a reflection of local customs and the vestiges of the past. But regardless of whether a country preserved the remnants of monarchy or aristocracy, the very "spirit" or character of lawful government entailed an obligation for the authorities "to change the government gradually and continually" so that it would conform to the "Idea" of a republic.[2] "Republic" derives from the Latin, *respublica*, a "public affair" or "public matter." It expresses the understanding, dating back to the ancients, that political rule is not a private business, directed to the private interests of the rulers, but an activity with public ends. It is directed to the good or to the moral improvement of the public, and laws have to be made on the basis of standards that express a "public" (or, we might say, in the language of morals, a "universal") good. Republican government is first and foremost a government of law, a constitutional order. It might be said that its first maxim, arising from the logic of morals itself, is that people in positions of authority should be compelled to cite some law beyond their own self-interest

---

[1] Immanuel Kant. *The Metaphysical Elements of Justice* [Part I of *The Metaphysics of Morals* (1797)], trans. John Ladd (Indianapolis: Bobbs-Merrill, 1965), p. 112; p. 340 of the RPA ed.

[2] *Ibid.*

as the ground of their official acts. In a republican government, leaders were restrained by law, and as Hobbes recognized quite clearly, a monarch who was restrained by law—who could be restrained by the authority of courts and parliament—was no longer, strictly speaking, a monarch.[3] For authority within the political order no longer emanated from a single source (there was no longer *mono arkhes*, the rule of one). As Kant observed, the "constitution" of a republic "is the only enduring political constitution in which the law is autonomous and is not annexed to any particular person."[4] Once the principle was admitted of restraining political power through the law, it would soon be discovered (as we shall see) that the notion of "equality before the law" is implicit in the idea of law itself. The idea of government by law would soon be connected, in other words, to the principle of "popular government." Once there were independent courts and parliaments, once the notion of government "by consent" was recognized, it remained only to elaborate on the scheme by enlarging or spreading the franchise.

Rousseau would not be speaking, then, in paradoxes when he would note that even a monarchy under the rule of law was a republic.[5] And, of course, no writer has written with more eloquence and force than Rousseau in tracing the premises of republican government back to the premises of lawfulness itself. In the opening sections of *The Social Contract* Rousseau managed to connect the problem of lawful government with the first implications that arise out of the very concept of morals:

> [W]e have come to speak of the Right of the Strongest, a right which, seemingly assumed in irony, has, in fact, become established in principle. But the meaning of the phrase has never been adequately explained. Strength is a physical attribute and I fail to see how any moral sanction can attach to its effects. To yield to the strong is an act of necessity, not of will. At most it is the result of a dictate of prudence. How, then, can it become a duty?
> ... [T]o admit that Might makes Right is to reverse the process of effect and cause. The mighty man who defeats his rival becomes heir to his Right. So soon as we can disobey with impunity, disobedience becomes legitimate. And, since the Mightiest is al-

---

[3] Thomas Hobbes, *Leviathan* (Oxford: Basil Blackwell, 1960 [1651]), pt. 2, ch. 19, pp. 125-26.

[4] Kant, *supra*, note 1, p. 113; p. 341 of the RPA ed.

[5] J.J. Rousseau, "The Social Contract" [1762], bk. II, ch. 6, n. 5, in *Social Contract*, ed. Sir Ernest Barker (London: Oxford University Press, 1960), p. 203.

ways right, it merely remains for us to become possessed of Might. But what validity can there be in a Right which ceases to exist when Might changes hands? . . .

. . . If I am waylaid by a footpad at the corner of a wood, I am constrained by force to give him my purse. But if I can manage to keep it from him, is it my duty to hand it over? His pistol is also a symbol of Power. It must, then, be admitted that Might does not create Right, and that no man is under an obligation to obey any but the legitimate powers of the State. . . .[6]

The point will become clearer, as we advance, that moral conclusions can be entailed only by moral propositions. They cannot be drawn from such distinctly nonmoral attributes as brute physical strength. The young boy who loses his first fight understands instantly that the success of his opponents cannot itself establish that they were "right" or "justified" in beating him up. In more exacting language, we would say that mere physical power cannot be the source of moral warrants. With Rousseau, we would say that power cannot be the source of its own justification: the fact that some men may have been successful in seizing and holding power over others cannot itself establish that they were *justified* in imposing their rule.[7]

The insistence of Rousseau, then, was that the exercise of political power by some men over others was something that called out for justification. An obligation to obey could be elicited only on the strength of a proposition of moral significance, which could explain why any particular set of leaders *deserved* to be obeyed. But when we say that it is necessary to establish the justice (or the "justification") of any plan of political rule, what we mean, precisely, is that it is necessary to render a justification or give reasons. Yet, to speak in that language and to set those requirements already presupposes something about the nature of the creature to whom the justification is addressed.

To put the matter more directly, it makes no sense to speak of

---

[6] *Ibid.*, bk. I, ch. 3, pp. 172-73.

[7] The rhetoric that flourished during the war in Vietnam once cast up the theory that the success of the Vietcong in guerrilla operations could not be achieved unless the Vietcong commanded a certain "support" among the Vietnamese in the countryside, and that support might be taken as a practical surrogate for free elections. In a strange inversion of Rousseau—and of moral reasoning—a success at arms would be taken as the measure of moral justification. A victory for the Vietcong would be enough to prove that they had deserved to win, and that their rule was legitimate. Apparently, Might would indeed be treated as a source of Right—so long as the forces possessing Might were sufficiently "progressive."

offering "justifications" to dogs, horses, and cows. The commitment to offer justifications makes sense only if we recognize, from the beginning, that we are dealing with creatures who can understand reasons, and it is only the prospect of ruling creatures of that kind which calls out for justification. Even in this advanced age of "animal liberation," it is doubtful that we will find many people signing labor contracts with their horses or cows, or seeking the consent of their dogs before they would presume to rule them. Nor is it likely that this franchise will be extended to animals a hundred years from now, even if the spirit of "reform" has diffused more widely in the land. But to say this is to recognize a fact of no small moral significance which is simply grounded in nature: the difference between creatures that have—and do not have—the capacity for moral judgment. As we have seen, that was the difference which proved critical for Aristotle in identifying the distinct nature in human beings that made polity both possible and necessary. For animals it was impossible, for gods it was unnecessary. As Madison remarked in *The Federalist* #51, "If men were angels, no government would be necessary."[8] If men were gods or angels, there would be no need for the restraint and teaching of law. But if men were beasts, if they were no different from other animals, there would be no use for the law, because men could not understand the moral teaching implicit in the law. Therefore, anyone who stands outside a polity, anyone who does not require the restraint of law—or who is incompetent to receive the teaching of the law— cannot be a human being. He must be, as Aristotle wrote, "either a beast or a god."[9]

IN THE TRADITIONAL understanding, then, polity was both possible and necessary for human beings because, while we are not gods, neither are we animals. And if one began with that sense of where humans stand in the rankings of nature, it was plausible to take the next step and draw the inference made by Locke, Rousseau, and the men who framed the American republic: that the inequalities which stand out so plainly in nature reveal, quite dramatically, the attributes in which human beings as a species must be regarded as *equal by nature*. The understanding could be expressed in this way: no man can be, by nature, the ruler of other men in the same way that God is by nature the ruler of men, and men are by nature the rulers of dogs, horses, and monkeys. Therefore, if a situation has come about in which some

[8] *The Federalist* #51 (New York: Modern Library, n.d.), p. 337.
[9] Aristotle, *Politics*, 1253a.

34

men have been placed in the position of exercising power over others, that situation could not have arisen from *nature*. It had to arise from convention or agreement; it had to arise, one might say, from *consent*.

In our own day, this traditional understanding has been restated with enhanced clarity by Professor Harry Jaffa.[10] But the classic texts make it clear that these were indeed the terms in which the foundations of government by consent were understood, even if that understanding has become less familiar to our own generation. After Rousseau recorded the premise that Might cannot make Right, he moved on to conclude that "since no man has *natural* authority over his fellows . . . the only foundation left for legitimate authority in *human* societies is Agreement."[11] In Locke the explanation took this form:

For men being all the workmanship of one . . . wise Maker . . . and being furnished with like faculties, sharing all in one community of nature, there cannot be supposed any such subordination among us that may authorize us to destroy one another, as if we were made for one another's uses, as the inferior ranks of creatures are for ours.[12]

. . . .

The *natural* liberty of man is to be free from any superior power on earth, and not to be under the will or legislative authority of man, but to have only the law of Nature for his rule. The liberty of man *in society* is to be under no other legislative power but that established by consent in the commonwealth. . . .[13]

To deny that understanding was to deny the things that separated human beings from animals. It was to suggest, as Jefferson said, that the "mass of mankind" had been "born with saddles on their backs," and that a favored few had been born "booted and spurred, ready to ride them legitimately, with the grace of God."[14] Those statesmen who understood that the difference between men and animals is the most decisive difference could write the document which founded a new political order on the proposition that "all men are created equal."

---

[10] See Harry Jaffa, *Equality and Liberty* (New York: Oxford University Press, 1965), pp. 137, 177-78.

[11] Rousseau, *supra*, note 5, bk. I, ch. 4, p. 173. Emphasis added.

[12] John Locke, "Second Treatise on Civil Government" [1690], bk. I, ch. II, in *Social Contract*, ed. Sir Ernest Barker (London: Oxford University Press, 1960), pp. 5-6.

[13] *Ibid.*, bk. I, ch. IV, p. 15. Emphasis added.

[14] Thomas Jefferson, letter to Roger Weightman (June 24, 1826), reprinted in Morton G. Frisch and Richard G. Stevens (eds.), *The Political Thought of American Statesmen* (Itasca, Illinois: F.E. Peacock, 1973), p. 13.

And on the basis of that premise they could draw the inference that the only legitimate governments over men are those which "deriv[e] their just powers from the consent of the governed." Anyone who would strike at the premises of popular government would have to deny that original understanding of the difference between men and animals. By the same token, anyone who would blur over that difference would have to call into question the foundations of free government.

Four score and two years later, the question was posed again in the debates between Abraham Lincoln and Stephen Douglas, and in the effort to render equivocal the wrong of slavery Douglas was moved to blur over the differences between the human and the subhuman. Douglas was compelled, that is, by his argument, to raise doubts about the human standing of the black man. Lincoln would later recall a remark by Douglas in Memphis that went unreported: "[Douglas] declared that while in all contests between the negro and the white man, he was for the white man, but that in all questions between the negro and the crocodile he was for the negro."[15] As Lincoln quickly pointed out, the implication was obvious: "As the negro is to the white man, so is the crocodile to the negro, and as the negro may rightfully treat the crocodile as a beast or reptile, so the white man may rightfully treat the negro as a beast or a reptile."[16] The defense of slavery could work only by assimilating black people to the things that were subhuman; only in that way could blacks be deprived of the rights that existed in all human beings *by nature.*

IN ORDER TO make his own case against slavery as a matter of *natural* right, Lincoln was compelled to return to the original imagery, to sharpen the awareness once again of the division in nature between human beings and animals. In a debate with Douglas in 1854, Lincoln put the question: if there is no sense of right or wrong attached to slavery, how would one account for the fact that in 1820 congressmen from the South joined those from the North almost unanimously in "declaring the slave trade piracy, and in annexing to it the punishment of death"? Why would they have done that, asked Lincoln, unless they recognized something wrong about slavery?—"The practice was no more than bringing wild negroes from Africa, to sell to such as

---

[15] *The Collected Works of Abraham Lincoln*, ed. Roy P. Basler (New Brunswick: Rutgers University Press, 1953), vol. III, p. 445.
[16] *Ibid.*, p. 446.

would buy them. But you never thought of hanging men for catching and selling wild horses, wild buffaloes or wild bears."[17]

Or again, Lincoln noted that

> there are in the United States and territories, including the District of Columbia, 433,643 free blacks. At $500 per head they are worth over two hundred millions of dollars. How comes this vast amount of property to be running about without owners? We do not see free horses or free cattle running at large. How is this? All these free blacks are the descendants of slaves, or have been slaves themselves, and they would be slaves now, but for SOMETHING which has operated of their white owners, inducing them, at vast pecuniary sacrifices, to liberate them. What is that SOMETHING? Is there any mistaking it? In all these cases it is your sense of justice, and human sympathy, continually telling you, that the poor negro has some natural right to himself—that those who deny it, and make mere merchandise of him, deserve kickings, contempt and death.
>
> And now, why will you ask us to deny the humanity of the slave? and estimate him only as the equal of the hog? Why ask us to do what you will not do yourselves? Why ask us to do for nothing what two hundred millions of dollars could not induce you to do.[18]

Lincoln was forced to return to this original imagery, which ran back to the understanding of Aristotle, because the heart of his dispute with Douglas was the question of whether the rights mentioned in the Declaration had a *natural*, or a merely conventional, foundation. Did those rights arise from the very nature of human beings, and would they be the same, then, wherever the nature of human beings remained the same? Or did those rights arise merely from the conventions or customs that were established in any society? In the debate between Lincoln and Douglas the problem was posed in this form: when the Declaration of Independence said that "all men are created equal," did it in fact mean "all" men, black as well as white? Or did it really mean—as Douglas professed to believe—"all white men" or "all British citizens"?[19] It was Lincoln's understanding that when the drafters of the Declaration said "all men," they meant, as an abstract, universal proposition, all men. As he persistently reminded his audience, that

---

[17] *Ibid.*, vol. II, p. 264.
[18] *Ibid.*, p. 265.
[19] *Ibid.*, vol. III, pp. 112-13.

proposition was never taken to mean that men were equal *in all respects*:

> [The authors of the Declaration] did not mean to say all were equal in color, size, intellect, moral developments, or social capacity. They defined with tolerable distinctness in what they did consider all men created equal,—equal in certain inalienable rights, among which are life, liberty, and the pursuit of happiness. This they said, and this they meant. They did not mean to assert the obvious untruth that all were then actually enjoying that equality, or yet that they were about to confer it immediately upon them. In fact they had no power to confer such a boon. They meant simply to declare the *right*, so that the *enforcement* of it might follow as fast as circumstances should permit.[20]

As we shall see more fully later, it cannot be possible to establish "principles" of justice, or "necessary truths," on the basis merely of "experience." Lincoln and the Founders were quite justified in their conviction that the proposition, "All men are created equal," expressed a necessary truth; but they recognized, just as surely, that they were not offering, in that phrase, an "empirical generalization," which summed up the experience of human nature. For the record of that experience encompassed many humans who did not exactly confirm the reputation of their species for moral reasoning. We may regard it as more apt, then, to say that we find reflected in our natures the awareness of reason and moral judgment. The connection between the two provides the foundation of our moral understanding, and the commands of morals that flow then, through the laws of reason, would stand on their own logic. They would hold for all moral agents, who have access, through their reason, to moral understanding. And their validity as laws would not be affected by any "evidence," easily assembled, that many human beings live out their lives with malice and willful ignorance, and with no strenuous use of moral reasoning.

But this is a problem which should be left more properly to the next chapter. We shall also find it necessary to consider then that the logic of "natural equality" cannot oblige us to place, on a plane of equality, the virtuous and the vicious, the innocent and the guilty. Nor would the notion of natural equality enjoin us to accord the same respect and affection to all of our acquaintances without any test of merit or moral desert. As we shall see, the logic of natural equality entails an

---

[20] *Ibid.*, vol. II, pp. 405-406 (speech on the *Dred Scott* case, June 26, 1857). Emphasis added.

equal claim to be treated justly—i.e., with justification. And when it comes to the matter of governance, it means that creatures who have the capacity to give and understand justifications do not deserve to be ruled in the same manner that we rule creatures which are incapable of giving or understanding reasons. Experience has shown that people in positions of authority are most likely to "give an account" of themselves and render a justification for their policies if they are compelled to seek support, in a free election, in order to remain in office. The claim to be ruled only with justification quickly translates into a claim to be governed only with one's consent, in a regime of law. As Lincoln once remarked, the black man in a condition of slavery may not be the equal of the white man who has had the advantages of freedom and education, but in his right not to be ruled without his consent and his "right to eat the bread, without leave of anybody else, which his own hand earns, *he is my equal and . . . the equal of every living man*."[21]

This right of the black man emerged simply from his nature as a being with the capacity to reason over matters of right and wrong, and therefore it would retain its validity wherever that capacity still marked the nature of human beings. The framers of the Declaration had no grounds on which to suppose that those capacities were somehow confined to the white people who were resident in the United States at that time. As Lincoln pointed out rather tartly, this brand of reasoning would not only withdraw blacks from the coverage of the Declaration; it would remove, also, all nationalities that were not represented in America and Britain in 1776: "The English, Irish and Scotch, along with white Americans, were included [in the terms of the Declaration] to be sure, but the French, Germans, and other white people of the world are all gone to pot along with [Douglas's] inferior races."[22]

In the academic argot of our own day, Douglas's argument represented the perspective of "cultural relativism," the view that there are no moral truths which hold their validity across cultures. Moral truths become "relative" to the understandings of "right" and "wrong" that are dominant in any culture. And what we would mean then by legal "rights" are not rights that are drawn from universal standards of justice, but the rights that are stipulated or "posited" by men in particular societies. In the old language of jurisprudence, the difference here coincided with the distinction between "natural law," the law

[21] *Ibid.*, vol. III, p. 16. Emphasis in original.
[22] *Ibid.*, vol. II, p. 407.

that arises for all men from nature, and "positive law," the statutes that have the standing of law only because they are "posited" or set down by the authorities in any country. Regardless of whether we preserve the old labels, the distinction between the two varieties of law (and rights) has an enduring relevance for us. We would assume, for example, that the foreign visitor who arrives in New York City has a right to be protected from lawless, unjustified assaults in the public streets. The fact that he is not an American citizen should have no relevance to the responsibilities of the police in protecting him from these crimes. But we would not think that the foreign visitor who steps off the plane would have the "right" to attend the City College at the same, subsidized level of tuition that is available to citizens of New York. This latter "right" belongs to those species of rights which are created in different communities for those people with whom the citizens of the community feel a special connection. These rights or claims depend on what the citizens of the community are willing to do for one another, and they may be withdrawn when they no longer have the support or sufferance of the community.

In Douglas's argument, all law became "positive" law and all rights were assimilated to this second category of "positive" rights. Whether it was right or wrong for blacks to be slaves—and, presumably, whether it was right or wrong for foreign visitors to be assaulted in the streets—did not depend on any claims that are intrinsic to the nature of human beings. The "right" not to be enslaved was a right only if it were recognized or created by the people who made the laws in any country, and of course that "right" could be withdrawn when it no longer commanded the approval of the community. In this respect, the tendency to view all law as "positive" law soon reveals the flaw that makes cultural relativism incompatible with the premises of constitutional government itself. If the understanding of right and wrong can be drawn only from the culture of any country, it may be asked, what are the authoritative sources of moral truth when the country happens to be divided in its moral perspectives? In the period leading up to the Civil War, the culture of the United States encompassed radically opposing views on the justification for slavery. Which of these cultural strands could be taken to represent the authentic view, settled in the culture, about the nature of right and wrong in regard to slavery?

With cultural relativism, there can be only one answer to that question: the most authoritative opinion about the nature of moral right and wrong would have to be that strand of opinion which is *dominant* in the culture. That, however, is simply another way of saying that what is right or wrong depends on those understandings of virtue and vice which are held by a *majority* of people within the country. What is "morally right" is then equivalent to "that which is approved by a majority," and what is "morally wrong" really translates as "that which is disapproved by a majority." And yet, with these premises it becomes logically untenable to question the judgments that are reached by majorities. The very fact that a judgment is supported by a majority becomes, of necessity, the sole and decisive test of whether the judgment is valid or justified. In that event, there could never be a possibility of restraining the acts of legislative majorities by appealing to a higher law of the Constitution or a Bill of Rights. There would be no ground, then, in principle, for calling into question any law passed by a majority. To invert Rousseau, power would become the source of its own justification: the power of the majority, which is necessary to establish a law, becomes the definitive measure of the justification for the law that is finally passed. We will have far more to say later, in a more systematic way, about the fallacies that afflict cultural relativism. It is sufficient to make the point at this moment that the premises of cultural relativism would cut the ground out from under constitutional government itself. And for those who would embrace cultural relativism, it may be posted as a sign of caution that they would have to attach themselves to the side of Douglas in the debate with Lincoln.

IT WAS precisely because Douglas found the source of all rights in "positive" law that he could profess not to "care" whether slavery was voted up or down in the territories of the United States, so long as the decision reflected the will of the local majority. But for Lincoln this was a thoroughgoing corruption of republican government. It implied that the only principle which defined democracy was a formal principle—viz., that the majority should rule—and it suggested that a democracy had to be indifferent, in principle, to the things that were willed by the majority. It was as though there were no *substantive* moral principles, implicit in the character of a democracy, which made some ends illegitimate and impermissible. In Douglas's view, it was perfectly proper for a democracy to make slaves of a minority so long as its measures were authorized in a formally democratic way, through the vote of a majority. During a debate in 1854 over the Kansas-Nebraska Act, Lincoln recalled that

> in the course of my main argument, Judge Douglas interrupted me to say, that the principle of the Nebraska bill was very old; that it originated when God made man and placed good and evil

41

before him, allowing him to choose for himself, being responsible for the choice he should make. At the time I thought this was merely playful; and I answered it accordingly. But in his reply to me he renewed it, as a serious argument. In seriousness then, the facts of this proposition are not true as stated. God did not place good and evil before man, telling him to make his choice. On the contrary, he did tell him there was one tree, of the fruit of which, he should not eat, upon pain of certain death. I should scarcely wish so strong a prohibition against slavery in Nebraska.[23]

As Harry Jaffa has commented on this passage, Lincoln was suggesting that the freedom of man, even under a free government, is "conditional upon denying to himself a forbidden fruit. That fruit was the alluring pleasure of despotism. . . . A democratic people must abide by certain restraints in order to be a democratic people."[24] A democratic people had to forgo the pleasures of despotism, and it could do that more readily if it understood that the restraint was made necessary by a principle that was integral to its own standing as a free people. What a free people had to understand was that it could not coherently choose slavery for some of its members or even for itself—it could not legitimately vote to deprive itself or the next generation of the right to government by consent. A majority may not properly waive its own freedom, because an act of that kind would be inconsistent with the premises that endowed the majority with the right to decide anything in the first place.

If we take Lincoln and the Founders seriously, the moral justification for democracy does not rest on any finding that it is the form of government which happens to be favored by a majority. The moral necessity of democracy derives, rather, from the fact that it is the only form of government which is suited to the nature of beings capable of giving and understanding justifications. The rule of the majority emerged only *after* the case for government by consent had been established, and it emerged because it is the only arrangement compatible with the premise of natural equality. The rightness of government by consent, therefore, is simply rooted in nature, in the things that make human beings different from animals, and it is beyond the competence of any man to repeal those parts of his nature that make him different from animals.

To invoke an old, but rarely understood, term, we have here a matter

[23] *Ibid.*, p. 278.
[24] Harry V. Jaffa, *Crisis of the House Divided* (New York: Doubleday, 1959), pp. 305-306.

of "inalienable" rights, rights that we are incompetent to alienate or forgo. We register our awareness of this old understanding when we refuse to honor the "right" of a man to contract himself into peonage or slavery.[25] But what can be said here for an individual must be said with equal force in relation to an aggregate of men and women collected in a legislative assembly or an electorate. Neither singly nor collectively do they have the competence to vote away freedom for themselves or for any class of innocent, competent persons within their midst. A free people would be obliged to forgo the impulses to despotism, because a free people would be obliged to respect in the first instance the premises on which its own freedom rests.

"As I WOULD NOT be a *slave*," wrote Lincoln, "so I would not be a *master*. This expresses my idea of democracy. Whatever differs from this, to the extent of the difference, is not democracy."[26] The same principle that makes it wrong for human beings to be ruled without their consent makes it wrong for human beings to be owned and ruled, without their consent, in the position of slaves.[27] The case for democratic government and the case against slavery are in point of principle the same. And it was the awareness of that necessary connection which brought forth the Republican party and accounted for the mission of Lincoln in our politics. What Lincoln and the Republicans understood was that the public could not be schooled to the acceptance of slavery without making itself suggestible, at the same time, to premises that are ultimately incompatible with republican government. For as Lincoln showed, there was no argument brought forward to justify the enslavement of black people which would not apply to many whites as well. In a fragment Lincoln wrote for himself on this point, he offered a model of what we may understand as a "principled" argument. He posed the question of how a white man could justify the enslavement of a black man:

> You say A. is white, and B. is black. It is *color*, then: the lighter having the right to enslave the darker? Take care. By this rule, you are to be slave to the first man you meet, with a fairer skin than your own.

[25] See *Bailey* v. *Alabama*, 219 U.S. 219 (1911).

[26] Lincoln, *supra*, note 15, vol. II, p. 532. Emphasis in original.

[27] As Lincoln wrote, "[A]ccording to our ancient faith, the just powers of governments are derived from the consent of the governed. Now the relation of master and slaves is, PRO TANTO, a total violation of this principle. The master not only governs the slave without his consent; but he governs him by a set of rules altogether different from those which he prescribes for himself." *Ibid.*, p. 266 (speech at Peoria, October 16, 1854).

You do not mean *color* exactly?—You mean the whites are *intellectually* the superiors of the blacks, and, therefore have the right to enslave them? Take care again. By this rule, you are to be slave to the first man you meet, with an intellect superior to your own.

But, say you, it is a question of interest; and, if you can make it your *interest*, you have the right to enslave another. Very well. And if he can make it his interest, he has the right to enslave you.[28]

A government that could make slaves of black men could, at the very least, begin restricting the franchise of poor whites; and as it created new categories of "disabilities," it could soon place large portions of the community under the permanent governance of a ruling class. As the government began to take all of the steps necessary to preserve a system of slavery, the democratic character of the regime would become muted, while the authoritarian features implicit in slavery would become more pronounced. In this way, slavery could bring about the corruption and erosion of republican government, because it would break the attachment of citizens to the premises that underlie their own freedom.[29] Lincoln spoke with a sober realism, then, when he remarked that "a house divided cannot stand": the political order could not exist half slave and half free; "it will become *all* one thing, or *all* the other."[30] The dynamic would soon have to move in one direction or the other.

Early in the Civil War, Lincoln was visited by a delegation of clergymen who urged him to elevate the moral purpose of the war by making the abolition of slavery the immediate cause for the prosecution of the war. That slavery was the ultimate cause of the conflict, few people at that time had reason to doubt. But to make abolition the immediate object of the war was to risk losing the adherence of border states like Kentucky and Missouri, which would fight for the restoration of the Union, but which would not take up arms for the purpose of abolishing slavery. Lincoln pointed out to the clergymen that "we already have an important principle to rally and unite the people in the fact that constitutional government is at stake. This is a fundamental idea, going about as deep as anything."[31]

It is not surprising, after all, that secession and the attack on law should have come from that party which sought to preserve human

[28] *Ibid.*, p. 222. Emphasis in original.
[29] See *ibid.*, vol. III, p. 95 (speech at Edwardsville, Illinois, September 11, 1858).
[30] *Ibid.*, vol. II, p. 461. Emphasis in original.
[31] *Ibid.*, vol. V, p. 424.

slavery in America. The defenders of slavery were moved to armed rebellion as a result of the election of 1860, in which they were as free as any other faction in national politics to persuade their fellow citizens and gain assent for their position. At the same time, as part of the processes of a constitutional order, the courts of law were always accessible to them, and as it turned out, the courts were mainly supportive of their interests. The partisans of slavery could not have been claiming, then, that they had been denied some essential freedom that it was the obligation of a constitutional order to provide. What they were claiming, rather, was nothing less than a right to win, a right to be ensured that the election would come out in their favor. When it did not, they rejected the obligation to obey the authorities who were lawfully constituted by those elections. But when the seceding states rejected, in this way, the claims of legitimate authority, they had to affirm, by indirection, the claims of *illegitimate* authority. Surely it was never their purpose to affirm the understanding that they had a right to prevail only when they had succeeded in persuading other citizens and gaining the assent of a majority. The act of taking up arms expressed eloquently—far more eloquently than anything the Southerners could merely say—their refusal to offer reasons and seek the consent of others, who were joined with them in a common polity. By necessity, the secessionists were asserting the right to prevail simply on the strength of their own action at arms. Rightness would be measured by success alone; the flexing of raw power would stand as its own justification. In short, Might—once again—would make Right.

Lincoln grasped here the connections that apparently eluded even some of the most zealous partisans of the Union: the secessionists could not attack the notion of law without striking at the premises of a government that was founded on "the consent of the governed." But law, of course, arose from the nature of "rational beings," who had the capacity to give and understand reasons; and a government by consent flowed, in the same way, from the recognition of what it was that made human beings different from other animals. The construction arranged itself with a perfect coherence: who else but the party of slavery would strike at the premises of natural equality that provided the foundation for law itself and the case for democratic government?

In his First Inaugural Address, Lincoln laid bare the implications of secession with a stringent clarity: "Why may not any portion of a new confederacy, a year or two hence, arbitrarily secede again, precisely as portions of the present Union now claim to secede from it?" Why couldn't South Carolina secede from the secession (in the way that "West" Virginia would secede from Virginia and the Confederacy)?

But then, why couldn't counties loyal to the Confederacy secede from South Carolina? Why couldn't towns secede from their counties—and individuals from their towns? "Plainly," said Lincoln, "the central idea of secession, is the essence of anarchy":

> A majority, held in restraint by constitutional checks, and limitations, and always changing easily, with deliberate changes of popular opinions and sentiments, is the only true sovereign of a free people. Whoever rejects it, does, of necessity, fly to anarchy or to despotism. Unanimity is impossible; the rule of a minority, as a permanent arrangement, is wholly inadmissable; so that, rejecting the majority principle, anarchy, or despotism in some form, is all that is left.[32]

If the existence of morals makes law justified and necessary, it is in principle legitimate for citizens to be bound by some legal process, so long as that process is itself compatible with the moral principles that underlie the notion of law. As Lincoln suggests here, the rule of the majority is not itself a principle; it is an *inference* from a principle. It is the only arrangement compatible with the principle of natural equality.[33] In the abstract, there is no reason to suppose that a minority, simply because it *is* a numerical minority, has a moral claim to rule the majority. If the choice had to be made on the basis merely of numbers, then with the premises of natural equality we should have to say that the "opinion" of the majority deserves precedence over the opinion of the minority. As Lincoln remarks, the requirement of unanimity would be impossible to meet; but quite apart from that, a requirement of unanimity would be merely another arrangement for the rule of a minority. For under one version of the rule of unanimity, the dissent of one person might be sufficient to bar any act of legislation; it may even be sufficient to block 99.99 percent of other citizens from forming a common polity and committing one another to a new constitution. One person, in effect, might rule the rest. That arrangement would have to be discarded, therefore, on the same grounds that would make the rule of the minority inadmissible as a permanent arrangement.

If the requirement of unanimity simply means that the law may operate, but that it will be valid only for those who accept it, then the arrangement would be incompatible with the very notion of morals and law. It would have to mean, quite exactly, that no rule may be valid or binding for a person unless he himself regards it as acceptable.

[32] *Ibid.*, vol. IV, pp. 267-68.
[33] See, on this point, Jaffa, *supra*, note 10, p. 149.

That is, of course, the "principle" that defines anarchy, and it explains at the same time why anarchy must be in principle wrong: not because it promises to create disorder, but because it rejects the very concept of morals. It must deny that there are in fact valid propositions about matters of right and wrong—propositions that command our respect because they do not depend for their validity on anyone's "personal" or "subjective" feelings. As we shall see presently, the existence of morals would stand as one of those "necessary" truths we are obliged to acknowledge, and any perspective in politics that ultimately rests on the rejection of a necessary truth is condemned, at its root, to incoherence.

If the rule of the minority and the rule of unanimity must be rejected on principle, that leaves only the rule of the majority—but the rule of the majority under a mandate with moral boundaries. As Lincoln made clear, the ruling majority is still a majority "held in restraint by constitutional checks and limitations." It is not a majority that is free to build its policies on premises which are inconsistent with the principles of a constitutional order. It is not competent, as we have seen, to legislate slavery for a minority or even for itself. And anyone who rejects this set of understandings has to fly, as Lincoln said, either to "anarchy or despotism." This scheme might be rejected, on the one hand, by denying that it is legitimate for anyone to be bound to rules that do not suit his interests, and which he cannot accept. That position literally rejects the concepts of morals and law, and is indeed the essence of "anarchy." On the other hand, the sense of an obligation to the law might be rejected by those rare people who insist that they are above the laws made for other men, that it would be radically unjust to impose upon them the regulations which are made, as Plato said, for people "in the bulk." Anarchy or despotism: with anarchy, there is no possibility of binding people to a common law, for in the logic of anarchy there are no moral truths, accessible to human beings, that make it justified for some men to rule or for other men to efface themselves in obedience. With anarchy, then, human beings are in a critical sense *beneath* the prospects for law. With despotism, certain men are *above* the law made for other people; indeed, they are almost a species apart. Anarchy, then, or despotism: man would be either beneath the law or above it. He would be, as Aristotle said, either "a beast or a god."

THE ATTRIBUTES in human nature that make law and polity necessary also establish, at the same time, that creatures with the capacity for reason may be ruled rightfully only with their consent. For Lincoln, as for Rousseau and Kant, the principles that establish the necessity of law also entail a commitment to republican government as the only form of government that is, in principle, legitimate. Of course the world is filled with governments that are conspicuously less than "constitutional orders," and many of them have to be tolerated out of prudence or necessity. But anyone who understands the principles on which a government of law is founded will understand also that those principles enjoin a regime of free elections and constitutional restraints. To demand the conditions of lawful government is to demand the conditions of republican government, and as enlightened men understood, the case for popular government and the case against slavery are in point of principle the same. They rest on the same premises, and those premises are grounded in nature, in the things that separate human beings from animals. For that reason, the case for republican government, like the case against slavery, would be everywhere the same. It would be valid in every place where the nature of human beings has remained the same and where men are still distinguishable from animals.

Lincoln had no reason to doubt, then, that the case against slavery was universal in its reach—that, in point of principle, slavery was as wrong in France or Afghanistan as it was in the United States. And so, if the United States did not take up arms for the sake of ending slavery wherever it existed in the world, it was not because we lacked the standards by which to judge that slavery was quite as wrong for other peoples, with customs and "cultures" different from our own. If the United States held back from a course of intervention abroad, it did not hold back then *out of principle*, but out of prudence. It held back because it lacked the means of establishing and preserving the conditions of freedom in countries distant from its own, and it did not wish to risk the survival of the republican experiment in the United States through a series of rash adventures abroad.

But if we understand, with Lincoln, that the case against slavery and the case in favor of democratic government are in principle the same, then a comparable argument applies to the defense of free government in the world. There is no reason to doubt that the case for republican government is as valid for other countries, with exotic customs and cuisines, as it is for the United States; that it is valid in the same way for France and Afghanistan—or Vietnam and Cambodia. And if the United States holds back from a course of intervention abroad, it cannot be because we lack the grounds on which to say that democratic government is in principle superior to any local despotism. If we hold back at all, it cannot be out of principle, but out of prudence: i.e., because we may doubt, in any case, that we have the means of achieving our ends. It must be said, however, that the means available to the United States in the middle of the twentieth century have been vastly larger than the means which were present in the nineteenth century. In our own time the United States has in fact been able to project its power successfully abroad, and in that way it has indeed managed to restore and preserve free governments. What had to be forborne in the nineteenth century out of a sense of prudence—out of a realistic reckoning of our capacities—may not be forborne in all places today with the same justification.

BY THIS MOMENT it should be plain that I have been alluding to the argument which arose over the American involvement in Vietnam. I shall have more to say later about the question of that war, which deserves to be treated with its proper degrees of complication. I wish merely to make the point here that, whatever the grounds on which the war in Vietnam may ultimately be defended or condemned, it could never have been tenable to argue against the war on the grounds that the United States was merely imposing its own "values" on a culture in which the principles of constitutional government bore no validity.

At the very least, it would have to be said that the propositions I have reviewed here all have political consequence. They would be bound, in fact, to arouse the most concentrated scrutiny and challenge among those who came to define themselves politically by their opposition to the war in Vietnam, and who have found the touchstone of their political understanding in the conviction that there are, strictly speaking, no moral truths (i.e., that there are no truths about matters of right and wrong that are universal in their validity). The most radical question that is likely to be raised against the arguments I have offered, then, is whether they can be *known* to be *true*. The universal validity of the case for democratic government and of the case against human slavery depends on certain propositions about human nature which Madison and Jefferson, Lincoln and Kant, understood to be *necessary* truths. The question, as Lincoln recognized, was whether the proposition "All men are created equal" really did express a "self-evident" truth or whether it was, in the words of Senator Pettit of Indiana, a "self-evident lie."[34] The proposition "All men are created equal," and the implications that arise from that doctrine, are drawn from the understanding of a creature with the capacity to reason over moral things. They would illustrate, in other words, part of Kant's contention

[34] Lincoln, *supra*, note 15, vol. III, pp. 301-302.

that all valid moral propositions must be drawn, as inferences, from the nature of a "rational being" and from the idea of morals itself. Whether these inferences have the standing of truths will depend, then, on whether the propositions that assert the existence of morals (and of beings with the capacity for morals) have the standing, themselves, of axiomatic truths. If these "first" truths can be established, they would confirm, at the same time, the truth of "All men are created equal"—and of all those other, politically interesting propositions which emerge in its train. Of course, if we can explain why moral propositions rest on "necessary" truths, we would establish even more. We would explain why moral propositions must have the quality of being universal *and* categorical—why they must be true in all times and places, and under all conditions.

IV

ON NECESSARY TRUTHS AND THE
EXISTENCE OF MORALS

Anyone who makes it his vocation these days to teach in the "moral sciences" will soon encounter a primate who protests that, after all, "there is no truth." The stock response of the philosopher, of course, is to ask whether *that* proposition is itself true: "The proposition that 'there is no truth': Is *that* proposition true?" If it is, then people will no doubt be pleased to discover that there *is* truth after all. We know then that we have at least one truth, and now it is a matter of discovering just how many more we know. If it is not true that "there is no truth," then it follows that there *is* truth.

The challenger who was seized with the revelation that there is no truth was not refuted with a mere play on words. He had simply put himself in the unenviable position of trying to deny a proposition that cannot be denied without falling into self-contradiction. The proposition "There is truth" is a proposition of that kind; and when we are in the presence of propositions that cannot be contradicted except with propositions that are themselves self-contradictory, we are in the presence of what Kant called an "apodictic," or necessary, truth. That Franklin Roosevelt was the thirty-second president of the United States is an incontrovertible truth. But it was hardly "necessary" that Franklin Roosevelt be our thirty-second president. It was not true in the way it must be true, as a matter of necessity that "two contradictory propositions cannot both be true." The law of contradiction expresses a necessary truth, and all efforts to refute it will fall into the embarrassment of self-contradiction. At the same time, it should be apparent that a truth like the law of contradiction is not merely an "analytic" statement in which the predicate is contained in the definition of the subject (e.g., "A triangle has three sides"). We do not start with a definition and then extract the law of contradiction; in fact, the law of contradiction is something we must be able to grasp on our own *before* we are capable of understanding or assessing "definitions." If our knowledge were built up simply through a system of definitions, without any mediating system of "logic," how would we be able to assess definitions that were internally inconsistent? In the naiveté of our youth, we might be told of a "squircle"—part square and part circle—a closed curve, all points of which are equidistant from a common center, but which contains, in addition, four equal sides. If we knew things only through definitions, we would have to nod credulously, add the "squircle" to the inventory of our "knowledge," and pass on to the next item (the "madcap insurance salesman").

What we discover, then, is that necessary truths, like the law of contradiction, must be understood before we are capable of understanding other things. They cannot be "demonstrated" in the sense of carrying out an experiment, because if these truths are not understood, anterior to experiments or "experience," we would have no basis on which to understand the experience. But when we speak in this way of propositions that must be grasped as necessary before we can know anything else—before we can know "secondary" truths—we are speaking, in the strictest sense, of "first principles."

Of course, there is an immanent risk in our day that the settled convictions of the educated classes will be disturbed by the suggestion that our understanding on any matter of consequence may be rooted in propositions that hold something more than a "relative," or decorously tentative, claim to truth. To ascribe to any true proposition the attribute of "necessity" is to stir incredulity or even alarm. And yet, we have long incorporated in our understanding the recognitions of "necessity" that Aristotle set forth in our first primers on the laws of reasoning. If a closed curve contains the features that define a "circle," then it will have to be regarded as a circle, and *by necessity* it will have to exhibit all of the properties that attach to circles. It would have to be true, then, that all of its radii will be equal to one another, as would be the case with any other circle. This kind of necessity has been labeled by some as "lexical necessity"—the necessity that arises from the logic of definition—and it acquires its necessity from the law of identity: that what is true of any thing must be true for any other thing that contains the same defining features. For Aristotle, this notion could embrace the necessity that attaches to any established fact from one moment to the next. Hence, "if it is true to say that a thing is white, it must necessarily be white."[1] Or, to put it another way, if it is Jones who is judged guilty of a crime, it must of necessity be the same Jones who is condemned to jail.

[1] Aristotle, *On Interpretation*, 18b; see also 18b20, 22a, 22a15, 23a20, 23b10; *Posterior Analytics*, bk. I, chs. 1-2, 6 ("Demonstrative knowledge must rest on necessary basic truths; . . . Now attributes attaching essentially to their subjects attach necessarily to them; for essential attributes are either elements in the essential nature of their subjects, or contain their subjects as elements in their own essential nature"); *Metaphysics*, bk. V, ch. 5, bk. VI, ch. 2; and D.W. Hamlyn, "On Necessary Truth," *Mind*, vol. 70 (1961), pp. 514-25.

Although the matter has not been entirely free of contention in some of its more refined domains, it has been conventional to apply the language of "necessity" to certain propositions of "entailment" or implication. If I wish to reach my car, it becomes *necessary* for me to leave my bedroom. The necessity in this case is "hypothetical": it arises only on the condition that I wish to reach my car, and it depends on the firmness of the connection between the end and the means. Even stricter relations of entailment would arise through the logic of a syllogism. And so, if "all men are mortal," and if "Socrates is a man," it must follow, with a *necessary* force, that "Socrates is mortal." The conclusion would flow, however, with the same necessary force if the syllogism had run: "All leprechauns are Irish," "Harry is a leprechaun"; therefore, "Harry is Irish." The logical necessity that attaches to a syllogism is quite independent of the question of whether the premises in the syllogism are true, or whether they refer to anything that really exists.

As we shall see, the propositions that may be extracted, as implications, from the "logic of morals" can claim this syllogistic force of validity even before we weigh the question of whether morals themselves exist and whether their existence can be known to us as a necessary truth. We shall find, for example, that the language of morals makes no sense when it is directed toward acts that are determined by the causal laws of nature. We could never sensibly say that the earth is *obliged* to revolve about the sun, and that it would be *wrong*—or worthy of blame—if it did not. The language of morals must presuppose, *of necessity*, a being who is free to choose one course of action or another. It is only because that being is free that he can be held responsible for his acts, and that he may, with coherence, be blamed or praised. When people are rewarded or punished not for their own acts, but for the accident of their racial background, they are not praised or blamed for anything that it was in their power to affect, and they are treated, therefore, as though they did not in fact possess the freedom or autonomy of moral agents. They are treated as though their acts were determined by causal laws beyond their own governance. As we shall see, then, the wrongness of this racial discrimination is rooted in the very logic of morals, and therefore it must be said that racial discrimination is wrong *of necessity*.

Those who may not be alert to the syllogistic nature of this judgment may make the mistake of supposing that we are offering merely an empirical assessment, and they may be tempted to argue that these propositions we put forth with the mandate of "necessity" are not so irresistible after all. In fact, as they may point out, we find people all around us who feel no special strain, and garner at times no small profit, in resisting these "commands" of moral necessity. But I hope it would be clear that this response to the problem must be forever inapt. That men are actually free to ignore the "requirements" of morals—that they will suffer no impediments from the laws of physics as they ponder their duties and their inclinations—is the very mark of their freedom as moral agents. But it is also the condition that engages their responsibility to reflect on the standards that must govern their judgments. And it cannot affect in any way the logical standing of those "requirements" or "laws" that are made necessary by the logic of morals itself.

They are made necessary, that is, once we have moral agents, who have access to moral understanding. I have no intention here of suggesting that morals have a kind of necessary ontological existence in the universe—that the laws of morals would exist even if there were no creatures whose conduct would lend itself to moral judgment, and who were capable in turn of reasoning over matters of right or wrong. But we would offer no concession here in the name of the "moral sciences" that could not be offered as well for any of the other sciences: it would be quite as apt to concede that, without the presence of "matter," there would be no laws of physics in the universe. If we take the universe, however, as we find it, it happens to be a universe that contains moral beings. They condemn and commend; and they apparently recognize, when they register their judgments of right or wrong, that they are expressing more than their personal, subjective feelings. When we begin with this logic of morals, the corollaries or implications we extract may claim that force of necessity which attaches to deductions that are validly drawn. The question remains of whether this "logic of morals," which we persistently recognize, can be regarded as anything more than a salutary fiction. If certain judgments can be said to flow, as a matter of necessity from the logic of morals, can it be said that the logic of morals does itself have the standing of a "necessary truth"? As I shall try to show, a matured reflection on this subject would lead us back to an ancient understanding: that the first truths or axioms of our moral understanding are bound up with those "first principles" of knowledge that stand at the foundation of any system of "understanding." These "first principles" of morals would become clearer to us, I think, if we were to return to the problem I raised earlier and begin to draw out the logic and properties of "first principles."

As I HAVE already pointed out, first principles cannot be "demonstrated" in the sense of being proved through experiment, because they must be known anterior to experience and experiments. The understanding behind these distinctions was set forth with an admirable clarity by Thomas Reid at the end of the eighteenth century. Reid noted that a first principle had to state a "necessary proposition," and that "propositions of this kind, from their nature, are incapable of proof by induction." They could not be demonstrated through experiments because experiments depended on experience, and "experience informs us only of what is, or has been, not of what must be":[2]

> Though it should be found by experience in a thousand cases, that the area of a plane triangle is equal to the rectangle under the altitude and half the base, this would not prove that it must be so in all cases, and cannot be otherwise. . . .

If it were strictly true that we can know anything only on the basis of experience, then what we know of triangles we would know only from the ones we have measured. We would not be able to speak about the properties of those triangles we may encounter next year, because we have not yet "experienced" the future. Through a series of trials and measurements, we may begin to form suspicions and draw generalizations about the triangles we have seen, but nothing in that generalization about past experience would "prove" the existence of properties that must hold true enduringly. Our confidence in the existence of those properties arises only when we have grasped the idea of a triangle or the principles that define its nature.[3]

The problem may be put in a better way when we consider how we arrive at the answer to the question, "Is there any number so large that one more may not be added to it?" If we sought to arrive at the answer by "experiment"—by recalling the largest number we knew and trying to add one more unit—we would still be here counting a week from now. Perhaps after a few operations of this kind, in which the incurable empiricist keeps building up his largest number, he will discover that, after adding one more unit to the highest number he can imagine, the result, persistently, is another number. At that point he may come to the recognition that the answer to this question did

---

[2] Thomas Reid, *Essays on the Intellectual Powers of Man* (Cambridge: MIT Press, 1969 [1814-15]), p. 654.

[3] H.J. Paton put it well, restating Kant on this point. "We may be obliged," wrote Paton, "to draw a triangle on a paper in order to help our imagination, but we are not thinking about the seen triangle. We are thinking about a triangle whose characteristics are determined only by the *principle* of its construction." Paton, *Kant's Metaphysic of Experience* (London: George Allen & Unwin, 1936), vol. I, p. 159. Emphasis added. See, also, pp. 140-41.

not depend at all on a series of "experiments." The answer flowed simply from a recognition of what was meant by a "number."

How did he grasp the notion of a number? Was it offered to him in a definition? If he were to consult the dictionary, he would discover that "number" means "a member of the set of positive integers; one of a series of symbols of unique meaning in a fixed order which may be derived by counting." But then, what elementary things would he have to know before he could understand the meaning of *one* member in a *series* of symbols with a *fixed order*? And when he derives numbers by "counting," *what* is it that is counted? He would have to be able to grasp the notion of a "one"—a unit—which may be added to others. That is, he would have to grasp the notion of a unit, separable from other units, and he could hardly do that without recognizing, instantly, the difference between "one" and "many." He would be bearing out, then, part of Kant's inventory of those understandings that must be accessible to us *a priori*—without dependence on experience—because without these understandings, we would be incapable of ordering the evidence of our senses and comprehending our "experience." Among these categories of understanding Kant placed the notion of *quantity*: that is, we are able to understand, *a priori*, the differences among singularity, plurality, and totality (one, many, and all).[4] Before the man in our example could comprehend the definition of "number" that was given in the dictionary, he had to understand these things. It should be evident, on reflection, that these points could not have been demonstrated to him or broken down into simpler components, which may be conveyed through definition. He had to understand these rudimentary things before he could understand a demonstration or a definition.

But he could not have grasped the difference between one and many—between unity and plurality—unless he had been aware of space or time. With the awareness of space, he could understand the separation between one unit and others. Without a recognition of space, he might still be able to understand the notion of number if he had an awareness of time: he might be able to recognize a succession of sensations or feelings, even if he did not perceive changes of objects in space. In that way, he could understand the notions of one and many. It is possible to understand a series of integers, as a strictly logical matter, without the need to assume a temporal sequence in which, say, 4 would have to come *after* 1 and 3. But if, as the dictionary suggests, we understand the notion of number more readily when we imagine a process of *counting* units in a series with a fixed order, we

---

[4] See Immanuel Kant, *Critique of Pure Reason*, A: 79-83ff.; B: 105-109.

must be presupposing then the existence of time. When we think of adding one number to another, we must conceive of a sequence unfolding in time. But to say that we "assume" or presuppose the existence of time is not to say that we indulge an arbitrary assumption whose truth cannot be known. It is to recognize, rather, that we are dealing with a necessary truth or first principle whose understanding provides the foundation for the understanding of all other things.

Consider for a moment the prospect of offering an explanation of these matters to the skeptic who would insist that he perceives the world as spaceless and timeless. One would have to wonder, of course, just how he manages to perceive the difference between himself and the person he challenges for an explanation. Putting aside, however, this minor hindrance, how would it be possible to offer an "explanation" to the skeptic without offering to him an arrangement of words and sentences? In order to form an explanation, the words will have to be arranged in a pattern that has meaning, and the sentences will have to be arranged in a sequence: an initial point will have to be followed by a development before we can present a conclusion. In order to carry on the conversation and exchange explanations, the skeptic would be compelled to assume that the words he is hearing are coming out in the sequence in which they are being offered; and if he raises skepticism on that point, he can do it only by offering, in turn, words arranged in a *sequence*. The person who denies the existence of time and space is speaking literal nonsense, and it is important not to delude ourselves into regarding it as anything else—as though any utterance, offered in a "philosophic mode," must be immanently plausible.

The man of understanding should cultivate an awareness of when he is urging on his listeners propositions that are "self-refuting." And he falls into contradiction, inescapably, when he seeks to reject the existence of time and space, which are necessary attributes of that world of objects in which he finds his place. As we try to trace back our understanding and recognize just what we must know before we can know anything else, we would retrace Kant's steps and come to the recognition, as he did, that behind his categories of understanding lay the even more fundamental awareness of time and space. H.J. Paton stated the point quite precisely, in a commentary on Kant, that "space and time are a fact, because experience is a fact: but they are not merely one of the many facts which we find in experience; they are the condition of all the other facts."[5] The recognition of time and space as necessary facts provides the foundation from which it is

[5] Paton, *supra*, note 3, p. 152.

possible to unfold Kant's understanding of the categories of understanding, the concepts of "pure" understanding that cannot be dependent on experience. If we are aware of time, it is because we
apprehend certain "constants," which may preserve their essential
character even while they are affected by change. And so it is possible
to conceive of an enduring "substance" of things that does not alter
with time or location: Socrates sitting is the same as Socrates standing;
the one who was Socrates last year is the same one who is Socrates
this year.[6]

This kind of recognition was placed by Kant under the category of
"relation," and along with our capacity to recognize the enduring
substance of things, he included our capacity to know the difference
between correlation and causation: between recognizing that one event
seems to be attended persistently by the occurrence of another, and
understanding that one event actually is the cause of another. The
state of mind of the person who confounds the two was reflected in
a sardonic sign I once saw in the office of a psychologist: "Experience
has proven that the beating of tom-toms during a solar eclipse invariably restores the sun." As I have become older, experience has impressed me with the sober apprehension that the Soviets create a military crisis with their forces in Cuba every time that neckties become
narrow. (It happened in the early 1960's, and when ties narrowed
again in 1979, the forces of History apparently moved the Soviets
toward adventurism once again.) It is one of the advantages built into
the "constitution of our natures" that we need not be prisoners of
such correlations. But the same understanding which allows us to
escape gullibility of this kind would also lead us to the rudiments that
are necessary to moral reasoning. If it is possible to speak of sequence
and causation, it becomes possible to speak of *moral* causation. It
becomes sensible to say, for example, that Smith hit Jones over the

---

[6] As Kant expressed the point, "Our apprehension of the manifold of phenomena is
always successive, and therefore always changing. By it alone therefore we can never
determine whether the manifold, as an object of experience, is coexistent or successive,
unless there is something in it which exists always, that is, something constant and
permanent, while change and succession are nothing but so many kinds (*modi*) of time
in which the permanent exists. Relations of time are therefore possible in the permanent
only (coexistence and succession being the only relations of time) so that the permanent
is the substratum of the empirical representation of time itself, and in it alone all
determination of time is possible. . . . If we were to ascribe a succession to time itself,
it would be necessary to admit another time in which such succession should be possible.
Only through the permanent does *existence* in different parts of a series of time assume
a *quantity* which we call duration." Kant, *supra*, note 4, A: 182-84; B: 225-27. Emphasis
in original.

head; that he *caused* the injury to Jones; and that he is therefore properly charged with the blame. And if the understandings necessary to moral reasoning are accessible to us *a priori*, as necessary truths, then we may be alerted once again to the implications of our natures: viz., that we are so constituted, as moral agents, that the rudiments of moral reasoning are necessary parts of our understanding.

WHETHER IT IS possible to speak of the difference between causation and correlation—or to regard causation as a necessary relation—is precisely what was at issue in the dispute between Kant and Hume. For Hume, the objects of human reason or knowledge arranged themselves into two categories: "relations of ideas" and "matters of fact." "Relations of ideas" involved what Kant would later call "analytic" propositions—statements in which the predicate is contained in the subject (e.g., all triangles have three sides). These propositions are found in subjects like mathematics; they can be discovered through "the mere operation of thought," without dependence on experience; and they express truths that will "for ever retain their certainty and evidence."[7]

"Matters of fact" referred to what we would call today "empirical matters," which are dependent on experience or the evidence of the senses. The statements that issue in this domain are what Kant would have called "synthetic"—they bring together concepts that are not connected by logical entailment, and they convey information. ("It was Booth who shot Lincoln.") But it was Hume's argument that knowledge in this field could not claim the certainty and necessity that characterized the propositions which arose under "relations of ideas."[8] The most significant propositions concerning matters of fact were propositions about relations of cause and effect, and it was Hume's argument that this kind of knowledge is inherently problematic. "I shall venture to affirm," he said, "as a general proposition, which admits of no exception, that the knowledge of this relation is not, in any instance, attained by reasonings *a priori*; but arises entirely from experience, when we find that any particular objects are constantly conjoined with each other."[9] Hume pointed out, for example, that a person would not know, without experience, that a transparent fluid such as water may suffocate him. But Hume went on from there to call into question the possibility of understanding a distinction between

[7] David Hume, *An Enquiry Concerning Human Understanding*, vol. IV in *The Philosophical Works of David Hume* (Boston: Little, Brown, 1854), sec. IV, pt. I, p. 30.
[8] *Ibid.*
[9] *Ibid.*, p. 32.

correlations—the frequent association or succession of two events—and the relation of two events that are connected through a principle of cause and effect. Hume went so far as to assert that "the mind can never possibly find the effect in the supposed cause, by the most accurate scrutiny and examination. For the effect is *totally different from the cause and consequently can never be discovered in it.*"[10]

What Hume suggested was that relations of cause and effect may be indistinguishable from random events, and the example he chose was the movement of billiard balls. One ball may be heading on a straight path toward another, and it may be predicted that the second ball will move off in another direction when the two balls collide. But Hume asked whether it is not possible at least to conceive of many other possibilities. Without knowing anything from experience about the movement of balls, why can it not be conceivable just as well that the two balls will meet and remain at rest, or that the first ball will hit the second and move back again without causing any change in the position of the second ball? None of these events, Hume suggested, is deducible from the notion of a moving ball, and so he went on to conclude that "every effect is a distinct event from its cause. It could not, therefore, be discovered in the cause, and the first invention or conception of it, *a priori*, must be entirely arbitrary."[11]

It was one thing, however, to suggest that the trajectory of a ball cannot be derived from the idea of a moving ball; it was quite another to suggest that it is impossible to understand the principle or "law" which accounts for the movement of bodies like the two billiard balls—laws which guarantee that the movement of bodies, under certain specified conditions, will not be random, but patterned or "lawful." Of course, we can know nothing *a priori* of objects such as billiard balls and their trajectories. On that point, Hume and Kant were in agreement. But in denying that it was possible to know *a priori* of cause and effect—to know that for every effect there was indeed a cause—Hume had to surrender to the measurement of correlations in every case. On Hume's premises it would not be possible to grasp the principle that connected two events without having to test that relation anew in each instance. It was as though we would have to keep meas-

---

[10] *Ibid.*, p. 34. Emphasis added. This part of Hume's argument was bound up with the question of "contiguity" and "succession" in the events that marked a causal sequence. This particular problem, as well as the larger question of Hume's teaching on causation, is treated with its proper complexity in Tom L. Beauchamp and Alexander Rosenberg, *Hume and the Problem of Causation* (New York: Oxford University Press, 1981), especially ch. 5.

[11] Hume, *supra*, note 7, p. 35.

uring each right triangle in order to be sure that the current triangle bears out the Pythagorean theorem in the way that all previous triangles have. It was precisely Hume's argument, however, that it is not possible to have knowledge of this kind about the material world—the world which makes itself known through the senses apart from pure reason—and therefore that it is not possible to have statements which are *both* synthetic and *a priori*. That is to say, in Hume's understanding, it is not possible to make statements about the world of empirical reality that can claim the standing of necessary truths.

But if there is no quality of necessity that attaches to the very notion of cause and effect—if it is impossible to speak of a connection in principle that joins two events (e.g., the striking of a match causing a flame)—then it is indeed doubtful that one can speak plausibly of one event "causing" another. And if it cannot be said with certainty that any event is caused, there can hardly be a ground on which to hold people responsible, in the domain of morals, for the harms they may be said to "cause." Thomas Reid made this connection at once, and he pointed it up with the devastating humor that Hume's doctrines were persistently able to inspire in him. "Suppose," said Reid, "a man to be found on the highway, his skull fractured, his body pierced with deadly wounds, his watch and money carried off." A coronor's jury is convened to consider the "cause" of this man's death—whether it was an accident or a deliberate murder. If the jury should happen to contain a person schooled in the teachings of Hume, he would have to be moved to challenge the premises of the inquest and ask whether there was *any* cause of the event. If that question were to be judged simply on the basis of past "experience," then, as Reid observed, "it is dubious on which side the weight of the argument might stand. But we may venture to say, that, if Mr. Hume had been of such a jury, he would have laid aside his philosophical principles, and acted according to the dictates of common prudence."[12]

Let us suppose we have a town that has suffered a serious problem of littering, and that a local empiricist had discovered a strong *correlation* between the appearance of political workers on the street, handing out literature, and a noticeable increase in leaflets and hand-

---

[12] Reid, *supra*, note 2, p. 659; cf. Hume, *supra*, note 7, sec. VIII, pt. I, pp. 104-109, especially 108-109. Reid (p. 658) observed tartly: "In great families there are so many bad things done by a certain personage called *nobody*, that it is proverbial, that there is a nobody about every house who does a great deal of mischief; and even where there is the exactest inspection and government, many events will happen on which no other account can be found: So that, if we trust merely to experience in this matter, nobody will be found to be a very active person, and to have no inconsiderable share in the

bills strewn about the street. Let us imagine that the town council, faced with this striking correlation, responded to the problem by banning the distribution of literature in the public streets. In fact, there have been cases of this kind, and they have raised questions about restricting, without a compelling justification, the right of people to engage in legitimate political expression by spreading leaflets. Regulations of this type would indeed be subject to a serious constitutional challenge, and we would probably urge the local authorities to find other, more direct means of dealing with the problem of littering without restricting legitimate expression. But if we were to make that argument, we would register our awareness that we are in fact able to penetrate the maze of "stronger and weaker correlations" and pick out the events that are more directly the *cause* of the littering. In that case, we would be more likely to treat the problem by putting a ban directly on littering—on the discarding of paper in the street—rather than punishing people for distributing or receiving literature.

The difference between the two responses would be reflected in the propositions that have to underlie the law in each separate case. One would be cast in the language of probability and uncertainty; the other would have the force of necessity. On the one hand the authorities might say, (1) "There is a strong possibility or likelihood that people who receive unsolicited material in the street will thoughtlessly throw it away on the spot." On the other hand it could be said, (2) "If people 'throw away' leaflets, and they mean, as they release them from their hands, to 'throw them away,' the leaflets *will fall down*. And once down, they will constitute litter." There is nothing in the least bit problematic about the principle that determines, for all present and future cases, that when objects like leaflets are released in midair, they are destined to fly *down*. Nor is there anything inscrutable, then, in

---

management of affairs. But whatever countenance this system may have from experience, it is too shocking to common sense to impose upon the most ignorant. A child knows that when his top, or any of his playthings are taken away, it must be done by somebody. Perhaps it would not be difficult to persuade him that it was done by some invisible being, but that it should be done by nobody he cannot believe."

Without fully addressing Reid's argument, Beauchamp and Rosenberg insist nevertheless that Hume's understanding did indeed accommodate the notion that "acts of free will aimed at human goals can be explained causally, while retaining their status as free acts for which we rightly hold persons responsible." See Beauchamp and Rosenberg, *supra*, note 10, pp. 315 and 292. The question, of course, is whether that accommodation is consistent with Hume's argument or whether it represents, as Reid suggests, a response to the command of "common prudence." On the issue of "causes," "reasons," and "determinism," see Daniel N. Robinson, *Philosophy of Psychology* (New York: Columbia University Press, 1985), ch. 2.

the differences between these two propositions. We recognize these distinctions, as we must, every day; and if we do, it is only because we are able to grasp in any case the sense of a principle that connects an event to its sequel as "cause and effect."

But to come to that recognition is to begin sketching the logic of Kant's answer to Hume on the question of "causation"—which was really Kant's answer to Hume on the question of whether it is possible to have necessary truths that are not merely "analytic." At the very least, Hume was willing to allow some credence to the notion that certain events seem to follow upon others in a regular way, and even if he were reluctant to assign the station of a "cause" to any event, he had to acknowledge that some preceding events bear a stronger influence than others on the events that follow. But then, it was quite proper for Kant to raise the question, in the first place, as to whether this elementary notion that certain events do indeed follow, with regularity, upon others is derived merely from "experience," or whether it is, in itself, nothing less than a *necessary* truth about the way the world has to be arranged.

If it could not be taken as a necessary truth that cetain events do objectively precede and follow one another, then even Hume's modified, "empiricist" version of cause and effect would have to be called into question. For we could no longer assume that the succession of perceptions we experience actually reflects the real ordering of things as events unfold before us. We think we see a ship draw its anchor and prepare to leave the harbor, and later we see the ship moving out to sea. And yet we would not be warranted in assuming that this order of events, as it appeared to our senses, was a product of anything more than our own subjective understanding. For all we *strictly* know (on the premises of Hume's argument), the ship moving out to sea might have *preceded* the drawing of the anchor and the preparation of the ship for departure. As silly as the prospect may be, Kant's point is that there would be no basis for asserting anything to the contrary as a necessary truth if we admit Hume's premise that what we know, we can know only on the strength of "experience." What must become apparent to us then, after a more rigorous reflection, is that if experience can really teach us that "something happens," it is only because, as Kant remarked, "we always *presuppose* that something precedes on which it follows *by rule*."[13]

Consider, for example, two contrasting cases offered by Kant. In one, we look at a house, and we may glance first at the roof and then

[13] Kant, *supra*, note 4, A: 191-97; B: 236-42. Emphasis added.

at the basement, or we may view the left side and then the right—or we may do all of this in reverse order, and nothing may be affected in our perception of the house. But in a second case we view a ship advancing down a stream, and the ship must be at point A before it can arrive at point B, further along in its journey. In viewing the house, no rule determined the order in which the perceptions had to be arranged for the sake of comprehending the house. In the case, however, of an *event*—the ship moving downstream—"there is always a rule, which makes the order of the successive perceptions . . . necessary." In viewing the movement of the ship, "it is impossible," as Kant said, "that the ship should be perceived first below and then higher up. We see therefore that the order in the succession of perceptions in our apprehension is here determined, and our apprehension regulated by that order."[14]

Of course, as Kant himself pointed out, the nature of the rule becomes more evident to us as we see it manifested in any experience (in the case, for example, of the ship moving downstream or a ball rolling down an inclined plane). But unless we understand already the immanent necessity of *a rule*—unless we presuppose that events are indeed arranged in a temporal order, with certain events A preceding certain events B and determining the position of B in the sequence— unless this elementary point is absorbed as a necessary truth, *it becomes impossible to impute any meaning to the succession of perceptions that flash before us*. As Kant remarked, "it is under this supposition only [i.e., the supposition that a rule of causation exists] that an experience of anything that happens becomes possible." The existence of the rule, as he said, became clearer through experience, but the awareness of the rule—the awareness of the very notion of causation— "was nevertheless the foundation of all experience, and consequently preceded it *a priori*."[15]

Professor Lewis White Beck has shown in a short, telling piece that this was the most decisive part of Kant's answer to Hume: viz., that Hume's own argument becomes intelligible only on the basis of Kant's understanding.[16] Before Hume could speak even of stronger or weaker

[14] *Ibid.*, A: 191-93; B: 236-38.

[15] *Ibid.*, A: 195-97; B: 240-42.

[16] Lewis White Beck, "Once More unto the Breach: Kant's Answer to Hume, Again," *Ratio* (1967), pp. 33-37. Professor Beck elicited an intriguing response from Professor Jeffrie Murphy, who thought it quite as plausible to argue that Kant's position presupposed Hume's premises. See Murphy, "Kant's Second Analogy as an Answer to Hume," *Ratio* (1969), pp. 75-78; for Beck's rejoinder, see the same volume, pp. 82-

correlations, before he could suggest that certain phenomena are likely to bring about others or influence their change, he had to presuppose a chain of happenings. He had to assume that certain events do indeed precede others objectively in a serial, temporal order—that correlations are not merely random events. And yet it should be plain that this assumption, which is absolutely necessary to the contention that experience yields "correlations," could not itself have been derived from experience. As Kant said, it had to be in place before experience could be understood. It had to be present *before* Hume could claim to extract the lesson from experience that there are, in the world, correlations, or regular conjunctions of events, which are distinguishable from random, unconnected happenings.

This predicament may be revealed to us, in one of its weightier applications, if we imagine for a moment that we are at Fenway Park and that a number of impressions on our senses suggested that Carl Yastrzemski is swinging a bat. It so happens that, on one occasion, we have the sensation that, after Yastrzemski swings, the ball winds up over the right-field fence. If we were seized with the premises of a radical skepticism, we might be obliged to hold back from cheering

---

86. The exchange is reproduced in Tom L. Beauchamp (ed.), *Philosophic Problems of Causation* (Encino, California: Dickenson, 1974), pp. 24-34.

It is interesting to consider that skepticism about the concept of causation became fashionable even among physicists and other scientists, as it has become fashionable among many people in the academy today. But there was one notable figure who broke away from this skepticism and returned to an older, classic view of causality, closer to the view of Kant. An illuminating account has been offered by Paul Forman, who observed that "philosophically, Einstein was much influenced [in his early years] by Ernst Mach (1836-1916) and Henri Poincaré (1854-1912), who persuasively expressed certain views which were widespread among late 19th- and early 20th-century physicists. Mach and Poincaré emphasized, on the one hand, that only concepts and constructs capable of being defined in terms of sensory experiences—i.e., in terms of possible experiments—were to be admitted into science. On the other hand, they believed, the actual choice of concepts, especially fundamental concepts, was to a large degree arbitrary, a matter of convention. But while his fellow physicists persisted in this view . . . Einstein himself gradually moved 'backward' philosophically to the *realist* view that scientific constructs—the conservation of energy, say, or the concept of the atom—approximate entities and connections that really exist.

"In one crucial respect, Einstein never deviated from that 'outmoded' realist metaphysics, namely, in his adherence to causality. In the years before the First World War, Einstein's contemporaries declared the notion of cause-and-effect to have no place in physics, which, they alleged, dealt only with functional relations. Yet in these years, Einstein framed profound questions and hypotheses based on the idea of causality, believing firmly that the world is necessarily thus and not otherwise. . . ." Forman, "Einstein and Newton: Two Legacies," *Woodrow Wilson Quarterly* (Winter 1979), pp. 110-12.

for Yastrzemski. For we would run the risk of giving him credit without warrant until we had the chance to consider the question, "What— or who—actually *caused* the ball to fly over the right-field wall?" We may be persuaded, after all, that what are often called "causes" must be measured, in an empirical way, by considering the clusters of correlations that attend the event. In this particular case, it might be observed that every time Yastrzemski has swung and the ball has gone over the fence, vendors were selling beer in the stands. It also turns out that on every occasion in which Yastrzemski has hit a home run, a little old lady sat praying behind home plate. On what basis, then, do we pick out from this cluster of correlations the act of Yastrzemski swinging the bat? Why do we regard that event as "causing" the outcome—unless we grasp a rule or principle that determines the relation between the hitting of the ball with the bat and the trajectory taken by the ball?

But let us suppose that we are in the company of a skeptic, who professes not to be "sure" that the impressions which register on his senses reflect events that are really taking place. Or, he may doubt that these impressions reflect the succession of events in the order in which they are actually unfolding. On what basis could we convince him that his senses have led him faithfully in this instance to recognize a rule of causation that exists in nature? What if we were to perform an "experiment" by reversing the order? What if we threw the ball over the fence to determine whether it was the flight of the ball that had *caused* Yastrzemski to swing? What if we compelled the vendors to sell beer and the little old lady to pray, under controlled conditions, with Yastrzemski at the plate? But if the flight of the ball over the fence was followed by Yastrzemski swinging, if the praying and the selling of beer were followed by Yastrzemski hitting the ball over the fence, how could we be sure that *these* events actually occurred in the sequence in which we were seeing them?

On the premises of the skeptic, no proposition about events can be assessed; for unless it is assumed, as a matter of necessity, that there is a rule which governs the sequence of events in nature, there literally cannot be any events, but merely a series of sensations without necessary connection. And, of course, if the premises of the skeptic are warranted, then as I indicated earlier, we cannot even accord any meaning to the challenge he seeks to raise. In order to express a proposition that registers his doubts, the skeptic is compelled to speak in sentences which are ordered in a sequence. As I asked earlier, how can we know that the words we are hearing are arranged in the order in which he is expressing them? And how can we know that his conclusion is being drawn *after* the statement of his premises and his reasons? By his own premises, therefore, the skeptic could not possibly claim to say anything that would be true and that could challenge the understanding, grounded in common sense, that the events are arranged, *by necessity*, in a serial, temporal order which makes it meaningful to speak of "causation." The notion of causation must be in us, so to speak, as a precondition of experience; it is one of those understandings, built into our natures, which makes it possible for us to "have experiences."

But to come to this recognition about the notion of causation is to confirm a synthetic, rather than a merely analytic, truth. We are not speaking here merely about "relations of ideas." We are expressing a truth about the real world—in this case, that the world is so arranged that every event has a cause. And the truth we express has an *a priori* standing: it does not depend on experience, and it has the force of necessity.

YET a questioner may ask whether the conclusions follow here simply from the first principles we have happened to define, or whether other conclusions might not follow if we had supplied a different set of axioms. An example commonly offered here is the difference between Euclidean and non-Euclidean geometry. In one "system" we assume that parallel lines can never meet, in the other we assume that they can; and on the basis of these different premises, we may extract some different conclusions.

I hope it would be clear by now, however, that this kind of argument misses the point. When we speak of "first principles" or the axioms of our knowledge, we are truly speaking of the most fundamental stratum of our knowledge: we are speaking of the things we must know before we are able to know anything else. If people broach the possibility of "shifting the premises of our system" and defining a different set of "first principles," the conversation cannot be intelligible unless there is some common ground on which we can speak about this change and assess its validity. If one invokes, after all, a new set of "first principles," providing a foundation of knowledge wholly different from any axioms now extant, how would the rest of us understand those new axioms or the case to be made for them? The change from Euclidean to non-Euclidean geometry might involve a shift in premises, but such a change would not involve anything that touches the level of genuine first principles or necessary truths. To confirm this point we need merely consider what we would have to know *before* we could understand the altered premise, in non-Euclidean geometry, that two parallel lines can eventually meet. What is conveyed here at the very least is a notion of extension—of parallel lines meeting at a distant point. But we cannot conceive of the separation between two parallel lines without assuming the existence of space, and we can hardly conceive of the distinction of *two* or more lines without being aware of the concept of "number." As we penetrate, then, to the level of what we may think, at times, are fundamental premises, we will often discover, with more reflection, that there are premises or assumptions that are even more fundamental yet; and those premises are part of the constitutive principles of our understanding.

In the same way, when we speak of the first principles of morals, we must be speaking of understandings that are drawn from "first principles" in the hardest and most fundamental sense. As Thomas Reid remarked, "whatever can, by just reasoning, be inferred from a principle that is necessary, must be a necessary truth."[17] Therefore, we cannot be speaking merely of one set of provisional "axioms" which may be replaced quite as well by another set of tentative premises, neither set having any stronger claim than the other to be "true." If they are validly drawn, the first principles of morals must have the same qualities of necessity that attach to other first principles. Moreover, as I suggested earlier, following Kant, moral propositions may claim this standing as true and necessary propositions only when they are drawn as necessary implications that arise from (1) the notion of a rational being (i.e., a being that can form moral judgments and reason over matters of right and wrong) and from (2) the idea of morals itself. I showed earlier that the first part of the Kantian formula—the notion of a "rational being"—lies behind both the proposition "All men are created equal" and the momentous implications drawn from that proposition. In raising the question for ourselves of how we may know first principles in morals, we might take, as a notable case in point, the question of how we come to know that the proposition "All men are created equal" does indeed express, as our Founders thought, a necessary truth.

As Locke understood, all men are created "equal" in the sense that they share "one community of nature" as beings possessed of "like faculties." By "like faculties," of course, he meant the faculties of a rational being who can reason over matters of right and wrong. Yet, Kant would make a telling point later when he warned against the temptation to deduce principles of moral judgment from "the par-

---

[17] Reid, *supra*, note 2, p. 616.

ticular natural characteristics of humanity" or the "particular constitution of human nature."[18] Human beings may indeed be the only
animals who are possessed by nature of the capacity to reason over
moral things; and yet it is evident that not all members of the species
share in that gift of reason. Some may be so diminished in their mental
powers that they are less acute than crafty animals. For them, it is
quite proper to be placed under the care and governance of others.

As Lincoln pointed out, the men who wrote the Declaration of
Independence understood all of this: "They did not mean to say all
were equal in color, size, intellect, moral developments, or social capacity." Still, they were not moved to proclaim that "*most* men are
created equal"—which was all they truly could have said if they had
been offering only an inductive truth and drawing a generalization
from the current experience of human beings. Through experience we
may be led to discover what it is that makes human beings decisively
different from other animals; but once we grasp the notion of a creature
endowed with reason and alert to the logic of moral judgment, we
may discover the grounds of our moral judgment, *a priori*, in the
notion of reason itself. We may draw out the logical implications that
mark the properties and "laws of reason," including the implications
that flow from the kind of being who has access, through his reason,
to judgments of right and wrong. We may not know how sagacity is
distributed among the natives of different places, but we do know that
the notion of morals must presuppose "moral agents"—beings who
have the freedom to choose one course of action over another, and
who are led to reflect, in their freedom, on the standards that govern
their choices. In the same vein, Lincoln could be well aware of retarded
and incompetent people who do not command the judgment to govern
themselves; and yet nothing in that recognition could dislodge the
understanding that moral agents—creatures with a faculty of moral
judgment—do not deserve to be ruled in the manner of creatures
who are devoid of understanding. I have suggested that the matter
could lend itself to a more precise statement, as follows: creatures
who have the capacity to reason over matters of right and wrong do
not deserve to be ruled in the way that one rules creatures which are
incapable of giving and understanding justifications. They deserve to
be ruled, then, only with justification, by a government compelled to
offer justifications for its acts. We may therefore understand "natural
equality" to mean that creatures with the capacity for morals deserve

18 Immanuel Kant, *Fundamental Principles of the Metaphysics of Morals* [1785],
trans. Thomas K. Abbott (Indianapolis: Bobbs-Merrill, 1949), pp. 42 and 58.

to be acted upon only in a moral way: they have an *equal right* to be treated *only with justification.*[19]

There is a need to be clear, though, about the ground of that claim to an *equal* right. That claim cannot really arise from a casual notion that each person is about as "good" as another, for anyone who takes questions of moral judgment seriously would be obliged to recognize that this simply cannot be true. Besides, the obligation to give justifications would remain the same in regard to bad men as well as good, and it is evidently quite compatible with the notion of "equality" that the good may be honored while the bad may be punished. I think it can be shown that the claim to equality arises in a rather different way, from the logic of morals itself. Consider the problem at work in an example that is less than momentous. It is not regarded as a violation of "natural equality"—as a denial of the fundamental principles of republican government—when teachers fail to assign the same grades to all of their students. Instead of observing the principle of equality by giving everyone an A or a B, they have regarded themselves as free to recognize the wide differences in the merits of their students by grading some of them with A's and others with D's and F's. The practice is understood as compatible with the principle of natural equality so long as the teachers apply the same standards to the judgment of each paper, and if they are capable of giving reasons or justifications for the grades they assign. But our question is, What enjoins the teachers to apply the same standards? The answer is implicit, I think, in the notion of assigning and *justifying* a grade. When a teacher arrives at the judgment that Jones wrote a "good" or "excellent" paper, a paper deserving an A, he must be able to say that the paper contains certain properties which define it as a "good" or commendable paper. If he means strictly what he says, he is not assigning the grade because of his personal fondness for Jones, but

[19] This is not to say, of course, that there is a license to inflict harm without justification in dealing with infants, animals, or even furniture, merely because the objects of this treatment do not give or understand reasons. But the prospect of dealing with creatures who are possessed of reason should stir the recognition, even among the obtuse, that the standards of justification in acting upon creatures of this kind must indeed be demanding. Not the least point in this exercise is that it may alert the actor himself to the implications of his own nature: it may remind him that, as part of the only species with a capacity for moral judgment, he has an obligation to act only with justification, on small creatures as well as great. It would not make sense for a man to seek the "consent" of a chair before he sat in it, but he would not necessarily have the "right" to disfigure or destroy a delicate piece of craftsmanship for no reason beyond his own whim; and what may be said in this respect for a chair must be said even more forcefully for animals and infants.

because Jones's paper provides an instance or example of the criteria that define a "good" paper more generally or universally. That is to say, when we define "goodness" in papers or anything else, we mark off the features that define the nature of goodness *universally* in objects of their kind. If the teacher thinks that Jones's paper exhibits the features that mark "good" papers, he must be implying that he would regard as "good" any paper which contains these same features, even if it is not written by Jones. If he were to encounter a paper with the same qualities, but esteemed it less, he would be obliged to explain why the standards that determined his judgment of Jones's paper do not govern the current case as well—or why the current paper bears defects that were not present in Jones's work. If we would act morally, then, we would be acting on the basis of moral *principles*, which are universal in their cast. And when we say that people have the right to be treated *equally*, we are really saying that they have the right to be treated morally or justly, with standards that happen to apply equally *because they apply universally*.

The proposition "All men are created equal" was a popular summary of a more precise set of propositions which ultimately expressed the injunction that men *deserve* to be treated equally, with justification. Whether that injunction itself is a true statement is dependent finally on the truth of the propositions from which it is drawn: (1) that human beings possess the capacity to reason, and (2) that morals exist. "All men are created equal" has the standing of a necessary truth, then, if these two propositions have themselves the standing of necessary truths.

THE FIRST proposition may be settled with a remarkable brevity, once we put the question of how we would go about proving to the skeptic that human beings possess the capacity to reason. I have usually asked the skeptics among my own students to consider just how they would wish to have this issue addressed, and they tend to be rather demanding about the terms. They will not be satisfied by an appeal to authority or belief, and they certainly will not permit the issue to be settled, finally, by the application of force. They typically insist that they be given evidence and reasons—that nothing less than evidence and reasons can decide so weighty a matter. They regard reason, then, as higher or more authoritative than brute force or personal belief. They will settle for nothing other than reason—and yet, to prove what point? That human beings are capable of reason. The very posing of the challenge already presupposes the answer that the skeptics are seeking to resist. And of course, who else but a *rational* creature would conceive of marshaling reasons at the highest level for the sake of resisting the proposition that human beings are capable of marshaling and understanding reasons? For Kant this was the instant, telling sign of an argument that reveals its own vacuity: it reduces to an exercise of "proving by reason that there is no such thing as reason."[20]

That human beings can reason, cannot be intelligibly denied. But they cannot reason over moral things unless morals themselves exist, and so everything must finally resolve itself into one question—How can we know of the existence of morals as a necessary truth?

To claim that morals exist is to claim simply that it is possible for human beings to understand the difference between acts that are justified and unjustified, right and wrong. It means that we can regard as comprehensible the difference between the two answers that may be given to this question:

(1) Why did you hit him? *To get his wallet.*
(2) Why did you hit him? *To keep him from jumping out the window.*

In the first case, a hurt is being inflicted on someone else for the sake of the self-interest or the benefit of the assailant. In the other case, the hurt is being inflicted—and inflicted, perhaps, with reluctance—for a reason that incorporates the good of the person who is being hurt. In the difference between these two cases we find the rudiments of a *justification*, and we recognize again the criteria that set apart justified (or moral) reasons from unjustifed (or immoral) reasons. If we regard the difference in these answers as plausible, if we think that human beings are able to comprehend that difference and reach a judgment about the two cases, then we are saying, in effect, that morals are understandable—that there is nothing inscrutable about the notion of giving a justification.

The person who is driven to deny the possibility of morals may be inclined to deny, in the first instance, that we are capable of giving and understanding reasons. Hence, we would be incapable of under-

[20] Immanuel Kant, *Critique of Practical Reason* [1788], trans. Lewis White Beck (Indianapolis: Bobbs-Merrill, 1956), p. 12; p. 12, also, of the RPA ed. More recently, Professor Alan Gewirth has expounded moral philosophy in the same vein, by seeking propositions with a *necessary* force which are grounded in the law of contradiction and the notion of a rational, moral agent. Gewirth has remarked that true answers can be given to the central questions of moral philosophy "if a supreme moral principle can be shown to be logically necessary so that its denial is self-contradictory. . . . And it is only by deductive rationality that such necessary truth can be established." See Gewirth, *Reason and Morality* (Chicago: University of Chicago Press, 1978), pp. 23-24, 42, 47, 166, 172-76.

standing the different reasons that are brought forth in these two cases of one man striking another. But let us assume here that the skeptic has grasped the first part of this argument—that he knows he would fall into contradiction if he should seek to deny his own capacity to give and understand reasons. His argument, in that event, would have to move to another level. He might concede that we can understand the reasons behind one course of action or another, and that we can understand the difference between hurting someone for the benefit of the assailant or for the benefit of the supposed victim. But what he might argue now is that we *cannot know* that it is *better* to act for the benefit of the victim rather than for the benefit of the assailant. He might insist that the preference here depends on the intervention of what is often called a "value judgment," and that "value judgments" are entirely the creation of persons or societies: they do not reflect any necessary part of human nature; they exist only because we choose to create them. By the same token, we may choose not to create or honor these moral "values," and in that case nothing would compel us to recognize their existence and to respect their maxims.

There are two kinds of responses that this argument might elicit. One line of response we may refer to as the "low road" because it is an argument drawn merely from *consequences*: it points out the consequences or implications that would arise if we were to assume that morals, in the most literal sense, do not exist. But this line of response does not strictly meet the argument because it does not trace its own reasoning back to first principles or necessary truths. The second response I have in mind (the "high road") would indeed reach that ground for its argument. The first response is worth considering for a moment, however, precisely because it does bring out the implications that would flow from rejecting the possibility of moral judgment.

If morals did not exist, then in all strictness there could be no ground of right or wrong apart from the feelings of any individual—which means that there could be no ground on which we could ever find fault with anything done by another person, especially if *he* happened to enjoy what he was doing. And so we might face a situation of this kind. We see one man assault another on a public street, without apparent provocation, and while the victim lies prostrate and bleeding in the street, the assailant removes his wallet. If morals do not exist, if there is no place for their logic in our understanding, then we could react by saying, "That really is an interesting event!" or, at the most, "That is an event which *I myself* find disturbing." But there could be no proper ground for *condemnation* here. In order to condemn, there would have to be standards of judgment which are not merely sub-

73

jective, standards which would allow us to judge that the act was wrong even though it gave the assailant pleasure and profit. We could not get around the problem by consulting the feelings of the victim, because we would expect him to be biased in this affair. It would be strictly necessary to ask the assailant what *he* felt about the act, and if he happened to like what he was doing, there would be nothing more to be said. For whatever the feelings of the victim, we could not say that the act of the assailant was wrong *for him* unless we acknowledge the existence of rules of right and wrong that are valid and binding for people quite apart from their subjective feelings. But, of course, that is precisely what is being rejected when one rejects the notion of "morals."

It would be possible for us to reject the existence of morals if we were indeed prepared then to live out the rest of our lives without the use of moral terms and the functions they serve. We would have to be willing to live without complaining or showing outrage, from the smallest villainies to the most massive evils—from being shortchanged at the supermarket, to encountering the horrors of genocide. We would have to cease condemning injustices, complaining about faults; we would have to stop despising what is hateful and loving what is admirable. In short, we would have to live a life barren of those things that give human life its special character, because we would rule out the one thing that is truly distinctive about human beings: our capacity for moral judgment.

FOR MANY people this argument, as far as it goes, has been quite enough. The prospects are sufficiently sobering that people will often back away from the rejection of morals and concede that there must indeed be knowable grounds of moral judgment. And yet the argument does not strictly make the case that morals exist—or that they *must* exist. It would still be open to the skeptic to argue that we have chosen to act *as though* morals exist because we have simply wished to avoid the disastrous consequences that would come from rejecting them. He might argue that morals are simply a fiction we have created for the sake of avoiding harmful consequences and securing our own benefit. Of course, the skeptic who offered in this way a "utilitarian" view of the reason for morals would still be left with the question of how he is able to speak of "good" and "bad" consequences without finally invoking the logic of morals.

But putting that matter aside for a while, the question would remain as to how we might show the skeptic that he must concede the existence of morals as a necessary truth. The skeptic would show very precise reflexes when he concedes our capacity to reason at the same time that he holds back from conceding our capacity to understand *moral* reasons. And yet the very act of holding back is the source of his undoing, because it implicitly concedes a critical premise in Kant's argument: the skeptic who holds back *manifests his freedom*. He implies that he is free to commit himself to one side of the argument or the other, depending on what is made persuasive to him. He reminds us that, in matters of morals, we are in fact in the world of freedom, and it is only in the world of freedom that the language of morals is at all relevant. Kant gave an important place in his own writing to the distinction between the world of freedom and the world of "determinism." That distinction turned out to be critical for the section in the *Groundwork of the Metaphysics of Morals* in which Kant wrote of "the two standpoints" from which we may view ourselves. And when we get clear on those two standpoints, I think we are led finally to the existence of morals as a necessary truth.[21]

The world of determinism is the world of natural laws, such as the laws which determine the speed at which falling bodies fall. The language of morals has no relevance to this world: if a person falls out of a window, we do not say that he is *obliged* to fall down; nor would we say that it is *right* for the earth to revolve about the sun. The language of morals comes into play only where people have a certain freedom or choice in forming their own acts. In those instances, it is plausible that the question should arise as to whether they are choosing well or badly—whether their freedom is being directed toward good ends or bad.

Kant reminds us that human beings are in both of these worlds at once, and so we must view ourselves from both standpoints. On the one hand, we must recognize that we are indeed part of the "sensible" world, or the world of sensation and determinism, and in that domain we are under the control of the laws of nature. If we fall out the window, we fall *down*; if we are hit in the face, we feel pain; if we eat something monstrous, we have a gastrointestinal reaction. But on the other hand—from the second standpoint—we belong to the "intelligible" world, in which we have access to the standards that govern our moral judgment. There is of course nothing concrete or empirical about moral standards. No one has ever seen Justice walking down the street, or Obligations falling out of the trees. There is no sensory receptor that records a sensation of Duty. Notions of justice, fairness,

---

[21] See Immanuel Kant, *Groundwork of the Metaphysics of Morals* [1785], trans. H.J. Paton (New York: Harper & Row, 1948), pp. 118ff.; pp. 450ff. of the RPA ed.

equity, justification—the properties that mark the moral dimensions of our acts—are all "supersensible." We cannot know them through our senses; we cannot touch, taste, or smell them; we can have access to them only through our reason or intelligence. They are part, as Kant would say, of the "intelligible" world. In that world alone may we discover the standards that measure our acts as "good" and "bad," and as we discover those standards of judgment we also become aware that we have the freedom to judge and to choose—that our acts are not entirely "determined" by the laws of nature. We are made aware, then, that in the intelligible world we are in the world of "freedom." In this world we are governed preeminently by *reason and argument.*[22]

If we keep in mind the differences between these two standpoints, we will become more alert to the properties of the sentences that are spoken by the skeptic as he attempts to deny the existence of morals. I suggested earlier that the skeptic may concede that he is capable of understanding the different answers to the question "Why did you hit him?" ("To get his wallet." "To keep him from jumping out the window.") The skeptic recognizes the difference between hurting someone for the benefit mainly of the assailant and inflicting hurt on another person for his own good. He understands that difference, but he denies that we can attach any *moral* significance to this disparity and say that one act is in fact "better" or more "commendable" than the other. He insists we cannot do that because we have not yet proven that morals exist, and only through the logic of morals can we assign a ranking to our acts as better or worse.

Just to get a bit more precise about the matter, the skeptic says he can understand the difference between the two reasons that are offered for hitting the man, but what he would say, in addition, is probably one or both of the following sets of sentences:

> (1) "I do not myself recognize or respect the force of any consideration except my own inclinations or self-interest. Nothing in the presentation of the two reasons *stimulates* any recognition in

---

[22] Kant expressed the matter in this way: "[Man] can consider himself *first*—so far as he belongs to the sensible world—to be under laws of nature (heteronomy); and *secondly*—so far as he belongs to the intelligible world—to be under laws which, being independent of nature, are not empirical but have their ground in reason alone.

"As a rational being, and consequently as belonging to the intelligible world, man can never conceive the causality of his own will except under the Idea of freedom; for to be independent of determination by causes in the sensible world (and this is what reason must always attribute to itself) is to be free." *Ibid.*, p. 120; pp. 452-53 of the RPA ed. See, also, Robinson, "Determinism, 'Hard' and 'Soft,' " *supra*, note 12.

me of 'moral' standards that must become engaged here as a matter of necessity."

(2) "No one would be *warranted* or *justified*, then, in holding me responsible for an obligation to give reasons and respect the logic of moral terms."

As we begin to weigh these utterances, we must ask, at the threshold of the problem, whether either one actually states an argument. If it does not, then it has no bearing at all on the dispute over the existence of morals. In this respect we must notice that the first statement does not strictly state an argument. It provides, rather, a report on the personal reactions of the skeptic. It is comparable to a narrative, offered by the skeptic, that when he is hit he feels pain, and when he falls, he falls down. It is merely an account of events in the empirical world; it is a descriptive report on the reactions of the skeptic in the world of natural events, the world of determinism. ("When I look into the sun, I squint; when I confront a so-called moral problem, I feel nothing at all—I feel no sense of what some people call 'oughtness' or outrage welling up within me.") His first statement says nothing on the point of whether the incident of a man getting hit on the head *ought* to have elicited a moral reaction in him or whether it was *justified* for him to detach himself from a moral judgment. Therefore, his first statement conveys no argument. We may say that it is no more relevant to an argument on this question than a report that a chimney is emitting smoke. It is simply another report on another event in the empirical world; and as an empirical account, it cannot even claim to report on whether any other person, apart from the speaker, responded in the same way and experienced no moral reaction in the face of a violent act. For all we know, then, he is the only one in the world who has experienced this peculiar reaction, while all other people might have discovered the engagement of their moral reflexes.

The skeptic does not move to the point of offering an argument until his second proposition: "No one would be *warranted* or *justified*, then, in holding me responsible for an obligation to give reasons and respect the logic of moral terms." This second proposition has the form of an argument, and it becomes relevant to the dispute only because the skeptic is *invoking the logic of morals and employing moral terms*. Central to his meaning here are the terms "warranted" and "justified": he is saying, again, that it would not be justified (or morally right) to hold him accountable to moral commands and treat him as though moral rules were indeed binding upon him. That is, it would be *wrong* for other people to impose obligations on him as though morals actually existed; and presumably he is saying that it would be wrong for people to treat him that way *even if they liked what they were doing*. In short, he is expressing the essential logic of morals; he is making nothing less than a moral argument in order to deny the existence of morals. The point here is that he is compelled to fall into this contradiction as soon as he states an argument that is at all relevant to the question of whether morals exist. For at that point it becomes necessary for him to use the form—and employ the language—of a moral proposition.

HOWEVER, there may be available to the skeptic one winding route of escape from behind this logical fence we have placed about him. This path of argument may be improbable in the sense that we are not likely to encounter anyone who would shape his own life to the contours of its maxims; but since it may furnish a logical route of escape for an incorrigible skeptic, it may be offered as a challenge to the understanding I have set forth. In forming this argument, the skeptic would seek to avoid the vulnerabilities contained in either one of the two lines of response I have described. On the one hand, he would not deny the existence of morals by citing merely his personal feelings or the state of his internal reactions. Instead of saying that he himself does not recognize the existence of moral propositions—that propositions so labeled evoke no feelings of obligation within him—the skeptic would now speak in an impersonal voice, and he would claim to speak in the name of a "truth" which is accessible to others as well as himself. But on the other hand, the skeptic would also deny that he must speak with any *moral* implication when he says that people would be "unwarranted" in imposing any obligations upon him.

His argument might run in this way. The skeptic could insist, as a factual matter, that morals do not exist—that they cannot be proven through experiment, that they cannot be grasped with the force of necessity which attaches to the recognition, say, of time, space, or the "law of contradiction." We deal here, we may notice, with a rather refined variety of skeptic: not only does he accept the possibility of knowing something, but he concedes that he is able to know certain propositions—e.g., the "law of contradiction"—quite independently of experience. This premise, as we shall see, is wholly necessary to the argument that the skeptic would have to make here, and yet, as we shall also see, it must be the source of deeper vulnerabilities in his argument. The skeptic could hold that the person who asserts the existence of morals simply makes a mistake, just as the man who denies the law of contradiction must be judged to have made, inescapably, a mistake. In both cases, he argues, the propositions are *false*, and it would have to follow that any actions predicated on these premises must be equally false or factually "unwarranted."

Let us suppose, for example, that we find a tribe in which the legislative majority proclaims, as a religious tenet, that the "law of contradiction" is false—that two contradictory propositions might both be true—and that anyone who denies these propositions should be punished with death. Of course, with the premises proclaimed by the majority it would not follow that anyone who *contradicted* the policy of the majority would have to be wrong. But by those same premises the majority still could not be judged "wrong" as it held, serenely, to these contradictory positions: (1) that the dissenters might be correct in their objections, but (2) that it could be right to punish them anyway! The urbane skeptic would have no trouble, then, in showing that the so-called ethical system of this tribe is contrived upon layers of nonsense. And because the postulates of the system are plainly vacuous, it would have to follow that the penalty of death for the dissenters must be thoroughly unwarranted or unjustified.

But our skeptic would hasten to point out that he uses the terms "unwarranted" or "unjustified" here without a trace of moral significance. Whether the penalty is morally right or wrong he cannot say, because he cannot say that there are morals. What he says is that the penalty is unwarranted, since it is founded on premises that are false. He does not venture to say whether it is morally "good" for people to avoid acting on false premises; he would say only that it is factually wrong (and unwarranted by the facts) to act upon premises that are mistaken. If Hitler's policies toward the Jews were based on a moral argument he fashioned about the evil of Jews, the skeptic could point out that those policies of genocide were unwarranted because they were based on a profound error (viz., the assumption that morals exist, and that a moral "justification" could be offered for the killing of Jews). By this reckoning, however, the Jews who resisted Hitler could also have been judged "wrong" or unwarranted if they were moved to their own acts of violence by a sense of injustice or moral outrage. For they, too, would have predicated their violent acts on an understanding that was mistaken. In the mind of the skeptic, the Jews might have been warranted in resisting, but solely because the policies they resisted were factually mistaken.

It is a curious understanding that can make no *moral* discrimination between Hitler and his victims; but it is precisely the *possibility* of moral discrimination that the skeptic means to reject. What may be even more curious, however, in the argument of the skeptic is that it makes no discrimination between the "mistake" committed by Hitler and the mistakes committed by a schoolboy doing his arithmetic. In the reckoning of the skeptic, they are both engaged in "mistakes." Some mistakes, clearly, are more serious than others; some are made on a grand scale. But in the world of our skeptic, the practice of cruel killing in mass numbers cannot affect any important distinction that may be drawn between Hitler and the schoolboy. It could not be the source of any judgment that might regard Hitler as a *worse* person, who is more deserving of our contempt and hatred than the schoolboy. For those judgments are rooted in the existence of morals, and while they might appeal to our imaginations with the same force as religious visions and literary fictions, they cannot claim the validity of propositions that have the cognitive standing of *truths*.

IT IS HARDLY a wonder that the skeptic I have described here does not have any historical embodiment. Apart from the accident of his absence from history, however, there is something in the logical construction of his position that would make him a curious figure even among the fraternity of fictitious skeptics that have sprung from the imaginations of philosophers. For in order to steer around the argument I have laid out, the skeptic was forced to take on premises that were awkward for skeptics. So, for example, it became necessary for him to avoid the claim that it is impossible to know the truth of any proposition concerning morals, for it would then have been impossible, by his own premises, to know the truth of his own argument about morals. His argument acquired its special force from the fact that he could speak in the name of a truth accessible to others as well as to himself. In making that kind of argument, he had to accept the existence of truths that did not depend for their validity on experience or feelings, even the experience and feelings of a majority. Yet, once that kind of concession is made, the skeptic has abandoned premises which have been enduring parts of the tradition of skepticism, and he would throw over most of the rationale for denying the existence of morals in the first place.

Consider, in this vein, the points that the skeptic would already have acknowleged: that there are grounds on which we can find that a majority has acted "wrongly" or "incorrectly," even when it is imposing punishment on people; that in some factual sense the act of the majority is "unwarranted" or "unjustified"; and that the act of the majority would have to be regarded as wrong even if the majority were subjectively convinced of the rightness of its course. The skeptic would concede, in other words, that there are standards of judgment, apparently universal in their reach, which allow us to judge acts to be "wrong" even when the actors themselves happen to approve of what they are doing. The range of those acts would encompass situations in which some men inflict harms on others, and it is the awareness of these harms that has marked, in our understanding, the threshold which defines acts of "moral" consequence. If the skeptic is willing to go *this* far—if he is willing to bring within his reach the judgment of harms—what remains for him to resist in the components that define the existence of "morals"? On what point, precisely, could he be holding back? Since he concedes the possibility of judging with universal rules of judgment, would he now simply refuse to recognize the difference constituted by the presence of suffering and harm? That is, would he be reluctant to say that the inflicting of a harm makes us warranted in treating that act as different in kind from other acts that may be factually wrong or unjustified? Is it inappropriate for us to place these acts on a different plane of significance by adding an edge of outrage or disapproval to the judgment we would render about the "wrongness" of the act?

And yet, if skeptics have been anything over the years, they have been empiricists. Empiricists have been united on the point that "sensation" and "sense data" are the ultimate sources of our knowledge; and, among the sensations that may impress our minds and form our motives, they have accorded a sovereign place to "pleasure" and "pain." The hideous crimes produced by the Nazis would register vividly in the understanding of the empiricist, and there could hardly be much doubt that, in the epistemology of the empiricist, the crimes wrought by Hitler would have a more pronouned cognitive presence than the mistakes produced by a student doing his sums.

In the school of the British "sentimental" philosophers, the awareness of the moral world began with those "sentiments" and sympathies which allowed human beings to recognize pain or suffering in others.[23] It was the recognition of that pain which triggered the demand for a justification—and with that, the full discipline that attaches to the logic of moral discourse. There was nothing in this understanding that could have been foreign to the confirmed empiricist, and it was hardly a coincidence that the most notable writer on "moral sentiments," Adam Smith, preserved the closest friendship throughout his life with David Hume, the preeminent figure in the tradition of empiricism. No heir to Hume could possibly fail to recognize the vast differences in

[23] See, for example, Adam Smith, *The Theory of Moral Sentiments* (London: H.G. Bohn, 1853), especially pt. I.

gravity that separate the "mistakes" of a Hitler and the mistakes of a schoolboy—to say nothing of the cruelty and wickedness that marked the acts of Hitler. The skeptic I have described is not likely to be any more blind to these differences than any other heir to the tradition of empiricism, and in that event his recognitions would have to bring him, as it brought his intellectual ancestors, to the border of moral judgment: the awareness of a vast harm knowingly inflicted would make it ever more plausible to demand a reason (if not, quite yet, a "justification"). And the demand for a reason must be strengthened by the further recognition—already conceded by the skeptic—that acts of this kind, which inflict harm on others, fall within that class of acts which can be judged by universal standards and reckoned to be "correct" or "incorrect," warranted or unwarranted.

From this point, the recognition of the moral world lies no further than the threshold of moral outrage, and that threshold can be reached with steps that would no longer mark any serious philosophic barriers for our skeptic. If he is sensitive (as his tradition makes him sensitive) to the creation of mass suffering, if he recognizes that the bloodiest torture and killing may be inflicted on people for reasons that are wholly thoughtless, vacuous, and therefore patently unwarranted, why would those recognitions not evoke from him a reaction that reflects more accurately the disproportion that exists between the gravity of the harm and the emptiness of the justification? That expression, properly measured, would have to be one of *outrage*. The temper of a moral reflex would then be added to the ingredients of a moral judgment, which are already in place. The skeptic who has admitted these points would soon be able to acknowlege that the man who inflicts pain for the sake of his own sadistic pleasure, or for the advancement of his own selfish interest, has fallen as far short of a justification—and quite as properly elicits our outrage—as the man who inflicts harm for reasons that are "mistaken." These grounds for condemnation would begin to fill out the language of our moral reactions, and yet they would not involve, for the skeptic, the incorporation of premises that are any more momentous than the ones he has already accepted in building his own argument.

A DECOROUS reserve holds me back from rejoicing here over the entrapment of a skeptic who is, after all, my own invention. But let me recall that the position of the skeptic was defined by arguments it was necessary to attribute to him if he would circumvent the case I set forth earlier for the necessity of morals. That case could not be resisted by an argument which disclaimed the possibility of knowing any truth beyond one's own internal feelings. The argument of the skeptic has to become, perforce, rather complicated, and it was compelled to absorb premises that would be, in turn, the source of its own unraveling. Hence the paradox that finally emerged. Our skeptic would not be compelled to invoke the logic of a "moral justification" in reaching his judgment, and he would not have to acknowledge the existence of morals. And yet, to produce this result, the skeptic would find himself accepting, in his premises, all of the ingredients that compose a moral judgment. Whether he finally invokes the label of "morals" or not, he will have conceded the points of understanding that are necessary to a moral judgment, and anyone who concedes all of these points could not have much reason any longer to reject the existence of morals.

Still, the skeptic would have rendered the service of making clearer to us just how very limited—how notably short of momentous—is the issue he would raise, even as he would seek to find a way around the argument for the existence of morals. To concede that there are truths which do not depend on the subjective feelings of any person, or on the opinions held by a majority, is to put the matter in its precise place. We remind ourselves that knowledge finds its beginning in certain axioms of understanding, which must hold true of necessity, and that moral truths are merely part of the universe of things we come to know in this way. Within that universe we simply mark off, as a different object of our interest, those acts which involve the inflicting of harms by creatures who had the freedom to hold back from harming. After all, pain and destruction may be wrought by falling bodies propelled by the laws of nature; it is not in the moral realm alone that harms are produced. But we are drawn, rightly, by a different fascination, to those acts of harming or helping that are produced by intention, by the fuel of motive, and by the conscious tailoring of means to ends. No falling rock reveals to us an incorrigible path of "cruelty"; but the world of cruelty and wickedness, of bravery and admiration, excites a different kind of wonder and engages a different part of our souls. And yet, that is all. The difference between our knowledge of moral and nonmoral things may ignite different passions and call forth different talents; but it does not remove us to a place beyond the axioms of understanding or the laws of reason, where we have no hope or prospect of "knowing."

Why, then, should there be any wonder that, at each moment of resistance, the skeptic finds himself backing into the grammar or logic of morals? We have the capacity for resistance and argument only because we have the capacity to give and understand reasons. As for the logic and language of morals, they are simply built into us. As Thomas Reid would say, they are part of "the constitution of our natures," and for that reason they are as much a part of our natural world as trees, rocks, air, and water. The person who seeks to deny the existence of morals will spend most of his days trying to flee from the perils of contradiction and the tangle of his own argument. He will discover, again, that for the man of reason the existence of morals must hold the place of a necessary assumption or a first principle in the ground of his understanding.

"To the Idea of freedom" wrote Kant, "there is inseparably attached the concept of *autonomy*, and to this in turn the universal principle of morality—a principle which in Idea forms the ground for all the actions of *rational* beings, just as the law of nature does for all appearances."[24] In this passage, Kant brought together again the two parts that form the foundation of all moral judgments: the idea of morals itself and the notion of a rational being. I have already shown how the case for republican government can be established as one of those implications which flow out of the notion of a "rational being." I have not yet shown how propositions of political consequence may be drawn from the idea of morals itself. I will turn directly to that task in the next chapter, but I will also make use of that demonstration to bring out some of the further implications or properties that attach to first principles in morals.

[24] Kant, *supra*, note 21, p. 120; pp. 452-53 of the RPA ed. Emphasis in original.

V

MORAL PRINCIPLES, VALID
AND SPURIOUS

As we have seen, Kant was able to establish, in his writing on "causation," that it was indeed possible to have synthetic *a priori* propositions: if "experience teaches us that something happens, we always presuppose that something precedes on which it follows by rule."[1] If we did not "presuppose" that events are arranged in a serial order, with antecedents and consequents, with an event A preceding an event B, with B following upon A according to rule, then our "experience" would consist of a "mere play of representations unconnected with any object." We would encounter a series of "perceptions" whose succession or sequence must ever remain in doubt. Therefore, it becomes *necessary* to suppose that events are arranged in a causal sequence, for it is only under this supposition "that an experience of anything that happens becomes possible."[2] As we saw in the notable case of Carl Yastrzemski at Fenway Park, it becomes incoherent to give an account of experience on any other supposition; and so it may be said, with Kant, that this notion of causation is "the foundation of all experience, and consequently [precedes] it *a priori*." At the same time, this necessary truth about causation cannot be merely an *analytic* proposition, because it states a truth about the way in which our experience in the world of sensation has to be arranged. Therefore, the proposition which affirms the existence of causation must be both *synthetic* and *a priori*.

Along with everything else, that necessary truth provides the foundation for our experience in the domain of morals as well, for there could be no ground of moral judgment—no ground for assigning blame and commendation—if moral agents were incapable of causing their own acts to happen. But beyond that, there is a *synthetic a priori* proposition which provides a distinctive, necessary ground for our moral judgments. When Kant set forth the proposition that "everything that happens . . . presupposes something upon which it follows by rule," he was stating one of the implications of saying that "causation exists." In the same way, those synthetic *a priori* propositions

---

[1] Immanuel Kant, *Critique of Pure Reason* [1781], trans. F. Max Müller (New York: Doubleday/Anchor, 1966 [1881]), p. 157 [A:191-95; B:236-40].

[2] *Ibid.*, p. 158 [A:195-99; B:240-44].

which form the "first principles" of moral judgment would be drawn as implications from the logic of morals—from the recognition that "morals exist" as a necessary part of our reason, as part of the "constitution of our faculties." For Kant, "the law of morality" was contained in the Categorical Imperative: "Act only on that maxim through which you can at the same time will that it should become a universal law."[3] To enjoin a person to act morally was to enjoin him to act in such a way that "the maxim of the action should conform to a universal law," and that practical principle constituted an *a priori* synthetic proposition: from the notion of a rational being, impelled by desire, and forming his will, we would not necessarily extract the notion of a being who seeks to conform his acts to a universal law of reason. A creature in the world of sensation could be moved, after all, by his inclinations and interests, by the commands of self-love or the things that give him pleasure. He could be ruled, in short, by motives quite apart from those which find their "seat and origin completely *a priori* in the reason," and which would "hold good for every rational creature."[4] Since the notion of acting upon a universal law is not contained in the very notion of a willing creature (or "actor"), this imperative could not be merely an *analytic* proposition. Kant was clear that the need to conform the maxim of the act to a universal law is a *necessary* commitment, arising from the logic of a "universal law," and that "law" found its origin *a priori* in reason itself. Hence, the imperative that enjoins us to respect the logic of morals has to be understood as a proposition that is both synthetic and *a priori*.[5]

We saw this same problem from its obverse side in the last chapter: the skeptic who sought to resist the logic of "obligation"—or the logic of morals—could not avoid the trap of contradiction. But that was another way of recognizing that the proposition which asserts the existence of morals (or the logic of moral propositions) must have the standing of a synthetic *a priori* truth. And so, in place of Kant's extended but elliptical constructions, we may put any proposition that conveys more directly the logic of morals. For example, we might say: "There are propositions that are set apart in their logic from statements of merely personal taste or subjective feeling. Those propositions establish the things that are universally right or wrong, good or bad, just or unjust—which is to say, good or bad, just or unjust, for others as well as for ourselves. And by their logic, therefore, those propo-

[3] Immanuel Kant, *Groundwork of the Metaphysics of Morals* [1785], trans. and ed. H.J. Paton (New York: Harper & Row, 1964), p. 88; p. 421 of the RPA ed.

[4] *Ibid.*, p. 29.

[5] See *ibid.*, pp. 57 and 71.

sitions can be valid and binding for us quite apart from our personal feelings or inclinations."

These sentences may be replaced with others more artfully or precisely arranged, but so long as they assert the existence of morals, and convey the "logic" of moral propositions, they will constitute a synthetic *a priori* proposition. And from that proposition—from the "logic of morals" itself—we can begin to draw, as implications, the principles of our moral judgment. As we extract these implications from the logic of morals, however, we become aware that the principles we derive in this way are part of the "intelligible" world, rather than the world of "sensation." They come to us through our reason alone and not through our sensory receptors. And because these understandings arise as inferences from necessary truths, they have the force of "laws" even though they are not drawn from mathematics or from the physical laws of nature. The "law of contradiction" has the standing of a necessary truth—and holds every proper claim to the label of "law"— even though people may fall into contradiction and "violate" this law without suffering any effects from the laws of physics. These are two different kinds of laws, one applying in the realm of determinism, the other in the realm of "freedom," and yet they are "laws" nevertheless. We might say with Kant, in that paradoxical expression, that the principles which govern our *moral* judgment are the "laws of freedom": we are obliged to respect their truth or validity as laws even though we are in the domain of freedom—even though our obedience cannot be ensured by the laws of physics. These two recognitions, taken together, make it necessary to supply a term that finds no place in the laws of determinism, namely, the notion of what we "ought" to do. We *ought* to obey the principles of moral judgment, we ought to regard them as binding on us, as entitled to our respect, simply because they are valid as *laws* of reason. And it becomes apt to enjoin ourselves to obey, to instruct ourselves on what we *ought* to do, precisely because we are free physically to ignore the commands of reason. We are governed, in this realm, by our moral understanding and not solely by the laws of physics.[6]

As Daniel Robinson has observed, in a commentary on Kant, the "sanction [of a moral imperative] comes from the very form—the very logic—of moral discourse. Stripped of it, an action may be wise, prudent, successful, and pleasurable, but it cannot be *moral*. . . . The

---

[6] As Kant sums it up, "Obligation is the necessity of a free action under a categorical imperative of reason." *The Metaphysical Principles of Virtue* [1797], trans. James Ellington (Indianapolis: Bobbs-Merrill, 1964), p. 21; p. 222 of the RPA ed.

specific action which an agent claims to be governed by it must *bear a logical connection to it*."[7] To take an example, "the mere *act* of setting buildings on fire is not a *maxim*, but proceeds from one. To the extent that the controlling maxim is self-regarding [e.g., the one who lit the fire might have sought to gratify his aesthetic sense or even to find a certain pleasure in destruction], it is not moral at all—it is amoral, perhaps immoral." The lesson might be clearer, however, in a case in which the maxim of an act bore, as Robinson said, a *logical connection* to the idea of morals or the "logic of moral discourse." As we have seen, the logic of morals comes into play only in the world of freedom, not in the world of determinism. The language of moral approval or disapproval makes sense only when it is addressed to beings who might have done otherwise—who were free to choose one course of action over another. It would be idle and senseless to invoke moral judgments in relation to acts that have been governed by the laws of physics. We would never say, for example, that it is morally right or wrong for the earth to revolve about the sun. If Smith were pushed from a window, we would not hold him responsible for any damage he caused in the course of his flight downward, for his movement, by that point, would have been quite beyond his control. From these elementary recognitions, which flow with logical necessity from the idea of morals, we can extract a number of interesting propositions, and they would include, as we shall see, one of those first principles of moral judgment which are evident even to the dimmest minds: viz., that people may not be held responsible or blameworthy for acts they were powerless to affect. If Henshaw was nowhere near the scene of the crime, if he was physically incapable of wielding the weapon, if he had no knowledge of the victim and no means of arranging for his murder, we would have ample grounds for regarding Henshaw as "innocent."

But what if it were argued that the "public good" would be served, nevertheless, by the punishment of Henshaw? It might be argued, for example, that would-be criminals are likely to be chilled by the recurring example of punishment, and from the standpoint of deterring criminals it may not be strictly necessary that only the guilty be punished. The decisive point, rather, is that punishments should be numerous and frequent. Henshaw, to be sure, would be punished unjustly. But what if it were argued here that the good of one person

[7] Daniel N. Robinson, *Toward a Science of Human Nature: Essays on the Psychologies of Mill, Hegel, Wundt, and James* (New York: Columbia University Press, 1982), pp. 88-89. Emphasis added.

may be overridden for the sake of producing a measurable good for the larger community in reducing crimes of violence?

This form of argument is not too remote from arguments that have been offered routinely nowadays, with a utilitarian cast of mind, to justify public policies. And yet, if we understand that the wrongness of punishing Henshaw arises as a necessary implication from the logic of morals itself, the argument for punishing this innocent man can be exposed, not merely as illiberal and unjust, but as incoherent. The case would begin to unravel as soon as it became clear that it seeks to offer a *justification*, and therefore that it is forced to incorporate the language and logic of morals. The claim, after all, is that a public "good" is to be gained, which "justifies"—which makes "just" or "right"—the act of punishing an innocent man. The proponents of this argument must make use of terms such as "good" and "right" and "just," and if they were pressed on the meaning of these terms, it would soon become apparent that these words do not convey merely a statement of subjective, personal feelings. Those who would punish Henshaw are not suggesting that innocent people should be punished when the punishment gives pleasure to the authorities. When they say that a larger "good" *justifies* the punishment of the innocent, they imply an understanding of "rightness" that is impersonal and universal: they suggest that *anyone* else, in their place, would be warranted in applying the same punishment. The argument could hardly make sense, then, if it were not in fact drawing on the logic of morals. But in that event, it must presuppose that there are indeed propositions which are valid and binding for people even when they run counter to personal feelings. It is only because there *are* propositions of that kind—because there are standards of judgment which are not merely personal—that it becomes possible to censure or restrain other people in the name of a "wrong" that runs well beyond subjective feelings. But with that unfolding of the premises contained in the argument, the problem comes full circle: the argument must presuppose the possibility of moral judgment, and yet it can scarcely be intelligible to offer moral judgments on people for acts they were powerless to affect. Anyone who would seek to explain, then, why it is "good" or "justified" to punish people for acts beyond their control is pursuing a policy that must be at war with the words they are using and with the logic that is implicit in their own "justification."

Whether a policy of punishing the innocent may produce "good" effects, is a matter, therefore, of utter irrelevance. Before we can know why it is "good," say, to reduce the incidence of violent crime, we must know the meaning of terms such as "good" and "justified." But as we come to know the meanings that must be absorbed into these moral terms, we also come to recognize why it becomes simply incoherent to invoke those words in support of policies that must be incompatible with the logic contained in these terms. It can be said, then, in all strictness that the wrong of punishing people for acts they were powerless to affect is a wrong that is rooted in the logic of morals, and from that central truth several other critical points emerge in marking the properties of a moral proposition. We are saying that an act is wrong when it is based on a maxim which is logically inconsistent with the idea of morals itself. In that respect, there is a distinctive moral ground for judgment: *the act is judged to be right or wrong solely on the basis of its logical connection to the idea of morals.* The rightness or wrongness of the act could not be contingent, therefore, upon any ancillary effects it happens to produce, for none of those consequences could affect in any way the ground on which we find the act to be wrong. And so we can say, for example, that the destruction of a racial minority, without regard to matters of innocence or guilt—the killing of people for attributes of race or color they were powerless to affect—is unequivocally wrong, even if it could be shown that the destruction of the minority and the redistribution of their property had the effect of enlarging cohesion in the rest of society and raising the standard of living for everyone else. This is not to deny that it may be good to enlarge the cohesion of a society or to raise the standard of living. It is to say, rather, that nothing in these consequences would affect the ground on which we judge the act of punishing the innocent. But when we recognize, in this way, that the maxim behind any act is to be judged for its rightness or wrongness on grounds that are quite independent of the consequences of the act, we grasp the force of Kant's explanation that moral imperatives are *categorical* rather than merely *contingent*:

> There is an imperative which commands a certain conduct immediately, without having as its condition any other purpose to be attained by it. This imperative is *categorical*. It concerns not the matter of the action, or its intended result, but its form and the principle of which it is itself a result; and what is essentially good in it consists in the mental disposition [i.e., the disposition to choose what is morally good out of respect for the requirements of goodness itself], let the consequence be what it may.[8]

If we were to encounter a businessman who studiously refrained from discriminating on the basis of race because he thought it was

[8] Kant, *supra*, note 3, p. 33.

good for business and his "public relations," he would be acting correctly, but he would be choosing to act in a moral way for some other purpose, of more uncertain moral standing. He would not be choosing to do what is right for its own sake, out of a respect for the principle that enjoins him not to discriminate on the basis of race. The distinctions involved here are ancient; they are not the invention of Kant, and they need not be confounded with parts of the Kantian teaching that may stir reservations (rightly or wrongly) among academics with tutored sensitivities. In the *Nicomachean Ethics*, Aristotle made the distinction between things that were good or bad in themselves and things that were good or bad only as means to other ends:

> Since there are evidently more than one end, and we choose some of these (e.g., wealth . . .) for the sake of something else, clearly not all ends are final ends; but the chief good is evidently something final. . . . Now we call that which is in itself worthy of pursuit more final than the things that are desirable both in themselves and for the sake of that other thing, and therefore we call final without qualification that which is always desirable in itself and never for the sake of something else.[9]

If the attempt were made, for example, to justify the killing of a racial minority for the sake of building cohesion in the rest of society and raising the standard of living, it would be quite apt to ask just why these results are regarded as "good." More precisely, we would have to ask whether they are good in themselves, or whether they are merely *contingently* good—whether they are good only as a means to another end which was good in itself. With further reflection, it would become apparent that "building cohesion" and "raising the standard of living" cannot be regarded as good in all cases. Cohesion and fraternity may be fostered in the excitement of a criminal project, and some people may raise their standard of living through simple plunder. Whether these ends are good would depend in turn on the ends to which they are directed, or on the character of the means by which they are pursued. "Why is it 'good' to raise the standard of living?" "Because that will be good for the retail business." "Why is it 'good' to improve the retail business?" "Because that will be good for morale in the community." "Why is it 'good' to raise morale in the community? Can morale be raised—can people become happy—in doing unjust things? In what kinds of projects do we wish people to lift their morale and enlarge their happiness?"

These questions would lead into an endless regress; they can find

---

[9] Aristotle, *Nicomachean Ethics*, 1097a, 25-36.

their terminus only when they reach the understanding of a good which is not merely contingent but good *in itself*. That kind of unalloyed good can arise from only one source: it must arise as a logical implication drawn from the idea of morals itself. As we have seen, the logic of morals stands as a necessary truth—as necessary as the notion of causation—and if our understanding of right and wrong is finally rooted in the logic of morals itself, our moral judgments will rest on a ground that is wholly indifferent to variations in place, culture, and circumstance. If it is wrong, say, to punish people for acts they were powerless to affect, if that wrong is rooted in the logic of morals itself, then it will be wrong wherever the logic of morals remains what it is. It will be wrong perforce in all places. Moral propositions, then, are universal and categorical precisely because they find their ultimate ground in propositions that must be true of necessity.

EVEN IN CIRCLES in which it is fashionable to be provocative, we never hear the question "How has the abolition of slavery *worked*?" We do not hear that question, I suspect, because people sense that the rightness or wrongness of ending slavery is wholly unaffected in principle by the extended consequences of that measure—whether the former slaves happened to prosper or grow poorer in their freedom. And yet it is quite common for people to ask whether policies of "reverse discrimination" or "busing for racial balance" have *worked*. In the difference between the two reactions we may find an indication that people have grasped, at least in a rough way, the logic of the difference between categorical and contingent propositions. On the one hand, they seem to understand the notion of things that are in principle good or bad, of things whose rightness or wrongness cannot depend on their consequences. On the other hand, they easily recognize things whose goodness or badness may be contingent on their circumstances or their consequences. They readily understand, for example, that the taking of an alcoholic drink may be benign or harmful, depending on whether it is done with moderation or carried to excess. But in contrast, they would never suppose that genocide, if practiced in moderation, would be harmless or inoffensive.

Men and women of the world have managed to understand these distinctions even without training in philosophy; yet, an understanding that has been accessible without strain to people of ordinary wit has been the source of the most serious confusion in our public discourse on law and public policy. When we say, for example, that it is "wrong" to separate children in schools on the basis of race, do we mean that it is indeed *categorically* wrong—wrong in principle, wrong in itself?

Or do we mean that it is only *contingently* wrong: it is wrong only because of its effects—because (in the words of the Supreme Court) it may affect the motivation of children to learn? Would a poor performance in school affect, in turn, the chances of black children to earn, in their maturity, incomes equal to those of whites? And if we attain an equality of performance in the schools, or a parity of income between the races, are those things good in themselves, or are they merely means to other ends? The questions lead on, once again, in a search for a final point, an understanding of something right or wrong in itself. To turn matters around, what if we were to discover cases in which the separation of students on the basis of race actually produced an improvement in the performance of black students? Would that finding establish that, in this case at least, the segregation of children on the basis of race had ceased to be wrong? When the wrong of segregation is understood to hinge upon its material effects, we must necessarily dissolve the conviction that the segregation of people on the basis of race is categorically, in principle, wrong.

The same confusion is present, of course, in the cases dealing with schemes of "racial entitlements" or preferences based on race. When we say that "it is wrong to assign benefits and disabilities to people on the basis of race," do we mean that it is equally wrong to assign benefits to blacks and disabilities to whites, or do we mean that this system of assignment is wrong only when it is used to the disadvantage of blacks? Would it be permissible, then, to take race into account, as some say, for the sake of opening up more jobs for blacks or bringing more black people into the professions? As the problem is cast in those terms, a critical shift takes place once again; and we find ourselves calling into question the conviction of an earlier day that the assignment of benefits and disabilities on the basis of race was indeed *morally* wrong, wrong in itself.

And yet, the confusion here is of no recent invention. It has been part of the litigation over racial segregation going back to the landmark case of *Plessy* v. *Ferguson* in 1896.[10] The heart of the problem was that the judges opposed to racial segregation never managed to get clear on the *principle* which defined the wrong of segregation, and after a while it became part of the strategy of litigation for the civil rights movement to avoid posing that question of principle. Instead, the legal tacticians of the civil rights movement helped lead the Court through a train of cases in which the Court would confront instances of racial discrimination in all their variety—in grade schools, colleges,

[10] 163 U.S. 537.

and law schools, in juries and elections—but without confronting the principle of which these cases were merely instances. As a result, the Court tutored a generation of lawyers and judges to put their focus on the material harms that were peculiar to each case, and that disposition of mind, confirmed over so long a period, has carried over to our own time. Rather than speaking of wrongs in principle which were independent of material injuries, the Court taught jurists to identify the wrong of these cases with harms which were often speculative and unprovable. And rather than invoking moral propositions, which had a categorical and *necessary* force, the Court continued to base its judgments on nothing more than a series of empirical predictions or conjectures that were, at their best, highly doubtful, and at their worst, comic.

"If Saks Fifth Avenue moves into the neighborhood, the whole neighborhood will prosper." That proposition may be true, but it need not be true. Whether it will be true or not is *contingent* upon a number of other events. It cannot be true as a matter of necessity—in the way that it must be true, for example, that "two contradictory propositions cannot both be true," or that people may not be held responsible or blameworthy for acts they were powerless to affect. The statement offers nothing more than an empirical prediction, *which cannot be anything more than problematic, even if it turned out to be true most of the time.*

The problem for our courts and jurists is that they have persistently confounded empirical predictions (or contingent propositions) with propositions that may claim the standing of authentic principles. The result has been that, in one domain of our law after another, the courts have been willing to settle their judgments not on propositions that have the categorical force of a principle, but on a series of propositions of the form "If Saks Fifth Avenue moves into the neighborhood, the whole neighborhood will prosper." And when those propositions are set forth with an attention to their logical form, it becomes plain that they state nothing of moral—and hence, jural—significance. Consider one or two cases in point. When the Civil Rights Act of 1964 was tested before the Supreme Court, it was necessary to explain how the law could reach incidents of racial discrimination in private establishments (such as inns, hotels, and restaurants) that were open to the public. Working with the conventional formulas of the Commerce Clause, the solicitor general and, ultimately, the Court were content to build their judgment on the following kind of argument. If blacks face the prospect of discrimination in public inns and restaurants, they might be discouraged from traveling among the states. If blacks are discouraged from traveling, the effect would be to reduce the total volume of trade available to restaurants, inns, and other places of public accommodation. In turn, that shortfall of trade would reduce the amount of orders that these businesses would place with other businesses (e.g., for meat, linens, furniture). The effect would be to depress even further the level of trade and, presumably, the general standard of living. In the eyes of the law, then, the problem of discrimination in places of public accommodation did not lie in any injustice that was done to black people, but in the interference it might produce in the interstate flow of meat![11] As a colleague of mine has pointed out, the problem stated here by the Court might have been dissolved quite as well if the racists in the country had simply made up for the shortfall by eating more meat.

In fairness, it must be said that many of our estimable judges and lawyers felt compelled to cast their arguments in this form, since they thought it was the only form that was either comprehensible under the Constitution or politically acceptable. But when the same people set out to explain "the principle" that defines the wrong of racial discrimination, they fall precisely into the same cast of argument that the courts have been employing for over forty years. Questions of principle have been confounded for so long now with empirical predictions or contingent propositions that even our best jurists are no longer clear on how to establish, as the foundation of their judgments, propositions that have a *necessary*, categorical force.

That difference may be brought out again, from another angle, if we recall one of the classic cases in the series on racial segregation, *Missouri ex rel. Gaines* v. *Canada*.[12] The state of Missouri, in the 1930's, refused to admit blacks to the law school supported by the state. Instead of establishing a separate law school for blacks, the state offered to pay "reasonable" tuition fees for any of its black citizens who gained admission to law schools in adjacent states where segregation was not practiced. The Court struck down this arrangement, and it argued that, in furnishing a law school for whites only, the state was establishing privileges or benefits for white students that it was denying to blacks solely on account of their race. (That is to say, the result was to deprive blacks of a material benefit.) But the Court skipped over an indelicate question. What if the law schools in neighboring states were in fact superior to the law school at the University of Missouri? If the case turned wholly on the question of whether

---

[11] See *Katzenbach* v. *McClung*, 379 U.S. 294, at 299-300, 303-304.
[12] 305 U.S. 337 (1938).

blacks were injured by being deprived of a legal education, then the embarrassing point was that blacks were not necessarily deprived of that education; they could in fact be "forced," in this arrangement, to attend a better law school than the one which was available to whites at the expense of the state. That this was indeed the actual experience in a number of cases was suggested recently in an interview given by Cecil Partee, a prominent black politician in the Cook County organization in Illinois. Partee recalled that he had graduated in 1938 at the top of his class at Tennessee State University. As a native of Arkansas, he applied to the law school of the University of Arkansas, but Arkansas worked under a policy similar to that of the state of Missouri. The state offered to pay Partee's tuition at another school. Partee happened to be admitted to the law schools at the University of Chicago and Northwestern University, both notably superior to the law school in Arkansas. Partee ended up choosing Northwestern and, as he later commented, "I laughed all the way to Chicago."[13]

Partee did not suffer a material injury as a result of being excluded on the basis of race from the law school of the state; but he was indeed *wronged*. That is to say, he was treated unjustly, he was treated according to the maxims of an unjust principle. If we seek to explain that principle which finally marks the wrong of racial segregation, we find that it could be drawn, as a necessary inference, from the logic of morals itself. The first thing that would have to be recognized in racial discrimination, as we have come to know it, is that it is meant to disparage or denigrate. It implies that if we merely know the race of the people we are dealing with, we also know something of moral significance about them—that they will be desirable or undesirable neighbors, good or bad colleagues. These moral inferences have not been drawn from the acts that people have performed or the infirmities we know they share. Disparaging all members of a certain race is not like providing punishments to all people who are arsonists or rapists; nor is it like restricting certain privileges for people who are mentally retarded. In racial discrimination there is a willingness to make hard predictions about the moral character of people on the basis of personal features that have no moral significance.

Most important, we are asked to assume that race exerts a kind of unfailing, *deterministic* control over the moral acts of each member of a racial group, in the way that the laws of physics "determine" the course of falling bodies. But as I pointed out earlier, the language of

---

[13] See the interview with Partee conducted by Milton Rakove in *We Don't Want Nobody Nobody Sent* (Bloomington: Indiana University Press, 1979), p. 156.

morals is entirely out of place with events in the world of "determinism." The language of moral judgment must presuppose that we are in the domain of freedom, and that we are addressing creatures who are in fact free to form their own acts and choose one course of action over another. Without that assumption, it would make no sense to assign credit or blame, or to hold people legally responsible for their acts.

The willingness to discriminate on the basis of race marks a rejection, then, of premises that are necessary, as suppositions, to the idea of morals itself—premises that cannot be rejected without falling into contradiction. Those who would establish disabilities, say, for blacks on account of their race would deny, in relation to black people, that moral autonomy which must be the mark of their nature as moral agents and the necessary premise of morals and law. If our moral acts were "determined" by our race as the path of a falling stone is "determined" by the laws of physics, then there could be no ground for outrage or condemnation—no ground, in short, on which to judge people for their acts. In fact, it could be said here that if racial discrimination is not wrong—if the premises of "racial determinism" are not false—then *nothing* could be wrong, for there could be no such concepts of "right" and "wrong" for which individuals could be held responsible. The wrongness of racial discrimination has little to do, then, with the question of whether the discrimination has actually caused a material harm, or whether the black victims find themselves happy or unhappy with the results. Cecil Partee "laughed all the way to Chicago," and yet the act of discrimination which produced that happy outcome was still wrong in principle.

We can put the matter to ourselves in yet another way by imagining for a moment that the level of violent crime is much higher in "Oriental" neighborhoods than it is in other parts of the city. Statistically, we would be correct in saying that the more Orientals there are in any neighborhood, the higher the probability that the crime rate will rise. Beyond that, let us assume that the chances are 70 out of 100 that the Orientals who wish to move in next door are likely to become criminals. Nonetheless, even if we know these statistics to be true for Orientals in the aggregate, we would grasp rather quickly the injustice of treating the new Chinese family in the neighborhood on the basis of what is known about Orientals *in the aggregate*. We would recognize that there is a chance that these new neighbors are part of the statistical minority who will be innocent, and we would be led to recognize further that these people deserve to be condemned or penalized only for their own acts. They do not deserve to suffer disabilities on the basis of what is known, in the aggregate, about the racial or ethnic groups of which they happen to be members.[14] What we seem to recognize, then, is that despite the racial or ethnic aggregates in which people happen to be classified, we are compelled to credit people with a certain autonomy—a certain capacity to disengage themselves on occasion from the dominant ethic within their group and to reach a different judgment on matters of right and wrong. In the riots of 1977 in New York City, there were many people who were poor and black who did not choose to loot or burn. If race and poverty "explained" or "determined" a tendency to engage in looting, it would be necessary to explain why most people who were poor and black decided to hold themselves back from the violence. The "explanation," of course, would be found in the most obvious things we take for granted about the capacity of any person to form his own moral judgments and choose his own course.[15]

The point is so axiomatic that it may elude, with its simplicity, some of the most instructed minds. Merely by knowing a person's race we cannot make any moral inferences about him. We cannot know that he has done a wrong and deserves punishment; neither can we know that he has suffered an injury and deserves compensation. And yet, this understanding has been ignored with the most righteous passion in recent years by colleges and offices of admissions throughout the country, as they have pursued policies of "racial preference." With the most generous intentions, these institutions have backed themselves into the old premises of "racial determinism," but with a novel slant: it is assumed now that if we know the race or the ethnic background of an applicant (e.g., that he is an Hispanic from Harlem), we can know also the likelihood that he will bring an interesting perspective to the classroom; that he will in fact be able to articulate a perspective; and that his presence in the class will tend to improve it. In this respect, we discover that there is nothing in principle that separates the offices of admissions these days from the racialists of old. On the main premise they both agree: viz., that race essentially determines, in a significant

[14] Once again, we would be compelled to recognize a decisive difference between membership in an ethnic group and membership in a voluntary organization, such as a gang of arsonists or terrorists, where the act of affiliation reflects the commitment to a common moral code and perhaps, also, the commission of the same criminal act.

[15] That elementary recognition might illuminate Immanuel Kant's observation that "the moral law expresses nothing else than the autonomy of the pure practical reason, i.e., freedom. This autonomy or freedom is itself the formal condition of all maxims" that convey a universal law which may govern our judgments. *Critique of Practical Reason* [1788], trans. Lewis White Beck (Indianapolis: Bobbs-Merrill, 1956), pp. 3, 33-34; pp. 4 and 33 of the RPA ed.

way, the moral character of individuals. The racialist and the dean of admissions differ from one another simply in the inferences they are inclined to draw from the same aggregate data (i.e., from the data which establish, at the same time, high levels of poverty and high levels of crime and violence). The dean of admissions assumes that the young man from the ghetto will bring into the classroom and dormitory the perspectives that are nourished in a lower-class setting. Those perspectives may be altogether novel for his fellow students, and for that reason it is hoped that the presence of the youngster from the ghetto will improve the education of his classmates. The racialist, on the other hand, may agree that the young man will carry with him the perspectives of the ghetto, but he believes that the fellow may bring with him, also, the less wholesome parts of that subculture. He may carry within him a sensibility formed by a lower level of literacy, as well as by the looser conventions about theft and violence that prevail in the ghetto. For that reason, the racialist thinks the young man is just as likely to pose a threat to his classmates and depress the levels of conversation and learning. And if we are making predictions about people simply on the basis of what we know, in the aggregate, about their racial or ethnic groups, the racialist is apt to be as right as the dean of admissions. The point, however, is that neither argument deserves to be credited, for they are in principle the same: both assume that race determines moral character. Both deny that notion of moral autonomy which stands as a necessary presupposition behind the idea of morals and law.

I HAVE DWELLED here on these points for the sake of bringing out more fully the difference between contingent and categorical propositions. The very fact that certain "goods" are merely "contingent" means that, under certain contingencies, they will cease being "good" and may even be productive of harm. At those moments, it may be found that certain contingent goods come into conflict (in the way that categorical "goods" cannot), and we are then compelled to choose between these contingent goods. In the nature of things, the standards that are needed to establish a hierarchy or ranking of preferences among contingent "goods" cannot themselves be merely contingent. Let us suppose that in a public square there is a sign saying, "Keep off the grass." The rule that forbids walking on the grass would serve a plausible and legitimate end: it is pleasant to have the beauty of the grass, and it is good to honor the work that went into the cultivation of the grounds. But in an emergency it might be necessary to run across the grass if that were the fastest way of reaching a phone to call an ambulance and save a life. We could argue that the good of preserving the grass should not take precedence over the good of saving a human life, and that it would be perverse to accord precedence to the interests of the grass.

But would that be merely a matter of opinion? The judgment would be taken widely as a product of common sense, and it is arguable that it rests on a necessary understanding of the interests that stand on higher and lower planes of importance. It is quite common to hear it said on occasions of this kind that "principles" are in conflict. I have been reserving the term "principle" to refer to propositions of a categorical nature that arise from necessary truths. If that understanding is taken strictly, there cannot be a conflict between real "principles" in this hard sense: by the law of contradiction it is not possible to have two necessary truths that are in conflict. Either one of the propositions may fail to state a necessary truth, or the two propositions may not be in conflict. In the case of running across the grass to call an ambulance, I would be more inclined to say that we find two "ends" (or contingent goods) in conflict, and that only by appealing to a "principle" of judgment can we find the basis on which to choose between these ends. The differences that arise in our choice of labels, however, should not obscure the underlying logic of what is being done here. Even the person who thinks that there are "principles" in conflict has to seek some standard—or some other set of principles— that will allow him to make a judgment. He may be tempted to call the principles that are in conflict "secondary principles," and when he finds the standards that allow him, finally, to judge between "secondary principles" in conflict, he may refer to those more fundamental principles as "first principles."

And yet, the logic of the inquiry is the same: whatever language we use, we will find ourselves making our way back to the logic of categorical propositions, or first principles, as the foundation for our judgments. At those moments, we must be able to tell the difference between propositions which may be cast in a categorical form, but which may be either valid or spurious. As I have tried to show, a valid moral principle will bear a logical connection to the idea of morals; it will state an implication that arises from the logic of morals itself. There is, of course, no mechanistic device for identifying these propositions and separating them from spurious moral principles. We must depend here on the disciplined uses of imagination as we become more practiced in reflecting on the problem and trying to trace our judgments back to the logic of morals. But one useful test in judging any proposition that is offered as a moral principle is to consider whether it is possible to act upon the maxim contained in the proposition while at the same time engaging in projects that are thoroughly evil. If it were said, for example, that "people ought to act in the way that is most likely to give them pleasure," we would recognize instantly that certain people may find their pleasures in perverse ways, in causing harm for others without justification. To put the matter more strictly, we notice that it is possible to act on the maxim of seeking one's pleasure while simultaneously acting on a maxim that is incompatible with the logic of morals itself—e.g., that "people ought to be free to kill members of a race they find disagreeable, even though it means killing people for attributes they were powerless to affect." To recognize that the two maxims can be reconciled—that we can act on both without conflict—is to recognize the plain truth that people may seek their pleasure unjustly. The second maxim is incompatible with the logic of morals, and if it is not in conflict with the first maxim, then we know that the maxim of "seeking pleasure" cannot arise as an implication from the logic of morals. Therefore the proposition that "it is good to seek one's pleasure" cannot stand as the statement of a categorical good; it cannot express an authentic moral principle.

We might consider the following list of propositions, which may be commonly thought to convey moral principles. It is useful to put the question as to which of these propositions would meet the exacting requirements that mark valid moral "principles." They all affirm something categorically, not hypothetically, and they all speak of moral "wrongs." But which of them can be said, accurately, to express an understanding of right and wrong that would hold true *categorically*, under all contingencies? The list would be:

(1) It is wrong to visit punishment on people
   without making reasoned discriminations between
   the innocent and the guilty.
(2) It is wrong to take things that belong to others.
(3) It is wrong to speak other than the truth.
(4) It is wrong to kill.

As it turns out, only one of these propositions—the first—states a valid moral principle. The notions of "innocence," "guilt," and "punishment" are bound up with the logic of morals. As John Stuart Mill remarked, "we call any conduct wrong, or employ, instead, some other term of dislike or disparagement, according as we think that the person ought, or ought not, to be punished for it."[16] When we say that "X

---

[16] John Stuart Mill, *Utilitarianism* (Indianapolis: Bobbs-Merrill, 1957 [1861]), p. 61.

is wrong," we mean that everyone ought, universally, to refrain from doing X; that anyone may rightly be restrained from doing X. If people are not left free to do X as it suits their own pleasure, then it must be legitimate to punish people who persist in doing X after they have been enjoined to stop. To mark off the difference between the guilty and the innocent is to describe the people who deserve—and do not deserve—punishment. Guilty people are those who do unjustified things; innocent people are those who refrain from unjustified acts. We show our respect for the difference between the innocent and the guilty when we insist on making that distinction only in the most sober and reasoned way, through a process of law, before we visit punishment on anyone. On the other hand, we would show contempt for that distinction if we were to inflict punishment in a sweeping, casual way, without making discriminations between innocence and guilt. One may be indifferent, then, to distinctions of innocence and guilt only if one preserves a fundamental contempt for the notion of morals itself, from which the difference between the innocent and the guilty is ultimately drawn.

The understanding contained in our first proposition would explain the traditional argument against lynching—against the willingness to inflict punishment without being overly fastidious about proving the guilt of the accused through the disciplined presentation and assessment of evidence. It would also account, at the root, for the wrong of genocide—that willingness to exterminate whole racial or ethnic groups, without judging whether the members of these groups actually committed a wrong that justified punishment. Once again we find a species of "group determinism": it is apparently assumed that membership in a certain racial or ethnic group impresses individuals with a character that will make them enemies of the regime in power. Thus Stalin could assume that any child who grew up in a family of small-holding peasantry would have an interest in private property, which would affect him with interests adverse to the interests of the Soviet regime. In the same way, it was assumed by the Nazis that any child who grew up a Jew would become an enemy of the "Aryan people" and the Nazi regime. Hence the resort to policies which swept broadly and destroyed children as well as adults, and which made no effort to tailor punishment to real crimes, or to matters of individual innocence or guilt. In this sweep of condemnation, this indifference to personal innocence and guilt, the mind directed toward genocide shows its ultimate indifference to the notion of "justification" itself.

Proposition 1 stands, then, as an implication arising from the logic of morals. For that reason, it holds true categorically and universally (which is why our judgment of genocide would be unaffected by matters of locale or by variations in regional "culture"). But the remaining propositions in the list are not propositions of that kind, even though they are widely taken as expressions of moral "principles." The second and third propositions—that it is wrong "to take things that belong to others" and "to speak other than the truth"—may alert us to the problem more easily, because they convey common notions in a phrasing that is noticeably unfamiliar. The more usual expressions would be that "it is wrong to steal" and "it is wrong to lie." But the difference in wording suggests the question to us: By "stealing" or "theft" have people not usually meant "taking things that belong to others"? By "lying" have they not usually meant "speaking other than the truth"? If not, then we have to state a bit more precisely the conditions that constitute "stealing" and "lying." Propositions 2 and 3 seek to define the nature of the wrong by describing the "act" that may constitute the wrong—but without making any reference to the intentions or reasons of the actors. What we discover again is that the outward act (or "mere behavior") cannot be invested with moral significance unless we know something, also, of the understanding that guided the actor.

To take the first example, would we apply the label of "theft" if we were given nothing more than this account of Smith's behavior?: "Smith went to the garage of his neighbor, Jones, and took Jones's hose." Obviously, we would not take these facts alone to define a theft. For all we know, Smith had permission from Jones to use the hose, and he intended to return it after he had made use of it. But what if Jones had not given his permission? What if a fire had broken out in Smith's house, and Smith quickly ran to borrow Jones's hose, even though Jones was not there at the time? Smith might not intend to keep the hose, and his use of the instrument without the approval of Jones could be "justified" by the seriousness of the emergency, combined with Jones's absence.

What we mean more strictly, then, by a "theft" is a taking of property "without justification." This definition of the wrong is easily satisfied in the case of muggers who take the wallets of people under coercion or assault—who appropriate to themselves the money that belongs to others even though they have established no claim to *deserve* that money. The next day we may witness a similar act on the street with one person assaulting another and removing his wallet; but this time it may be the victim of the previous day who is doing the assaulting, and it is mugger of the day before who may be suffering the assault. The original mugger, however, would not be a "victim"; the original victim would not be a "mugger" or a "criminal." The victim

103

did indeed have a moral claim to recover the money that was taken from him unjustly, and his act of vindication could not be considered a "taking of property without justification." Whether a taking of property is wrong, then—whether it constitutes a "theft"—turns entirely on the question of whether it is done with or without "justification." Hence our labeling and judging of the act would have to depend ultimately on what we know about the standards of "justification"—i.e., about the kinds of considerations that truly constitute "justifications."

The same thing would have to be said in regard to "speaking other than the truth." Very early in *The Republic*, Plato raised the question of whether justice inhered in always speaking the truth, and he had Socrates put the question: What if a friend, whom you knew to be deranged, asked you the whereabouts of a weapon? Would you be obliged to tell him the truth?[17] The answer, of course, was no: the telling of the truth, in that particular case, could produce an unnecessary, undeserved harm, and so the telling of the truth would not have been warranted. As a matter of common sense, we do not consider people immoral on every occasion in which they "speak other than the truth." We find the presence of a lie, rather, when people speak falsely in the service of unjust ends—when they deceive others, for example, for the sake of defrauding and serving their own interests. But that is simply to say that a lie consists in speaking other than the truth *without justification.*

If it were categorically wrong to speak other than the truth, we would be faced with this moral inversion: we would have to indict as immoral the people of Holland who hid Jews in their homes during the Nazi occupation, and who did not tell the truth to the agents of the Gestapo who appeared at their doors. To treat the injunction against speaking falsely as a categorical imperative, one would have to place the Dutch householders on the same moral plane with the Nazis. We are obliged, rather, to say that it may be justified at times to speak other than the truth. If the Dutch citizens had told the truth to the Nazis, they would have made themselves, in effect, agents or accomplices for the purposes of the Nazis. The aim of the Nazis was genocide, and as we have seen, genocide is a categorical wrong; its wrongness arises as a necessary inference from the idea of morals itself. For that reason, there must be a justification for resisting acts that are at war with the very notion of justification. But my concern, again, is with the form of our reflection here. In order to reach a

---

[17] Plato, *The Republic*, bk. I, 331c.

judgment in this particular case—in order to decide whether it would be justified, on this occasion, to speak falsely—we would have to be drawn back to first principles in explaining just why the ends of the Nazis were categorically wrong; why those ends could never have been justified under any contingency; and why the insistence on speaking the truth could not have been the mark, in this case, of a man who was morally good.

YET IT WOULD strongly appear—and it is widely taken for granted—that Kant's teaching would have urged the Dutch householders to tell the truth to the Nazis at the door. In Kant's understanding, the categorical proposition in regard to lying did indeed coincide with the third proposition listed earlier. As he wrote in *The Metaphysical Principles of Virtue*, "no intentional untruth in the expression of one's thought can avoid this harsh name [of 'lying.']" For Kant, the wrong of speaking other than the truth is utterly indifferent to the question of whether the act is harmless or harmful. As he put it, unambiguously, "the injury to other people which can arise from lying has nothing to do with this vice. . . . Lying is the throwing away, and, as it were, the obliteration of one's dignity as a human being":[18]

> A man who does not himself believe what he says to another . . . has even less worth than if he were a mere thing; for because of the thing's property of being useful, the other person can make some use of it, since it is a thing real and given. But to communicate one's thought to someone by words which (intentionally) contain the opposite of what one thinks is an end directly contrary to the natural purposiveness of his capacity to communicate his thoughts. . . .

Even in Kantian terms, however, this passage is rather curious. The "natural purposiveness" of the human "capacity to communicate" is not merely to convey information. Its most distinctive purpose—and its highest end—is to arrive at an understanding of right and wrong. As we shall see, Kant recognized an obligation flowing from the logic of morals itself to do "good" where we can. And as one careful student of Kant has noted, Kant's injunction to seek the happiness of others—or to make ourselves "useful" to others—must still assume that we are putting ourselves in the service only of *legitimate* ends. Kant could not be read to prescribe an obligation to help others in carrying out

---

[18] Kant, *supra*, note 6, p. 91; p. 429 of the RPA ed.

criminal projects.[19] For the same reason, a person cannot preserve his "integrity" or enlarge his "dignity" by making himself an accomplice in wicked acts, as he surely would if he insisted on tendering, truthfully, to the Nazis the information they would find useful in tracking down their innocent victims. If this is what Kant's teaching would have prescribed, we are tempted to say that, even on his own terms, Kant must have been mistaken.

In its main formulation by Kant, the Categorical Imperative was stated in this way: "Act only on that maxim through which you can at the same time will that it should become a universal law." When it comes to the question of speaking falsely, it is tempting to apply the Categorical Imperative in the most sweeping manner and say something like the following: "We cannot coherently will, as a universal law, that everyone should speak falsely, for life would become unworkable. We could not assume, in that event, that any item of information is true. Bus schedules, menus, balances in banks, records in hospitals—none of these could be relied upon, and we could not manage our existence." The point is correct, but this understanding of the "maxim" is needlessly broad, and for that reason it is not a response to the more precise justifications that are usually offered for speaking falsely. In the case of hiding Jews, the Dutch owner of the house is not affirming that it is justified to speak falsely *on all matters* or to speak falsely when it serves one's own interest. The fact that he speaks falsely in order to protect innocent victims cannot imply a license for everyone else to convey falsehoods for any other kind of purpose. He is claiming only that there is a justification for speaking untruths when they are necessary to save victims from genocide. In that case, the more precise statement of the categorical imperative would be, "It is wrong to speak other than the truth *without justification*." But we ought to be clear that this formula would not permit us to fill in the "justification" with any reason we could invent. When we say that an act is "without justification," we mean to say, more strictly, that the maxim behind the act is incompatible with the idea of morals or with the very idea of a "justification"—precisely in the way that genocide, as we have seen, is incompatible with the logic that is built into the notion of a moral justification.

A question may be raised as to whether the categorical proposition, in this form, is still categorical. It does not brand as wrong all "intentional untruth in the expression of one's thought," and it seems to pick out only certain instances of speaking falsely. But the heart of

[19] See H.J. Paton, *The Categorical Imperative* (London: Hutchinson, 1947), p. 173.

the problem here, as I have already indicated, is that we cannot attribute moral significance to outward acts alone. Before we are warranted in invoking the language of morals, we must know the reasons that animate the act. To discover more precisely what those reasons are is not to convert a categorical statement into a proposition that is merely "conditional" ("X is wrong *on the condition* that it is done without justification"). Rather, it is to fill in the pertinent description of the act, which allows us to see more exactly the kind of problem raised by the case and the principles that become relevant in arriving at a judgment. As Kant suggested, we canot pass judgment on any act unless we can extract the maxim that is disclosed in the act, and the maxim can be revealed only by a statement of reasons. And so, when Kant applied the Categorical Imperative to matters such as "lying," the moral judgment was not addressed to a plain, unembellished act called "lying." The act of speaking falsely would occur in a setting, or under certain circumstances, and it would be accompanied by a reason. If we were to reject the reason or the maxim that describes the act, we might end up saying something like this: "Contrary to what you say, it is always wrong to speak falsely under condition X (e.g., when it injures someone else), for reason Y (e.g., solely for the sake of advancing your own interests)." This condemnation of speaking falsely would be pronounced in the name of the Categorical Imperative, even though it would not cover, in a sweeping way, all cases of speaking falsely. The prohibition on speaking falsely would be narrowed by the fact that it addresses the maxim which defines, as a class, only *these acts* of false speaking. Nevertheless, the prohibition attains the quality of a categorical statement because it applies, *universally, to all of the cases of false speaking that come within this class* (i.e., to all cases in which people speak falsely for the purpose of misleading and injuring others, and serving their own interests).[20] And when we say that this kind of false speaking is wrong, we are saying that it is wrong under all circumstances and conditions, that its wrongness would not be affected by matters of degree.

After all, the condemnation of *lying* did not lose its categorical force for Kant because it was narrowed to a particular species of wrongdoing. In the same way, the proposition I have set forth here would not lose its categorical quality because it picks out for condemnation only that class of untruthful speech which can be regarded, unreservedly, as wrong. This understanding of the matter may also help to defend the notion of a "categorical" imperative from the kind of

[20] In this vein see Kant, *supra*, note 3, pp. 89-90; pp. 422-23 of the RPA ed.

mistaken criticism that could be offered even by a figure as estimable as Hegel: viz., that as soon as *content* is added to an imperative, the proposition has to become contingent rather than categorical. Hegel argued, for example, that the injunction against lying would still be "contingent" on the prospect that the actor *knew* what was true. In that event, he says, "speaking the truth is left to the chance whether I know it and can convince myself of it; . . . This contingency in the content has universality merely in the propositional form of the expression; but as an ethical maxim the proposition promises a universal and necessary content, and thus contradicts itself by the content being contingent."[21]

And yet, the contingency Hegel had in mind has nothing to do with the *principle* that stands behind the imperative, and it has no bearing on the categorical nature of the moral proposition that emerges. But then we are simply reminded that no real principle—no proposition with a universal and necessary force—could possibly incorporate a reference to events that are merely empirical and contingent. It could never be said with a categorical logic that "it is always wrong to speak falsely to people who appear at your door hunting for refugees." The categorical quality of a moral proposition can arise only from its expression of a principle, and a principle cannot be expressed unless the proposition conveys, in relation to its subject, an implication that arises out of the idea of morals itself. That requirement would not be satisfied by a proposition which merely states, without elaboration, that "it is wrong, on all occasions, to speak other than the truth." The statement would not attain the character of a valid moral proposition until it was recast in a form more nearly like the following: "It is wrong to speak falsely when the intention is to harm others or to damage other people in their legitimate interests, and when the animating purpose behind the falsity is to advance one's own interests." When the proposition takes on a form of this kind, it does not become defectively narrow or particular: it simply states, for the case at hand, an understanding that is implicit in the idea of morals. Its sweep would be universal, its logic categorical, because it would apply, comprehensively, to all instances of false speaking that are morally relevant.

As it turns out, Kant's own teaching on this matter was not so unequivocal as it might have appeared from the nature of his "cate-

[21] See G.W.F. Hegel, *Phenomenology of Mind* ("Reason as Lawgiver"), trans. J.B. Baillie (New York: Harper & Row, 1967), p. 442.

gorical" affirmations. As he came to elaborate his argument on "lying," Kant showed himself unwilling to condemn, categorically, all instances of speaking "an intentional untruth in the expression of one's thoughts." In his lectures on ethics, Kant remarked that "if we were to be at all times punctiliously truthful we might often become victims of the wickedness of others who were ready to abuse our truthfulness."[22] There was, for Kant, no obligation to speak the truth for the sake of furthering the work of criminals, and the criminals had no "right" to receive the truth. And so, as Kant said, if an enemy were to grab him by the throat and ask where he kept his money, "I need not tell him the truth, because he will abuse it; and my untruth is not a lie (*mendacium*) because the thief knows full well that I will not, if I can help it, tell him the truth and that he has no right to demand it of me." Kant went on to say that if force were used to extort a confession from him, "if my confession is improperly used against me, and if I cannot save myself by maintaining silence, then my lie is a weapon of defence. The misuse of a declaration extorted by force justifies me in defending myself."[23] The sense of being coerced toward an unjust end is enough to remove the act of speech from the obligations of truthfulness that must attach to the speech of communication and exchange, the speech that is directed toward legitimate ends.

It might have been taken for granted by Kant that it is wrong to speak falsely when the deception would cause injury or deflect people from legitimate ends, but that "moral" requirement, built into the Categorical Imperative, deserved to be made explicit. For it would have become clear then that Kant could not really have rejected, categorically, all departures from truth, and that understanding would have clarified a deeper truth about the Categorical Imperative itself: viz., that the Categorical Imperative does not sanction any maxim, in a mindless, formalistic way, so long as the actor is sufficiently willing, in his perversity, to make it universal. With this kind of reasoning, it has been easy to fall into the assumption that the Categorical Imperative would have sanctioned the proverbial "conscientious Nazi," the man who was willing to be killed if a Jewish ancestor were discovered in his own background. In the course of his many commentaries on the Categorical Imperative, however, Kant wrote of the "fitness" of

---

[22] Immanuel Kant, *Lectures on Ethics*, trans. Louis Infield (New York: Harper & Row, 1963), p. 228. The lectures collected in this book were offered by Kant between 1775 and 1780; the quotations here are drawn from Kant's lecture "Ethical Duties towards Others: Truthfulness."

[23] *Ibid.*, pp. 227-28.

any maxim to be established as a universal law.[24] As Kant made clear, the objects of inclination were quite mutable and contingent. Even if people universally chose to do the right thing in any case, not because it was right, but because it *pleased* them, they might cease to act rightly at another time when acting rightly ceased to please them.[25] The object of the Categorical Imperative was not to make private enthusiasms global; it was, rather, to direct our will to the maxims that are fit to be installed as universal laws because they have been drawn from the idea of morals and the commands of reason alone.

Anyone who views the Categorical Imperative strictly must understand, also, that it expresses the logic of morals and that its requirements presuppose creatures with the competence for moral judgment. It would be incoherent, therefore, to respect the formal properties of the Categorical Imperative while at the same time willing ends that are incompatible with the very idea of morals or with the notion of a "rational being." And so, the same principles which enjoin us to act in a principled way and employ the Categorical Imperative would establish why it is wrong at the same time to will a policy of genocide, *even if we were disposed to will that policy universally*. It would be as contradictory to will genocide under the terms of the Categorical Imperative as it was contradictory, earlier, to say that a free people may be free to choose slavery so long as the choice is made in a formally democratic way, through the votes of a majority. As we saw earlier, there are certain substantive ends that cannot be pursued through the principle of "rule by majority." By the same logic, there are certain substantive ends (such as slavery and genocide) that may not be pursued properly through the use of the Categorical Imperative.

With these points in place, it may be easier to see why Kant's Categorical Imperative would not have enjoined us to speak the truth in the service of immoral ends. Kant came closer to the language of

---

[24] Kant, *supra*, note 3, p. 57. See, also, Mary J. Gregor, *Laws of Freedom* (Oxford: Basil Blackwell, 1963), pp. 38-39.

[25] "Practical precepts based on [principles of self-love] can never be universal, for the determinant of the faculty of desire is based on the feeling of pleasure and displeasure, which can never be assumed to be universally directed to the same objects.

"But suppose that finite rational beings were unanimous in the kind of objects their feelings of pleasure and pain had, and even in the means of obtaining the former and preventing the latter. Even then they could not set up the principle of self-love as a practical law, for the unanimity itself would be merely contingent. The determining ground would still be only subjectively valid and empirical, and it would not have the necessity which is conceived in every law, an objective necessity arising from a priori grounds. . . ." Kant, *supra*, note 15, p. 26; pp. 25-26 of the RPA ed.

this chapter when he observed that "not every untruth is a lie."[26] Still, it was a measure of this good man's straining over this question that he insisted on regarding people as liars, even when he conceded that they had not told lies. It was Kant's conviction that, even when it was justified to speak falsely, the act of departing from truth violated "the right of mankind." But those Dutch citizens who misled the Gestapo did not deflect the Nazis from any end they had a "right" to pursue. And since the act of misleading was morally justified, it could not strictly be said that the Gestapo had been "injured" by the deception. Beyond that, the Dutch who hid Jews furnished no precedent, they offered no principle, for those who would deceive for the sake of doing injury. Kant might have done better to honor more fully his own recognition that to speak falsely at times may be *justified*, and that the term "lie" should be reserved for those intentional acts of deception which are done "without justification."

OUR LANGUAGE has preserved these distinctions which turn on matters of justification: not all takings of property are "thefts," not all instances of speaking falsely can be counted as "lies," and not all killings can be called "murders." We speak of "justifiable homicide," which may be carried out in self-defense, and we assign the label of "murder" only when it has been established that there was an intentional act of killing, carried out "without justification." Once again, the proper form of the categorical proposition would not be "It is wrong to kill," but "It is wrong to kill without justification." We will have occasion later to encounter the argument that the only principled opposition to war must rest on the unqualified conviction that "it is wrong to kill—anyone, anywhere." This argument rests, however, on a deep misunderstanding of the properties of a principle; and it is usually placed beyond the canons of reasoned argument by being classified in the domain of "belief." But as we shall see, the argument cannot be sheltered from its defects merely because it is placed under the rubric of "religious belief."

To say that "it is wrong to kill" is to invoke the logic of morals: the proposition speaks of what is "wrong" and it implies, then, the existence of morals. To recognize the existence of morals is to recognize, as we have seen, that it is possible to speak of acts which are justified and unjustified. It would be possible, in that event, to speak of certain takings of property which are justified and unjustified, just as it would be possible to speak of acts of violence which may be

---

[26] Kant, *supra*, note 22, p. 228.

warranted and unwarranted. We can advance up a scale, beginning with minor villainies and injuries, and eventually we may reach acts of acute malice and severe harm. But then we would seem to be told that, as we ascend the scale in this way, the language of morals must suddenly cease when we arrive at those material injuries which are the most substantial and irreparable: as soon as we speak about the taking of life, it is no longer possible to make distinctions and speak about *lethal assaults that may be justified or unjustified*. And yet, if it is possible to speak intelligibly of an ordinary assault that was launched "without justification"—e.g., for the pleasure or benefit of the assailant—then the assault can surely be judged for its justification even when it acquires a lethal possibility. The person who resists an act of injustice cannot, by definition, be unjustified, and we would accord him the right to use the same magnitude of force, in his resistance, that his assailant is willing to use against him (if, in fact, that level of force would be necessary to resist the assault). It is on those premises that we have accorded the right to certain people threatened with death to kill in self-defense.

But if we insist that all killing is wrong, without gradations or distinctions, we would have to place on a level of moral equality the killing done, say, by a Hitler and the killing done by those who would resist being killed by a Hitler. That kind of parity could not be established without ruling out, from the beginning, any notice of the differences in motive and justification that separate the two sides. And once again it must be said that we cannot blind ourselves to these distinctions between the malicious and the innocent without showing a profound disrespect for the notion of morals itself, from which the difference between the guilty and the innocent is ultimately drawn. The logic of morals compels us to make the distinction between Hitler and his victims, which means that we are obliged in turn to distinguish among lethal acts animated by purposes that are "justified" or "unjustified." If the command "Thou shalt not kill" is understood to be directed at the potential victims as well as the potential assailants, then it cannot be a moral command in the truest sense. And if the proposition "It is wrong to kill" leads to the judgment that the resisting victims of an evil maniac are criminals on the same plane with the maniac himself, then it cannot be a *moral* proposition, speaking in the name of a truly moral understanding.

THE LAST THREE propositions in my list fail to state valid moral propositions because they fail to express propositions that could hold true categorically. The correct form of the categorical proposition in morals

112

will always be, "It is wrong to do X without justification."[27] "X" may signify "take property," "kill," or "walk on the grass." Or, to borrow from Woody Allen's list of villainies, it may even encompass "dialing information for numbers you could look up yourself." It may be helpful to conceive the form of the proposition here to be comparable to an equation which arranges itself in this way:

$$\text{It is wrong} = \text{to do X without justification}$$

Both sides of the equation ultimately reduce to the same thing: to say that something is wrong, or "without justification," is to say that it is incompatible with the logic of morals (or the very notion of a "justification"). This statement of the problem may have the advantage of reminding us that we arrive at an understanding of what is categorically wrong by drawing out the implications that are locked away in the idea of morals itself. I have tried to show, in a few instances, how we may go about that task of extracting moral propositions from the logic of morals. I have reviewed the classic case for republican government and the arguments that can be drawn against slavery, genocide, and racial discrimination. I meant this demonstration, of course, to be suggestive rather than exhaustive. I tried to suggest the nature of the reflection that is needed in order to find the ground of our judgments, but I did not mean to imply that we could provide a complete inventory of the first principles of morals and justice. Experience may not be the source of our knowledge of principles, but it does provide the occasions which inspire reflection, and we can expect that thoughtful people, as they work within a tradition of moral reflection, may discover more of the implications which arise from the logic of this enterprise of giving and understanding reasons.

Often, they will come to recognize, as "first principles" or necessary truths, understandings that they have simply taken for granted. I will suggest in a while what some of those understandings may be, and I will take the occasion to summarize some of the first principles that have already been brought out in the course of these chapters. In all

---

[27] "X" may not, however, include things like "genocide," "lying," and "theft," because the choice of those words already indicates that the acts in question have been judged to be "without justification." To say that genocide or theft may be "justified" would be to say that "unjustified acts of killing (or taking property) may be justified." Beyond that, if we were to say that "genocide may be justified under certain conditions," we would be implying that genocide is only contingently, not categorically, wrong. And so, it must be understood that we exempt from this formula ("It is wrong to do X without justification") terms which are used in our language to mark off things which are categorically wrong.

strictness, it is not possible to establish a hierarchy of first principles, since they are all derived from the same core (i.e., from the logic of morals). Some of the inferences that arise as first principles, however, may have the effect of settling a wide range of understandings or sweeping away a large portion of the fallacies that distract our moral judgments. And one of the most useful recognitions in this respect is the one that it was the purpose of this chapter to establish: viz., that any categorical proposition in morals will have to be drawn, as an inference, from the idea of morals itself (or the very concept of a "justification"). A proposition which cannot be traced back to that core cannot have any pretension of expressing a valid moral statement. That elementary recognition would be enough to rule out most of the bogus systems of ethics which have been propounded over the centuries as writers have sought to remedy what they thought was vague or uncertain in morals by making ethics more "objective." They have sought, in various ways, to advance this mission by translating moral terms into nonmoral measures. And so, instead of clarifying the implications of "goodness" or "justice," they have sought to define goodness or justice as the things that make men "happy" or "harmonious"; as the measures that produce the "greatest satisfactions or pleasure for most people"; or as the policies that bring about, as nearly as possible, an equality of income or reward.

What has been neglected over the years is the possibility that the logic of morals bears within itself a hard logic which cannot be compatible with all meanings or interpretations, and only this irreducible "logic of morals" can provide the foundation for a body of knowledge which is distinctively "moral." Surrogate moral theories persistently fail to connect their judgments, in a necessary way, to the idea of morals, and when they fail to make that connection, they merely end up reducing the moral to the nonmoral. They offer us judgments, enveloped with the passion of moral claims, but utterly lacking in moral content. Hence the enduring embarrassment for these nonmoral formulas of morals: that they are quite compatible with policies which are substantively unjust and thoroughly evil. The "harmony" and "cohesion" of a society may be fostered by lynching members of a racial minority; "the greatest pleasure of the greatest number" may be achieved through policies of genocide. If there are any grounds on which these policies may be challenged, they must be distinctively moral grounds, and they will have to lead back to the logic of morals itself.

Oddly enough, the people who have been most disposed in modern times to fall into these common fallacies are the very people who have

114

been most inclined to affirm the old distinction between "facts" and "values." They have been most inclined, that is, to warn that we are not warranted in extracting "ought" statements (propositions about the way things *ought* to be) from "factual" statements (propositions about the way things actually are). But in the search for what they have fancied to be a more "objective" ethics, they have been willing to invest with moral significance measures and standards that have no moral content whatsoever. On the basis of what has been established here so far, I think we are in a position to make a more precise statement about the error contained in the old distinction between "facts" and "values." But what remains plausible in that ancient doctrine is the awareness of the point that certain kinds of factual propositions simply cannot entail moral conclusions. And when we settle that understanding, we can render ourselves immune to most of the brands of silliness that have been pressed by earnest people under the name of "ethical theory."

VI

ON "VULGAR SYSTEMS OF MORALITY": THE MYTH OF "FACTS" AND "VALUES"

Somewhere in this land there is a man at a cocktail party, leaning against a wall with drink in hand, confident that no moral argument may be posed against him or his enthusiasms, so long as he invokes the venerable, "unchallengeable" truth that there is a difference between "facts" and "values" and that one moral judgment cannot be shown to be truer than another. It could not have been David Hume's mission long ago to provide a license for the thoughtless to evade the discipline of moral discourse; but by the time his thought was diffused to the multitude, he managed to furnish the reigning clichés on matters moral for many people who would not have known his name. Rightly understood, Hume's thought would have helped to avoid much mischief in the world. But one wonders just how many infirm arguments have drawn their ultimate points of conviction from those notable passages in the *Treatise of Human Nature* in which Hume insisted that "morality is not an object of reason":

> Take any action allowed to be vicious; willful murder, for instance. Examine it in all lights, and see if you can find that matter of fact, or real existence, which you call *vice*. In whichever way you take it, you find only certain passions, motives, volitions, and thoughts. There is no other matter of fact in the case. . . .
> . . . In every system of morality which I have hitherto met with, I have always remarked, that the author proceeds for some time in the ordinary way of reasoning, and establishes the being of a God, or makes observations concerning human affairs; when of a sudden I am surprised to find, that instead of the usual copulations of propositions, *is*, and *is not*, I meet with no proposition that is not connected with an *ought*, or an *ought not*. This change is imperceptible; but is, however, of the last consequence. For as this *ought*, or *ought not*, expresses some new relation or affirmation, it is necessary that it should be observed and explained; and at the same time that a reason should be given, for what seems altogether inconceivable, how this new relation can be a deduction from others, which are entirely different from it. But as authors do not commonly use this precaution, I shall presume to recommend it to the readers; and am persuaded, that this small attention would subvert all the vulgar systems of morality, and

let us see, that the distinction of vice and virtue is not founded merely on the relations of objects, nor is perceived by reason.[1]

In warning against the facile leap from the "is" to the "ought," Hume should have said enough to ward off the kind of gullibility that could make us suggestible to "vulgar systems of morality" on the order, say, of Social Darwinism. Even if the "survival of the fittest" or the "law of the jungle" describes the evolution of living things, it is invalid to convert that statement of "fact" into a moral imperative: viz., that human affairs *ought* to be governed by the survival of the fittest, in accordance with the "laws" disclosed in nature. But in his insistence that moral judgments are divorced from reasons and facts, that they turn on "feeling" or "sentiment,"[2] Hume anticipated the later teaching of the "logical positivists" that statements about "values" are essentially emotive: they express the feelings or emotions of the speakers, but they cannot be reckoned as true or false. That someone has a strong passion for cauliflower may be a fact. But that he *ought* to have that passion, that he is warranted in his tastes, is not open to *judgment*.

Over the last thirty years the teaching of the positivists has been called into serious question, and along with that critical challenge has come a certain questioning of the old distinction between "facts" and "values."[3] That distinction has been challenged from a number of different angles, but the criticism which accords most closely with the argument established in these chapters has been offered by John Searle in his book *Speech Acts*. Searle put forth a series of propositions, all factual in nature, but culminating, unmistakably, with an *ought* proposition:

(1) Jones uttered the words "I hereby promise to pay you, Smith, five dollars."
(2) Jones promised to pay Smith five dollars.
(3) Jones placed himself under (undertook) an obligation to pay Smith five dollars.
(4) Jones is under an obligation to pay Smith five dollars.
(5) Jones ought to pay Smith five dollars.

[1] David Hume, *Treatise of Human Nature*, vol. II in *The Philosophical Works of David Hume* (Boston: Little, Brown, 1854), sec. I, pt. I, pp. 230-32. Emphasis in original.

[2] *Ibid.*, p. 231.

[3] I have discussed the issue between the positivists and their critics in my book *The Philosopher in the City: The Moral Dimensions of Urban Politics* (Princeton: Princeton University Press, 1981), pp. 69-74. See, also, Leo Strauss, *Natural Right and History* (Chicago: University of Chicago Press, 1953), ch. II.

The last proposition, that Jones "ought" to pay Smith five dollars, follows from this series of propositions as soon as we establish the meaning of the phrase that Jones "promised"—or "undertook an obligation"—to pay Smith. As Searle remarks, "The whole proof rests on an appeal to the constitutive rule that to make a promise is to undertake an obligation, and this rule is a meaning rule of the 'descriptive' word 'promise.' "[4] If Jones concedes that he did in fact make a promise, that making a promise means undertaking an *obligation*, then it follows that he does have an obligation—he ought to pay Smith. Searle conceives of a situation in which it is the seventh inning and he has a big lead off second base.

> The pitcher whirls, fires to the shortstop covering, and I am tagged out a good ten feet down the line. The umpire shouts, "Out!" I, however, being a positivist, hold my ground. The umpire tells me to return to the dugout. I point out to him that you can't derive an "ought" from an "is." No set of descriptive statements describing matters of fact, I say, will entail any evaluative statements to the effect that I should or ought to leave the field. "You just can't get evaluation from facts alone. What is needed is an evaluative major premise." I therefore return to and stay on second base (until no doubt I am shortly carried off the field).[5]

He would be carried, rightfully, off the field because he failed to honor what Searle called an "institutional" fact: that in agreeing to enter the game, he implicitly accepted all the rules that define the game, much in the way that Jones, when he made a "promise" to repay Smith, accepted the meanings built into the word "promise." But what if someone should take the position of a skeptic and ask why we are *obliged* to honor these "institutional" facts? Why *ought* we accept an obligation to obey merely because other people think that the sense of an obligation is built into the meaning of a "promise"? Searle imagines a skeptic saying of Smith, "He made what they, the people of this Anglo-Saxon tribe, call a promise." But how do we know that a "promise" deserves to be treated with the same logic by all other tribes? As Searle comments, the skeptic might as aptly say that when a local man declares "X is a triangle," he might mean no more than that "X is what they, the Anglo-Saxons, call a triangle." But nothing in that mere assertion would establish that there are two

[4] John R. Searle, *Speech Acts* (Cambridge: Cambridge University Press, 1969), pp. 177 and 185.

[5] *Ibid.*, p. 185.

senses of a "triangle."[6] In the same way, one may try to assert that the meaning of "promise" or "obligation" alters with each tribe or culture. But nothing in that mere assertion can efface the essential logic of an "obligation," or establish that there is more than one sense of what we mean by a "promise."

The heart of the problem, then, is whether there are terms, such as "obligation" and "promise," which draw their meaning from the logic of morals, and which would therefore remain the same in all places. An "obligation" is the source of a duty because the notion of a moral *commitment*—or the sense of an *ought*—is built into the meaning of the word. If Jones knew that he was making a "promise," as that term is understood, then the promise was indeed the source of an obligation, and it could be said that Jones *ought* to pay. The only ground on which the skeptic could offer a challenge would be the ground of insistence that the idea of morals is no more than a fiction, and that words which carry moral commitments (e.g., "promise") cannot be binding on Jones if he himself does not recognize the existence of morals. Yet, as we have seen already, that path of resistance would have to be foreclosed once it is established that the skeptic cannot tenably deny the existence of morals. But if we come to recognize again that the existence of morals must stand as a necessary truth, then it would become more evident, at the same time, that the problem of "facts" and "values" must dissolve. For the decisive point then is that the existence of morals is itself a momentous, ineffaceable *fact*. Some people may wish to restrict the definition of "facts" to cover only empirical truths, which are accessible through the senses. In that case, of course, moral principles would not be facts, because there is nothing merely "empirical" about them. But they are not, on that account, in the realm of fantasy; they are simply part of the things that can be known to us through our reason, without the aid of touch, sight, or smell.

And so, whether we refer to morals as empirical "facts" or not, the critical point is that the existence of morals stands as a *truth*. For that reason, the propositions which flow, as inferences, from the logic of morals may not be consigned to the domain of opinion or feeling, as though there were some doubt about their cognitive standing as *true* propositions. I sought to show, for example, in the preceding chapter that the case against racial discrimination arose, in this way, from the logic of morals itself. If that argument was validly drawn, the prop-

[6] *Ibid.*, p. 196.

osition that declares the wrongness of racial discrimination would have the standing of a truth, no less certain than any "empirical fact."

Whether we speak, then, of "facts" or "truths," it becomes important to acknowledge that there are true propositions built into the logic of morals itself, and with that understanding secured, we may return to Hume and state more precisely what his original argument may or may not establish for us. It would have to be said first that Hume was in part correct: certain facts cannot entail moral conclusions. In this respect, Rousseau was thoroughly right when he argued that the mere *fact* of physical power cannot provide a warrant for its exercise. But it must be said, also, that the reason this fact cannot entail moral conclusions is not *because* it is a fact. The more precise point is that the existence of brute force cannot entail a moral conclusion because it represents no truth of moral significance. We have already seen that, from the "fact" or the truth constituted by the existence of morals, we may draw the standards of judgment which can settle cases or entail conclusions on matters of moral consequence. But no other source could furnish the ground for a distinctly "moral" judgment. If we set about, then, to draw up an inventory of first principles in morals, this recognition should claim standing in the list: "All moral propositions must be drawn as implications that arise from the idea of morals itself, or from the notion of a 'rational being.' And no proposition which is drawn from any other kind of 'fact' can claim the force of a moral proposition. No facts without moral significance can entail 'ought' statements or moral conclusions."

Once that understanding can be settled, it will establish a barrier against a surprisingly large portion of the fallacies that have been put forth over the years as surrogates for moral understanding. We would not have to linger very long then in weighing arguments to the effect that "harmony" is the highest good, or that men should be governed foremost by their feelings and emotions rather than by their reason. As I suggested earlier, harmony may be founded on a variety of principles, and it may embrace the evil as well as the good: a society may find its harmony and cohesion, after all, in terrorizing the members of a minority. And if there were no standard of goodness beyond harmony itself, we could not judge the difference between the harmony of a criminal band and the harmony attained by a court of wise men. As for the people who are inclined to cast their lot with the party of "feeling" and "emotion," it turns out, on reflection, that they are not uniformly willing to respect all positions that are advanced with passion. They may not, for example, respect the passions and emotions of the people who turn over school buses in order to protest court orders on busing, and certainly they would not respect the feelings that animate a lynch mob. The simple fact of the matter, which seems oddly elusive, is that people are not generally willing to offer their respect in the face of "passion," "intensity," or "sincerity," as though those qualities alone can render an empty argument plausible. That a mob may be sincere or intense establishes nothing about the *justification* for what it is doing. The decisive question, rather, at all times, is whether the passions and intensities of people are being aroused by a proper understanding of what is just, and whether their feelings are being guided by a sense of decent ends.[7]

THE FALLACY of reducing moral standards to nonmoral formulas has exerted a powerful temptation. It has lured even a figure such as John Stuart Mill, whose mind was tuned to recognize, at a distance, most of the fallacies that ran across his age. But it may be said for Mill that his affair with "utilitarianism" was in large part inherited from his father, in the manner of a bizarre, cumbersome heirloom, whose enduring value was dubious, but which could not decorously be cast aside. What remained was to put a rather different face on things—in the case of "utilitarianism," to redefine it to the point that it was no longer really utilitarianism in anything more than its veneer. Filial duty could not be preserved in this instance by an intellect of the first rank, for Mill could hardly be persuaded by any theory that would proffer "happiness"—even the happiness of the "greatest number"—as the measure of moral goodness.

Without an excess of decoration, Mill offered to explain "What Utilitarianism Is," and he provided, in a compressed space, as much as one would probably wish to say about the meaning of "utilitarianism":

> The creed which accepts as the foundation of morals "utility" or the "greatest happiness principle" holds that actions are right in proportion as they tend to promote happiness; wrong as they tend to produce the reverse of happiness. By happiness is intended pleasure and the absence of pain; by unhappiness, pain and the privation of pleasure. . . . [Mill went on to say that] the theory

[7] It was the problem of penetrating this elementary point which accounted for the enduring inability of the late Edward Westermarck to understand Kant's argument and to comprehend why Kant should resist a point that was so plain to Westermarck: viz., that the source of our moral judgment is to be found in personal emotions and nothing more. See Westermarck, *Ethical Relativity* (Paterson, New Jersey: Littlefield, Adams, 1960 [1932], chs. III, VIII-IX.

of life on which this theory of morality is grounded [is that] pleasure and freedom from pain are the only things desirable as ends; and that all desirable things . . . are desirable either for pleasure inherent in themselves or as means to the promotion of pleasure and the prevention of pain.[8]

In the tradition of moral philosophy a distinction was made between the pleasant and the good, and that distinction marked the awareness that the things which give us pleasure are not necessarily "good." Unless "utilitarianism" sought to repeal that distinction, it would have no meaning; if it did seek to deny that understanding, it would be rendered indefensible. Mill was, of course, an uncommon man, and he never supposed for a moment that the things which made yahoos happy also defined, at the same time, the things that were *good* for them. Men in the bulk could find their pleasure in torturing animals; they could find their main source of entertainment in watching gladiators disembowel their professional colleagues in a public arena. The classic understanding of morals did not take its measure of "good" from the things that made people, subjectively, happy; it enjoined people, rather, to find their happiness only in doing things that are innocent or just. It encompassed the recognition, then, that men can hold themselves firmly to a course of moral duty without securing their own profit or enlarging the sum of human pleasure.

Mill understood that point as well as any other worldly man, and so the preservation of his "utilitarian" faith required a larger exertion of intellect than the credulous would think necessary or possible. Mill acknowledged that the man who acts nobly may in fact suffer for his nobility (he could become a martyr, for example, to irascible authority). And yet, Mill had no doubt that it was "good" to act nobly even at the cost of pain, even at the cost of suffering and death.[9] But in that event, the moral goodness of the act would be quite detached from matters of pleasure and pain, and the teaching of utilitarianism would be overturned. Mill's judgment could be reconciled with utilitarianism only on the assumption that a precedent for noble acts could encourage emulation: if many people follow the example of acting nobly, the number of noble acts might be multiplied, and so the consequences which flow in the long run from that noble sacrifice may serve the interests and happiness of the mass of mankind. The noble act may help secure, after all, the happiness of the "greatest number."

[8] John Stuart Mill, *Utilitarianism* (Indianapolis: Bobbs-Merrill, 1957 [1861], p. 10.
[9] *Ibid.*, p. 16.

It was precisely in this way, of course, that the distinction arose between "act utilitarianism" and "rule utilitarianism." When it was recognized that any particular act might produce suffering, even while it was directed toward benevolent, unselfish ends, the utilitarian doctrine was modified, for some writers, to a form closer to this proposition: "An act is right if, and only if, it conforms to a set of rules general acceptance of which would maximize utility."[10] As it turns out, that would not be enough to save even modified utilitarianism from complications which would expose its tendency, as David Lyons put it, to become "incoherent in a special way."[11] But whatever modifications are made, the differences between the two forms of utilitarianism would prove negligible when compared to the one critical point they still share: as Lyons remarked, "the rightness or wrongness of acts [would still turn] in some way, directly or indirectly, upon their being conducive to the product of the best effects."[12] The lens could be widened or narrowed in viewing the field of relevant consequences, but the test of consequences would remain decisive. That cardinal point would finally prove crippling to the argument for utilitarianism, and it must be said, in this respect, that no recent version of utilitarianism has added any novel ingredient which could possibly rescue the argument from the flaws that were made evident already—and with an admirable clarity—in the writing of Mill.

It was Mill's task to explain why the noble act could be regarded as "good" even though it brought suffering or death to the one who

[10] This formulation was offered in David Lyons, *Forms and Limits of Utilitarianism* (Oxford: Clarendon Press, 1965), p. 136 and ch. IV more generally. Lyons pointed out that, for this proposition to be true, it was not enough that the rules be *generally accepted*. It was necessary also that they be *practiced*. In that event, the proposition had to be modified to this form: "An act is right if, and only if, it conforms to a set of rules general *conformity* to which would maximize utility" (p. 137; emphasis in original). The proposition ceases to offer a guide to moral practice if the actor cannot assume that others, more generally, are acting upon the same rules. But in that case we reach this paradox: the rule may not be valid in a population that has not yet come to believe in the rules of utilitarianism.

[11] *Ibid.*, p. 142. On the distinction between "act-" and "rule utilitarianism"—and the problem of discovering a tenable standard—see J.J.C. Smart, "Extreme and Restricted Utilitarianism," *Philosophical Quarterly* (October 1956), pp. 344-54; his essay, "Utilitarianism," in *The Encyclopedia of Philosophy* (New York: Macmillan, 1967), vol. 8, pp. 206-211; and Richard Brandt, "In Search of a Credible Form of Rule Utilitarianism," in G. Nakhnikian and H. Castaneda (eds.), *Morality and the Language of Conduct* (Detroit: Wayne State University Press, 1963), pp. 197-240.

[12] Lyons, *supra*, note 10, p. 136. A recent, penetrating criticism of utilitarianism and "consequentialism" can be found in John Finnis, *Fundamentals of Ethics* (Washington D.C.: Georgetown University Press, 1983), ch. IV.

acted nobly. But as Mill pursued the question, he was compelled to cast his argument in the form of a contingent proposition rather than as a statement of principle. By his own premises, he could not profess to know that there were grounds of principle on which noble acts could be said to be good in themselves. For if they were good in themselves, their goodness would not depend at all on their consequences, and as a utilitarian, he could profess to know what was "good" only on the basis of consequences. But it is one of the defects of "consequences," as a standard of moral judgment, that they are never "all in." As a colleague of mine has put it, we are still experiencing the extended consequences of Caesar crossing the Rubicon. Operationally speaking, we cannot know the precise date at which the consequences will be reckoned, the balance sheet will be closed, and no further consequences will be considered.

The reliance on consequences as the foundation of moral judgment also converted Mill's own proposition here from a moral statement into an empirical prediction. Instead of saying that "it is good in principle to act nobly," he was merely offering a descriptive statement in the form of a prediction: "If Jones does X, Y, and Z, which constitute the features of a 'noble' act, there will be more people in the future who will perform X, Y, and Z, and the world will be a happier place." However, we still do not know why X, Y, and Z should define something "good." Nor do we know why there must be a necessary connection between the doing of X, Y, and Z and an enlargement of the feeling of happiness in the world. If Mill had spoken in the voice of principle, he would have told us why it was good as a matter of necessity to act nobly. But as a contingent proposition or an empirical prediction, his advice to us was inescapably *problematic*: at best he could say only that it *might* be good to act nobly. It would be good *only on the contingency* that the precedent of acting nobly is witnessed and emulated, and that it begets a larger volume of similar acts in the future. As the statement of a contingency, that is notably less than a ringing moral judgment. And as a contingent statement it would be hostage to all the accidents of experience that contingencies produce. The man who acts nobly may be martyred in silence, without the knowledge of the world, so that no precedent is created, no example is established, no emulation takes place. In short, no good consequences emerge; and so, by the calculations of the utilitarian, it could not be said that the noble act had been "good."

It should be evident, therefore, that it could not have been on the basis of "experience" that Mill could profess to know that noble acts were "good." Even if Mill had experienced all the consequences that could have issued from "noble" acts, he would have been faced yet with the task of explaining why *those consequences* were "good." But without principles of moral judgment—without some antecedent understanding of what defines "good" and "bad"—he would have had no basis on which to judge the difference between good and bad consequences. Mill might indeed have possessed a faith that good acts would produce, in the long run, good consequences; but that faith became comprehensible only because there were grounds on which he could presume, with a sense of surety, that he could tell the difference between results that were right or wrong, better or worse. And it had to become clear, with further reflection, that his conviction on these matters was not derived from a tallying of consequences.

That conviction was revealed in Mill's remarks on the ranking or hierarchy of pleasures. Since Mill could not reduce the test of moral goodness to the things which induce giddiness among the common folk, he was naturally led to insist that there is a hierarchy in the varieties of happiness. Some forms of happiness had to be counted as higher or more desirable than others, and if that were the case, there would be no need to lower the standards of the moral world to coincide with the pleasures of the vulgar. The search for those standards could begin, in the spirit of the ancients, with the things that separate the human from the subhuman. "It is better," said Mill, "to be a human being dissatisfied than a pig satisfied; better to be Socrates dissatisfied than a fool satisfied. And if the fool, or the pig, are of a different opinion, it is because they only know their own side of the question. The other party to the comparison knows both sides."[13]

It is certainly within the range of possibility that human beings are capable of "knowing" the pleasures of wallowing in the mud; and if that is not the way most of us spend our weekends, it is not because of an epistemological barrier which prevents us, as a species, from glimpsing that alternative. As Mill remarked, "Human beings have faculties more elevated than the animal appetites," and the pleasures of a beast "do not satisfy a human being's conception of happiness." Even the Epicureans, who were committed to the cultivation of pleasure, did not think that all pleasures stood on the same plane: "There is no known Epicurean theory of life," wrote Mill, "which does not assign to the pleasures of the intellect, of the feelings and imagination, and of the moral sentiments a much higher value as pleasures than to those of mere sensation."[14]

[13] Mill, *supra*, note 8, p. 14.
[14] *Ibid.*, p. 11.

125

If a choice has to be made between the pleasures of appetite and the pleasures of acting nobly, it cannot be pleasure alone that establishes the difference and governs the judgment. Mill could assign human pleasures a higher standing than the pleasures of animals because he could say with confidence that the pleasures of intellect are higher than the pleasures of appetite unaffected by intellect. And it was precisely on the same ground of conviction that he could regard some human pleasures as higher than others: the pleasures of moral understanding are higher than the pleasures of bodily comfort; the pleasures of forgoing one's own interests, out of a respect for duty, are higher than the pleasures of pursuing one's own, most contracted self-interest; the pleasures of respecting a rightful law beyond oneself are higher—and here I risk the credulity of close friends—than the pleasures of a royal flush.

It is evident, of course, that Mill's understanding follows exactly along the line of the classics: what makes humans higher than animals is the capacity for reason, but even more decisively, the capacity to reason over moral things. The refinement in the answer does become critical, I think, when it comes to answering the question "What makes the pleasures of the intellect *higher?*" They are different, we know, from the pleasures of sensation (the pleasures, say, of the royal flush or of cheesecake from Zabar's); but on what ground can it be said that they are higher? To say that something is "higher"—that it is superior to other things—is to invoke a moral judgment, and as we have seen, a moral conclusion cannot flow from facts having no moral import. An attempt might be made to argue that the pleasures of intellect are higher than the pleasures of sensation because the pleasures of "knowing" are higher than the pleasures of ignorance, but it could be pointed out in return that it is not always better simply to "know." The knowledge of vice may be worse, quite often, than the ignorance of vice. Nor would it always be good to have unsolicited, embarrassing knowledge of the private lives of other people, including things we have no need or right to know.

The pleasures of knowing or the pleasures of intellect can be assigned a higher standing only when they are connected to the idea of morals itself. What can be said, more accurately, is that the knowledge of right and wrong is higher than moral ignorance; the knowledge of what justice commands is higher than an indifference to questions of justice. And if we were asked, "What first principle makes these conclusions necessary?," the answer would be that these judgments are entailed by the logic of morals itself. In the logic of morals, what is good or just is that which ought to be favored universally over things that are bad or unjust, or over things that are morally indifferent.

What is good must be higher than—and superior to—what is bad. What is just must be higher than what is unjust. In the most literal sense, there can be nothing "better" than goodness or a moral life. But in that case it must follow that the understanding of what is "good" or "just" would have to be regarded as higher than the ignorance of right and wrong. And it would follow, with equal force, that the pleasures of moral understanding must be regarded as higher than the pleasures of ignorance or the kinds of pleasures that are not affected in any way by moral understanding.

Mill's "refinement" in utilitarianism really depends, then, on the classic understandings that formed the core of his education. But when his own understanding is traced back to its root, it becomes clear that his teaching rests on a foundation that is decidedly not utilitarian. He did not draw his judgments of right and wrong through an endless canvassing of "results" or consequences. Nor did he take the measure of goodness from the things that make people "happy," without regard to the goodness of the things that inspire pleasure. His estimate of good and bad consequences was drawn from principles of judgment which do not depend on the measuring of "benefits." Indeed, the things he honored as "good" may be good even though they bring suffering rather than pleasure. His principles of moral judgment were ultimately drawn from (1) the logic—or the idea—of morals itself and from (2) the nature of that creature who alone has access to the pleasures of moral understanding. In short, Mill had to make his way, in the end, to the ground marked out by Kant: he finally drew his principles of moral judgment precisely from the two points Kant set forth as the ultimate foundation of our moral judgments.

WHEN WE TRAVERSE these steps and establish the understanding from which Mill's argument was drawn, we would virtually reconstruct an older, more celebrated argument, which may hold even more interest in the politics of our own day: namely Plato's argument on the equality of women. In Book V of *The Republic*, when Plato was reaching the end of the discussion of the equality of the sexes, he had Socrates say that it is the equality of women which is in accord with "nature" and justice. At the same time, he insisted that the current conventions of society—the conventions that prescribed the inequality of women—were "unnatural" and wrong.[15] In this classic passage, Plato seems to have provided a dramatic example of the rejection of cultural relativism. The equality of women—or, more precisely, the equal claim of women to exercise political authority—was clearly not supported by

---

[15] Plato, *The Republic*, bk. V, 456c.

the dominant opinion in Plato's own land or in the civilized world as he knew it. Serious questions have been raised as to whether Plato himself fully accepted the argument he put forth in the portrayal of Socrates.[16] But the argument *is* brought forward in *The Republic*; it emerges comprehensibly from the premises of the dialogue; and whatever question we may have about Plato's real intention, the argument deserves to be considered on its own terms. For even one who doubted—as Plato very likely did—that the natural differences between men and women could be reduced to a plane of sameness could still find himself drawing on the argument he set forth in explaining why certain women, no less than certain men, would be competent to the tasks of governing.

When Plato said that the current conventions of his society—the conventions that prescribed the inequality of women—were "unnatural," and therefore unjust, he implied that he could appeal to "nature" as an independent source of understanding of the things that are just and unjust. The nature to which he appealed was the same nature that Aristotle would later take as the beginning of his political teaching: viz., the nature which separates human beings from animals and which endows human beings with the capacity to reason over moral things. Once again, the differences that made human beings higher than animals corresponded with the faculties that are higher and lower in humans. The capacity for wisdom was higher than that capacity for brute physical force that humans share with animals; the capacity for lawfulness deserved to be sovereign over the inclinations or mere appetites. As Plato understood, the proper ordering of the soul depended on the proper ordering of the human parts: a person whose judgment was ruled by his passions or his appetites was disordered within himself. The health of the individual soul was marked by that state of affairs in which passions and physical strength are governed by the faculty of reason and understanding. Under those conditions, people

---

[16] Alan Bloom has argued that, in this section of *The Republic*, Plato was seeking to counter the derision cast by Aristophanes on the claims of philosophy to understand the world of human things. The denigration of philosophy was portrayed rather notably in *The Clouds*, where philosophy was derided in the person of Socrates. In Bloom's reading, Plato sought to counter Aristophanes by showing the superiority of the philosopher in producing a comedy, but a comedy which also contained a more profound commentary than anything produced by a comic poet. Plato has Socrates undertake, in a serious vein, an argument that would have been regarded instantly as absurd in the Athens of his time: viz., that the barriers to the equality of men and women are to be found in convention more than in nature. See Alan Bloom's "Interpretive Essay," at the end of his translation of *The Republic* (New York: Basic Books, 1968), pp. 381-82 *et passim*. See also, *The Republic*, bk. V, 455d-e.

would be more truly in command of themselves; they would possess the harmony wrought by a "constitutional government within them."[17]

Of course the moral principles that established the proper ordering of individuals would apply to the larger community as well. As in the case of the individual soul, the polity was properly ordered within itself when it was governed by its wise and reflective parts, rather than by the forces of brute strength. Since reason properly claimed sovereignty over strength, people who were gifted with a larger measure of reason and wisdom were more suited to the office of governing than those people who were distinguished chiefly by their physical strength or their martial arts. Most women were physically weaker than most men, but it was not physical strength that counted decisively in the competence to govern. Plato observed at one point that there are undeniable "natural" differences between a bald man and a man with hair; but nothing in those natural differences bears on the competence of the bald man to be a shoemaker. In a similar way, there are undeniable differences in nature between men and women, but nothing in those natural differences provides a ground on which women could be disqualified, properly, from the exercise of authority. As Plato has Socrates say, it was necessary to pay heed "solely to the kind of diversity and homogeneity that was pertinent to the pursuits themselves," and if men and women differ only in the respect that "the female bears and the male begets, we shall say that no proof has yet been produced that the woman differs from the man for [the purposes of governing], but we shall continue to think that our guardians [i.e., officers of government] and their wives ought to follow the same pursuits."[18] Plato was willing to suggest that most women were not as intelligent as most men,[19] but he was apparently willing to allow, at the very least, that *some* women possessed those aptitudes of reason and reflection which made them qualified, by nature, for the discipline of governing.[20] If things were so arranged then in the world that women were not admitted to positions of official authority, that state of affairs could not have arisen *from nature*. That situation, which was everywhere sanctioned by custom, was contrary to nature and therefore wrong.

BUT WHAT IF we should learn that the inequality of women had been sanctioned not only within Athens, but all over Greece and the civilized world? What would have been the standing of this argument, recorded

[17] Plato, *The Republic*, bk. X, 591a.
[18] *Ibid.*, bk. V, 454c-e.
[19] *Ibid.*, 453c-d.
[20] *Ibid.*, 456a-b.

by Plato, for the equality of women, if indeed this argument had been universally ignored or rejected? We would have to say, in all strictness, that the validity of the argument could not have been affected at all by this news on the state of the world. The fact that this question arises so often is a mark of the confusion that persists between propositions that are "universal" in the sense that they are universally *valid*, and propositions that are universal only in the sense that they are universally accepted.

This confusion is probably typical of a time in which the premises of modern anthropology have been widely absorbed. And so, when the anthropologist Ralph Linton sought to discover the moral understandings that were "universal," it went virtually without saying that the only way he could conceive of going about the task was to carry out a survey of all "cultures": the "universal" moral "values" would turn up in those practices (e.g., incest) which might be condemned in all societies.[21] The minor defect, of course, in this conception is that a "value" ceases to be "universal" as soon as we discover one country—or one individual—who rejects it. The major defect lies in the failure to recognize that this method of assessing the problem converts the issue from a moral question into an empirical question. Instead of asking whether certain practices are truly right or wrong, justified or unjustified, we would seek to measure just how widely they have become accepted in the world. The fact that there is no society in which questions of moral justification are not raised is a fact that should stir the most serious reflection. But at the same time, if genocide were suddenly approved strongly in all parts of the world, nothing in that universal acceptance could establish the rightness of genocide. The survey which revealed that universal acceptance of genocide would merely provide evidence of the progress of corruption in the world.

The root of the problem, once again, is that there has been little recognition of the existence of necessary truths in the domain of morals. No anthropologist would think for a moment of doing a study to see whether the Pythagorean theorem enjoys a universal acceptance. But if such a study *were* carried out, and if it located an insular tribe in Brazil that did not "believe" in the Pythagorean theorem, no one would take that evidence as a ground on which to call into question the universal validity of the Pythagorean theorem. As Karl Popper would remind us, knowledge in the objective sense is "totally inde-

[21] See Ralph Linton, "Universal Anthropological Principles: An Anthropological View," in Ruth Anshen (ed.), *Moral Principles of Action* (New York: Harper, 1952).

pendent of anybody's claim to know; it is also independent of anybody's belief, or disposition to assent." In fact, "knowledge in the objective sense is knowledge without a knower."[22] The truths that are known do not depend for their truth on the presence of any particular "knower." If we grasp the universal truth of the Pythagorean theorem, it is because we understand that the validity of the theorem depends ultimately on the truth of those axioms from which it is drawn. In that event, we recognize that the truth of the theorem is quite independent of the question of who articulated it—of whether it was Pythagoras, or anyone else, who "said it." Still less would we be inclined to identify the theorem as a "Greek understanding" of triangles. But if we recognize, in the same way, that our moral understandings are drawn from certain axioms which must hold true of necessity, we should not label them as "Western values," as if they were valid only in the place where they were first articulated. These understandings would not depend on the "authority" of those who first pronounced them—whether it was Aristotle, Aquinas, or Kant. They would depend, rather, on the axioms from which they arise, and if those first principles are true, the moral understandings they support will be quite as indifferent as the Pythagorean theorem to the vagaries of local opinion.

Plato addressed the same kind of question by drawing, as an analogy, on the understanding of a circle. We may all have accessible to us the *idea* of a circle: a closed curve, all points of which are equidistant from a common center. In the real world, however, even a circle that is drawn mechanically may show, at the closest inspection, an ever so slight touch of straightness, the smallest departure from perfect roundness. That says nothing, of course, of the man with the unguided hand and the casual standard, who persistently draws oblongs where circles should be. But even though a perfect circle cannot be achieved in the world of experience, the host of imperfect circles that abound in the world cannot be taken as evidence for the proposition that "the circle" does not exist.[23] The idea of a circle is accessible to the mind; it is understandable on its own terms. If it were not understandable, then the observer would not be able to recognize, in the oblong or in the kidney-shaped figure, a failed attempt to render a circle. In the same way, there may be an understanding of the idea of morals or justice— and of the kind of community that would be constituted on the prin-

[22] Karl Popper, "Epistemology without a Knowing Subject," in his *Objective Knowledge* (Oxford: Clarendon Press, 1972), pp. 106-150, at p. 109.

[23] Plato, *Epistles*, VII, 342b-c, 343a.

ciples of morals and justice. The fact that the world is littered with imperfect and corrupt political orders—with flawed or even grotesque efforts to render a circle—cannot in itself invalidate the idea of morals or the understanding of a just political order. What it indicates instead, as Plato recognized, is that in place of a true understanding of the principles that define a good political order, we find in the world a multitude of imperfect "opinions" about the nature of a good regime.

There was no indulgence, then, on Plato's part of the fallacy that forms the central premise in cultural relativism: namely, that the presence of disagreement confirms the absence of truth. That is, the variety of opinion which exists on the nature of virtue and vice is usually taken in itself as proof of the proposition that there are no understandings of morals that are universally true. On this undefended premise, as far as I can see, rests much of modern social science. It remains undefended in part because it is never brought to the level of an explicit proposition, and in part because it is at root indefensible. If it were stated in the form of a proposition, it would probably look something like this: "The presence of disagreement on matters of moral judgment—the sheer variety of opinion that exists in the world on these questions—is sufficient to indicate the absence of universal moral truths." For reasons I have already set forth, that is a proposition I cannot endorse, and the critical question may be how my own refusal to agree with this proposition would affect its validity. My disagreement establishes that the proposition does not enjoy a universal assent, and by the very terms of the proposition, that should be quite sufficient to determine *its own invalidity*. Are we likely to find, though, that the people who have adhered to this proposition—who have absorbed it as a tenet of their lives—are apt to be shaken in their confidence by this news? They may be more disposed to think that the refusal to accept the proposition is the result of a "mistake" in reasoning, if not a certain dimness of mind. In any event, they have come to harbor a conviction whose truth is unaffected by the presence or extent of disagreement. Willy-nilly, they may have backed themselves into the discovery of a proposition that is true "in the nature of things," a proposition that would apparently hold true of necessity—a proposition, then, that would be universal in its validity.

The same predicament would arise for the votaries of "cultural relativism" if their argument were stated in this way: "There are no truths of moral significance that hold across cultures." They would be faced, in turn, with the awkward question of whether this proposition itself does not purport to state a truth of moral consequence that holds across cultures. If it does, then the doctrine of cultural relativism refutes itself. If it does not, then the "truth" affirmed in cultural relativism might be nothing more than a "local persuasion." It might itself be the product of only our own culture, and so we could not suppose it to be true of any culture outside our own. For all we would know, all cultures outside our own—all cultures that may not be affected by our fashionable brand of "cultural relativism"—find no strain in recognizing moral truths that hold across cultures.

This is but a taste of the perplexities and the innocent pleasures that await us all if the practitioners of this modern school of anthropology—and the spokesmen for cultural relativism—would try to bring to an explicit statement the premises on which they earn their livings and offer teachings to the world. It is mainly because the effort has rarely been made that the merriment has not yet broken out. But in the interests of science and the memory of vaudeville, we shall consider in the next chapter, in all its philosophic terrors, the case put forth for cultural relativism.

VII

THE FALLACIES OF CULTURAL
RELATIVISM; OR, ABBOTT AND COSTELLO
MEET THE ANTHROPOLOGIST

The question posed by cultural relativism is whether there are moral truths that hold true universally, or whether those truths are only "relative" to the culture in which they are held. This question received its most powerful expression in our politics in the debate between Abraham Lincoln and Stephen Douglas, where it was cast as a dispute between "natural" and "positive" rights—between the rights that exist for all men everywhere, by virtue of being human, as against the rights that are merely "posited" or established in different societies by the will of the local majority. Before this issue was raised during the crisis of our "house divided," it received an elegant statement earlier in the century, at the hands of two of our most accomplished jurists, in cases involving slavery and international law. In both cases, the judges had to pronounce upon the standing of the African slave trade in international law. Since the jurists could not be governed by the laws of any particular country, they were drawn back to the sources of law. In the celebrated case of *La Jeune Eugénie*, in 1822, Joseph Story argued, in the tradition of natural justice, that the law may not incorporate what is by nature wrong (or, as Lincoln would later put it, that there cannot be "a right to do a wrong"). Story appealed to "the first principles which ought to govern nations":

> [The trade in slaves] is repugnant to the great principles of Christian duty, the dictates of natural religion, the obligations of good faith and morality, and the eternal maxims of social justice. When any trade can be truly said to have these ingredients, *it is impossible that it can be consistent with any system of law*, that purports to rest on the authority of reason or revelation. And it is sufficient to stamp any trade as interdicted by public law, when it can be justly affirmed, that it is repugnant to the general principles of justice and humanity.[1]

Two years later, in the case of *The Antelope*,[2] Chief Justice Marshall wrote with uncharacteristic strain as he sought to defend a notably

[1] 2 Mason 409. Emphasis added.
[2] 10 Wheaton 66 (1825).

134

different doctrine. On the question of natural law, or the commands of natural justice, he could not disagree with Story. "That [slavery] is contrary to the law of nature," Marshall wrote, "will scarcely be denied. That every man has a natural right to the fruits of his own labor, is generally admitted." The enlightened nations had incorporated that understanding into their national policies and they had sought, in varying ways, to suppress the trade in human beings. The question, though, was whether the commands of natural law, embodied in the laws of some nations, became binding on other nations through international law. But unlike Story, Marshall did not locate the binding quality of law in those principles of right and wrong which, by their very logic, command obedience. He found the sources of law, rather, in the logic of an *interstate system*. For Marshall, it might have been said, international law was international before it was law: instead of beginning with maxims that were universal in their validity, the law of nations began with the awareness of sovereign nations arranging their relations according to conventions, or "laws," that were compatible with their sovereignty. By this understanding, a "law" was universal in its reach only if it were universally accepted, and as Marshall remarked, "no principle of general law is more universally acknowledged, than the perfect equality of nations":[3]

> It results from this equality, that no one can rightfully impose a rule on another. Each legislates for itself, but its legislation can operate on itself alone. A right, then, which is vested in all by the consent of all, can be devested only by consent; and this trade, in which all have participated, must remain lawful to those who cannot be induced to relinquish it. As no nation can prescribe a rule for others, none can make a law of nations; and this traffic remains lawful to those whose governments have not forbidden it.

But what if this root principle of the sovereignty or the "perfect equality of nations" should cease to be accepted universally? What if it came to be rejected, in fact, by a majority of nations? Would the majority have been free then to impose laws on the minority—to restrain, say, the trade in slaves, or to abolish slavery altogether? It is clear that, in Marshall's understanding of international law, the majority of nations could not claim such an authority to override the

---

[3] *Ibid.*, at 122. For a classic discussion of the differences between Story and Marshall in these cases on the slave trade, see Benjamin Munn Ziegler, *The International Law of John Marshall* (Chapel Hill: University of North Carolina Press, 1939), ch. XI.

sovereignty of any single nation.[4] That is to say, the ultimate sovereignty of each nation—the principle that Marshall regarded as the father of all principles in international law—did not depend for its validity on its universal acceptance. That proposition was apparently to be accepted as a proposition true in itself, true in the nature of things, and it would continue to be true—it would continue to define the law of nations—even if it were rejected by most communities that were constituted as nations. But if the root of international law had to be found in principles of lawfulness that did not depend on universal agreement, would Marshall not have had to concede, finally, the *ground* of Story's argument? The only question remaining was whether the wrongness of slavery is grounded in one of those truths that do not depend on universal acceptance; and if it is, why should it not have been incorporated, as Story thought, in the principles that compose "the law of nations"?[5]

Marshall's version of legal positivism fell into contradiction because it denied, in the field of international law, a proposition that stands as necessary truth: namely, that there are in fact propositions about the things that are universally right and wrong. Legal positivism shares with "cultural relativism" this need to deny the existence or logic of morals. Without that denial, either doctrine loses its rationale. Both doctrines suffer the same flaws and fall into the same contradiction. Yet, both doctrines are widely diffused today, and they continue to affect matters of consequence. And so, as the nations of the world seek to establish a new "law of the seas," a question arises about the terms, say, on which minerals may be mined in international waters. Might this work be pursued through the application of slave labor? If this new regime of international law were to be founded on the principles of natural justice, it could bear no tolerance for slavery. But many nations (including, most notably, the Soviet Union) make use of forced labor. If international law is to be constituted merely by the understandings of right and wrong that are accepted by the members of the United Nations—if it is to be an international law founded on the premises of cultural relativism—then it will be a law that may have to accommodate some new styles of involuntary servitude.

In another case, a liberal voice of protest in South Africa, a thoughtful professor of law, argues that the courts in his country have made an accommodation more easily with the policies of racial apartheid

---

[4] See 10 Wheaton 66, at 120-21; Ziegler, *supra*, note 3, p. 304.

[5] For an extended, sensitive analysis of the case of *The Antelope*, and for the mixture it offered of jurisprudence and politics, see John Noonan, *The Antelope* (Berkeley: University of California Press, 1977).

because, since the very inception of the South African state, the reigning orthodoxy in the schools of law has been legal positivism.[6] Under that doctrine, the courts became pliant tools in the service of the ruling majority that *posited* the laws on apartheid. And yet, when Professor John Dugard sought to break the sovereignty of this false teaching, even he was reluctant to appeal to an understanding that moved beyond the terms of legal positivism. So infirm, apparently, was his surety about the sources of natural law that he finally could recommend nothing more than a "new relativist natural law" (the legal equivalent of a square circle). What he sought was a law that was not indifferent to its moral content—a law that could reflect something more than the habits of the local tribe, whatever those might be—but he feared that the foundations of this new law would be open to irresolvable doubt unless they could be rooted, say, in "the legal values of Western civilization."[7] What he offered, then, was merely the definition of a more extended "tribe." But the source of law would still be found in the opinions that were accepted by a majority within this culture. It was a pretense born of hope that our understanding of justice could attain the foundation of the natural law, that it could claim sources of truth beyond the opinions that were dominant in any place, while at the same time claiming no conviction about its validity outside something called "the West."

This diffidence, this immanent sense of the limits of place that confine moral conviction, can be seen, finally, with even vaster consequence in the agnosticism that seems to affect so many political commentators when they come to judge the ultimate objectives of the United States and the Soviet Union. Both countries seek ever more advanced weapons; they dirty their hands in clandestine, lethal projects, and in collaboration with regimes they can hardly find congenial. They do these things in the service of their national interests, to defend themselves against the potential strength of the other. If one abstracts from the differences of principle that separate these two nations—if one could put out of mind the way of life that each seeks to defend— it may be tempting to conclude that both nations are driven by the interests that animate any great power, and that they are equally at fault for the dangers that are generated in this competition. But if the ends of the two nations are not on the same plane, if the kind of world supported by the strength of American arms has a claim to be regarded

<hr/>

[6] See John Dugard, *Human Rights and the South African Legal Order* (Princeton: Princeton University Press, 1978).

[7] *Ibid.*, pp. 398, 400.

as superior morally to the kind of world sought through the extension of Soviet power, then we cannot cast blame with an even hand or with a mindless neutrality. The state of mind that would have us reserve our judgment would urge us to be cautious in judging between the United States and the Soviet Union. That state of mind cannot be understood apart from the modern persuasion of cultural relativism, which enduringly counsels us to be humble or modest before we judge other nations with standards drawn—as we are sure now they must be drawn—only from our own experience.

THE ISSUE OF cultural relativism did not recede, then, from our political life when Lincoln won the political fight against Douglas. It must be left to the mavens of "the history of ideas" to explain why the persuasion of cultural relativism has preserved such a hold on the educated classes in our own time when its political association with slavery has been notorious, and when the doctrine of cultural relativism has never even had the benefit of a serious philosophic statement. When it has become necessary for philosophers to cite the most explicit defense of cultural relativism, they have not been able to cite the work of other philosophers. What they have been compelled to cite, persistently, is the work of two anthropologists. Professor Edward Westermarck offered his classic survey on *The Origin and Development of the Moral Ideas* in 1906, but Richard Brandt later remarked, with charity, that this influential work was "methodologically somewhat unsophisticated."[8] Westermarck acknowledged that the "great variability of moral judgments does not of course *eo ipso* disprove the possibility of self-evident moral intuitions."[9] Still, he could not shake himself from the apprehension that a *disagreement* among experts—among those who are sufficiently informed to have opinions worth pondering—must be a decisive piece of evidence in establishing the absence of truth on any matter.[10] Westermarck was convinced that there are no "objective" standards of moral truth, that all moral judgments are relative to the emotions. And yet his "proof" of that thesis consisted mainly in a survey of the diversity of beliefs among different societies, and of the disagreements that have marked the writings of moral philosophers. As he himself recognized, however, such "proof" was irrelevant in principle to the philosophic point that had to be

---

[8] Richard Brandt, "Ethical Relativism," *The Encyclopedia of Philosophy* (New York: Macmillan, 1967), vol. 3, pp. 75-78, at 78.

[9] Edward Westermarck, *Ethical Relativity* (Paterson, New Jersey: Littlefield, Adams, 1960 [1932], p. 42.

[10] *Ibid.*

established. As Westermarck sought to fashion his own argument, he took it for granted that moral judgments contain certain distinct properties—they are universal and impartial in their coverage, they are obligatory and binding, they apply to acts of volition rather than to accidents.[11] These properties he regarded as part of the "logic" of moral judgment, which permitted him to be sardonic in dismissing those who were too dim to grasp these points. Westermarck apparently knew then as a writer what he did not officially know as an anthropologist of morals: that there is a logic in moral judgments which does not depend for its truth on the emotions of any person—a logic which is "intersubjective" in its validity, and which cannot therefore be "relative" in any way to persons or cultures.

The writing that is cited most often, in authoritative places, as "one of the most vigorous contemporary defenses of relativism,"[12] is Melville Herskovits's book *Cultural Relativism*.[13] In any anthology on the subject, a selection from this book can usually be counted on to provide the only unreserved defense of cultural relativism. Herskovits deserves close attention for a moment because he does draw out, with a rare explicitness, some of the bizarre implications that must be contained in the argument for relativism. But Herskovits is interesting, also, because he reveals—apparently without comprehending the depth of his concession—that even a cultural relativist may take for granted certain truths of moral significance that hold across cultures.

In the course of his argument Herskovits observed: "The proposition that one way of thought or action is better than another is exceedingly difficult to establish *on the ground of any universally acceptable criteria*."[14] With that reflection he affirmed, as a matter of course, a premise that would render any moral judgment vacuous. For he assumed that the only plausible moral standards with a universal reach are those standards which are accepted universally. By this reasoning, a moral standard is instantly discredited as a moral standard as soon as we find one country—perhaps even one person—that rejects it. At that moment it becomes clear that this standard cannot have the import or *function* of a moral standard: it cannot be used to condemn or commend or judge. If our surveys were to suggest, for example, that incest is universally condemned, but we then discover an isolated country where incest is generally approved, we could not use our "moral" standard to condemn or denounce the conventions of this

[11] *Ibid.*, pp. 123, 173, 178-79, 277, and especially 131.
[12] Brandt, *supra*, note 8, p. 78.
[13] New York: Vintage Books, 1972.
[14] *Ibid.*, p. 23. Emphasis added.

exotic land. By the simple force of an aberrant case, this country would have shown that the rejection of incest does not indeed reflect a "universal" truth. The condemnation of incest could not therefore claim to issue from any valid *moral* principle.[15]

To his credit at least for drawing the apt conclusions from his own premises, Herskovits recognized that this was indeed the kind of conclusion to which he was driven by the logic of his argument. As he said, with a sobering directness:

> [C]ultural relativism is a philosophy that recognizes the values set up by every society to guide its own life and that *understands their worth to those who live by them*, though they may differ from one's own. Instead of underscoring differences from absolute norms that, however objectively arrived at, are nonetheless the product of a given time or place, the relativistic point of view brings into relief *the validity of every set of norms for the people who have them*, and the values these represent.[16]

By the terms of this argument, of course—and Herskovits surely must have recognized it—a policy of genocide would have been "valid" in Germany if it stemmed from a "set of norms" accepted by the German people. The withholding of moral judgment here is a necessary part of the cultural relativist argument, and Herskovits found something redeeming in this recession from moral judgment, for an "emphasis on the worth of many ways of life, not one, is an affirmation of the values in each culture."[17] But to find, as Herskovits did, an equal dignity or "worth" in each culture is to do nothing less than reach a moral judgment about cultures other than one's own. And it is apparently a judgment that was meant to be universal in its validity, for

[15] The same "reduction" takes place in the understanding offered by Ruth Benedict, who evidently reflects the views of other anthropologists, that the proposition "X is wrong" means merely that X is in conflict with the "norms" held in a certain group. And so if we were told, say, that two people were in a moral disagreement on abortion, that would translate to mean that each one has expressed the understandings dominant in his own group. But as G.E. Moore pointed out, in an analogous criticism of Westermarck, this understanding would deprive the event of any intelligible meaning as a "moral dispute." The only possible argument between the parties is over the question of whether they genuinely reflect the views of their respective groups. What is ruled out is that the parties may say anything in this exchange which bears on the rights and wrongs of abortion. For Moore's argument, see Westermarck, *supra*, note 9, pp. 142-43. For Benedict, see her essay "Anthropology and the Abnormal," reprinted in Richard Brandt (ed.), *Value and Obligation* (New York: Harcourt, Brace & World, 1961).

[16] Melville Herskovits, *Cultural Relativism* (New York: Vintage Books, 1972), p. 31. Emphasis added.

[17] *Ibid.*, p. 33.

it would affirm the equal worth of *all* cultures. In this same vein, Sir Bernard Williams has pointed out that cultural relativism is founded in contradiction to the extent that it holds, as one of its main premises, that "it is wrong for people in one society to condemn, interfere with . . . the values of another society." As Williams remarks, this persuasion would make a claim "about what is right and wrong in one's dealings with other societies, which uses a *nonrelative* sense of 'right' "—a sense that should not be permitted by its own premises.[18]

Williams refers to this brand of cultural relativism as "vulgar relativism," and it is notable, I think, that in a recent collection of writings, brought forth by philosophers who strained to establish what may be plausible in the case for "relativism," no one sought to defend this radical (or "vulgar") form of cultural relativism. No one was prepared, that is, to deny altogether the possibility of passing judgment on the policies of another country. But for all of his philosophic innocence, Herskovits had the virtue of being clear in his definition as a relativist. In contrast, the persuasion that emerges from the recent labors of these philosophers is "relativist" only in the most trivial sense, if indeed it can be regarded as "relativist" in any intelligible form.[19] As in the case of Westermarck, the writers who sought to offer

---

[18] Bernard Williams, "An Inconsistent Form of Relativism," in Jack W. Meiland and Michael Krausz (eds.), *Relativism* (South Bend, Indiana: University of Notre Dame Press, 1982), pp. 171-74, at 171. Emphasis in original.

[19] A case in point is provided in a recent work on moral relativity by David Wong, whose self-proclaimed "relativism" is able to encompass these ingredients: that "most of the moral issues that confront us in our daily lives *are* capable of rational resolution by reference to facts"; that it is possible to judge—and to "criticize as false"—the moral understandings held by people in different cultures and moral traditions; and that we are not required, by relativism, to regard all moral views as equally plausible or "permitted." See Wong, *Moral Relativity* (Berkeley: University of California Press, 1984), pp. 138, 63, 73, 75; emphasis in original. For Wong, relativism simply comes to mean that, on certain issues, people disagree in their moral judgments, and that there does not seem to be a rational or principled ground on which to resolve the disagreement (see, for example, p. 175). That people disagree, however, is less than a momentous discovery; still less—as Wong knows—is it a discovery that proves the absence of true answers to moral questions. I have suggested in this book that when we are in the presence of a dispute which yields no principled solution, we may conclude that we are not in the presence of a *moral* dispute. And in that event we may recede, quite properly, from a moral judgment. Wong does not explain why it is necessary to leap instead to the inference he draws: that there are moral issues with no principled ground of resolution. The more illuminating question is just how Wong is able to know—and know, apparently, with unshakable confidence—just which disputes among people have a *moral* character. For that, Wong must have a clear notion of the character or the logical properties of moral questions—properties, as it turns out, that Wong regards as holding true across cultures. See *infra*, note 35.

even a lame good word for relativism found themselves depending, at critical points, on assumptions that admitted no "relativistic" caviling. Philippa Foot was convinced that "local truth is the only substantive truth that we have." She wondered why it should not be enough to "claim relative truth for our moral judgments," taking them as true "relative either to local standards or to individual standards."[20] On the other hand, she also thought that the Jews killed at the orders of Himmler were "indisputably innocent,"[21] and that "it was impossible, *logically speaking*, . . . to argue that the killing of millions of innocent people did not need any moral justification."[22] These are not phrases tinged with relativistic doubt, and if Foot was, as she says, "logically speaking," it is hard to see why the condemnation she expressed in regard to the Nazis would stand on nothing more than a "local truth"—which, as she intimates, may be no truth at all.[23]

The same curious mixture of convictions was presented by Gilbert Harman, who has been credited with offering a case for moral relativism which is at least "lacking any obvious inconsistencies."[24] And yet Harman could complain that "there is a prima facie arbitrariness and lack of generality in a plan that involves avoiding cruelty to people but not to animals."[25] Moral judgments are apparently to be regarded as flawed or suspect if they are affected by "arbitrariness" rather than logical consistency, if they are wanting in "generality" (and are therefore partial, rather than universal), and if they blind us to the existence of unwarranted "cruelty." These ingredients in Harman's argument are not evidently afflicted with "relativism," and so they may properly make his argument accessible to any fair-minded reader who is open to persuasion. Both Foot and Harman find the root of relativism in the assumption, unexplained and unjustified, that the standards for recognizing true arguments can only be "shared" standards—which is to say, standards that require the agreement of a group or a society.[26]

[20] Philippa Foot, "Moral Relativism," in Meiland and Krausz, *supra*, note 18, pp. 152-66, at 161.

[21] *Ibid.*, p. 159.

[22] *Ibid.*, p. 163. Emphasis added.

[23] *Ibid.*

[24] David Lyons, "Ethical Relativism and the Problem of Incoherence," in Meiland and Krausz, *supra*, note 18, pp. 209-225, at 209.

[25] Gilbert Harman, "Moral Relativism Defended," in Meiland and Krausz, *supra*, note 18, pp. 186-204, at 202-203. His essay originally appeared in *Philosophical Review* (1975), pp. 3-22.

[26] Both writers might have been affected by the concern, arising from Wittgenstein, for "private languages." Once it is recognized that the life of moral judgment is bound up with the giving of reasons or justifications, it must be recognized also that this life

142

At the same time, both expend their powers in seeking to make their views persuasive to readers who may not understand or *share* their convictions. Presumably, those who can be addressed, those who can enter the conversation, are thought to *share* enough understanding that they may be brought, through argument, to the discovery of a novel truth. By that reasoning, however, moral truths would be valid potentially for anyone, anywhere, to whom they might be explained. Neither writer, of course, betrays a hint of doubt that there is anything "relativistic" or problematic in the truth they would urge upon their readers. Foot is convinced that there are "good reasons" that would persuade us of the truth of moral relativism. But to be sure (or, rather, to be unsure) she is prepared to concede, in the spirit of relativism, that those reasons may not hold for anyone apart from herself. Nevertheless, she would insist that they may still be considered "good reasons." Then again, we should be indecorous were we to attribute to Foot a willingness to persuade us to a position which she regards as no more likely to be true than a position she would reject. And only a writer of sublime cleverness would wish to recruit us to the conviction that "we may be mistaken—and we may be mistaken that we are mistaken."[27]

So far as I can tell, the only version of "relativism" that survives the efforts of these philosophers is the kind recognized by Plato and Aristotle: viz., that the goodness or badness of certain acts will be contingent on their circumstances.[28] But as we have already seen, the recognition of certain rights and wrongs as contingent is quite compatible with the recognition of other rights and wrongs that are immutable and categorical, and that are not affected by changes in setting

---

depends on discourse and language. Language is, of course, irreducibly social; it depends on conventions of meaning that must be shared. From that point, however, some philosophers may go on to make the (unwarranted) inference that moral understanding itself must be irreducibly conventional. As one commentator has put it, the mistake here is to assume that because moral terms may be grammatical fictions, the understandings they represent are also ontological fictions. Societies may contrive different symbols and sounds in place of our language of "rights" and "wrongs," but the functions of commending and condemning, of demanding and offering justifications, are present in all languages, for they arise from the constitution of our natures. See Daniel Robinson, *Philosophical Psychology* (New York: Oxford University Press, 1985), ch. IV.

[27] A close equivalent to this dictum has been offered in a recent work on moral relativity. That author claims, for his "relativist analyses," that they would "preserve a good deal of moral objectivity while making possible an explanation of why some of us would think there is a single true morality that everyone has reason to follow, even if there is not." See Wong, *supra*, note 19, pp. 120 and 153.

[28] See, for example, Bernard Williams, "The Truth in Relativism," in Meiland and Krausz, *supra*, note 18, pp. 175-85.

and circumstance. In fact, some writers have taken the existence of contingent rights and wrongs as variations that merely cast in relief the enduring notions of right and wrong that we use to guide our judgments in shifting cases.[29] Whether I rush an innocent victim to a hospital may depend on what I know about the competence or corruption of the doctors (perhaps their willingness to act as servants of a brutal state in treating a political enemy). But nothing in the variation of my response would imply anything mutable in the logic that *obliges* me to act, where I can, to save an innocent life. It requires no special arts of philosophers to establish this notion of "relativism," but it is a notion that has never properly claimed the name of "relativism." It has nothing in common with that moral relativism which has rendered so many people so diffident on the large political questions of our day. One can only wonder why seasoned philosophers are willing to take the chance that, as they render relativism plausible by making it trivial, they make the public suggestible to a relativism which is far from trivial, and which cannot be reconciled with the moral premises that support constitutional government.

WHETHER OR NOT Herskovits was able to notice these implications, he had the merit at least of conveying, unalloyed, the premises that had to stand behind cultural relativism. He seemed serenely unaware that he was offering a moral judgment with universal reach when he affirmed the equal *worth* of all cultures; and so he could move on, with a comparable innocence, revealing something more about the epistemology of cultural relativism, as he sought to explain how he knew such remarkable things. How did he know, for example, that the moral codes in all cultures were valid for the people who lived under them? That conclusion seemed to flow from the proposition, put forward early in his essay, that "judgments are based on experience, and experience is interpreted by each individual in terms of his own enculturation."[30] It was possible, of course, to hold that knowledge begins with "experience," but to acknowledge at the same time that there is a material world out there, beyond the psyche of the individual, and that material world can place hard limits on the range of "experience" accessible to any person. But in his need to affirm that *personal* experience is the source of all knowledge, Herskovits was willing to entertain a more radical notion—viz., that even the

[29] See Jonathan Harrison, *Our Knowledge of Right and Wrong* (London: George Allen & Unwin, 1971), pp. 79-80.
[30] Herskovits, *supra*, note 16, p. 15.

facts of the material world may be altered, in their standing as facts, by the subjective understanding of individuals:

> When we reflect that such intangibles as right and wrong, normal and abnormal, beautiful and plain are absorbed as a person learns the ways of the group into which he is born, we see that we are dealing here with a process of first importance. *Even the facts of the physical world are discerned through the enculturative screen,* so that the perception of time, distance, weight, size, and other "realities" is *mediated by the conventions of any group.*[31]

Happily for us all, this argument is fatally vulnerable to the recognition, accessible to the educated, the uneducated—and even, at times, to the overeducated—that there really is a material world out there. That world happens to be filled with facts that do not depend for their existence as facts on the "experience" or the subjective "perceptions" of individuals. Even if the "enculturative screen" of Jersey City affected its natives with fanciful "perceptions" of "distance," the actual distance between Jersey City and Paris is very likely to remain the same. And so Thomas Reid could aptly remark, with the empiricists of his own day in mind, that when we trip over a rock, we trip over a rock, and not over the concept of a rock. But if the brute fact of the material world tells against Herskovits's argument, so too would Kant's account of those truths which we cannot know merely through experience—and which we must be able to know before we are capable of having "experiences." In that respect, one may be indecorous enough to point out that Herskovits's own assertion of the worth of *all* cultures is a proposition that cannot strictly be derived from experience. Herskovits could not possibly have experienced all cultures himself, or even scanned secondary accounts of all cultures. What he was asserting was a principle, which covered countries he did not know and would never know, a principle that would hold true for all cultures now and in the future. He offered, in effect, a statement of a necessary truth, which could not, by definition, be drawn from anything known to him through his "experience."

But Herskovits gave the game away himself and made, probably unwittingly, the decisive concession to Kant here. Herskovits remarked at one point that "the facts about many cultures demonstrate that all peoples *at times* think in terms of objectively provable causation, just as *at times*, they indulge in explanations that relate a fact to an *ap-*

---

[31] *Ibid.* Emphasis added.

parent cause."[32] Hume to the contrary, Herskovits was admitting that, quite regardless of the wide variations in culture or civilization—quite apart from the varieties of personal and social "experience"—people everywhere recognize the concept of causation. The capacity to recognize the difference between causation and correlation seems to be part of the understanding built into the constitution of their natures, quite apart from the special impress that is made upon their sensibilities by the local cuisine or indigenous rituals. This concession by Herskovits is enough to spark the imagination of the urbane bookmaker, who, sensing a rare possibility, may offer a wager to the professor or his successors. Our bookie may propose that we hire a team of anthropologists, set them loose in a variety of settings that are sufficiently exotic and improbable, and see what evidence they turn up about other parts of the Kantian inventory. Herskovits already conceded that people in all cultures understand the concept of causation. We may place the wager now that people in all cultures will also understand the concepts of number, space, and time; that they will understand the difference in saying that something is true, that it is true only within certain limits, or that it is true as a matter of necessity; and that along with their understanding of time, sequence, and causation, they will understand *moral* causation: they will assign blame and fault, and they will insist on raising questions about the grounds on which certain acts may be justified. In short, we may make a wager on the question of whether people everywhere will recognize the concept of justification—or the idea of morals—in the same way that they recognize other necessary truths, such as the existence of time, space, and causation.

And yet, Professor Herskovits conceded the point here himself, even though he did not manage to extract its full significance for his own argument. Opinions about the nature of virtue and vice may vary from one society to another, but Herskovits observed that "morality is a universal, and so is enjoyment of beauty, and some standard for truth":[33]

> The many forms these concepts take are but products of the particular historical experience of the societies that manifest them. In each, criteria are subject to continuous questioning, continuous change. But the basic conceptions remain, to channel thought and direct conduct, to give purpose to living.

[32] *Ibid.*, p. 27. Emphasis in original.
[33] *Ibid.*, p. 32.

In other words, even though people in different societies may come to different moral judgments, there is a universal disposition among human beings to raise questions about the things that are good or bad, justified or unjustified. The *concept of morals*, then, is accessible to people in all societies. Of course, the fact that people universally raise moral questions does not itself prove the existence of morals, any more than the existence of morals would be disproved if it were shown, through an amassing of evidence, that most people in the world fail to consider the justifications for their acts. But to recognize that people in all societies are aware of the concept of justification should at least stir some serious reflection among those having a touch of imagination. If we understand that the concept of morals exists in all societies, then we recognize again that the logic of morals is everywhere the same, and that people are capable of extracting, in all places, the implications that arise out of the idea of morals. People who have the wit to ask for justifications when they are assaulted have the wit to recognize the difference between acts that are justified and unjustified, between people who are innocent and guilty. They know all they need know in order to recognize why it is wrong to visit punishment on the innocent and the guilty alike. Which is to say, they should be capable of drawing out those inferences from the idea of morals which establish, categorically, the wrong of genocide. By the same token, they should be able to draw the case against slavery, the case for republican government—in short, they should be able to draw out the inventory of moral truths that people anywhere can extract from the logic of morals itself.

It is only to be expected that different societies will prove more or less imaginative in this exercise, and the task is likely to be aided in those societies in which people of reflection may build upon a long tradition of writing in moral philosophy. In principle, though, it is possible for men anywhere to begin with an awareness of the concept of justification and to draw out its implications. What we notice, in fact, is that many common threads, many similarities, become visible from one society to another, and that evidence may merely confirm an ancient recognition: the multitude of people in the world differ widely in their understanding—they may see "as through a glass darkly"—but what they glimpse, with varying degrees of clarity, is the idea of justice itself in its elementary logic. The principles that grow out of this understanding may attach themselves to different objects in different places, depending on the material conditions of life. In some societies a "wrong" may be manifested in the use of a Xerox machine to reproduce, without permission, copyrighted material; in another place, it may be found in the purloining of a banana. But the considerations that ultimately define "thefts" or other *wrongful* takings of property would be indifferent to the technical means through which these wrongs are acted out. The first Neanderthal who is hit on the head and utters the equivalent of "Why did you *do* that?!" marks an awareness of the moral world. What he demands is a "justification," and as he does that, he recognizes the same logic of morals that may produce, with further refinements in the chain of reasoning, the laws against corporate embezzlement.

I think we would be in a position, then, to add a further, radical statement to the argument we have already assembled against cultural relativism. We have established up to now that moral truths must in fact hold their validity across cultures, and that the existence of those truths is sufficient to refute the doctrine of cultural relativism. We have also seen that the proponents of cultural relativism fall into the fallacy of presuming that there can be no universal moral truths if different societies display different moral codes or different principles of justice. I think we may now take an additional step and say that spokesmen for cultural relativism have been fundamentally mistaken in their factual understanding as well: there have never been, in fact, different "moral systems" in the world. The conventions of different peoples have of course varied widely, and no one will mistake the Incas of Peru for the denizens of Fresno. But nothing in those differences can establish the proposition that the various peoples in the world have been separated by different "principles" of justice, or by a different understanding of the concept of morals. As I have already suggested, there has been from the beginning, for the Neanderthal as well as the corporate executive, only *one* moral system—only one logic of morals, only one set of concepts that arise from the idea of "justification." The mistake of the cultural relativists can be found in the kind of evidence they are willing to accept for the existence in the world of diverse moral systems, governed by divergent moral principles. Whatever the differences that might separate countries, those differences cannot be traced back to concepts of "justification" which differ fundamentally from our own, or to "necessary truths" which vary in any way from the truths that are necessary in our own land.

THE PHILOSOPHER Wittgenstein once asked a friend, "Tell me, why do people always say it was *natural* for men to assume that the sun went round the earth rather than that the earth was rotating?" His friend replied, "Well, obviously, because it just *looks* as if the sun is going round the earth." To which Wittgenstein responded, "Well, what would it have looked like if it had looked as if the earth was rotating?"

Why has it seemed so natural to assume that the variety of customs and social conventions in the world reflects the existence of different "value systems," predicated on different concepts of morality? The most obvious answer is that people have been impressed by the sheer variety of the differences that separate one society from another. In one society, a widow is burned on the funeral pyre of her husband; in another, she is burned on the beach in Miami. In one society, people complain to the chef about the roast beef; in another, they send back the roast beef and eat the chef. That there are differences no one will doubt, but the question is whether these differences mark the presence of different notions of the meaning of "morals." We saw earlier that it was unwarranted to draw moral inferences about an event on the basis of outward "behavior" alone. I suggested the example of Smith going to the garage of his neighbor, Jones, and taking the hose stored in the garage. Whether that taking of property was a theft or a borrowing turned on the understanding that animated the actors. It was entirely possible that the outward acts, in two separate cases, could be virtually identical—e.g., someone went to a garage and took a hose—but the two events might have an entirely different moral significance, and they would lead to moral judgments that were markedly different.

The same understanding would apply when we compare the outward behavior of societies in an effort to give an account of their "cultures." We may find two societies, for example, in which the populace turns away from eating the flesh of animals. Would we say that we have here two societies which share a certain moral or cultural perspective? It may turn out that in one society the people turn away from the eating of animals out of a sympathy for living creatures which share, with human beings, a capacity to suffer pain. In the other society, the people refuse to eat animals because they are under the persuasion that "you are what you eat," and so they eat only other humans— and preferably those with academic degrees more advanced than their own. The two societies contain people who seem to "behave" in the same way, but we would be mistaken to conclude that they share a common moral perspective.

The same understanding would hold quite as well in the obverse form of the problem, which is the form that bears more directly on the question of comparing "cultures." It is possible that two societies may exhibit practices which are strikingly different in their outward character, but that their differences may not stem from any disagree-

149

ment about the meaning of morals. And so, even though the contrasts in social practice might be dramatic, we could not conclude that we are in the presence of different "moral systems." In one society, grandfather, when he turns 65, is given retirement benefits and Social Security. In another, grandfather is left at the shore to die while the rest of the group moves along to the next grazing land. As we inquire more closely, we discover, to our surprise, that the people in this nomadic society display the attitudes we usually associate with a "respect for life." They think that the taking of life must carry the heaviest burden of justification; they sternly proscribe abortion and infanticide; and they refuse to regard the retarded or the handicapped as representing "lives that are not worth living." They are also convinced that people are responsible for their acts of omission, and that anyone who knowingly abandoned an infirm person and left him exposed to the elements would be held responsible for his death. But then, why do these understandings not work to protect grandfather at 65? It turns out that, in addition to all of the other tenets of this society, its people also believe that humans cease to be truly alive or distinctively human after the age of 65.

Now it could not be accurate to say that we are divided from the people of this society by fundamental differences in moral understanding. It is apparent, in fact, that these people are working with moral premises—and perhaps, one may say, with an apparatus of moral reasoning—that is identical to our own. Our differences are focused entirely on the question of whether these people are justified in the judgment they have reached about the terminus of human life. It may not be wholly clear, just yet, whether the mistake we think they are making is traceable to an error in their factual understanding or to a defect in their grasp of "principled" reasoning. But it should be clear that we have not reached an impasse, marked by differences of a "religious" nature, in which reasoned exchange must be suspended. If we were to find in our country a religious sect which believes in the ritual sacrifice of people over 65, it is inconceivable that the civil authorities would stand back and permit the ritual acts of killing to go forward simply because they would take place under the auspices of religion. The claims of "religion" or "belief" may not insulate from the law acts of killing that cannot otherwise be justified. And so it would be thoroughly proper to insist that we are not in the presence of differences that are intractable and irreconcilable. We cannot know whether we have reached that point until we have learned something more about the reasoning that underlies the judgments of our nomads with respect to life after 65.

We would be warranted, in other words, in putting the question: "Why is this judgment justified? On what basis do you conclude that grandfather ceases to be alive or distinctively human on the day of his 65th birthday? Is it really conceivable that grandfather has all the attributes of a human being at 64 years and 364 days, but that he will lose them at midnight of the 365th day?" The reflective nomads may respond that they are being guided here by experience and by a cluster of empirical findings. They claim that people, when they turn 65, become slower and not very productive; that it becomes rare for them to emit any sentence worthy of human beings, or even anything mildly interesting; and that they have an incurable tendency to watch daytime game shows.

In the face of this kind of reasoning, however, it would be proper for us to point out that the nomads are not honoring the principled implications of their own argument. Surely, we might protest, there would be people far younger than 65 who are slow and unproductive, who seem incapable of uttering an interesting sentence, and who show a disposition to take in the lesser offerings of daytime television. Of course, the nomads may respond to this criticism by applying their policy of abandonment more thoroughly and consistently to all those who display these characteristics. But in that event we would be moved to a more decisive criticism about the foundation of their policy: we could point out that there is nothing of moral significance disclosed in the report that people are infirm of body or mind. Nothing in that condition can establish the ground for the moral conclusion that these people *deserve* to perish.

As Americans, we might be placed in a singularly awkward position in raising these arguments. The nomads might point out that, for more than a decade now, the American courts have employed the same kind of reasoning used by the nomads, but at the other end of the age scale. Instead of saying that a member of the species *Homo sapiens* ceases to be human at age 65, the courts insist that a member of this species is not yet human at 8 months and 29 days, but that it becomes incontestably human—and subject to the protection of the law—only at 9 months of age, or when it finally emerges from the womb of its mother. Whether it is found inside our outside the womb is a matter merely of location, which says nothing about the *nature of the organism* at 9 months or at 9 months lacking a day. Our nomads might claim that a 65-year-old, placed outside the society and left by the shore, ceases to be a "viable" human being; but, again, the shift in location is irrelevant to any judgment about the nature of the being who is abandoned. The question of abortion will be taken up fully

151

later; I would simply point out here that, with the argument for abortion, or with the argument put forth by our hypothetical nomads, neither side may close itself to the demand for a further, reasoned exchange merely by invoking personal "beliefs" or "religious convictions."

What would be the nature of the dispute, then, between the nomads and those of us who would find fault with them? It would not be that the nomads are working with moral concepts fundamentally different from our own. The problem lies, rather, with defects in their moral reasoning. Our nomads are far from clear about the criteria that define the nature of "humans"; they are infirm in their principled reasoning, in applying those criteria consistently; and they have made a serious mistake in drawing moral conclusions (i.e., about the fitness to live or die) from facts which have no moral significance (in this case, the infirmities of people). In short, the difference between the nomads and us would arise mainly from the fact that the nomads are not well instructed in the properties and requirements of moral reasoning. But the difference in that respect would not indicate that we are separated from the nomads by different "moral systems" or even by different "cultures." As I have suggested, the same differences may separate the proponents and opponents of abortion in our own country, and we would hardly claim that the division between those two sides reflects a division in the United States between two different "cultures" built upon different moral premises. The two sides obviously draw on many common moral understandings, and they would not be so exasperated with one another if they thought that their opponents were simply incapable of understanding the issue because they were immured, irrecoverably, in an alien culture.

Of course it was never easier to suppose that the United States was breaking into rival cultures and moral systems than during the crisis over slavery which brought on the Civil War. But we know that sentiment on this question was not uniform in the North or the South. As Lincoln pointed out, the large numbers of free blacks were living testimony to the moral understanding that affected many former owners of slaves, who were finally moved to free their slaves even at vast cost to themselves. The historian Kenneth Stampp recalled a North Carolinian who provided for the unconditional emancipation of his slaves and who left a record of his reasons: "Agreeably to the rights of man, every human being, be his or her colour what it may, is entitled to freedom. . . . The golden rule directs us to do unto every human creature, as we would wish to be done unto; and sure I am, that there is not one of us would agree to be kept in slavery during a long life.

... I wish every human creature seriously to deliberate on my reasons."[34]

This fragment bears a faint similarity to the exercise Lincoln wrote out for himself, in which he tested the justification for making slaves of black men. Lincoln had not owned slaves; the Southern author of the fragment cited by Stampp did in fact own slaves. Up to the time that the Southerner wrote that fragment for himself, worked out the syllogism, and drew the decisive conclusion, what was it that separated him from Lincoln? He could not have been part of a separate culture built upon radically different moral premises. He showed, in his fragment, that he accepted the premises which underlay the "natural equality" of blacks, and that he was versed in the same canons of moral reasoning which guided Lincoln. He understood the meaning of a "principle" that would apply to himself as well as to others; he understood the form of a syllogism; and he understood what it meant to demand a "justification." In demanding the same justification from himself as he would demand of others, he showed, quite tellingly, an understanding of the logic of morals. If there were cultural differences which separated Lincoln from this Southerner, they could not have been differences which impaired in any way the capacity of people in the North or the South to understand the rudiments of moral reasoning. One would be compelled to conclude, then, that the only thing which separated Lincoln from this Southerner up to the time he wrote his fragment on slavery was simply that *he had not yet written his fragment on slavery*: he had not posed the issue to himself in the most rigorous, reasoned way and drawn the conclusion that was commanded by reason.

But if we can have proper doubts about the "cultural" differences that separated the North from the South, it should be all the easier to resist the same facile explanations of the differences that may separate our own generation from the statesmen of our past. We know, for example, that the Republican leaders who framed the Fourteenth Amendment and passed the Civil Rights Act of the 1860's never supposed for a moment that anything in those legal measures forbade the separation of children in schools on the basis of race. That same understanding, affirmed in our own time, would be taken as the mark of the most obdurate reactionary. And yet these men, we know, were the most progressive men of their age. If we should seek to account for the differences between them and us—differences that would surely

[34] Quoted in Kenneth Stampp, *The Peculiar Institution* (New York: Vintage Books, 1964), pp. 235-36.

open them to the most severe moral censure in our day—we could not say that they lived in a culture radically different from our own. Nor could we say that they were acting on the basis of moral premises strikingly at odds with our own. Our premises are their premises. In fact, they became our premises largely because these men taught us that they *should* be our premises. The precise accomplishment of these statesmen was to establish more explicitly principles that should have been understood to be part of the Constitution all along. Without their work in framing the Fourteenth Amendment and reshaping the American political order, it would have been harder for the Supreme Court to take the steps it would take in later years in filling out the understandings entailed by "the equal protection of the laws."

If these Republican leaders are to be faulted, then, they are to be faulted mainly for *incomplete* reasoning: they did not fully grasp the nature of the principle which underlay their own legislative achievements. Or, to put it more charitably, they did not see the fuller implications which arose from the principle they were affirming. As defects go, these were not all that bad—certainly not bad enough to override the major good that was accomplished in establishing the Fourteenth Amendment. And, of course, none of us ever succeeds in drawing out all the implications that arise from the principles of morals. That is the enduring work of moral philosophy, a work that is never finished; and it is a work that will always be bequeathed as a challenge to the next generation. It can hardly be a damning criticism, then, to say that these Republican statesmen were not able to see as clearly as later generations the implications of their own work. Still, there is no gainsaying that, between ourselves and the Republican statesmen of the 1860's, there are differences in judgment which cannot be regarded today as morally trivial. And yet, as I have tried to argue, these points of divergence could not have arisen from any fundamental difference in moral premises which separated their age or "culture" from our own.

I have made the same argument concerning the differences that separate us from the nomadic tribe described above and from the Southerners who held slaves. Again, the differences could not have been counted as morally insignificant, and yet it would have clothed them in a false grandeur—and obscured a vital truth—if these differences were taken as the marks of societies which were separated from one another by a radical disagreement in their moral premises. The truth that would have been obscured here is that in all these societies, distant as they have been in time and space, there has ever been but *one* set of moral premises, *one* understanding of the logic of morals.

If these societies have not been in agreement, I have suggested that the causes are to be found in matters far less portentous than a difference in moral premises. The disagreements can be attributed, without pretension, to faulty or incomplete reasoning from right premises, or to an insufficiently cultivated sense of the canons and requirements of moral reasoning.

But if we were to be strict about the matter, we would have to go on to say that in the presence of a palpable ignorance on one side of a disagreement, it is false and misleading to describe this divergence as a "dispute." It would be false, that is, if we meant to convey anything more than the obvious point that the two sides do not coincide in their judgments. If we suggest that two people or two cultures are "in disagreement," we run the risk of implying that this lack of agreement is rooted in different premises or doctrines which reach a philosophic core. And yet that suggestion might endow this simple discrepancy with far more significance than it could rightly claim. To take an innocent case, let us suppose that the question is put, "Who is likely to be regarded, fifty years from now, as a more admirable figure: Martin Luther King, Jr., or Jesse Jackson?" Imagine that one man affirms his choice of King and sets forth his reasons, including a review of King's efforts in the civil rights movement. A second man derides the judgment of the first and insists that Jackson will have to be estimated as a far more dynamic figure. In partial evidence for his judgment he recalls "Jackson's three home runs during the World Series of 1978." A disinterested observer, who knows something of the larger world, quickly points out that the second man has described the wrong Jackson: he has mistaken the Rev. Jesse Jackson for Reggie Jackson, late of the New York Yankees. Until the recognition was offered, however, the second man had no doubt that he was engaged in a heated dispute with the first man, in which the soundness of his personal judgment was being gauged. Yet, nothing in their exchange should have been dignified by the label of "disagreement" or "dispute." For the exchange never rose to the level of a genuine dispute: the second man simply did not understand what he was talking about and, therefore, he never said anything of relevance to the question.

In a similar way, we could imagine an exchange with a member of our nomadic tribe which believes that human beings, at age 65, cease to be human. Let us suppose that we inquire about the reasons that support this judgment, and we ask whether those reasons can satisfy the requirements of a principled argument. The nomad does not comprehend what we are asking, and he turns us away with a smile, saying, "Obviously we have reached a point of disagreement." He may be

155

convinced, wrongly, that there is no relevance in an exchange of reasons over issues that come down ultimately to matters of "belief." He may also betray a certain conviction that, so long as matters of belief cannot be tested with reasons, he is safely beyond any critical challenge. But this surety on his part would be as unwarranted as the dignity he claims for his position: for he fails even to engage the question in a manner which would allow us to say that a "disagreement" is present, much less a disagreement which can reach a point of principle and claim the name of a "moral disagreement."

Were we to find civilized nations surrounded then by barbarian hordes pretending to be nations, it would not be accurate to say that the international community is divided by serious disagreements over fundamental moral principles. It may be, in certain cases, that the civilized are merely confronting countries that are rendered barbaric by their own ignorance. On the other hand, we have thus far left out one explanation from the inventory of things that may account for the serious moral differences between societies: those differences may arise not from ignorance or incomplete reasoning, but from plain malevolence or evil, knowingly applied. The burglar who enters a house under cover of darkness knows he is doing something wrong. He may suffer, for all we know, from a diminished moral imagination and incomplete reasoning; but he knows he is harming others, and that he is doing it for his own benefit or satisfaction. He knows, in other words, the grounds on which his action is wrong, and he confirms to us that he knows these things when he shows outrage over the theft of his own property.

No one who seriously read Adolf Hitler's *Mein Kampf*, could have harbored any doubt that the author was quite aware of the logic of "justification." He had constructed over the years a comprehensive indictment of the "injustice" of the Treaty of Versailles, and he was not without emphatic judgments on the "wrongs" he found so pervasive in German life. On the "social question," Hitler seemed to have drawn from Plato the image of people born into the humble orders, but whose souls were fashioned out of gold and other precious metals. The test of a just society was whether it would raise these people to the stations to which they were suited by nature, quite apart from their lowly origins. Hitler was no stranger, then, to the rudimentary logic that was built into the concept of "justice" and "justification." Any man who understood what Hitler did, understood the most fundamental things he had to know in order to come to the understanding of why genocide is wrong. Nothing in his culture cut him off from that moral understanding; he came from the same country in which

Kant had lived and taught. If Hitler embarked then on a policy of genocide, it was not because his culture had been shaped by moral postulates different from our own. With all of our inclinations these days to seek the sociological or nonmoral explanation for moral events, we often overlook an explanation that must remain immanently plausible: that certain people do injustice not because they fail to understand what they are doing, but precisely because they do understand. They do it for their own gain or aggrandizement, and they may do it for the sadistic pleasure they find in the suffering of others. They may do it, in some cases, for the love of evil itself.

Among the fictions which may cover over these severe truths are the kinds of theories that would sweep away the recognition of moral depravity and suggest that the differences that matter in this world arise from the existence of different moral principles (or "value systems") which cannot be reconciled. But as I have tried to suggest, none of the empirical evidence brought forth on this point can possibly establish the truth of that proposition. No evidence amassed by anthropologists or historians will show that there is, or ever has been, anything more than one moral system, which traces back to the same understanding of the logic of morals or the meaning of a "justification." The rudiments of that system are acknowledged anywhere and everywhere, whenever an injured person feels the passion of outrage and demands a *justification*. For he affirms his understanding that morals exist; that a justification is different from a report on causes; that the pleasure of the assailant does not constitute a justification; that moral judgment proceeds through the giving of reasons; that the standards of moral judgment are not subjective (otherwise, reasons could not be given or judged); that the assailant is a creature with the freedom or autonomy to form his own act (he had been free to assault or to refrain from assaulting); and that the assailant, therefore, may be held responsible for his act. We could go on drawing out the implications, but the elementary point should by now be in place. By demanding a justification, one acknowledges all of the components that are built into the logic of morals, which means that one acknowledges all of the groundwork that is ever necessary for extracting categorical propositions in the domain of morals. And by the testimony of the most radical "cultural relativists," there is no society in which the demand for a justification is not heard; there is no "culture" in which the logic of morals is not acknowledged.[35]

[35] This is a point that seems to have been neglected by Professor Wong in his recent work on moral relativity (*supra*, note 19). Apparently, he overlooked the fact that the

The moral differences that are displayed in a comparison of countries can be understood, then, only as a measure of the relative progress those countries have made in drawing the implications which arise out of the idea of morals itself. But of course, the exercise of morals consists in the task of drawing, from the logic of morals, those necessary truths which stand as "first principles." As we apply principles to cases, we find that we may clear away the distractions to our best judgment if we can identify instantly the fallacies or the spurious arguments which stand in contradiction, ultimately, to necessary truths. When those distractions are swept away, it becomes possible to focus more precisely on the questions which are more truly in dispute. These points will be borne out, I think, when we turn to the section on applications: we will enter a chain of connected cases, beginning with the problem of "conscientious objection" and ending with the question of abortion. In each instance, we will have the chance to show how "first principles" must affect the way in which the problem is posed to us, and we will have the chance to test or amplify those principles as we move along. And at times, through the novel circumstances of cases, we may be led to discover some further implications which arise from these "first principles." But before we turn to the cases and applications, I will pause briefly, in the next chapter, to summarize some of the "first principles" we have already accumulated here.

---

societies he pointed to, as examples of different "moralities" or moral traditions, shared the same understanding of the logic and properties of a "justification." These societies might have differed in their judgments about rights and duties, but they all understood questions about the just and unjust uses of authority, and about those acts which call out for justification. Wong himself assumed that the question of justification would have to arise in all places (p. 56); that "moral systems are all action-guiding systems" which seek to establish the standards of what is right or justified or defensible (p. 45); that questions about the way in which we "ought" to act are bound up with the enterprise of giving reasons (p. 36); and that the judging of reasons must be affected by tests of universality, logical consistency, and "moral relevance" (p. 57). In fact, if Wong's understanding were not informed by such a sense of "moral relevance"—if he did not work with an understanding of the logic and properties of a "moral" question— how would he know just which parts of the experience of other societies are pertinent to the ongoing dispute over "moral" truth? In short, Wong's own argument fails to be comprehensible except on the basis of an understanding of a "logic of morals" which holds true across cultures. Once that logic is understood, as an old saying used to go, "the rest is commentary."

VIII

FIRST PRINCIPLES: A PROVISIONAL
SUMMARY

A student of mine, who came from Africa, took in the argument on cultural relativism, but he still found it hard to accept the notion of moral principles extending across cultures. I confessed to him that I knew almost nothing of the customs of his own country, but I wondered what the conventions of his society were on a matter firmly placed in the American understanding. In my own country, I explained, it is understood that if a burglar were to enter a man's home and force him, at the point of a gun, to sign over a deed to his home, the courts would not regard that arrangement as a valid "contract" enforceable at law. My student reported that the same understanding was followed in his own country. I went on to explain another "convention" in American law. If Jones is thrown out of a window and on the way down lands on Smith, we would not hold Jones liable for "assault"; that is, he would not be responsible for acts he did not intentionally perform and which he was powerless to resist. As it turned out, this understanding, too, was accepted, as a principle of law, in my student's native land.

These propositions seem so obvious or elementary that we may hardly be aware of them most of the time as moral propositions. And yet, the fact that we assume these propositions as a matter of course, as propositions that could hardly be otherwise, may merely be another indication that we are dealing with "first principles." In the case of Jones falling on Smith, we saw earlier that the notion of morals presupposed a world of freedom rather than of determinism. When Jones was thrown out the window, his subsequent "behavior" in falling down was governed by the laws of nature; he was, at that moment, incontestably, in the world of determinism. If we understand the very idea of morals, we understand that it must presuppose, as a moral agent, a being who has the freedom to choose a course of action and reach judgments of right and wrong. Thomas Reid was quite correct, then, to state, as a necessary "first principle" in morals, that "what is done from unavoidable necessity . . . cannot be the object either of blame or moral approbation."[1]

[1] Thomas Reid, *Essays on the Active Powers of the Human Mind* (Cambridge: MIT Press, 1969 [1788]), p. 361.

159

In regard to the making of contracts, of course, we recognize that a promise signed at the point of a gun is not freely tendered. But then we realize that the notion of a contract must also presuppose a creature with the "freedom" to form his own acts and make judgments about the kinds of ends that may *properly* be the object of his promises. To make a promise is to encourage another person to stake his interests on the expectation that you will keep your word. If you do not keep your promise, you run the risk of inducing another person to accept an injury for the sake of *your* own interests. For that reason a promise is enveloped with moral significance, and so, too, is the "obligation" that issues from a proper contract. But a contract entered into under duress can be no contract. It would be merely a device that seeks to impart a legal consecration to an act of theft. As Rousseau understood, brute coercion cannot be the source of a moral obligation; therefore, it cannot be the source of that obligation which arises uniquely from a promise. A contract, properly understood, must imply a creature with the "competence to contract," or to offer his consent. We do not make contracts with dogs and horses, we do not consider them creatures with the competence to offer their consent, because they lack the moral competence that is necessary to the forming of a moral intention and to the knowing tender of a promise.

It should be no surprise, then, that when the idea of a "contract" is understood in its essential logic, anywhere in the world, it is understood to imply consent freely given. If that much is clear—as it was to my student—then why should it be so strange to contemplate the same point made about that form of government which has often been conceived in the terms of contract and consent? If human beings are understood to be creatures competent to contract, they deserve not to be ruled or forced into "contracts" at the point of a gun. And if they deserve not to be coerced into contracts, then they deserve not to be ruled, more generally, without their consent. If the very logic of a contract requires, in all places and cultures, that contracts be voluntary, why should it be so hard to grasp, by the same reasoning, that the notion of legitimate government requires, in all places and cultures, a government of "consent"? If consent is manifested in the process of elections, the same reasoning would establish why those elections must in turn be *free* elections, in which citizens are insulated as much as possible from the influence of coercion.

All of these considerations, then, arise as implications from first principles. The points they establish are hardly trivial, even though they are so taken for granted in our lives that we are hardly aware of them any more as propositions with moral significance. Just how many of these propositions we have, we cannot say with confidence, because their discovery may depend on our imagination, and our imagination may be inspired by cases unique to the times. But the core of such propositions remains the same: these principles will all derive ultimately from the idea of morals itself and from the notion of a "rational being" with a capacity for moral judgment. Since the propositions that emerge here are drawn from the same core of necessary truths, they cannot be in conflict with one another. Nor can they really be placed in a hierarchical order, because they are all drawn, as implications, from the same source.[2] It may not make much of a difference, then, as to the order in which we unfold this series of propositions, but some steps might follow more clearly when others have preceded them. And so we may take stock of some of the first principles we have encountered, and we may arrange them provisionally in the following order, beginning with the logic of morals itself:

1. By "moral" and "immoral" we refer to the things that are universally good or bad, right or wrong, justified or unjustified. Because they are universal, the propositions that express moral understandings apply to other people as well as ourselves. And when we invoke this language of morals, we mean, as Thomas Reid says, that "there are some things in human conduct, that merit approbation and praise, others that merit blame and punishment."[3]

[2] Aquinas expressed the same sense of the matter in his discussion of "natural law," or the law that arises from the nature of human beings as creatures possessed of "reason": "Apparently natural law does not contain several precepts, but only one. . . . Were there serveral precepts of natural law it would follow that there were several natural laws. . . . [N]atural law is a corollary to human nature, which is one because man is a single whole and manifold because he has many parts. Either there is one precept of the law of nature on account of the first or there are many precepts on account of the second. . . . In addition, it has been said that law is from reason. For all humanity this is one and the same. Therefore there is but one single precept of natural law." *Summa Theologiae*, Ia2ae, 94, 2.

[3] Reid, *supra*, note 1. I should point out that even after we have set forth the "logic of morals" and the properties of moral propositions, someone may still ask what we mean by "good," "bad," "justified," "unjustified"? Here we have to understand that we are in the presence of what might be called "primary" concepts, which have to be grasped on their own, for the obvious meaning they hold in our language, and we will discover that other definitions are built upon them. And so, for example, if I look up the word "pain" in the dictionary, I learn that it means "suffering." If I look up "suffering," I discover that it means "to feel pain." We understand notions such as "pain" or distress in contradistinction to "pleasure" or happiness, much as we understand "up" by coupling it with "down," and "good" by recognizing its opposite, "bad." If we look up the meaning of "good" in its moral definition, we learn that it refers to

We recognize, at the core of the logic of morals, that we are moving beyond statements of merely personal preference or subjective taste. We speak in a universal voice about the things that are right and wrong for all people who are similarly situated. We imply that the standards of moral judgment are not inscrutable or idiosyncratic, but that they are knowable "intersubjectively"; they are accessible, in principle, to others as well as ourselves. And because moral propositions speak about the things that are universally right or wrong, they entail commitments or obligations. Hence:

2. When we say that something is morally right or wrong, we mean that it is *universally* right or wrong—that *everyone* is obliged to do what is right and refrain from what is wrong (presuming that it is within his means to do one or the other). Therefore, as Lincoln said, there cannot be "a right to do a wrong."

(The logic here may be put in another way by saying that what is morally right must be regarded as higher than—or superior to—what is wrong. From this proposition a string of corollaries may follow. For example: the understanding of goodness or justice must be preferable to an ignorance of moral things; a life governed by an understanding of the principles of morals must be better than a life led in moral ignorance or with an indifference to questions of right and wrong.)

It was this "first principle" of morals which defined the fallacy that Lincoln exposed in Stephen Douglas's argument: it was incoherent to say, at the same time, that slavery was "wrong," but that the separate territories should be left free to decide whether they would vote slavery up or down. This is the "first principle" that expresses the logical connection between morals and law. Once we establish that "X is wrong," the logical implication is to remove X from the domain of personal taste or private choice. We may forbid X, then, for everyone, with the force of law.

As we shall see, many of the participants in the current debate over

---

what is "justified" or "virtuous" or "right." If we look up virtuous, it refers to what is "good" or "right"—and on it goes. The exercise does not prove that definitions are circular; nor does it prove that "the good" is indefinable. It merely means, I suggest, that we are in the presence of primary terms, which are built into the logic of our language and "the constitution of our natures." At some point, all definitions must find their origin in words that cannot themselves be defined. Otherwise, how could we know the words used in the *first* definition? We must acknowledge certain terms which are needed in building the understanding of other words and concepts; and the words associated with morals—good and bad, right and wrong, just and unjust—are among those irreducible terms.

abortion are apparently unaware of this "first principle," which was made explicit more than a hundred years ago in our politics by our most distinguished public man. Lincoln had no training in the classics or in medieval philosophy; but what he expressed here, out of his native understanding, was the proposition that Aquinas had set down, six hundred years earlier, as nothing less than "the first principle for the practical reason" (*primum principium in ratione practica*): "that good is to be sought and done, evil to be avoided" (*bonum est faciendum et prosequendum, et malum vitandum*). To put it back in our own terms, we cannot recognize certain acts as "right" or "wrong" and continue to treat them logically as matters of taste or indifference; to recognize the logic of right and wrong is to recognize a logic that obliges us to do what is right and resist what is wrong. Aquinas regarded that proposition as the first to be derived from the logic of morals, and he saw it, in turn, as the source from which all other imperatives of practical reason are to be drawn. Several hundred years later, in the middle of the eighteenth century, Blackstone would seek to explain "the law of nations," and he found the beginning of that law in "this principle, that different nations ought in time of peace to do one another all the good they can; and, in time of war, as little harm as possible, without prejudice to their own real interests." And from what source was this first principle of international law drawn? Not strictly from the agreement of nations, but from "the law of nature and reason."[4] Exactly who had first stated this principle did not matter; what remained was the conviction that it arose as a necessary implication from "reason" itself. But what deserved to be made more explicit, in the tradition of moral reflection, was that this imperative did not merely arise from reason, but from the "logic of morals."[5]

[4] William Blackstone, *Commentaries on the Laws of England* [1769] bk. 4, ch. 5. I use here the edition of the University of Chicago Press (1979), pp. 66-67.

[5] In a curious turn of reasoning, Philippa Foot has sought to weave an argument for moral relativism through the use of Aquinas's first principle. She has offered this paradox: by the first principle of practical reasoning, even a man who wills an evil project would be obliged to act upon his notion of a good, for if he did not, he would be refusing to respect the logic that attaches to the notion of what is morally good or "right." Foot would seek to coax us, then, into a relativistic posture of conceding something morally defensible even in the acts of a wicked man. I offer no commentary here on the merits of this argument; I would merely point out what is deeply curious in an argument for relativism that depends, at any point, on "the first principle for practical reason," which Aquinas regarded as true of necessity, true in itself, quite beyond demonstration—a proposition, in short, that has nothing "relativistic" about it. See Foot, "Moral Relativism," in Jack W. Meiland and Michael Krausz (eds.), *Relativism* (South Bend, Indiana: University of Notre Dame Press, 1982), pp. 152-66, at 158-60. For Aquinas see *supra*, note 2.

As we saw earlier, it was that "logic of morals" which furnished the ground for Mill's argument on utilitarianism and for Plato's treatment of the equality of women. Both depended on the understanding that human faculties and distinctly human pleasures were higher than the brute force and appetite of animals. The ascendance of what was human depended on the higher standing of the capacity for morals, which human beings alone possessed. But the higher standing of that capacity for morals derives from the logic of morals itself. It derives, that is, only from the understanding which establishes that knowledge of what is good must be higher than any other kind of knowledge. That knowledge is higher than technical knowledge, because technical knowledge may be applied to evil ends if it is not guided ultimately by an understanding of the things that are right and wrong. The knowledge of driving a car may be useful, but whether it is good or bad depends on the ends to which it is directed—whether it is used, say, to drive a getaway car or to drive children to school. What must be higher than the knowledge of driving is the knowledge which tells us whether we are using our technical skills in the service of justified or unjustified ends. That knowledge of the goodness or badness of our ends must be regarded, finally, as the most sovereign among the kinds of knowledge we possess.

The same logic of morals ultimately explains also what is fundamentally mistaken in arguments to the effect that "there is something higher than morals," or "there is something higher than principle." Whether or not we use the label "morals," we are speaking of moral judgments whenever we speak about the things that *ought* to be regarded as "higher" or "better" than others. Anyone who would argue, say, that "tolerance" should be regarded as a "virtue" higher than "goodness" or "justice" would have to explain why tolerance ought to be regarded as *good*, and why he is *justified* in giving it an ascendant place. Without seeming to speak in the language of morals, he would nevertheless be articulating a moral judgment; and as he sought to explain the grounds on which that judgment would be justified, he would be articulating nothing less than a *principle*, which would govern all similar cases. And so the man who insists that "there is something higher than principle" ends up articulating a principle, and what is put in the place of "principle" turns out to be . . . but another principle.

Somewhat later, we will see at work an additional corollary of this first principle, when we consider the "obligation to rescue." That obligation finds its source in this first law of practical reason because the logic of the principle tells us, as Kant once put it very simply, that we are obliged to do good where we can.[6] That understanding may deserve a separate statement, for it is connected also to the notion of "proportionality," which everyone grasps instantly as a requirement that is built into the logic of morals:

> 3. Since we are obliged, by the logic of morals, to do what is good and refrain from what is bad, we are obliged, where we can, to do more good rather than less, and to do less harm rather than more.

If a person is faced with an unjustified assault on his life, it seems to be widely understood that he may be justified in using lethal force against his assailant. But when an assault is far less than lethal, we would not think him justified in using lethal force. We know that it is justified to resist an unjustified act, but we easily recognize that it would be bizarre to respond with lethal force when someone keeps books overdue from the library, or when he commits the offense of jumping ahead in the queue at the movies. I once compiled a list for my students of some of the more notable excuses offered at murder trials in Chicago, and in one case, when the question was put, "Why did you kill him?" the reply was: "Because he ate the last piece of pizza." In another case, this reply was offered: "Because he wouldn't turn down his stereo." These "excuses" never failed to elicit laughter, and the laughter marked a natural recognition that such violent responses were vastly out of proportion to the original offenses. We generally assume that force should be modulated, that penalties should bear some proportion to the crime. This understanding even finds a reflection in the U.S. Constitution, in the provision of the Eighth Amendment which bars "cruel and unusual punishment."

What is important to recognize is that this commitment to punishment in proportion to the offense does not arise simply from prudence; nor does it reflect a vague, inexplicable sentiment which marks the evolution of our "humane" qualities as a society. This commitment, we ought to be clear, arises from an understanding that is immanent in the logic of morals. In another one of its variants, it would tell the person who is faced with the choice of saving one innocent person or thirty that it may be better for him to save the thirty. That does not spare him the task of considering whether the "one" person happens to be a doctor, who could eventually help him save twice thirty, or a statesman whose presence might be needed to save hundreds of thou-

---

[6] Immanuel Kant, *Groundwork of the Metaphysics of Morals* [1785], trans. H.J. Paton (New York: Harper & Row, 1964), p. 66; p. 398 of the RPA ed.

sands. Nor does it oblige him to save a gang of thirty killers in preference to one innocent person. It would still be necessary for him to know that he is making a choice between victims who are equally "innocent." But where there are no moral reasons for preferring one set of victims to the other, or where the rescuer cannot establish anything about the moral claims of the potential victims, he would be warranted in seeking to do more good and avert more harm. In other words, we can understand and apply this principle without persuading ourselves of the crude notion that moral judgments are arrived at by making calculations of consequences in a mechanistic way. And as we have seen, the justifications of any act cannot hinge entirely on an estimate of its consequences, because the consequences are never all in. We may not know whether the noble act will encourage other noble acts, or whether the gross national product will rise as a consequence of one person acting nobly, now. What we come to consider is whether there are grounds on which to say that the noble act is intrinsically good, good in itself, quite apart from its consequences. And so, we come to recognize that

4. Moral propositions, in the strictest sense, are *categorical* in nature, rather than hypothetical or contingent. They speak of the things that are right or wrong, good or bad, under all contingencies, at all times and places. Moral propositions have this force because they are drawn as implications from the logic of morals itself. They ultimately rest, then, on the necessary truth which affirms the existence of morals; and as Thomas Reid reminds us, "whatever can, by just reasoning, be inferred from a principle that is necessary, must be a necessary truth." Whether an act is judged good, bad, or morally indifferent depends on whether the maxim underlying the act bears a logical connection to the idea of morals. Without that connection, an act may produce pleasure or success, but it cannot be regarded as "good" or "justified." For that reason it becomes incoherent to speak of doing a categorical wrong for the sake of a "higher good." The grounds on which we can judge the results of any act to be "good" would also establish the grounds on which we can recognize the act itself to be wrong. Therefore it must be said, simply as a logical matter, that the judgment of any act as categorically right or wrong must be unaffected by the ancillary consequences produced by the act.

We were alerted long ago to the distinction, grounded in common sense, between things whose goodness or badness hinges entirely on their effects—things which are good or bad only as a means to other ends—and things that are good or bad in themselves. As we have seen, we cannot conceive of a chain of merely contingent goods, one leading to another. That chain must find a terminus somewhere, in the understanding of things that are good in themselves, or else the whole chain is rendered meaningless. Without this logic of things that are categorically right or wrong, we would not be able to explain, say, why slavery should still be regarded as wrong even if it had the effect of making the slaves healthier, more literate, and happier. It would explain also why genocide would not become harmless or inoffensive if it were practiced in moderation; for the wrongness of certain acts must indeed be understood as independent of matters of degree and circumstance.

When we draw our standards of moral judgment from the logic of morals itself, we recognize, in the first instance, that the existence of morals must imply the existence of moral agents—beings who are free to choose one course of action rather than another, and who may therefore be led to consider the standards that ought to govern their choices. From this notion of a moral agent, or a "rational being," many other implications may be drawn, and so it probably deserves a separate elaboration:

> 5. The notion of morals would be meaningless—and the language of morals would exist in vain—unless it presupposed creatures whose acts were not *determined* entirely by natural laws, but who were sufficiently free or autonomous to choose between alternative courses of action. It makes no sense to condemn people, after all, for acts they were powerless to affect (e.g., falling after being thrown out a window). The existence of freedom creates the possibility of choice, but animals may be free also without being subject to moral judgment. Moral judgment becomes apt only when there are also creatures with the capacity for reason—creatures who can apprehend, with their reason, the justifications for acting one way rather than another.

As we have seen, the case against racial discrimination flows from this understanding. Racial discrimination, like many other forms of discrimination, implies a theory of "determinism": in this case, that *race* essentially determines the moral acts and the character of individuals. The same logic is at work in other kinds of discrimination, when it is thought that we can make relevant inferences about the character of people if we merely know some nonmoral attributes that connect them with a group. And so, people who merely fall into groups defined by age (say, those "under 18" or "ages 19 to 25") may be

167

denied a license to drive automobiles, or they may be required to pay higher rates of insurance, even though they are as careful and competent drivers as people who fall into other age brackets defined by age. The same assumptions of "group determinism"—the same tendency to assume that membership in the group determines conduct or character—can be found in many discriminations based on ethnicity, class, or sex.

Any understanding which is rooted, in this way, in premises of "determinism," is incompatible, then, with the idea of morals and with the understanding of a "rational being," who has the freedom or autonomy to disengage himself from a group and reach his own judgments of right and wrong. Any acts that are grounded in premises of determinism are therefore wrong as a matter of necessity. And if it is true, as Lincoln said, that we cannot have a right to do wrong, it may be said, correlatively, that we can claim, at the very least, a "right not to be wronged"—a right not to be treated unjustly. A right not to be wronged is tantamount to a right not to be treated on the basis of maxims that are inconsistent with the logic of morals and with the nature of a being who has the capacity to reason over moral things. As we have seen, our right not to be bound to a contract we did not freely accept, or our right not to be ruled without our consent, are rights that flow in this way out of the very nature of a "rational being," who has the capacity to give and understand reasons. At the same time, we are justified in holding people responsible for their own acts only when we are dealing with moral agents, who are indeed free to choose one course of action over another, and who can understand the reasons that govern their choices.

ONCE WE ARE clear that moral propositions of a categorical nature can be drawn only from the idea of morals or from the notion of a rational being, we are in a position to draw perhaps the most serviceable of our first principles, which arose in the preceding chapter:

6. No moral conclusion can be entailed merely by facts or by factual propositions of a nonmoral nature. Moral propositions are grounded ultimately in facts or truths, but they can be derived only from the necessary truth which affirms the existence of morals or explains its essential logic.

The failure to recognize this implication of morals is probably responsible for the failure to see through most of the fallacies that have masqueraded over the years as theories of morals. I had occasion earlier to mention the tendency to reduce the understanding of morals to nonmoral measures, such as "happiness," pleasure, prosperity, or even "harmony" and civic "cohesion." The same kind of fallacy is engaged in the tendency to attach moral justification to mere physical or military power, as though the power was the source of its own justification. We find here the ancient argument that justice reduces to the rule of the strong, that success in any contest at arms proves the wisdom or rightness of the cause. (The obverse statement of the same fallacy has been served to us recently in heavy doses in relation to the war in Vietnam: viz., that a *loss* in a contest at arms had to prove the *wrongness* of the cause.)

The impulse to reduce moral propositions to nonmoral measures arises quite often out of the mistaken conviction that morals can be rendered in this way more objective and less subject to dispute. That impulse merely distracts us, however, from the kind of deliberation that would connect the maxims of our acts to a distinctively *moral* ground of judgment. But so long as people are diverted from addressing moral questions with a distinctly moral reflection, we should not be surprised to see many people distracted by such arresting formulas as "the greatest happiness of the greatest number" or "the conditions that enlarge the wealth, the peace, and the harmony" of the nation. All of these formulas may be satisfied by the peaceful acceptance of a regime of the most thoroughgoing evil, and it may take special drills to keep reminding ourselves that all of these qualities or conditions, taken by themselves, have no moral significance whatsoever. We will have the occasion to notice, when we consider the problem of conscientious objection, that another one of those spurious moral tests, as false as it is popular, is the test of "sincerity." This can be a vexing matter, and I will try to treat it with its proper complication and delicacy. But it is important to recognize that, when we consider the question in the most rigorous light, "sincerity" cannot stand for a moment as a plausible substitute for moral justification. Few doubt that Hitler was sincere or that the cadres of the Ku Klux Klan are motivated by the highest degrees of earnestness. But when we confront these sincere people we usually have no trouble in recognizing that their sincerity cannot possibly supply a justification that is otherwise wanting in their acts.

Finally, I would add one further statement to this provisional list of first principles:

> 7. It is precisely because of the *universal* quality of moral propositions that they must be indifferent to the question of who the agent is who vindicates rights and wrongs.

Once again, the proposition is simple, but it displaces an enormous mass, it might be said, in our body of moral and legal understandings. For one thing, it explains and justifies, more powerfully than anything else, the common law "rule of rescue." If a man were set upon by a mob that sought, without justification, to take his life through a lynching, we could concede to him the right to use lethal force in defending himself from this unjustified assault. When we say that it would be justified for him to resist, we move once more into the universal terms of a principled argument. The man does not draw his justification for resisting from the fact that he is Harry Jones, a salesman passing through town, and that it is *his* body which is under attack. Rather, his justification is drawn from the fact that he is innocent of any crime; that he is being set upon unjustly; and that, in resisting an injury, he is warranted in inflicting on his assailants injuries commensurate with the injuries they would inflict upon him. But what if Jones is overwhelmed by the mob and is too weak to vindicate his own rights? The understanding in the law has been that a third party may intervene for the sake of saving Jones, or vindicating Jones's rights, and the intervener would be warranted in using the same level of force that Jones himself would be justified in using if he were in a position to defend his own rights. This third party might not himself be the object of an attack, and so it may not be the case that his own "self-defense" would be engaged. This recognition may finally permit us to see that the notion of "self-defense" has misled us in the past in explaining how violence may be justified, even on the part of the original victim of the assault. That justification, to repeat, cannot be drawn merely from the fact that one's own "self" is being threatened. That reason could not justify the violence that may be used by the disinterested third party, whose "self" is not being threatened in any way. The justification for the use of force must be drawn from the franchise that *anyone* could claim, morally, to vindicate a wrong. If it is wrong to assault Jones, it is wrong for *anyone* to carry out that assault, and by the same logic of a moral principle *it would be right for anyone* to help Jones in resisting the assault.

We shall have occasion later to consider the argument, drawn from first principles, that would justify people in using lethal force not merely to preserve their lives, but to preserve the moral terms of principle on which human beings deserve to live. That understanding would be necessary in justifying the resistance to a tyrannical government, and the same principle would explain why the runaway slave would have been justified in using lethal force for the sake of resisting his return to slavery. As a child of the American Revolution, Lincoln had understood that argument. And yet, if we add to that understanding the principle of moral agency we have set forth here, we discover a serious challenge to the argument Lincoln made against the abolitionists of his own day, the men who were willing to use violence outside the law for the sake of freeing slaves. As these men acted out their disrespect for law, Lincoln saw them as striking at those premises of natural equality and lawfulness that are bound up with the moral case against slavery. But Lincoln's formidable argument may begin to unpeel once the principle of moral agency is brought into play. Would the runaway slaves have been justified themselves in using deadly force in order to resist the slave catchers who were carrying out the Fugitive Slave Act? If they *would* have been justified, and if they could not themselves have matched the forces arrayed against them, could their rights not have been vindicated, properly, by anyone who might act on their behalf? Might the abolitionists have been justified, then, in using, as third parties, the force that the victims themselves would have been warranted in using had they been in a position to defend their own rights?

More recently we have seen an intriguing—and potentially explosive—application of this principle in the matter of abortion. In one case in Virginia, a local judge dismissed the charges against a group of people who broke into an abortion clinic for the sake of disrupting the business of the clinic and preventing the abortions that would have been carried out that day. The defendants argued that if the fetuses were understood to be human, abortions would be seen more clearly as operations directed toward the taking of innocent human life. And if the fetuses were not in a position to defend themselves, either against the mothers who ordered the abortions or the physicians who were carrying them out, then any third party would be justified in intervening to vindicate the rights of the victims. The judge upheld this argument by finding in it an expression of the common law "rule of rescue." If the decision of the judge had been appealed to the Supreme Court, the Court would have been forced to consider the root question of whether the human standing of the fetus could really be denied. But the operators of the clinic decided to move their facility to another town, outside the jurisdiction of this judge, rather than force a decisive test in the courts on appeal.

I would point out here, lastly, that there is a challenge to the root doctrines of traditional liberalism in the simple principle that the vindication of rights and wrongs is indifferent to the identity of the agent. Traditional liberalism has marked off the limits of the law in the harms that one person inflicts on another. It has sought to insulate from the

171

reach of the law the harms which a person inflicts upon himself, or which "consenting adults" inflict on one another. This traditional posture of liberalism depends on a critical act of forgetting, and what is forgotten is the strict meaning of a principle; for once we are clear on the universal import of a *wrong*, it is a matter of utter irrelevance if the wrong is inflicted by a person on himself. If it is wrong, for example, for *anyone* to make slaves of a human being, then "anyone" encompasses the slave himself, and the principle must forbid a person from contracting himself into slavery. Hence the logic of "inalienable" rights—rights we are incompetent to waive, or "alienate." What we must recognize, however, is that any principle becomes the foundation of inalienable rights. To the extent that anything stands in the class of a wrong, it stands there only by virtue of a principle, and the validity of that principle is not suspended because a person becomes willing to inflict that wrong on himself.

It soon becomes apparent, of course, that this understanding would have to affect the practice of suicide. It may not strictly rule out all suicide, any more than the principles of morals would rule out all killings. But in the same way that it is possible to judge some acts of killing to be unjustified, it is possible to employ the same principles in weighing the justifications that may be offered for the destruction of oneself. And so if we tell Cavendish, a homocidal professor of English, that it would be wrong for him to kill people merely because they persistently, incorrigibly, split their infinitives, the same principle would have to restrain Cavendish himself. If Cavendish suddenly found himself lapsing, incorrigibly, into the splitting of infinitives, he would not have a justification for taking his own life. And since a moral principle is indifferent to the matter of agency, we could not permit Cavendish to make use of proxies, in an extension of his will, if he himself were incapable of carrying out his intentions. If Cavendish were attached to an artificial respirator necessary to preserve his life, he might be inclined to ask his physician or his family to have the equipment removed because he cannot live any longer a "life worth living" (i.e., a life free of the blight of split infinitives). But we could not honor such a request by his family or physician, as the guardians of his interests, any more than we could honor a request by Cavendish to assist him in a suicide as his response to the split infinitive.

As I HAVE suggested, the list of first principles put forth here may easily be augmented. As we confront novel cases, we may be led to discover implications we had not noticed before in the logic of morals; and of course I may have overlooked, in this provisional list, corollaries that are evident right now to someone else. Since all of these first principles derive from the same core, they are all consistent with one another, and as I have said, the order in which they are arranged should not make much difference. But someone may find a more artful way of stating these propositions or a more inspired way of arranging them, one which would reveal more fully the directions in which they may yet be unfolded. Still, however one states them, the main items in the list would cover the same ground and bear the same logic as the propositions I have set down here.

I should caution again that these propositions are not meant to provide an exhaustive code that could govern all events in our lives. It is one of the attributes of a genuine discipline of morals that it makes the requirements of a moral principle very stringent, and it warns us against invoking the language of morals all too casually to cover subjects that do not really lend themselves to moral judgment. Whether we spend our evenings listening to Beethoven or watching the Orioles, whether we make our living by practicing dentistry or washing windows, none of these choices will pivot on a moral principle. Fortunately, large domains of our lives may be filled out with choices of this kind, which do not happen to rest on categorical propositions. But, of course, we are never liberated from the responsibility to consider whether the choices we are making are indeed choices among *legitimate* things: that our entertainments do not include Russian roulette or lynching, along with Beethoven and baseball, and that our ways of making a living do not include the recruitment of children for pornography, as well as the care of teeth or the washing of windows. The principles of morals do not cover everything, but they do mark off the boundaries between the legitimate and the illegitimate, and they do help make clear to us the breadth of that terrain in which we are in fact free to choose among many legitimate things. At the same time, they help to avert the injustice that is committed when we legislate too casually and restrict, without compelling justification, the freedom of individuals to make their own choices and cultivate their own preferences.

But if the principles of moral judgment do not cover everything, and if the first principles I have set down here do not exhaust the range of moral considerations, I think we will discover that these first principles manage to prove decisive in a surprisingly large amount of cases. Many cases may actually turn on considerations as elementary or fundamental as the propositions contained in my small inventory. In some instances these first principles serve to counter many clichés or fallacies that may distract our judgment; and as they clear away what is spurious, they may allow us to see more plainly the moral considerations that ought to govern our judgments. In other instances, they may sweep away a deceptively simple formula for deciding a moral question, and they may then compel us to discover just how complicated, just how resistant to facile solutions, the case truly is.

My design now is to move through a connected series of cases in order to show how these principles come into play and bear on the judgment of substantive questions. We may discover, along the way, some further implications of these principles, and we may subject the principles themselves to a severe test. These principles may be tested at the outset, in the sternest way, by considering the grounds on which people may be obliged to commit themselves on matters of life and death. We shall consider, as the beginning case, the problem of "conscientious objection" and the question of whether people may justly be obliged, through the law, to take the lives of others and to risk their own.

PART TWO
CASES AND APPLICATIONS

IX

ON THE GROUNDS FOR EXEMPTION FROM THE LAW: IS CONSCIENTIOUS OBJECTION MORAL?

In December 1967, Guy Porter Gillette was ordered to report for induction into the armed forces of the United States. To respond to the notice and serve in the armed forces was to accept, at the time, the prospect of serving in the war in Vietnam, and it was Gillette's conviction that the American involvement in Vietnam was unconstitutional, illegal, and immoral. Gillette did not challenge the notion that he could be called on, properly, to defend his country when it was under attack. He professed a willingness, also, to take up arms against a country that had not attacked the United States if there were a finding by the United Nations that aggression had been committed and that the peace of the world had been endangered. Gillette did not claim an aversion to war in general, or at least he did not deny that it would indeed be justified on certain occasions for nations to go to war. What he argued, rather, was that *this particular war*, the war in Vietnam, was not in fact justified as a military venture for the United States.

That judgment, of course, was at odds with the judgment reached by the president and the Congress; and while Gillette held to his own assessment of the war, he could not divine any grounds that would oblige him to obey his draft notice and report for induction. Consequently, he was prosecuted by the government. The prospect of testing his obligations in a legal forum furnished him with the chance to address, in a careful way, the grounds on which he could be exempted, justly, from obligations that were being enforced through the law on many other young men as well as himself.

One of the questions that should have been posed, at the threshold of the case, was whether Gillette would have claimed an exemption from the law (1) for himself alone, (2) for all young men currently subject to the draft, or (3) for only those young men who shared his views on the war in Vietnam. It is not clear from the record that this question, at the threshold of the case, was ever considered by Gillette and his advisers in a demanding way. The answer to the question was provided, implicitly, by the way in which the argument for Gillette was framed. Gillette chose, in effect, to seek an exemption for himself

177

alone, and if his appeal succeeded, he would have established, at most, an exemption for anyone else who came into a court and claimed to share his views on the war. This character of Gillette's appeal was shaped by the fact that he decided to cast his argument as a special variant on "conscientious objection," and that decision, as we shall see, mattered profoundly for the properties—and the special frailties—of the argument he was making.

By his own admission, Gillette did not bear convictions, of a religious or philosophic nature, which moved him to reject the justification for all wars. He "objected" to the particular war fought in Vietnam by the United States, and he complained that the government discriminated, without warrant, between two kinds of "conscientious" objectors: the government was willing to grant an exemption from military service to the objector who cited religious tenets and rejected participation in all wars; but it would not honor with the same exemption people like himself, who objected to certain wars on grounds that were also, arguably, "conscientious." Under the Selective Service Act of 1967 the grounds of exemption for "conscientious objection" were expressed in this way:

> Nothing contained in this title shall be construed to require any person to be subject to combatant training and service in the armed forces of the United States who, *by reason of religious training and belief, is conscientiously opposed to participation in war in any form.* As used in this subsection, the term "religious training and belief" does not include essentially political, sociological, or philosophical views, or a merely personal moral code [*sic*].[1]

Gillette's objections to the war in Vietnam did not fit the definition of religious conviction that was set forth in the statute. Gillette professed to found his judgment on what he described as a "humanist approach to religion." He did not rely, that is, on doctrines cultivated in schools of theology or associated with organized churches. What he did rely on, precisely, was never made clear, because the trial court did not permit Gillette to set forth the reasons that constituted, in his judgment, a "humanistic" ground of "religious" objection. This disposition of the court did not flow from any reluctance to consider novel forms of "religious" conviction. By statute and judicial construction, the law had long since moved away from the practice of

---

[1] Quoted in *United States v. Gillette*, 420 F. 2d 298, at 299, n. 1 (1970). Emphasis added.

178

tying religious exemptions to membership in particular sects. For that matter, the law no longer even required any particular views about the nature of God or a "Supreme Being" as part of a "religious" persuasion. Whether Gillette's views were sufficiently "religious," within the standards of the law, the court did not have to determine, for whether they were religious or not, the statute clearly provided exemptions only for those people whose religious beliefs commanded an opposition to "participation in war in any form." It was Gillette's view, apparently, that the law created, in this way, two classes of religious belief and honored only one. For the courts, on the other hand, the refusal to participate in *any* war in *any* way seemed to be the decisive mark of "conscientious scruples." Religious beliefs were not always accepted as grounds of exemption from the law; and in the judgment of the court, religious beliefs would not be allowed as a ground of exemption from the draft unless they met the criteria of "conscientiousness," or scrupulosity, on the question of war.[2]

This reasoning proved to be decisive, also, when the case was appealed to the Supreme Court, and in this respect it must be said that the federal courts, at all levels, permitted their judgment to rest upon a mistake. The courts converted "religious belief" into "conscientious scruple"—which is to say, they confounded matters of private, religious belief with the requirements of a "principled" argument, and then went on to show that they were seriously misinformed about the properties of a principled argument. That their judgment was founded ultimately in error did not, however, make Gillette's position any more defensible. It is ironic, though, that the main defects in principle in Gillette's argument would have been far easier to see if the courts had been able to recognize what was fundamentally spurious about the ground on which they were content, by and large, to reject his claim.

IN UPHOLDING Gillette's conviction, the Supreme Court sustained the argument that "conscientious objection" could not properly encompass the "selective" objection to particular wars. Justice Thurgood Marshall wrote for the majority that the distinction drawn in the statute did indeed mark off the difference between "those whose dissent has some conscientious basis [and] those who simply dissent."[3] In the understanding, apparently, of Marshall and his colleagues, a "conscientious" and principled objection to war had to reject, in a

---

[2] *Ibid.*, at 299-300. The phrase "conscientious scruples" appears in Mr. Justice Marshall's opinion for the majority in *Gillette* v. *United States*, 401 U.S. 437, at 443 (1971).
[3] *Gillette* v. *United States*, 401 U.S. 437, at 457.

categorical fashion, the fighting of *all* wars, under *all* circumstances, with no consideration of the ends or justifications that might separate one war from another. That was, as we have seen, a faulty understanding, and as Marshall sought to elaborate the reasoning behind his position, he helped to make explicit, at the same time, what was problematic in his understanding.

Marshall observed, quite accurately, that disputes over particular wars would open draft boards and courts to a vastly larger number of considerations that might be brought forth to show why any particular war was justified or unjustified. It might have been an overstatement on the part of Marshall to say that "a virtually limitless variety of beliefs are subsumable under the rubric 'objection to particular war' ";[4] but there was no doubt that the number was at least as large as the number of reasons that might be brought forth as justifications for the use of arms. Marshall's fear was that once the gates were thrown open in this way, the grounds of objection could then encompass "factors that might go into conscientious dissent"— i.e., considerations that have little to do with religious belief. They might embrace judgments about the political ends of a war or even assessments of military strategy. It was entirely possible, as Marshall also noted, that an exemption "might be based on some feature of a current conflict that most would regard as incidental, or might be predicated on a view of the facts that most would regard as mistaken."[5] An objector might conclude that the Allied bombing of Dresden in the Second World War was so brutal and unnecessary that it collapsed the difference that separated the Allies from the Nazis. Another objector, with an active imagination, might believe that the war was being controlled by a Zionist conspiracy, and on that basis he might resist being drafted into "a war for the Jews."

Of course, no government clothed with the authority of law could be obliged to honor just any objection that might be offered in this vein, without judging its plausibility. But this is quite different from saying that arguments over military operations may never touch on questions that are bound up with the justification of a war. It was no doubt true, as Marshall said, that judgments made about particular wars at particular times must be by "nature changeable and subject to nullification by changing events."[6] And yet, what is changeable here are the circumstances in which principles have to be applied to cases.

[4] *Ibid.*, 455.
[5] *Ibid.*, 456-57.
[6] *Ibid.*, 456.

There would be nothing contingent or changeable, however, in the *principles* of judgment themselves. It was hardly warranted, then, to draw the conclusion, reached by Marshall, that we cannot speak seriously about the justification for particular wars without falling back upon standards that are "ultimately subjective."[7]

To recall an example that arose earlier, we may receive a variety of answers in response to the question "Why did you hit him?" The answers might include "To get his wallet" or "To keep him from jumping out the window." But the fact that the responses may differ in any case cannot itself establish that there is anything "subjective" about the reasons offered, or that it is impossible for the rest of us to judge those reasons. We can take evidence in these cases; we can consider whether certain assaults are provoked or unprovoked; and we can test reasons or excuses by the canons of justification.

If Marshall were taken at his word, he would have to mean that there is no real possibility of moral judgment in particular cases—that we are strictly incapable of rendering judgments about the justification for *particular* assaults, for *particular* takings of property, for *particular* restrictions of personal freedom. But the life of morals consists precisely in the task of applying principles of moral judgment to the particular incidents that arise in our day-to-day lives. As we have seen, a categorical proposition derives from the logic of morals, and as it bears on any particular case it enjoins us not to do anything that is inconsistent with the notion of justification itself. And so the proper form of the categorical proposition here would not be "It is wrong, in all circumstances, to kill," but rather "It is wrong, in all circumstances, to kill *without justification*." We had occasion earlier to see why the proposition "It is wrong to kill" becomes virtually incoherent as a moral proposition: it invokes the language of morals; it suggests that we can make distinctions between acts that are justified or unjustified; but then it suggests that the language of justification suddenly ceases to apply as soon as we confront lethal assaults. At that moment, we are apparently asked to believe that we can make no distinction between those who would kill for sadistic and unwarranted reasons and those who would kill as the only means of resisting their own destruction at the hands of the wicked. The false categorical proposition exposes its own vacuity as a moral proposition by asking us finally to ignore the differences that separate assailants from victims, the guilty from the innocent. And no proposition can abstract from

[7] *Ibid.*

those kinds of differences while claiming, at the same time, to be a moral proposition.

The irony, then, is that Justice Marshall and his colleagues on the bench have accepted, as the only true form of a categorical proposition or genuine principle, a proposition that is simply invalid and incoherent as a categorical proposition. In a manner laden with paradoxes for a court of law—for an institution that seeks to establish principles of law in settling concrete cases—the judges presumed to settle this particular case against Gillette by holding that it is impossible to reach "conscientious" or principled judgments in particular cases.

THE JUDGMENT that was cast against Gillette depended, therefore, on premises that were untenable at their root. But that ultimate defect in the holding of the Court did nothing to establish the validity of Gillette's argument. In fact, if the judgment of the Court hinged on a certain ignorance about the properties of a "principled" argument, the same standards of scrutiny would have exposed even more serious defects in Gillette's argument. Gillette might have sought to counter the position of the government by showing that it was indeed possible to reason over the justification for particular wars, in the same way that it was possible to reason over the justification for particular assaults. He could have claimed that it was possible to articulate reasons X, Y, Z as the justification for any act, and that it was possible for those reasons to be understood or judged. They would be intelligible to others because they would depend on criteria and evidence that are not inscrutably private and subjective, but accessible to others as well as oneself. And on that ground, the reasons could ultimately be judged for their validity.

As we shall see, however, that is exactly the kind of argument Gillette was barred from making by the very nature of his position as a "conscientious objector." For if Gillette had decided to cast his argument in this form, he would have been indistinguishable from the litigant who might come into court to challenge the legality of the war or the authority of the government to commit him to military service. Of course, the conventions that have been established in our legal system have made the courts reluctant to interfere with the management of military operations in the field, or even to involve themselves with judgments about the justification for military actions. And yet, in principle, it is not inconceivable that challenges on these matters may be brought into court (e.g., on the grounds that a certain military venture is in violation of a treaty or—in more recent times—that the president has exceeded his authority under the War Powers Act).[8] For all we know, Gillette might have avoided the kind of argument that would have placed him in this position because he was advised that this form of challenge was not likely to prevail. But challenges of this kind *were* brought during the Vietnam war, which means that it was open to a litigant to consider whether this particular form of challenge was not in fact more faithful to the premises on which he claimed exemption from the law.

It is worth reminding ourselves, then, of what the differences in principle were between the different forms of arguing the case. If Gillette had challenged the legal justification for the war (and for conscription) his claims would have taken the form of a principled argument. That is, his claims would have depended in no way on the state of his own feelings or personal beliefs. His argument would have been directed wholly to the substantive grounds on which the war could have been said to be justified or unjustified. He would have presented reasons X, Y, and Z in making his case against the war, and it would have been the responsibility of the Court to judge the validity of those reasons. If the Court found those reasons valid, if it agreed that the war was not legally justified, then the consequence would have been to declare the war, as a project, unjustified; to order the government to stop prosecuting the war; and to stand ready to block the efforts of the government to draft anyone into the war. Gillette would have gained his exemption from military service—but by virtue of the fact that *everyone* would have been exempted, because the war itself would have been declared, in principle, wrong.

Yet, that was not the result which would have flowed from the claim made by Gillette as a conscientious objector. If the claim to exemption turned on the state of Gillette's *personal* beliefs, then the exemption would have been granted only to Gillette or, at most, to those who claimed to hold beliefs similar to Gillette's. (Of course, if Gillette's claim had been accepted by the Court, we could expect that many other people would have discovered that they held, after all, those selfsame beliefs. Still, we must be clear that the ground on which the exemption would be offered would not apply, in principle, to everyone.) The innovation suggested by Gillette in claims of conscientious

[8] Two members of the Surpreme Court indicated, during the Vietnam war, that they were prepared at least to hear arguments on the substantive question before they reached a judgment as to whether the problem ultimately lent itself to a judicial decision. See the remarks of Justice Douglas and Stewart in *Mora et al.* v. *McNamara*, 389 U.S. 934 (1967).

objection was that his own case would turn on the *reasons* he professed to hold in objecting to a particular war. But whether that claim to novelty was valid or spurious depended critically on the status of those reasons. Was the exemption to be granted because the reasons he offered were *substantively valid*, or were his reasons to be honored solely because *he held to them* "conscientiously"? If the first, then Gillette, as I have suggested, would not have distinguished himself in any way from the person who challenged the legal justification for the war.

But that cannot be the kind of argument Gillette was making, and the proof can probably be found in response to this problem: if Gillette were really offering a principled argument about the justification for the war, if he were setting forth reasons X, Y, and Z, was it his understanding also that those reasons could be examined and *judged* by the courts? If the courts came to the judgment that Gillette's reasons simply failed as reasons, that they were substantively invalid, would Gillette have been prepared to accept that judgment, not only as the judgment that settled the case, but as the *only* kind of judgment that could properly settle the case? If we assume that Gillette understood what he was doing when he decided to represent himself as a "conscientious objector," rather than as a litigant challenging the legality of the war, we must suppose that these arrangements could not have been acceptable to him. As a "conscientious objector" he would have been compelled to argue that the reasoning of the Court was at best interesting, but not ultimately authoritative. Regardless of what the Court thought about his reasons, he would likely have insisted that he "conscientiously" believed in those reasons nevertheless—that they were "valid" in his own mind, according to his own beliefs, even though the Court could not bring itself to respect those reasons.

But in that case, the differences between "general" and "selective" conscientious objection would essentially dissolve. The fact that the "selective" objector offers a set of reasons about a particular war represents a difference, finally, that is merely superficial and spurious. In the end, both selective and general conscientious objection come down to the same thing: they both involve a claim to be exempt from the obligations of the law, not on the strength of reasons that can be tested for their validity, but on the basis of personal feelings or beliefs that cannot, ultimately, be examined or judged. That claim, as stated in its root form, cannot possibly stand. And it fails not because it is inexpedient, not because it may undermine respect for law and generate adverse consequences, but because the principle it expresses is incompatible with the concept of morals itself. It stands in contradiction, therefore, of a necessary truth.

THE LOGIC behind this conclusion may come through more clearly if we consider for a moment the alternative ways of construing the claims of the conscientious objector. If the argument is really meant to turn on the "sincerity" of the objector, it would be hard to understand why a court could not employ devices such as truth serum or lie detector tests in order to establish veracity or "sincerity." It quickly becomes apparent that "sincerity" is not to be judged; it is to be accepted on its face if it is offered as part of a statement of personal faith or conscientious belief. All of this is another way of saying that claims to inner belief are simply not to be judged. But as we have already had occasion to see, "sincerity" is irrelevant, in point of principle, to the validity of any proposition. In this case, sincerity becomes relevant only if we are not asked to judge the validity of the reasons that are offered in objection to the war in Vietnam. That may stand as another indication of the fact that, for the conscientious objector, the reasons, strictly speaking, do not matter. What the courts are asked to honor is the avowal of belief itself.

It is often suggested that the conscientious objector is really posing a problem of prudence to the government and the military: a man who cannot make himself fight on the battlefield will waste the resources of the government in his training, and if he is placed in combat he may be a hazard to his fellow soldiers. But, of course, this argument states no moral ground for an exemption; it merely offers an empirical prediction: viz., that people who profess themselves to be conscientiously opposed to war will turn out, in fact, to be incapable of fighting. It does not take much experience, however, to recognize that this proposition falls far short of an apodictic truth. And if the argument is put forth as an empirical prediction, it would be quite proper for the government to insist, in turn, that it be tested as an empirical prediction. Here the argument would be open to the inventory of methods that has been accumulated under the arts of "operant conditioning." A young graduate student in sociology may not be able to imagine himself under the discipline of the military, much less engaged in combat. But if he were subjected to an intensive period of basic training; if he were drilled in the use of weapons and then placed in a combat situation, in which he had to fight to protect himself and his comrades, he might discover that he was not so incapable of pulling a trigger as he may have thought.

185

If the argument for conscientious objection comes down then simply to a prediction rather than an argument, it would be fair enough for the government to insist on having that prediction tested in each case. But beyond that, it would become apt for the government to ask just why the scruples of the objector would not lead him to focus his objections more precisely on service *in combat*. Why would it be necessary for him to reject the military altogether? He could serve in the military, after all, and he could support the armed forces in a mission of national service, even if he were not in combat. The answer, proffered quickly and often, is that the objection is precisely against supporting the war effort, and that *any* service in the military would support that effort. Service in an administrative role, or assignment in another theater, would merely free other people from those jobs and allow them to be shifted into combat. But if that is indeed the understanding which guides the objector, his withdrawal would have to advance quite beyond participation in the military. For he could serve the war effort by working as a civilian in production related to the war; or, even if he were working in production unrelated to the military, it is arguable that he would free up workers for activities related to the war. He would also help the government sustain the war by continuing to pay taxes and by adding to the productivity of the economy. To escape involvement, he would be driven finally to two choices: (1) he might emigrate (though even that may not end his support for the American economy), or (2) he might refuse to pay that portion of his taxes which goes to the support of the war.

It should occasion no surprise that many acts of opposition to war, which begin as arguments for "conscientious objection," eventually carry over into a demand for exemption from taxation. During the Civil War, for example, Lincoln's aid was sought for members of the Society of Friends of Ellwood Township, Illinois, who refused to join the army, and who made it difficult to raise other volunteers. As it was explained in a letter to Lincoln, "The township is unable to raise sufficient funds without the aid of the 'Friends' to obtain volunteers to fill their quota, and the 'Friends' are not only conscientiously opposed to bearing arms, but they are opposed to voluntarily furnishing money to pay others. . . ."[9] A connection has been made in the past, then, between the refusal to participate in a war and the refusal to support that war with money; and this connection is likely to be made in the future, simply because it is immanent in the logic of "consci-

---

[9] *The Collected Works of Abraham Lincoln*, ed. Roy P. Basler (New Brunswick: Rutgers University Press, 1953), vol. VIII, p. 290n.

entious objection." But when that connection is made, the argument for conscientious objection shows its resemblance to other demands that have been made over the years, in which people have sought to withhold that portion of their taxes which goes to the support of policies they find objectionable. Those policies have ranged from the welfare system to the support of the United Nations, but the concern in any case is to avoid being implicated, through the tax system, in policies that are regarded as morally abhorrent.

If these demands were acquiesced in, they would establish the relation between the citizen and the community on a radically different foundation. In the terms we set forth earlier from Aristotle, the citizen would have merely a *contractual* relation to the community. He would be obliged to support only those programs and policies to which he has consented in any case. As Aristotle understood, that arrangement would mark the end of a polity because it would mark the displacement of "law" by arrangements of contract or covenant. For in the strictest sense there could be no law any longer: there could be no such notion as a rule that is binding on people even when they disagree. What is implicit, after all, in this scheme of contractual relations, is that no one may be bound in cases in which he refuses to be bound. As we saw earlier, that understanding is incompatible with the notion of law because it is incompatible with the notion of morals itself. Law, we may recall, emerges from the logic of morals: it is necessary and proper to bind someone to a common rule only if there are, in fact, propositions that establish things which are *universally* right or wrong. If they are indeed valid and universal propositions about right or wrong, they will be valid even for people who fail to understand them, who find them disagreeable, or who simply refuse to honor them. That is not to say, of course, that the government can never be wrong. It is to say, rather, that no defensible ground of opposition to law can ever be based on the proposition that "no rule is valid or binding for any person unless that person accepts its validity." That proposition, in its literal significance, would simply be incompatible with the logic of morals; therefore, it cannot be reconciled with the very notion of "law."

WHEN THE ISSUE is finally put in that way, the grounds on which the "conscientious objection" is rejected will stand out with far more clarity. For it should be plain by now that the issue cannot hinge merely on fears or predictions about the consequences of allowing some people to have these exemptions. It is indeed possible that the granting of such exemptions will cause resentment among people who are not favored with them, and it may encourage other people to deny their obligation to respect laws they find uncongenial. But whether any system of exemptions will generate disrespect for law is a problematic matter, in the realm of prediction. An argument based on such predictions would present us merely with a *contingent* proposition rather than a statement of principle. What should be evident now, though, is that the case against conscientious objection would stand entirely on a principle. It would rest on showing that the maxim which underlies conscientious objection is quite literally inconsistent with the meaning or logic of morals.

We would discover, then, that there is a radical difference between "conscientious objection" in its recent meaning and the claims of "conscience" as they have been traditionally understood. In the classic case of Thomas More, the integrity of "conscience" simply meant that a person should not be forced to avow convictions he does not hold. More was willing to swear an oath recognizing the right of Parliament to establish the succession to the English throne on the children that Henry VIII would have with Anne Boleyn. More would not, however, swear to the Act of Succession so long as it declared Henry's previous marriage to have been invalid, and while it repudiated, in that way, the supremacy of the pope. As minister of state, More had shown no tolerance for sedition or disobedience even while he disapproved of the act of his sovereign. He was prepared, to the end, to respect the law, and he would not cast judgment on those who could swear, in good conscience, that Henry's first marriage had been invalid. But he was adamant in refusing to swear an oath that ran counter to convictions which were rooted in principle and firm in his conscience. His conscience could not be coerced, his judgments could not be misrepresented in public with his own endorsement; but he would never claim a "right" to be released from the obligations of law when the law came into conflict with his own judgments.[10]

It has been commonly said, of course, that "conscientious objection," in its more recent meaning, may be tolerable for us because it has not generated a mass disrespect for law and it has not made it impossible to put an army in the field. But that kind of argument, it should be plain, misses the point in principle. Whether the precedents for conscientious objection become contagious is largely a matter of happenstance. As we shall see in a moment, though, the effects of these precedents are starting to spread, as the doctrines fashioned by

[10] R.W. Chambers, *Thomas More* (London: Jonathan Cape, 1935), p. 396, and see also pp. 303-305.

the courts are applied to other areas. If the consequences of these principles have not yet broken the bonds of law that connect citizens to one another, it is not for want of anything sufficiently corrosive in these principles. Our good fortune here seems to result mainly from the moderation of the American people, coupled with a benign absence of awareness on the part of most people of what their privileges really are under the principles that have been established for conscientious objection.

The fact that other people do not rush forward to claim comparable exemptions for themselves can be taken, only through a perverse turn of mind, as proof for the argument that no harm has been done. The essence of the problem here is that an *injustice* has been done: an exemption has been granted without justification. As that injustice translates into the terms of material injuries, it means that certain members of our population have been asked to bear serious burdens and risks—indeed, to give up their lives—while another part of the population has been spared those risks and burdens. And the ground on which we assign these awful burdens to some people and lift them from others *cannot itself be justified*. When it comes to people who are physically incapable of serving in the military, it is evident that we would not be justified in imposing responsibilities on those who cannot bear them. But there is no comparable justification in relation to conscientious objection. We could not be warranted in assuming that the people who seek these exemptions display a more cultivated moral sensibility—that they are more humane and caring people—than those who did not claim conscientious objection. We can make these kinds of moral discriminations only on the basis of a moral proposition, which can tell us why conscientious objectors are more justified, or more worthy of our esteem, than people who have not sought exemptions as objectors. It is precisely that moral proposition, however, which the objector refuses to supply. For it would not be consistent with the character of his claims if he were to offer reasons that could be judged for their validity *as reasons*. Without the benefit of those reasons, we would be invited to excuse people from their obligations mainly because they have sensibilities that should be spared this experience. And yet, even if the objectors did possess more humane sensibilities, that alone could not stand as a ground of exemption from the burdens—and the grave risks—that are cast upon others. To share the responsibilities of citizens for the defense of their country surely cannot be regarded as a mission reserved to the most depraved among us.

Still, there is a lingering disposition to believe that people who claim standing as "conscientious objectors" must be on a higher plane than people who would conscientiously object to other public policies, and this question deserves to be considered seriously. On what basis would it be argued that the conscientious objector reflects a higher moral concern than other kinds of objectors, whose claims we would not honor? For example, how would we distinguish the conscientious objector from the taxpayer who objects "conscientiously" to being taxed for the purpose of supporting people on welfare who keep having illegitimate children, or the taxpayer who does not wish to be committed, through the tax system, to the support of abortions? In both cases, people are moved to opposition on the strength of considerations that are quite plausibly moral, and they are reacting to the peculiar reality of the tax system in committing their personal resources, against their own wishes, to ends they find morally indefensible. If "conscientiousness" is the ground of exemption in one case, how do we know "conscientiousness" when we see it, and why would conscientiousness not furnish a proper ground of exemption in these other cases as well?

We must remind ourselves here that the root of "conscientious" or "conscience" is in the Latin *conscire* (to be conscious of, *to know*). It involves knowledge, not feeling; it involves the kind of understanding that is not merely subjective and ineffable, but capable of being explained to others. In short, it is the kind of knowledge we can give an account of to others, and which can be judged to be true or false. And that possibility of imparting and judging may be the source of our conviction that we do not merely "feel" something to be true, but *know* it.

If the conscientious objector presents us with claims based wholly on his inner feelings, then he offers a claim whose worth and validity we cannot really *know*. For the same reason, we cannot know that his feelings deserve to be treated with a respect that we do not confer on other kinds of feelings. The argument may be made that the conscientious objector draws the dignity of his claims from the subject that inspires his feelings: the matter of taking other human lives. But when the conscientious objector seeks to address the subject of his feelings by speaking in propositions, his main point of conviction is that "it is wrong under all circumstances to kill"—a proposition, we have seen, that simply cannot be coherent as a moral proposition.

If the conscientious objector is to be distinguished, then, from other objectors, it cannot be on the ground that his beliefs or moral convictions are more valid than theirs. The attempt has usually been made to draw these distinctions in another way. The most prominent and accepted distinction has been formed on the grounds of "religion."

190

The contention has been offered that "conscientious objectors" have been animated by beliefs of a religious nature, and that a decent society should go as far as it practicably can in permitting them to honor their beliefs. Where it can be avoided (the argument has run), the law should not compel people to perform acts that are repugnant to their religious convictions.

Of course, this formula is not quite so simple as it might appear. In the first place, it has long been understood that people cannot be given a franchise to commit any atrocity they wish so long as they claim to be acting in the name of religious belief. If a law is underlain by principles that do not depend for their validity on religious beliefs, a decent society cannot permit the law to be violated, it cannot allow wrongs to be done, on the strength mainly of convictions of faith which cannot be judged for their validity. More than a hundred years ago, the Supreme Court declared that the authorities could not stand back and permit a widow to be burned on the funeral pyre of her husband, even if the ritual were carried out under the auspices of religion. In the same case, the Court upheld the ban that the civil law placed on polygamy, even though the law would restrict the freedom of the Mormons to engage in a practice that was sanctioned by their religion.[11] And in a line of cases extending through the years, the courts have made it clear that they would not grant exemptions on religious grounds to many varieties of statutes which reflected a legitimate legislative purpose. In that vein, the courts refused to permit an exemption, on religious grounds, from a public program of vaccinations,[12] and they have also refused to allow a Jehovah's Witness to ignore the laws on child labor by having her 9-year-old niece work with her in proselytizing.[13]

In one case in New Jersey, a woman who was in her eighth month of pregnancy began to hemorrhage, but she refused to have a blood transfusion because it was counter to her faith as a Jehovah's Witness. And yet, the court overrode her religious convictions because the transfusion was necessary to save the life of her unborn child.[14] It is plain, therefore, that the law will not honor any course of action that can be "justified" only through an appeal to religious tenets. No religious belief could validly deny the proposition that "two contradictory propositions cannot both be true," and in a similar way, no religious belief can make legitimate in the law propositions that are incoherent or

[11] See *Reynolds* v. *United States*, 98 U.S. 145, at 166 (1878).

[12] *Jacobson* v. *Massachusetts*, 197 U.S. 11 (1905).

[13] *Prince* v. *Massachusetts*, 321 U.S. 158 (1944).

[14] *Raleigh–Fitkin–Paul Morgan Mem. Hospital* v. *Anderson*, 201 A. 2d 537 (1964).

indefensible. The question may be raised as to why the courts have not treated cases of conscientious objection with the same logic they have applied in these other cases involving claims to religious exemptions? The answer may be that the courts have simply not had an accurate understanding of the properties of a categorical proposition in morals and, therefore, they have not been able to recognize that the central tenet of conscientious objection—the conviction that it must be wrong under all circumstances to kill—is simply invalid as a categorical proposition. What they have not understood is that the proposition is no more plausible, as a statement of religious conviction, than a denial, on "religious" grounds, of the law of contradiction.

THE ARGUMENT for religious exemptions suffers a further complication in the concern about an "establishment of religion." If the government should decide, for example, that an exemption from military service could be granted most appropriately to people who share the tenets of Seventh-Day Adventism, we would not be surprised to encounter a sudden rush of conversions to that faith. When the government bestows on certain sects the favor of official policy, it may create inducements for people to attach themselves to those sects. With an awareness of that peril, the government has been careful in recent years not to connect the exemptions for conscientious objection with membership in particular churches. The Draft Act of 1917 removed the obligation to military service from objectors who belonged to "any well-recognized religious sect or organization." But by 1940 the Selective Training and Service Act accepted exemptions for those whose objections to war flowed simply from "religious training and belief."

Implicit in this movement, in other words, was a broadening of the definition of "religion" to encompass more than formal doctrines of theology associated with particular churches. But the same dynamic that led to a broadening in the definition of religion would push on eventually toward a legal understanding of "religion" that was virtually indistinguishable from "private beliefs" of any kind. As the courts confronted cases on the establishment of religion, they came to deny even the propriety of prayers in the public schools that were offered simply to God, without any sectarian embellishments. They also regarded as unacceptable those prayers or public regulations which merely affirmed the existence of a "Supreme Being." In these instances, the courts saw a tendency to favor beliefs that were irremediably "religious" in the sense that they signified some rather emphatic views about such subjects as God, heaven, redemption, the Beginning and the End. All of this the courts thought too unfair, on

192

the whole, toward atheists: for the public schools to favor "prayers" with even a small residue of religious significance was to suggest to children and citizens that the state favored religion over irreligion.

There is ample evidence, of course, that this was indeed the preference of the men who framed the Constitution and accepted the First Amendment. They did in fact think that the moral foundations of a republic are more secure when citizens can find, in the existence of God, the guarantor of a final moral reckoning. The Founders could hold, as a general matter, that religion was better than irreligion, even while insisting that it was improper for the state to favor one sect over another.[15]

But the courts, in the maturing years of the twentieth century, found no grounds on which to favor religiosity over atheism, and in one matter, at least, they were accidentally right. When it came to offering exemptions from military service, there was no warrant for placing heavier burdens on atheists than on people with religious convictions. And so the courts began to remove the vestigial tests of religion that remained in the laws on the military draft. In 1948 the Congress sought to clarify its current understanding when it explained that "religious training and belief" referred to "an individual's belief in a relation to a Supreme Being involving duties superior to those arising from any human relation, but [not including] essentially political, sociological, or philosophical views or a merely personal moral code." In 1965, in the case of *United States* v. *Seeger*, the Court was faced with a claim of conscientious objection on the part of three young men who did not profess a belief in a Supreme Being. One avowed his skepticism about the existence of God, while affirming a faith in "goodness and virtue for their own sakes." Another stated his belief in a "Supreme Reality," an "Ultimate Cause for the fact of Being of the Universe." And a third claimed to derive his convictions from a source of moral guidance he was content to call "the supreme expression of human nature"—a notion sufficiently mystic to move beyond man without implying God. All three spoke vaguely of certain causes or forces in the Universe, which might have been enough, with a generous construal, to bring them within the terms of the statute. But none of the petitioners was prepared to say (in Woody Allen's phrase) that the First Cause was God or a stiff wind, and strictly speaking, none of them thought that the moral laws governing his life emanated from a Lawgiver. Still, the judges found something redeemingly inscrutable

---

[15] The case here has been made persuasively in Walter Berns, *The First Amendment and the Future of American Democracy* (New York: Basic Books, 1976), ch. 1.

in their arguments. The Court was convinced that the young men were moved, sincerely, by beliefs which held a place in their lives "parallel to that filled by the orthodox belief in God." With the inspiration of this example, the Court was willing to argue now that the statutory reference to a "Supreme Being" should not rule out beliefs informed by a "broader concept of a power or being, or a faith, 'to which all else is subordinate or upon which all else is ultimately dependent.' "[16]

After this decision in *United States* v. *Seeger*, the Congress amended the law to remove the reference to a Supreme Being. But it held to its understanding that "religious training and belief" could not be reduced to "essentially political, sociological or philosophical views, or a merely personal moral code." The Court, however, managed to remove even that minimal test of a conviction that was distinctively "religious." In 1970, in the case of *Welsh* v. *United States*, the Court dealt with a conscientious objector who emphatically denied that his views had any foundation in religious faith. Justice Black held, for the Court, that the pronounced convictions of this young man on the question of taking life could not be regarded with less respect than convictions of a similar nature that were inspired by religious belief. Black was willing, then, to exempt from military service "all those whose consciences, spurred by deeply held moral, ethical, or religious beliefs, would give them no rest or peace if they allowed themselves to become part of an instrument of war."[17]

With literary license, but with tolerable accuracy, Justice Harlan remarked that Black had "performed a lobotomy" on the statute by removing the requirement of a theistic religion. Still, Harlan was willing to acquiesce in the result as the only way of "salvaging a congressional policy of long standing that would otherwise have to be nullified."[18] He acquiesced, apparently, because he thought that it was legitimate to offer exemptions from military service on the strength of personal "beliefs," and that it was unjustified to discriminate, in this matter, in favor of *religious* convictions. The result, however, was to reduce "religious belief" to any belief of a personal nature that could not be examined or judged by others—and to offer exemptions from the law to anyone who would merely assert this kind of belief. What Black, Harlan, and their colleagues were willing to create, then, was a ground of exemption from the law that was neither religious nor moral. It was not religious, because it did not require any reflection

16 *United States* v. *Seeger*, 380 U.S., 163, at 174 (1965); see also 165-69.
17 *Welsh* v. *United States*, 398 U.S. 333, at 343 (1970).
18 *Ibid.*, at 346.

194

about the nature of God or, for that matter, about spiritual forces in the universe. As the Court redefined religion now for its own purposes, "religious" beliefs could legitimately encompass homilies that were read on the backs of cereal boxes. There was simply no ground on which to make distinctions between kinds of belief—there was no way of distinguishing the reflections of a theologian from the inspirations gleaned from fortune cookies—because the sources of validity for these beliefs were understood to be wholly "personal" and "private." And for that reason, these convictions could not claim a "moral" standing either. As far as anyone could say, no belief would be more or less valid, more or less elegant, than another. In the moral world reshaped by the Supreme Court, the law would be obliged to grant exemptions from military service on the basis of beliefs that could incorporate almost any variety of nonsense.

With the best of intentions, but with the most infirm understanding of the properties of a moral proposition, the courts have now absorbed into the law premises that are incompatible with the very idea of morals and law. It is no wonder that, two years after the Welsh case, the Supreme Court was willing to take a further step and grant an exemption on the basis of religion to a valid statute that did not involve service in the military. In *Wisconsin* v. *Yoder*, the Supreme Court dealt with a member of the Old Order Amish, who refused to permit his 15-year-old daughter to attend high school. The Amish were willing to have their children attend school through the eighth grade, but they thought their religion and way of life were incompatible with the unofficial ethic that prevailed in American public high schools. The conflict between the Amish and the authorities could have been dissolved if the courts had come to the judgment that the policy of compulsory schooling imposed unwarranted restrictions on the religious freedom of groups like the Amish. In that event, however, the policy of required schooling would have been struck down for everyone, not merely for members of certain religious sects. But if the courts did not wish to overturn the entire edifice of compulsory education, it was tempting to escape from the constraints of principled argument by invoking the kind of "religious" exemption which had become familiar in the cases on "conscientious objection." That was, as it turned out, precisely what they did. For the first time outside cases of military conscription, the Supreme Court was willing to uphold a radical claim of that kind. Still, for Justice Douglas, the ruling of the Court held too narrowly to a *religious* ground of objection. In that respect, he pointed out, the decision failed to reflect the "advances" that had already taken place in the cases on conscientious objection.

As Douglas put the question, Why should the Court limit the ground of exemption to religion in these cases of compulsory schooling, any more than it limits the ground of exemption to religion in the cases on military service?[19] Why not accept, once again, a release from the obligations of law when those obligations run counter to "personal beliefs" that are firmly held?

And indeed, why not? For the Court has now created a basis of exemption to laws of any kind on the basis of beliefs of any kind. What logic, then, would confine this new "principle" to questions of military service? As Walter Berns commented on the *Yoder* case, "[I]s it not strange to be told—after eighteen years of the efforts to integrate the public schools . . . that it is unconstitutional for a state to require children (or, at least, some children) even to go to high school? Is it not strange that they be permitted to segregate themselves from the rest of the American community?"[20]

Picking up Berns's cue, what if we were suddenly faced with the formation of a new religious sect that established, as one of its articles of faith, an opposition to any commerce with blacks? Let us assume that the members of this sect object "conscientiously" to any law which would forbid them to discriminate on grounds of race in arranging their affairs, from the selling of their homes to the selection of schools for their children. The fact that this is a new sect would be utterly without significance, for the same doctrine that forbids us from judging the validity of beliefs would also prevent us from making any discrimination between revelations old or new.

THE PUBLIC at large may not be attentive to the holdings of the courts, but it may find fresh evidence every day of the way in which these exemptions are finally manifested in practice. When people have before them the example of their fellow citizens enjoying special advantages in the law for reasons that strike them as frivolous and unpersuasive, we should not be surprised to discover that they may shed their sense of embarrassment and take advantage of the same inanities in the law. Knowing nothing of recent cases, they may show an inventiveness that is wholly spontaneous, and they suddenly discover that the claims they devise, with a combination of irreverence and chutzpah, fall easily into the allowances that have been created by the Supreme Court.

A wondrous lesson in this respect was taught inadvertently several

---

[19] *Wisconsin v. Yoder*, 406 U.S. 205, at 248-49 (1972).

[20] Walter Berns, "The Importance of Being Amish," *Harper's* (March 1973), pp. 39-40.

years ago by the yeomen of Hardenburgh, New York. In 1976 the citizens of the town began to grow resentful because their property taxes were nearly doubling, while some of the largest estates, owned by religious groups, were exempt from taxation. As it turned out, most of the $21 million in property in Hardenburgh had been held by Buddhists, Tibetan monks, and other religious groups, which had bought the property as rural retreats. In response to the inequity of the situation, a large number of residents in the town declared themselves to be ministers of a new church in which services would be held in their respective homes. As the *Washington Post* reported, half the residents in the town were "ordained in a mass ceremony conducted in a cocktail lounge by George McLain, a tatooed plumber who is a bishop in the Universal Life Church. The church, which does most of its business by mail, subscribes to no specific beliefs." One of the new ministers insisted, though, that the churches were being formed for "good moral purposes, and one of our purposes is to seek equality for all." Each minister was expected to hold a church service in his own living room about "once or twice a month." The living room in each house was to be designated as a "church meeting hall," and the rest of the house would be described as a "parsonage." On this basis, at any rate, the new ministers applied for exemptions from their taxes, and the town assessor approved their applications.[21] Indeed, given the standards that the courts have adopted in defining "religion" and granting exemptions from the law, the assessor could hardly have done anything else, for there is no legal ground now on which these claims could be regarded as illegitimate.

In a society with sensible laws, this kind of burlesque would be unworthy of grownups. And yet one can hardly fault these people for acting out, with its full silliness, what the courts have propounded for their guidance under the name of "jurisprudence." It is only the limits of public awareness that keep the example of Hardenburgh from spreading to other areas and other questions of law. If it does, then we will encounter nothing less than the erosion of law and the disappearance of any notion of legal obligation. But this unraveling of law would not mark the fact that the American people had suddenly become lawless or unscrupulous. It would be a reflection, rather, of the fact that the courts had merged their tenderness toward "conscientious objectors" with their literal ignorance of moral principles. On the premises accepted by the Court, there is no way of knowing just who the conscientious are, or of making distinctions between the

[21] *Washington Post*, December 6, 1976.

197

conscientious and the unscrupulous. The result has been to cast favors on some and impose burdens on others, on grounds that carry no evident justification. And when the law becomes detached in this way from the discipline of justification, the truly conscientious may be able to protect their own interests only by taking advantage of the same amoral premises that have become established now as the foundation of the law.

THE QUESTION was raised as to how we might distinguish conscientious objectors from people who object conscientiously to the use of their tax money to sustain the public funding of abortion or to support unwed mothers who keep having illegitimate children. We would conclude that the distinction could not coincide with a difference between religious and nonreligious beliefs. Even when the distinction between the two kinds of persuasion is drawn more clearly than the Court wishes to draw it, a religious ground of belief could not provide a tenable basis of exemption from a statute that is constructed on valid moral grounds. If there is a valid moral proposition that furnishes the ground for a statute, that proposition may be limited only by another plausible set of reasons. I would arrive, then, from a somewhat different path, at the same judgment reached about twenty years ago by Philip Kurland: that, as a general matter, claims to exemptions and special privileges in the law which are based solely on religious belief ought not be accepted.[22] We may wonder just why this conclusion should be so startling in relation to military service when it was evidently understood by the first generation of American statesmen. When the Bill of Rights was being debated in the First Congress, an attempt was made to attach a provision on conscientious objection to the section concerning the rights of the people to keep and bear arms. As the debate proceeded, the congressmen came to discover many of the considerations that we have unfolded here; and as a result, the provision on conscientious objection was eventually deleted from the Bill of Rights.

The pertinent section read in this way: "A well regulated militia, composed of the body of the people, being the best security of a free state, the right of the people to keep and bear arms shall not be infringed; but no person religiously scrupulous shall be compelled to bear arms."[23] Congressman Gerry of Massachusetts objected at once

[22] See Philip B. Kurland, *Religion and the Law* (Chicago: Aldine, 1962).

[23] Bernard Schwartz, *The Bill of Rights* (New York: Chelsea House, 1971), vol. II, p. 1107.

to the provision on religious exemptions. He seemed to fear that, unless the privilege were attached to membership in particular sects, the exemption could be claimed by nearly everyone.[24] And yet it became apparent that there was no disposition to attach the privilege to particular sects, because a provision of that sort would establish, in effect, churches favored by the state.

Congressman Jackson thought that the issue would not be a serious practical concern, since most people in the country were not likely to belong to the Quakers or to other sects that professed scruples against war. But he acknowledged that a grave question of equity would arise. One part of the population would have to take the risks of war and the burden of defending the country, including the defense of those who would not defend themselves. That arrangement he thought patently unjust, unless a person who was exempted from military service might be obliged to pay a certain sum to support a soldier in the field. It was quickly pointed out, however, that the same people who would refuse to fight would refuse also to pay for others to fight in their place.[25]

As the debate wore on, Congressman Benson finally moved to strike out the passage that provided for religious exemptions. Benson observed, quite rightly, that the debate had revealed an intractable problem in establishing a principled ground of justification for the provision on conscientious objection. If the exemption were allowed to stand, it would stir endless arguments over equity, it could foster litigation over nearly all matters involving the militia; and these persistent controversies surrounding the military would be traceable to the fact that the original provision for religious exemptions had not been settled on any clear ground of equity. The claim to conscientious objection involved, as Benson said, a "religious persuasion," but it marked no "natural right."[26] If the subject were removed from the Bill of Rights, it would be clear that when a legislature respected these claims of conscientious objection, it would be respecting them wholly as an "indulgence" and not as a matter of "right." In closing the argument, Benson brought the question to the root that proved decisive in our own consideration: "It is extremely injudicious," he observed, "to intermix matters of doubt with fundamentals."[27] That is to say, it is a mistake to confound matters of personal belief with moral propositions and necessary truths, and it is untenable to establish privileges

[24] *Ibid.*, p. 1108.
[25] *Ibid.*
[26] *Ibid.*, p. 1109.
[27] *Ibid.*

in the law on the basis of articles of faith that cannot finally be judged or justified on grounds accessible to other men.

In one interesting twist, it was even suggested in the debate that a serious danger could come into being if it were pretended that the exemption from military service stood on a principled ground. For in that case it would have been entirely reasonable for the government to test the earnestness of the claims to exemption. As an example, the government might test the convictions of the "objectors" by forbidding them to own or carry arms. If the objectors protest that they need guns for their own protection, if they show they are not averse to killing when it may be justified, why should they not also serve in the army? But then, if the standards of religious exemption were to become very loose and almost everyone were willing to claim the exemption, a large portion of the population could unwittingly disarm itself. In that event, the government would be left with an even larger preponderance of force, and the purposes of the Second Amendment could be, in effect, subverted. A law that permitted an unprincipled release from its obligations might tempt citizens to indulge their self-interest at the expense of their public duties, and citizens who were tempted into corruption could forgo at the same time the means of resisting a tyrannical government.

And so, when Congressman Scott offered the final words in the debate, he found no assurance in the estimate, made by some of his colleagues, that the issue would simply disappear over time. Religion, they thought, was on the decline, and therefore they reasoned that fewer people would be claiming religious exemptions. But if it were true that religion was on the decline, then it seemed plausible to Scott that the consequences could be quite the reverse: that "the generality of persons will have recourse to these pretexts to get excused from bearing arms."[28] With the decline of religion, there could be a weakening, also, of the convictions that supported a more exacting moral temper, and people might be more unembarrassed by the claims they were willing to make in the name of religion.

IF AN EFFORT were made, then, to preserve a distinction between the conscientious objector and the taxpayers who object to being implicated in other kinds of policies, the argument would have to move to some ground other than religious belief. There would be an attempt, very likely, to draw the distinction between the two sets of objectors, not by the sources of their convictions, but by the injuries that would

[28] *Ibid*, p. 1126.

confront them. The argument has been made that the taxpayers are threatened only with a loss of money, and the loss would be trivial at that, when we consider the amount that any one taxpayer would pay in supporting any particular policy, such as Aid to Families with Dependent Children. That is the reasoning, in fact, which used to explain the unwillingness of the courts to accord to taxpayers a "standing" to sue.[29] In contrast, the involvement of the conscientious objectors in policies they regard as abhorrent would be far more substantial and direct. They may be placed in a position that compels them to take the lives of others, rather than merely paying to support a war, and of course they would expose themselves to the danger of suffering death.

This argument, in turn, contains levels of complication, and one must be careful, first, not to be too facile in measuring a moral interest by the severity of the material interest that is at stake. Madison once remarked that the uncommon statesmanship of our revolutionary leaders was revealed in their wisdom in recognizing, in a tax of three pence on tea, the full magnitude of the evil comprised in the precedent.[30] A government that was not constituted with the consent of the governed did not become less offensive merely because it was moderate in its exactions. If that government could legitimately lay taxes of three pence on any citizen, it could just as well lay taxes of £3,000. The revolutionary leaders did not make it their business to haggle over the price; their objection was with the terms of principle on which they were to be governed by the British Parliament. In a similar way, the issue for those who object, say, to the public funding of abortions, is not with the pennies that they are contributing to the project. Their concern, rather, is that the tax system represents, in a concrete way, the moral nexus between the citizen and the policies that he is being obligated, through the law, to support. Whether that support amounts to three cents or $3,000, his concern is that he is linked to the political community on terms of principle which compel him to support policies he finds morally repugnant.

The requirement of "standing" arises plausibly out of the design of the Constitution; it helps to mark off a separate sphere for judges by confining the courts to the discipline of judging cases in controversy. But this requirement has been eroded over the years precisely because the material stake in the outcome is no measure of the moral interests

[29] See *Frothingham* v. *Mellon*, 262 U.S. 447 (1923).

[30] See Madison's "Memorial and Remonstrance against Religious Assessments," cited and reprinted in *Walz* v. *Tax Commission*, 397 U.S. 664, at 719-27 (1970).

201

at stake or of the moral claim of the "citizen" or "tax objector" to raise a challenge.[31] The argument may be made, though, that the conscientious objector should not be compared to the objecting taxpayer; a more apt comparison may be made to the doctor who is opposed to abortion and yet serves in a hospital that may be obliged to perform such operations. The prospect no longer seems quite so likely as it appeared earlier, since Congress has affirmed its refusal to fund abortions and the Supreme Court has upheld that refusal.[32] But while there was a prospect that the federal government might be compelled to fund abortions, and while the former Department of Health, Education, and Welfare showed a determination to make abortions available, there was the need to contemplate cases in which federal aid might be removed from hospitals that refused to perform abortions. The prospect, at any rate, was sufficiently lively that medical schools began to inquire into the convictions of their students on this question, and the message was conveyed that doctors who were opposed to abortion could be liabilities to hospitals that might come under a legal obligation to offer these operations. Both the doctor and the draftee could be placed then in positions in which they would be asked to serve directly as agents in what they understood to be the taking of life.

The comparison is sufficiently apt that it has become the source of a serious problem among people who conventionally count themselves as supporters of conscientious objection. And so Professor Richard Flathman was willing to bring to the point of explicitness a question that people might have been embarrassed to pose in public not too long ago: "Does a woman have a right to demand an abortion from

---

[31] There are cases, after all, in which the Constitution may be violated blatantly and yet no one may be injured materially by the violation. That state of affairs arose when President Franklin Roosevelt appointed Senator Hugo Black to the Supreme Court, in a clear violation of Article I, Section 6, paragraph 2, of the Constitution, which states that "no Senator or Representative shall, during the Time for which he was elected, be appointed to any civil Office under the Authority of the United States, . . . the Emoluments whereof shall have been encreased during such time. . . ." We may not think that this particular issue is as momentous as it was thought to be by the men who framed the Constitution; but it remains in the Constitution nevertheless, and the question is whether citizens may not have interests *as citizens*, and not merely as taxpayers, in preserving the integrity of the Constitution that defines the polity in which they are citizens. If they can be conceded such an interest, how would that interest be affected in any significant way by the question of whether they are also threatened with a material injury? The question of Justice Black's appointment to the Supreme Court was challenged in *Ex parte Levitt*, 302 U.S. 633 (1937), where the Court rejected the standing of taxpayers to bring the constitutional challenge.

[32] See *Harris* v. *McRae*, 65 L. Ed. 784 (1980).

a medically competent (and otherwise available) individual who personally believes that abortion is morally wrong?" Flathman has made clear his own understanding that the possession of a "right" on the part of one person must imply a correlative "duty" on the part of someone else to render what is due, or at least to avoid obstructing the satisfaction of that right. Flathman happens to regard the case for abortion as strong, and for that reason he thinks there is a strong "right" to an abortion. Therefore, he would argue that there is indeed an obligation to perform abortions, even on the part of doctors who profess to be morally opposed to them.[33]

Flathman likens this matter to the obligation that is enforced against conscientious objectors to participate in a just war: if their services can be spared, the society may honor their sensitivities and try to accommodate these people. But there is no endorsement of their objections in principle. What Flathman clearly understands is that if a war is justified in principle, the government would be justified in using the legitimate means that are necessary in fighting the war, and those means must include the commitment of one's own citizens to serve in the military. In the same way, it could not strictly be said that a person has a "right" to an abortion if all practitioners who were competent to perform the operation were *justified* in refusing to perform it. Implicitly, Flathman rejects the premises that are most decisive to the position of the conscientious objector: he recognizes that it is logically contradictory to say at the same time that the government would be justified in enforcing a law and that people may be free to dismiss their obligation to that law simply by invoking their personal, subjective beliefs. What Flathman understands, in other words, is that the question can be addressed, finally, only at the substantive level. Whether one is justified in refusing to perform an abortion must depend wholly on the question of whether abortion itself is justified or unjustified. And whether one is justified in refusing to serve in the military depends on whether a nation may be justified in using military force, whether it is justified in prosecuting the particular war that is at issue, and whether it may commit its citizens to the support of its legitimate ends.

Unless questions of that kind were resolved, Flathman was not about to grant special rights of "conscientious refusal" to public officers, who are charged with a "direct" responsibility to vindicate the rights

[33] Richard E. Flathman, "The Theory of Rights and the Practice of Abortion," paper delivered at the panel "Abortion and Jurisprudence" during the meetings of the American Political Science Association, Washington D.C., September 4, 1977, pp. 25-26.

of citizens. There are social workers who directly administer public welfare; there are lawyers in the Department of Justice who enforce laws against racial discrimination; there are postmen who may be asked to deliver publications they find objectionable. The fact that these people bear direct responsibilities for the administration of services they may find uncongenial cannot itself confer upon them a privilege of refusing to carry out their responsibilities solely because of personal feelings that cannot be imparted or justified to others. To put it another way, the "directness" of their responsibilities cannot be enough to establish, *for citizens or officials*, an excuse to avoid their obligations under the law merely by invoking personal beliefs which cannot be examined or judged by others. A conscientious objector may not dissolve, in that casual way, the obligation to military service that comes to him through his office of citizenship, any more than a public official may evade his duty to administer his own, public obligations.

There is one last feature, however, which separates the conscientious objector at once from the objecting taxpayer; from the official who bears a "direct" responsibility for policies he finds repugnant; and from the doctor who may be ordered to suppress his moral convictions and carry out abortions. And that one noteworthy feature is that the conscientious objector who encounters the military draft is faced with the prospect of suffering violent death. For many people, of course, that injury stands in a class apart from all other injuries, and it is the source of franchises that do not flow so easily from the risk, say, of losing money, or even from the risk of being made the agent of an immoral purpose. The argument may be offered at least for consideration that this danger of suffering violent death may excuse acts of withdrawal, based on private fears or aversions, which would not be acceptable in the face of any other obligation. At the same time, there happens to be an argument of ingenious construction and philosophic power that yields the same judgment: Thomas Hobbes's classic argument in *Leviathan* would seem to provide, on its face, the most impressive solution to the problem faced by the conscientious objector. No one has been more forceful than Hobbes in insisting on the stark preeminence, among all other injuries, of the suffering of violent death. Hobbes's argument would have to work ultimately to protect the conscientious objector who would resist service in the military; but it would also turn back, with contempt, any effort on the part of other people to deny their obligations to the law when faced with any risk notably short of death. With all of its terrors, Hobbes's argument may hold a curious appeal for certain "liberal" factions in our politics, for

it would allow the government to use the instruments of legal com-
pulsion in supporting regulations based on race and policies of redistribution, but it would remove the authority of the government to
commit its citizens to service in wars.

Yet, I think we will discover that Hobbes can produce these remarkable results only on the bases of premises that should not be
tolerated for a moment by liberals *or* conservatives. Those premises
cannot be tolerated, at any rate, by anyone who takes seriously the
notion that political life must imply moral foundations and that it
must be attended by moral requirements. At its root, Hobbes's argument presents the most explicit challenge to the premises of political
life set forth by Aristotle. And for that reason Hobbes makes clear,
far more powerfully than anyone else, just what consequences arise
when distinctively moral ends are ruled out of political life.

X

CAN THERE BE AN OBLIGATION TO RISK ONE'S LIFE FOR ONE'S COUNTRY? THE ATTRACTIONS AND DANGERS OF HOBBES'S TEACHING

For Aristotle, as we have seen, the polity found its rationale and justification in the existence of morals itself. The existence of morals virtually entailed the existence of law, and the capacity of human beings for morals made it possible and necessary for human beings to be governed by law. In this classic perspective, the purpose of the polity was to vindicate rights and wrongs. A polity constituted on these premises would of course seek to protect people from unwarranted assault, but it would seek to protect people in this way as a part of a larger mission to secure its members from all varieties of injustice that come within the practicable reach of the law.

For Hobbes, on the other hand, the polity found its rationale and justification solely in the effort to protect people from violent death. Hobbes could reduce the ends of politics in this way precisely because he detached the character of political life from the moral premises that were at the foundation of Aristotle's understanding. For Aristotle, humans were suited *by nature* to live in a polity because they can distinguish between good and evil—and give reasons. But for Hobbes that common nature in which all men are equal was not the capacity for moral judgment, but the capacity to kill one another: even the "weakest" of men "has strength enough to kill the strongest, either by secret machinations, or by confederacy with others, that are in the same danger with himself."[1]

Years later, Hegel would caustically remark upon the tendencies of the "contract" theorists to construct a "state of nature" antecedent to civil society and then to abstract, from that primitive, "natural" condition of human beings, the capacity for morals that was also part of our "natural" world.[2] It was only with such rarefied assumptions

[1] Thomas Hobbes, *Leviathan* (Oxford: Basil Blackwell, 1960 [1651]), pt. 1, ch. 13, p. 80. Cf. Hobbes, *De Cive*, ed. Sterling Lamprecht (New York: Appleton-Century-Crofts, 1949), ch. I, para. 3, p. 25.

[2] G.W.F. Hegel, *Natural Law*, trans. T.M. Knox (Philadelphia: University of Pennsylvania Press, 1975), p. 66. As Hegel put it, "The absolute Idea of ethical life . . . contains both majesty *and the state of nature as simply identical* [emphasis added],

that William Blackstone could remark, in his famous *Commentaries on the Laws of England*, that when humans leave the state of nature and enter civil society, they surrender their "natural" liberty to do "mischief" in exchange for a larger measure of "civil liberty," the liberty that arises when they, as well as others, are restrained by law. In his polite incredulity on this point, James Wilson managed to reveal the persistence, among our own Founders, of the moral perspective inherited from the classics. "Is it part of natural liberty," he asked, "to do mischief to any one?"[3] For Wilson, apparently, it was still possible, even in the "state of nature," to tell the difference between an unprovoked assault and a "justified" act of resistance. And if it was possible to tell the difference between justified and unjustified acts, it was possible to say that assailants were "wrong" when they attacked unjustly, and that victims would be "right" in defending themselves. The assailant, therefore, had no rightful "liberty to do mischief"; he had no right to do a wrong, regardless of whether a legal order had yet been constituted. Even in the state of nature there was no "right," say, to rape or assault; and the wrongness of these acts was entirely unaffected by the presence or absence of government. The advent of government merely enlarged the chance of securing the right of victims to be protected against wrongs. But the moral understanding that made it possible to speak of justice and injustice, of criminals and victims, did not come into existence only with the creation of civil society. In the classic perspective, it was that understanding which explained, in the first place, why human beings were enjoined to create a civil society and to be governed by laws which reflected moral imperatives.

BUT FOR Hobbes there was, in the strictest sense, no moral understanding in the absence of formal government. As he put it very directly, "The desires, and other passions of man, are in themselves no sin. No more are the actions, that proceed from those passions, *till they know a law that forbids them: which till laws be made they cannot know.* . . ."[4] Under these assumptions, the "state of nature" could hardly be anything other than the terrifying jungle described by Hobbes. For not only were people unrestrained by law, they were also

---

since the former is nothing but absolute ethical *nature*; and in the realization of majesty there can be no thought of any loss of absolute freedom, which is what would have to be understood by 'natural freedom,' or of any sacrifice of ethical nature."

[3] James Wilson, "Of the Natural Rights of Individuals," in *The Works of James Wilson* (Cambridge: Harvard University Press, 1967), vol. II, p. 587.

[4] Hobbes, *Leviathan, supra,* note 1, p. 83. Emphasis added.

ungoverned by any moral sense of their own. One could not afford to assume, under these conditions, what anyone else was likely to assume. Everyone had to be counted as a potential enemy, and so it was plausible to believe, with Hobbes, that the state of nature would be marked by the "war of every man, against every man":[5]

> In such condition, there is no place for industry; because the fruit thereof is uncertain: and consequently no culture of the earth; no navigation, nor use of the commodities that may be imported by sea; no commodious building; no instruments of moving, and removing, such things as required much force; no knowledge of the face of the earth; no account of time; no arts; no letters; no society; and which is worst of all, continual fear, and danger of violent death; and the life of man, solitary, poor, nasty, brutish, and short.

For Hobbes, the most fundamental "law of nature" was the law that impels each person to seek his own self-preservation, and under the conditions of the war of "every man, against every man," each man would have the right, by nature, to use all means necessary to his own defense. Since each man was a potential enemy, the doctrine of necessity would encompass what is known these days as "preemptive war": in the interests of defense it would not be irrational to attack people who could be a threat in the future to one's self-preservation. As Hobbes put it, "every man has a right to every thing; even to one another's body."[6]

That prospect, overall, was immanently frightening, and "as long as this natural right of every man to every thing endureth," wrote Hobbes, "there can be no security to any man."[7] For the sake of solving this problem, man wills the existence of a government or sovereign with the power to preserve order and law. That is, he wills the existence of government as a projection of his self-interest in avoiding violent death. This understanding of the genesis of the political order makes a profound difference in understanding the limits of political authority or, conversely, the limits to the obligation of citizens to obey. As I pointed out in Chapter VIII, our "right" to resist attacks on ourselves does not arise simply from the fact that our "selves" may be under assault. Our franchise to use violence in these cases arises from our right to resist "injustice" of any kind, including "unjustified" attacks

---

[5] *Ibid.*, p. 82.
[6] *Ibid.*, pt. 1, ch. 14, p. 85.
[7] *Ibid.*

on ourselves. In this understanding, the vicious criminal who is justly sent to the gallows may not claim the "right" to kill his executioners as a matter of "self-defense." But with Hobbes, the law of self-preservation would indeed encompass the right to kill in situations of this kind, or in any other case in which killing may be necessary to one's own self-preservation.

Hobbes removes, in other words, any *moral* discrimination that may be made between acts of self-preservation that are justified or unjustified. If we understood, in the first instance, that we will the existence of a government for the sake of securing only our "just" interests, the legitimacy of the government would hinge upon the "just" uses of authority. The government could not claim the obedient submission of its citizens to *any* policy directed to its own "self-preservation" or to the protection of its citizens, for a government might pursue those ends, in certain instances, through means that were unwarranted and illegitimate. By the same token, citizens could not be released from their obligation to the law unless they were able to show that the law would commit them unjustly—that it would commit them to *wrongful* ends. The irony in Hobbes is that he constructs a political order in which government and citizen alike may exercise a license unaffected by moral restraints. The government need not be obliged to establish any moral justification for its policies so long as it can tenably claim to act for the sake of "preserving" the lives of its subjects. And citizens need never be obliged, in any strict sense, to engage in activities that would threaten their self-preservation. All of this became clear, of necessity, as Hobbes sought to explain the rights that were not "alienable"—the rights that no man could waive as the condition for entering civil society.

FOR HOBBES and other "contract" theorists, men moved to government and civil society from the "state of nature," and in making that transition individuals would transfer to the sovereign a portion of that liberty they possessed before the invention of government. Still, there were certain imperatives, rooted in the nature of man, which could not be effaced, and there were certain rights that could not be surrendered. A man may be moved to surrender part of his liberties for the sake of securing the protection of his life; nevertheless, he could not suppress his natural inclination—his "natural right"—to seek his own preservation. And so, while the sovereign might command a man to do many things, the government could not legitimately order him, as Hobbes said, "to lay down the right of resisting them, that assault him by force, to take away his life; because he cannot be understood to aim thereby, at any good to himself."[8] Nor would a man be obliged to obey if he were ordered "to kill, wound, or maim himself; . . . or to abstain from the use of food, air, medicine, or any other thing, without which he cannot live."[9]

In entering civil society, a man supposedly transferred to the sovereign that right to use violent force which he himself exercised without restraint in the state of nature; and yet, it was plain that he could not have transferred to the government his right to use the kind of force that might be necessary at times to preserve his own life. In the same way, a man supposedly ceded to the government the right to make laws binding on him; but on Hobbes's premises the question had to be raised as to whether the government could lawfully command its citizens to risk their lives. The same premise that would allow a citizen to "take the law into his own hands" and resist a lynch mob may justify the citizen in refusing to accept a military draft and to be placed, in battle, on the beaches of Normandy. At that moment, the Hobbesian citizen might remind the government that it was constituted in the first place for "nothing else but the security of a man's person, in his life, and in the means of so preserving life, as not to be weary of it."[10] And if there was "nothing else," if no other end justified the creation of a polity, then how indeed could the polity order a man to risk his self-preservation without becoming destructive of that end for which government had been instituted?

It would furnish no coherent response for the government to say, at this point, that it is necessary to put an army into the field for the sake of preserving the country as a whole, including those who were too infirm to defend themselves. That response would provide no tenable answer because the Hobbesian citizen did not will the government into existence for the sake of *someone else's* self-preservation. He willed the government into existence for the sake of his *own* preservation. If he had entered the civil order out of the sense of a good that encompassed the well-being of others apart from himself, that would have implied a notably different understanding about the foundations of polity. It would have suggested that government had its origins in the recognition of *moral* principles, which could make it necessary at times for some people to surrender their self-interest for the good of others. That kind of explanation cannot be reconciled with the premises of Hobbes's argument. Nor can it be recast plausibly in Hobbesian terms by suggesting that the government is really acting,

[8] *Ibid.*, pp. 86-87.
[9] *Ibid.*, pt. 2, ch. 21, p. 142.
[10] *Ibid.*, pt. 1, ch. 14, p. 87.

after all, for the long-run self-interest of the citizen himself when it drafts him into the military and places him on a battlefield in Normandy. The government would be offering here nothing more than an empirical prediction—and a dubious one, at that. The citizen could reason, with far more persuasiveness, that his self-interest would enjoy far better odds if he remained at home while someone else was put on the beach at Normandy. All things being equal, he might prefer to be in Philadelphia. And if the matter turned solely on his self-interest, or on the prospects for preserving his own life, it is hard to see how the government may compel him to land at Normandy.

There is a serious question, then, as to whether a political order constituted on Hobbesian premises could establish any "obligation" on the part of its citizens to render military service and risk their lives. Hobbes wrote at times as though an obligation of that kind could exist in his scheme; but a closer reading will show, I think, that where Hobbes is most adamant about an obligation to military service, the language of "obligation" would really be out of place. The hard truth here, which could not be evaded by Hobbes, is that the notion of an obligation to risk one's life is dissolved by his own premises.

Before Hobbes addressed the question of service in a war he referred, in one passage, to a situation in which a number of men were "manifestly too weak to defend themselves united." Under those conditions, he said, "everyone may use his own reason in time of danger, to save his own life, either by flight, or by submission to the enemy, as he shall think best; in the same manner as a very small company of soldiers, surprised by an army, may cast down their arms, and demand quarter, or run away, rather than be put to the sword."[11]

Hobbes seems to have in mind here virtually hopeless situations, when even brave men would be wise to back away or surrender out of prudence. But some men may be keener than others in estimating a situation on the battlefield. They may understand, long before others, that the battle cannot be won and that their lives would be expended in a futile effort. It is hard to believe that Hobbes would have contempt for their prescience, or that he would be able to condemn them if they should honor their judgment and flee earlier, even though they might be endangering the comrades they leave behind. If the decisive point here is self-preservation, Hobbes could not decorously quibble over these calculations, or permit a less generous license to people whose arts of self-preservation were more finely cultivated. For much the same reason, he was bound to insist that an allowance be made, even in time of war, "for natural timorousness; not only to women, of

[11] *Ibid.*, pt. 2, ch. 20, p. 134.

whom no such dangerous duty is expected, but also to men of feminine courage":[12]

> When armies fight, there is on one side, or both, a running away; yet when they do it not out of treachery, but fear, they are not esteemed to do it unjustly, but dishonourably. For the same reason, to avoid battle, is not injustice, but cowardice.

To act cowardly would not be manly or desirable, then, but it apparently could not be "wrong" or "unjust". Therefore, it could not represent a failure to perform anything one was "obliged" to do. Hobbes could not overlook, of course, the strong interest on the part of the government in preserving a competent military force. The "sword of the law" was bound up with the fundamental reasons that justified a political order in the first place. To refuse to obey military orders may frustrate, as Hobbes said, "the end for which the sovereignty was ordained; then there is no liberty to refuse: otherwise there is."[13] Hobbes went so far as to say that a soldier who refuses, when commanded, to fight against the enemy may be punished rightly with death. But the rationale for this punishment, as we have shown, would be difficult to justify in a polity established to *preserve* the lives of its subjects. The teaching is immured in paradox, and one may ask, Under what conditions may a citizen justly refuse, as Hobbes says, to participate in the military?

Hobbes allows, first, that a citizen may refuse without injustice if he provides another soldier in his place; for in that case "he deserteth not the service of the commonwealth." The citizen may sustain in this way his service to the commonwealth, but the concession removes any sense of an obligation to risk one's life in military service. It would be replaced, rather, by an obligation merely to support the effort of one's country at war. As Hobbes goes on, he makes his allowance again for the man of "timorousness" or "feminine courage" who would also be relieved of any obligations to risk his life if that prospect should affect him with an overpowering fear. And yet, for reasons that remain inscrutable, Hobbes refuses to honor these appeals to fear when they are made by a man who had volunteered for military service. That man, Hobbes insists, "is obliged not only to go to the battle, but also not to run from it, without his captain's leave."[14] Perhaps it was assumed by Hobbes that, in the act of enrolling in the army, the man had affirmed his emancipation from "timorousness" and "feminine

[12] *Ibid.*, ch. 21, p. 143.
[13] *Ibid.*, p. 142.
[14] *Ibid.*, p. 143.

courage," and so if he refused now to stand and fight, his refusal would have to stem from less forgivable motives. But by the terms of Hobbes's own argument, it could not be supposed that the man waived his right to self-preservation when he entered a contract for military service, any more than when he entered the compact that formed civil society. If Hobbes was willing to respect the impulses that move men to flee from the terrors of the battlefield, his imagination should have been able to encompass the possibility of scenes that would strain the courage of even the most hardened veteran.

A point was reached, however, for Hobbes at which an obligation to bear arms became unequivocal and unqualified. That was the moment at which the entire commonwealth seemed to be in grave danger, and that situation, he declared, "requireth at once the help of all that are able to bear arms." He went on to insist that the obligation was universal: "everyone is obliged; because otherwise the institution of the commonwealth, which they have not the purpose, or courage to preserve, was in vain."[15] The obligation would be borne, in other words, even by those who had not enrolled, of their own volition, in military service. Apparently it would also be a stringent obligation: there seem to be no allowances here for "timorousness" and "feminine courage," no excuse for those who would calculate the odds and fly from a difficult battle. But then how could all of these allowances, so plainly drawn from the warrants of self-preservation, be cast aside in such a sweeping way, with a rule that recognized no shadings or exceptions?

The answer, I think, is as woven in the design of Hobbes's argument as all of the allowances he would now sweep aside. For Hobbes seemed to have in mind here a kind of Carthaginian war, in which the entire population runs the risk of extermination. At that moment, there is no longer any tension between the commands of the sovereign and the interest of the citizen in his own self-preservation. The danger is not confined now to soldiers in the field, for if those soldiers were to be overcome, the citizens would be compelled to pick up their own weapons and fight to the end, much in the way that Jews were compelled to fight or die in most countries occupied by the Nazis. The citizen would fight, in this war, as a natural reflex of his own, ineffaceable instinct toward self-preservation. For Hobbes, after all, the impulse to self-preservation was a fundamental "law of nature." In all strictness, then, it was inconceivable to Hobbes that people would face any choice over the question of whether they should defend themselves against assaults on their lives. Anyone who understood the laws

[15] *Ibid.*

of nature would recognize why human beings could hardly do otherwise. That is why the universal "obligation" to fight in a Carthaginian war could be set forth so emphatically, without a hint of the problematic: it was predictable that everyone *would* fight, and that no sane person would have to be forced to defend himself.

Yet, did it make sense any longer to speak of an "obligation" to fight? If the impulse to fight in these circumstances was governed by an unremitting force of nature, the act of fighting would be "determined" by the "laws of nature" quite as much as the flight of falling bodies. As we have seen, however, the language of morals is out of place when we speak of acts "determined" by the laws of nature. Hobbes was willing to declare an "obligation" to military service in the most unqualified terms only in those circumstances when—he had no doubt—people would be driven to fight as though impelled by a law of nature. Under those terms, the language of "obligation" becomes detached from its meaning.

By any stern test, therefore, Hobbes offered no case in which a person may strictly be "obliged" to risk his life in military action. For there was no case, in Hobbes, in which a citizen could have been enjoined to fight out of respect for a principle, quite regardless of his own self-interest. Hobbes might have a certain attraction, then, for those people who have sought to deny any ground of obligation to participate in a war. But at the same time, his teaching would offer no support for those who would wish to be released from their obligation to obey other laws they may find uncongenial. There would be no comparable privilege, in other words, for people who might object (on what they think are moral grounds) to the "welfare" system or to laws that forbid discrimination on the basis of race in the sale or rental of housing. The same premises in Hobbes that would dissolve any obligation to risk one's life would also justify the government in rejecting out of hand any claim to resist the obligation of the law on an issue involving anything other than the risk of violent death. But once those premises are made clear, the costs in principle of Hobbes's argument become even more evident, and we come to understand once again why neither liberals nor conservatives could afford to embrace Hobbes's argument, even if it should produce, on occasion, outcomes they might welcome.

ON THE MATTER of raising a challenge, in any instance, to the binding authority of the law, the teaching of Hobbes can be stated briefly. There was no provision whatsoever for any challenge of that kind. There was no willingness, for example, to contemplate the kind of legal challenge that is routinely permitted with the institution of an independent judiciary. It was unthinkable that any ordinary citizen could challenge in a legal forum the legal justification or the author-itative standing of any law. Nor was it imagined that a litigant might compel attorneys for the government to appear and show why the government would be justified in committing him to the policies es-tablished in the law. For Hobbes, these performances would have been acts of incoherence. The sovereign authority was willed into existence by the citizens themselves as an agent of their most fundamental in-terest, the interest in their own personal security. The authority of the sovereign could not be called into question without weakening the power that was created as the strongest guarantor of one's own life. And to suggest that the agent of one's own, most important interests was treating one unjustly was virtually equivalent to saying that a man could treat himself unjustly. As Hobbes understood the matter, "every subject is . . . [the] author of all the actions, and judgments of the sovereign" that he helped to institute. "It follows," said Hobbes, "that whatsoever [the sovereign] doth, it can be no injury to any of his subjects; nor ought he to be by any of them accused of injustice." Hobbes continued: "He that complaineth of injury from his sovereign, complaineth of that whereof he himself is author; and therefore ought not to accuse any man but himself; . . . It is true that they that have sovereign power may commit iniquity; but not injustice in its proper signification."[16]

Taking this argument to its limit, Hobbes averred that the sovereign might decide to put a subject to death, but he would not be committing a wrong against the subject. The killing of Uriah by David was contrary to equity, said Hobbes; yet it was not an injury to Uriah, but to God—not to Uriah because the right to do what he pleased was given to David by Uriah himself. (That is to say, Uriah had "authored," along with other subjects, the existence of a sovereign that would protect them all.)[17]

This is, to put it mildly, a rather rare and sobering perspective on the matter of political obligation. The subjects of the polity would not be conceded the right to question whether the ruler might have made a mistake, whether he might have misconceived the facts, or whether he was directing his power toward ends that were incompatible with the character of his mandate to govern. The tremors wrought even by questions of that kind apparently threatened to undermine the solid

[16] *Ibid.*, ch. 18, pp. 115-16.
[17] See *ibid.*, ch. 21, p. 139.

wall of authority which alone sheltered the individual from lawlessness and the war of all against all. Of course it was not beyond the imagination of Hobbes that rulers made mistakes, or that they could become corrupted in their exercise of power. But the stake of the citizen in remedying these defects was insignificant when compared with the vast interest he bore in preserving, unshaken and unimpaired, the authority necessary to protect his life.

That sense of the immanent fragility of civil order no doubt colored Hobbes's understanding of how portentous it was to challenge the authority of the law; and so he was moved finally to deny that the sovereign ever received his power *on condition*. In the first place, he took care to argue that the sovereign authority did *not* come into existence as a result of a contract between the ruler and his subjects. To accept that metaphor was to conceive a state of affairs in which the ruler and his subjects stood on the same plane, as two equal parties competent to contract. With an understanding of that kind, it might indeed be legitimate for subjects to raise pointed, carping, endless questions. They might flatter themselves to believe that they surrendered some of their liberties to the government in consideration for certain services that were to be rendered in exchange. They might think themselves enfranchised, then, to ask persistently whether their conditions were being met, whether the exercise of authority was ultimately compatible with the purposes for which that authority had been granted. Hobbes preferred to argue, rather, that the compact was made *among the subjects*, as they merged their concerns and consented to the creation of a government that would safeguard the natural interests they all shared.[18]

For all his craftiness in weaving arguments, however, Hobbes did not quite meet the point. Even a stranger in the street who might restrain another person in his liberty or cause him some harm would be obliged to offer a justification. That much is implicit in the sense of morals itself whenever one person affects another in an injurious, or even annoying, way. The obligation to give reasons would arise even if the offense came from one who held no responsibilities as an "agent" in the affairs of the victim. But it would require the most exotic understanding of political life to regard the government as bearing no responsibilities as an agent or custodian for the interests of its subjects. The government must surely have as much standing as an "agent" as the babysitter who acts out Wittgenstein's celebrated example: the parents instruct the babysitter to "teach the child a game"

---

[18] *Ibid.*, ch. 18, p. 114.

while they are gone; the babysitter, in their absence, teaches the child how to shoot craps.[19] From the outrage of the parents, several plausible questions emerge. Were the parents really obliged to spell out, in advance, every act that could not be performed under the character of the "mandate" they had left with the sitter? Could the sitter not be depended on to have some understanding of the things that separate legitimate from illegitimate "games," or of the considerations that might urge him to avoid any game that could be on the borderline of offensiveness? Beyond all that, was it not legitimate for the parents to raise these questions and ask for a justification? And if so much may be said even in relation to a babysitter, surely it may be said in relation to those figures who are invested with the authority to rule over their fellows with the force of law. So much must be implicit in the logic of a government of law, even without the metaphor of a "contract." So much must be implicit in the logic of morals itself.

But for Hobbes, the authority of the ruler stood on a foundation that was antecedent, as we have seen, to all laws and even to the advent of morality. For that reason, arguments about the obligations arising from compacts revealed themselves to Hobbes as a species of refined nonsense. From his most fundamental premises, he could extract the telling point here with the force of necessity: viz., "that covenants being but words and breath, have no force to oblige, contain, constrain, or protect any man, but what it has [sic] from the public sword; that is, from the untied hands of that man, or assembly of men that hath the sovereignty, and whose actions are avouched by them all, and performed by the strength of them all, in him united."[20]

A contract may be virtually meaningless without a superintending authority which has the power to guarantee or *enforce* the obligation of the contract. Contracts become possible, in other words, only *after* the government has been established. As Hobbes remarked, there was no obligation of contract in the state of nature. In the absence of an authority to enforce contracts, no one could assume that anyone else would keep his promise when it did not suit his interests. That was part, after all, of what made the state of nature such a hazardous place. Therefore it became, for Hobbes, a special kind of incoherence for the citizen ever to challenge the faithfulness of the government to the social compact. That very challenge would serve to weaken the authority which alone made it meaningful to speak of any obligation

[19] Ludwig Wittgenstein, *Philosophical Investigations* (New York: Macmillan, 1953), p. 33n.

[20] Hobbes, *Leviathan, supra*, note 1, pt. 2, ch. 18, p. 115.

arising out of a contract. Hobbes was led then to insist that "there can happen no breach of covenant on the part of the sovereign," because without the sovereign there could be no contracts in the first place.[21]

But in that event, the question must be asked: what kind of obligation could have attached to that "original" contract—*the contract that preceded all other contracts*, the contract that was made among the subjects themselves to establish a sovereign authority? If Hobbes is to be taken at his word, no obligation could exist until after a government was constituted. Was there an "obligation," then, in any strict sense, to carry out that original contract in the interval between the forming of the agreement and the steps that actually brought a government into being? And if there had been no strict obligation to respect the terms of the original contract, could we not question the *obligation* to respect all of those other commitments of law that flow out of the original contract?

Hobbes's answer to this question would be inescapable. The motive to respect the original contract would depend on the most basic of all motives: the motive that could ensure a universal interest in respecting the contract even if a government did not yet exist. To put it another way, the binding force of the contract would depend on that motive or passion which needs no further inducement or incentive to support it—the fear of violent death. People are moved inexorably to will the existence of a government as a projection of their own, most compelling self-interest.

But what could motives of this kind have to do with the character of an "obligation"? We have the occasion here to recall that no moral significance attaches to acts that are "determined" by the laws of nature. If people are moved, irresistibly, to form the original contract, it would be inapt to say that they are morally "obliged" to respect it. Besides, as we have pointed out, a moral obligation cannot be generated by an act of coercion. As Rousseau reminded us, we would not be "obliged" to hand over our money to the highwayman who held us up at the point of a gun; nor would we be obliged to honor any "contract" he made us sign under those conditions.

To say that fear or coercion can be the source of moral obligations is to deny the most elementary understandings contained in the logic of morals. And yet, Hobbes's argument is built precisely on a denial of that kind. For it is Hobbes's argument that fear and coercion may in fact provide valid bases for contracts and obligations. Hobbes pays

[21] *Ibid.*, p. 114.

218

lip service to the notion that a "choice" is necessary to a contract, but his notion of a free choice is rather eccentric. A man may be taken prisoner and given a choice between death and the paying of a ransom. If he promises to pay the ransom, Hobbes insists that he is bound by the promise he made under these conditions.[22] For he was given a "choice," after all, between death and ransom, and he chose to pay the ransom in order to live.

The choice between death and ransom, however, can hardly be regarded as a free or meaningful "choice," and by the terms of Hobbes's own argument, he surely could not have thought that the prisoner would "choose" anything other than his own preservation. This notion of a contract, in short, is unthinkable. Yet, it is the foundation of Hobbes's conviction that an obligation may flow to a government that is established out of fear,[23] and it becomes a necessary part of Hobbes's argument once one accepts his main premise: that the highest interest we have is the avoidance of death. For only if that premise is absorbed can one hold, with Hobbes, that the man who has it in his power to kill you, but holds back, has done you a favor. Only when we assume that we have no interest more preeminent than the avoidance of death can we feel grateful to the thug who spares our life (just as many hostages have felt grateful to the gunmen who released them after theatening to take their lives). And gratitude may impart, in turn, a sense of attachment and obligation. A sovereign who has the power to kill his subjects, but who uses that power instead to protect them, would seem to have the most compelling claim yet to the obedience of those subjects. For their very survival would furnish a testament to his sufferance and self-restraint. It would indicate that he has fulfilled the purposes of his mandate. But then the following line of reasoning becomes irrefutable: the sovereign who enlarges his capacity to protect his subjects enlarges his claim to their obedience; he enlarges his capacity to protect them as he enlarges his capacity to kill or to use the instruments of coercion in the most decisive way. As Hobbes understood, the sovereign would be in a better position to protect his subjects if he were freed from those legal restraints which would check his power and create doubts about his authority. It would follow, then, that as the government frees itself more and more from legal restraints, it would raise to the highest level its capacity to offer protection; and, therefore, the government that would have the highest

---

[22] *Ibid.*, pt. 1, ch. 14, p. 91.
[23] See *ibid.*, pt. 2, ch. 20, p. 130.

claim to the allegiance and obligation of its subjects would be the most thoroughgoing absolutist government.

But then, what if the government turned itself into a Nazi-like dictatorship for the sake, ostensibly, of protecting its citizens? Would there be any ground on which it could be proper or legitimate for the citizen to complain? On the premises of Hobbes's argument, the answer would be unequivocal: there could be no ground on which to raise such a complaint, because it would mark a concern for the *character of the regime* or the *terms of principle* on which people are to be governed. That kind of question was thrust into a secondary place once it was established that the preeminent interest in our lives is the avoidance of death. If that is indeed our paramount interest, then Hobbes is correct: that interest prescribes a government with untrammeled, undivided authority; and the more absolute it is, the more suited it is to its overriding mission. To insist on raising questions now about the nature of the regime would imply a radically different ordering of premises and the displacement of Hobbes in favor of Aristotle. It would be to say, with Aristotle, that the purpose of the polity is not merely to preserve life, but to establish a *good* character of life. That is, it would be to say that far more important than the preservation of our lives must be the terms of principle on which those lives are led. The highest part of our nature is our capacity for moral judgment; therefore, it cannot be a matter of indifference as to whether the conditions of our lives are consonant with the character of rational, moral beings or whether those lives are permitted to subsist only on conditions of slavery and abasement.

Observations such as these are wholly out of place in Hobbes's argument, for the same reason that they are central for Aristotle. Hobbes's design for absolute government becomes plausible only when we abstract from the nature of human beings as moral beings. His design can be regarded as plausible and compelling, in other words, only when it has banished from the body of its argument any recognition of the logic of morals itself.

But once the logic of morals is recognized, it establishes its own hierarchy of judgments, which must be incompatible with the construction of Hobbes. It would establish, as we have seen, that the life led with a concern for questions of morals and justification must be higher than a life led with indifference to moral questions. And as we follow out the implications which flow from that understanding, we are compelled to elevate Aristotle above Hobbes: we are properly concerned with the preservation of our lives, but that interest cannot be given an ascendent place over the concern for the moral character of our lives or for the terms of principle on which a political community shall be governed. As we shall see, this does not mean that we would regard as insignificant the taking of human life. It would mean, quite to the contrary, that we would pose severe and demanding questions about the grounds of principle on which any act of killing can be justified. But the justifications for taking life would have to encompass the preservation of free governments, which are founded on the premise that their citizens are endowed with moral competence.

As I HAVE suggested, the doctrines of Hobbes may exert a certain appeal to those who would seek to deny an obligation to participate in a war, because the ground of Hobbes's argument would foreclose altogether any obligation of that kind. The teaching of Hobbes would produce this result precisely because it incorporates, as its decisive premise, the notion that there is no higher interest than self-preservation. But the same premises that dissolve any obligation to serve in the military would also cut the ground out from under constitutional government itself. For they would deny that it is legitimate to challenge the government and raise questions about the terms of principle on which the community is ruled, so long as the government seeks to keep most of its citizens alive. And if that sovereign test is satisfied, there would be no justification for taking up arms "merely" for the sake of resisting a tyranny and changing the character of the regime.

We have already established why it is incoherent to state, as a categorical proposition, that it must be wrong, under all circumstances, to take human life. We have shown why it must be justified to use lethal force in resisting unjustified assaults. Now we may add, as an implication arising out of the logic of "first principles," that it would be justified to take human life for the sake of preserving a regime of law, or a government by consent, as the kind of political regime that is suitable, in principle, for beings who can give and understand reasons. Without this inference from first principles, we would not be able to explain why it is legitimate, for example, for the runaway slave to defend himself with lethal force against the slave catchers who seek to return him to slavery. It is worth recalling that the fugitive slave was not faced, in the first instance, with a threat to his life. He had value to his captors only if he was alive. It was their primary interest to restore him to his master as a living slave, not a dead one. But they would have preferred to have him dead rather than permit him to remain free. They were willing to kill the slave, then—and they were a threat to his life—only if he resisted. And so, in the current language of "rights," they might have spoken to him in this way: "We are

221

seeking, at most, to deprive you of a 'property right'—namely, your property in yourself and in the earnings produced by your labor. Would you use lethal force against us—and deprive us of our 'life rights'—merely for the sake of preserving your right of 'property' in yourself?" This question may have the advantage of reminding us of what we understood long ago: that our rights of property began with our right of property in ourselves. If we understand that it was legitimate for the slave to use lethal force for the sake of preserving his personal freedom—his ownership of himself—then we would understand at the same time why it would be justified for a people to use lethal force in preserving a free government, even if their own lives would not be threatened by the installation of a totalitarian regime.

If people may be justified in taking up arms to resist the imposition of an unjust regime, it must also follow that they would be justified in taking up arms whether the threat of that change emanates from within or without—whether it comes from local guerrillas or from enemies abroad. But then, what of the rest of the problem? If a nation may be justified in going to war and taking lives for the sake of preserving a free regime, may it *compel* its citizens to risk their lives, and possibly take lives, in defense of their country? As it turns out, that problem requires but a short, additional step once we have established that there are in fact moral grounds on which it may be *justified* to take life, and that it may be justified for a nation to engage in war for the sake of preserving a good regime. Once those fundamental points are in place, the rest of the question can be answered with a variant of Lincoln's rejoinder to Douglas on the logic of morals itself: if we can say that X (slavery) is wrong, we cannot say at the same time that everyone must be free to choose X or not according to his own sense of what suits his interests. In a similar way, we might say that "the government would be justified in establishing a policy of support for the poor and disabled," but we could not insist at the same time that "people must be free to contribute to the plan or not, according to their own sense of what suits their interests." To say that the government would be "justified" in carrying out the policy would have to imply that the government would be justified in using all means that are necessary and legitimate in seeking that end. If private charity proves to be quite sufficient to meet the needs of the poor and disabled, it may no longer be *necessary* to meet those needs through a program of taxation or compulsory support. Nor would the government be warranted in raising the needed revenue for such a program through arbitrary, unjustified methods—e.g., through laying especially heavy taxes on Orientals and Armenians. It could not be legitimate to impose far heavier costs on certain groups without any justification for picking them out, among all others, for these special burdens. But where the means are legitimate, where they are rationally related or necessary to their ends, the government would be warranted in using those means so long as the end is in fact "justified."

The obligation on the part of citizens to render military service would be covered by this same set of general propositions. If a nation is justified in undertaking military action, then it would have to be justified also in committing its citizens to the support of its policies. It would not be necessary or legitimate to conscript for service in combat people who are disabled, and certainly it would not be legitimate to impose military service through a system of classification that arbitrarily draws on one ethnic or racial group rather than another. The obligation to serve, in other words, may be justly established as an obligation under law, and it may be contravened only in those instances in which exemptions can be shown to be warranted.

There has been much nonsense of late, on the political Right as well as the Left, which has characterized the obligation to military service as a form of "involuntary servitude." It would be quite as tenable to describe taxation as a form of "involuntary servitude," since it extracts from people the fruit of their labor, compelling them, in effect, to work for a portion of the year in order to support purposes that may not be theirs. In point of fact, taxation *would* represent a form of involuntary servitude if certain conditions could not be met: the money must be necessary to support projects that the state is *justified* in undertaking, and it must be extracted through a process that is legitimate and equitable. As with anything else, the end of taxation becomes justified when it can be traced back to a moral principle. Without a principled ground of justification, taxation would indeed be merely a form of theft with legalistic trappings. In any theft, the thief appropriates to himself the fruits wrought by the labor of his victims; in supplying the wants of the thief, the victims are subjected to involuntary servitude. The difference, then, between involuntary servitude and the exactions made upon free citizens in the form of obligations turns wholly on the matter of whether the exaction was made by lawful authorities, with legitimate means, for justified ends.

Once again, the same reasoning would cover the matter of military service. Citizens are not converted into slaves when they are placed under the *just* obligations of law. (They are nothing less than slaves, of course, whenever they are compelled to obey unjustified laws.) But when citizens are called upon by their government to participate in a justified war, when conscription is administered through legitimate

223

procedures, then the obligation to serve in a war—the obligation laid upon citizens and enforced through the law—cannot be properly likened to involuntary servitude.

IT FOLLOWS from everything we have said that no one may strictly be obliged in principle to obey any law that is unjustified. That proposition follows as a necessary inference from the logic of morals. The difficulty, of course, is that it cannot be reduced to the proposition "No one may be obliged to obey any law that *he thinks* is unjustified." As we have seen, it cannot be consistent with the logic of morals to grant people a franchise to exempt themselves from the commands of law and moral propositions merely on the strength of personal beliefs. Nor could a release from obligations be granted on the basis of attributes that are utterly lacking in moral significance—e.g., the "sincerity" with which people hold their convictions, or even "their willingness to go to jail in support of their views." The conscientious objector who preferred to go to jail rather than go to war against Hitler would not have proved, by going to jail, that it was wrong to fight Hitler. The act of going to jail did not supply the substantive argument that would have been necessary to establish why it was unjustified to resort to war in resisting Hitler.

If we are to respect the character of morals, we must turn from the false sentimentality which has led us to accept features such as "sincerity" as the surrogates for a valid argument and a moral justification. Our willingness in the past to live with flawed conventions of this kind has pointed up the insoluble nature of the problem that arises when the government feels pressed to grant exemptions from the law even when the case for an exemption rests on no ground of principle that the government and the public have been able to comprehend.

The problem has rarely been put as deftly as it was by Plato in the *Crito*. This dialogue was set at the time just after Socrates had been sentenced to die for corrupting the young and teaching disrespect for the gods of Athens. Crito, one of his young followers, urged Socrates to flee before the sentence was carried out. Crito argued that Socrates would dishonor his friends in failing to escape, because "most people will never believe that it was you who refused to leave this place." They were more likely to believe that his friends had failed him, that they had not cared enough to spend the money and secure his escape.[24]

Socrates' response to this first line of pleading was to ask Crito why he placed so much importance on what "most people" thought. To

[24] Plato, *Crito*, 44b-d.

make that consideration decisive was to concede a certain moral authority to public opinion, and yet why should one respect an opinion uninformed by understanding? It was precisely that concern for the opinion of the public which had moved the authorities to prosecute Socrates. Should he now shape his own acts out of respect for that same opinion of the multitude?

And yet, as Plato drew the dialogue on, this initial argument of Socrates would in the end be overturned. Socrates came to concede, implicitly, the main concern in Crito's pleading: ultimately, Socrates' argument would indeed be governed by a concern for the effect of his act on the public understanding. At one moment, Socrates conceded to Crito that if he were in fact justified in running away from the prison, then he *ought* to run away. But as he held back from acting on that proposition, he seemed to hold back out of a concern for prudence in its highest and best sense: he held back, that is, out of a concern that his act would be destructive of the very principle he meant to vindicate. And it would be destructive because of the way in which the act of running away was bound to be misunderstood by the public at large.

The intractable problem for Socrates might have been put in this way. If the public and the authorities understood that he would be justified in fleeing, they would have to understand that he had been prosecuted unjustly. In that event, there would be no need to run away; he would be officially discharged from prison. But if he were not freed, it would be because neither the authorities nor the public thought that Socrates had been prosecuted unjustly. If Socrates fled under these circumstances, the public would not understand the principle that made it justified for him to run away. The only conclusion the public would be capable of drawing is that Socrates left when the restrictions and obligations of the law did not suit his interests. And if this franchise could be claimed by a teacher of right and wrong, why should it not be claimed by others, who may also encounter a tension at times between the commands of the law and their own self-interest?

That prospect was portentous, not merely because of the consequences it might produce, but because of the principle it would seem to affirm in public. The consequences were evident enough: if the obligations of the law may be cast aside when they are in conflict with anyone's interests, then the laws—all the laws—would be weakened at their foundation. As Socrates put the question, rhetorically, to Crito, "Do you imagine that a city can continue to exist and not be turned upside down, if the legal judgments which are pronounced in it have no force but are nullified and destroyed by private persons?"[25] Socrates imagines an anguished conversation with The Laws of Athens, suddenly embodied and standing before him, threatened by the prospect of his treason. As Plato quickly has Socrates concede, his quarrel indeed was not with the laws—not with the laws that provided for the nurturing and education of the young; not with the laws through which his own parents had married and begotten him; and not with the laws under which he was content to raise his own children. If Socrates had a quarrel, it was not with the laws in general *or with the principle that enjoins the existence of laws.* His quarrel was with the particular judgments rendered by particular men under the laws.[26] But in that event, Socrates would run the risk of creating vaster evils than the injustice done in his own case: in vindicating the wrong done to him, he would strike at the foundation of *all* the laws.

And yet, beyond the estimate of these sobering consequences, the prospect of leaving prison only through an escape had to be unacceptable to Socrates in point of principle. So long as the understanding of the public remained defective, the act of running away could be fathomed by the public only as an expression of this proposition: that Socrates did not respect any law as valid or binding on him if it ran counter to his own interests. Unless the public was willing to regard Socrates as a superior man, who was properly beyond the laws made for other men, it would be compelled to extract the more general lesson: viz., that in the judgment of Socrates, there were *no* laws that were valid and binding when they came in conflict with one's own self-interest. *But that was to say that there were no morals in the strictest sense.* How could that be the last dramatic lesson taught in public by a man who had devoted his life to moral teaching? How could his last act as a teacher and a citizen be to shake the public from its conviction that there are indeed moral imperatives and moral obligations?

Socrates could properly be warranted in leaving prison, then, only when he received, as he said, an "official discharge"—only when the judgment of the authorities could sustain the justice of releasing him and inform the understanding of the public. That event could take place only if Socrates were able to "persuade" the authorities to let him go; if he were to escape without seeking to offer that persuasion, Socrates was convinced that he would do a serious injury to the laws.[27]

[25] *Ibid.,* 50b.
[26] *Ibid.,* 50b-d, 54b-c.
[27] *Ibid.,* 49e-50a.

In four separate places, Socrates affirms that he would not be justified in leaving prison without "persuading" the authorities, the city, or "the laws" that his release would be justified. The commitment to persuade marks the commitment, in moral discourse, to offer reasons, and it marks the high prudence of political life in seeking the consent of the multitude.[28]

THE SAME insolvable problem that faced Socrates would have to face any person seeking an exemption from military service under a government of law. As we have seen, that exemption could not be granted merely on grounds of "personal belief" without denying the concept of morals itself and the very notion of law. In many cases, of course, an "exemption" is not the proper action to seek, because the purpose is not to win an exception from an otherwise valid law, but to challenge the justification for the law itself. For that reason, the challenge pressed by ordinary litigation or by "civil disobedience" is more aptly tailored to the moral requirements of contesting the law. The challengers put themselves in the position of breaking a law they regard as wrong, and when prosecuted, they would compel both the government and themselves to offer reasoned justification in a legal forum.

It also becomes critical, in these situations, that the violation of the law is managed in such a way that the parties are required to direct their arguments to the validity of the law under challenge. When Martin Luther King forced his arrest for riding in the front of a bus in Birmingham, Alabama, the case that moved through the courts on appeal had to focus at some point on the question of whether it was justified to require, by law, the separation of the races in public conveyances. When students protested the draft by refusing to carry draft cards, courts had to deal with the question of whether it was justified for the government to administer a military draft. But when students blocked the road to an Air Force base in Massachusetts for the sake of protesting the war in Vietnam, the courts had to confine themselves to the question of whether the government had a legitimate interest in preserving access to a military base. Nothing in that ritual act of violating the law could have compelled a court to address the legality of the war in Vietnam.

In a free society with open courts, the citizen may not have to wait until he can persuade a majority of his fellow citizens in a free election before an unjust law can be overturned. But if he failed to persuade either the courts or the electorate, he would be faced precisely with

[28] *Ibid.*, 49e-50a, 51b, 51c, 51c-52a.

the problem that afflicted Socrates. To the public and the government, which still do not see his claim as justified, he would be asserting that no law has the authority to elicit his obligation when it runs counter to his judgment. Rather than teach a lesson as untenable and destructive as that, a citizen in certain cases may choose, out of prudence, to hold back from a course of disobedience. Or, if the disobedience is necessary to avoid an egregious, evil act, he may console himself, in jail, with a Platonic understanding: it may at least be better that he suffer injustice than that he *do* injustice. For the hard fact of the matter is that there is no way, consistent with the character of morals, that exemptions from the law can be conferred outside a process of "justification." If the process should fail to sustain a valid challenge to an unjust law, the man of understanding may indeed find some consolation in suffering imprisonment, rather than establishing a principle that is incompatible with the notion of law or, on the other hand, making himself the agent of an evil purpose.

On the question of civil disobedience, of course, there is far more to be said. The science of moral reasoning cannot displace the arts of conjecture and practical wisdom that are indispensable to citizens and statesmen alike; and it is through these arts of judgment that people must calculate whether they can serve their principled ends better by holding back, out of prudence, or whether the situation is ripe in any case for a dramatic show of disobedience and reasoned challenge. A public gesture of disrespect for law is implicit in every public act of civil disobedience, and the casual resort to this device may have the effect of eroding that reverence for the law which is necessary to any decent society. The plain, unyielding fact is that these gestures can be justified only when the laws they attack are indeed unjustified; when these gestures are not warranted, they will be mischievous and destructive in their tendency. In a society without law, there may be nothing to lose. To interfere with the shipment of Jews to the killing centers of the Nazis was not to engage in lawless acts, but to honor the principles of lawfulness in a society without the restraint of law. And yet, what if the same spectacle should take place in a country with an elected government and with courts that were independent but unsympathetic? Under those conditions would a person have a diminished obligation to interpose himself, where he could, to save the victims? But we need not put the question to ourselves by contriving, in our imagination, the displacement of the Holocaust to America. It is sufficient to consider the situation that confronts those people in our country today who see, in the accumulating volume of abortions year by year, a massive taking of human lives that rivals the scale of the Holocaust. Would these people be well advised to throw their bodies in the way of the machinery of killing by blocking and disrupting the abortion clinics—perhaps even destroying them? Or would such efforts have to be seen merely as acts of lawlessness by those who have not come to see abortions in the same way as the taking of human lives? In that case, the opponents of abortion may merely burden their own cause and make it harder in the long run to achieve their principled ends. They might be better advised, then, to take the counsel of Socrates: to stay scrupulously within the law and concentrate their efforts on "persuading" their fellow citizens toward a change in the law. For if a change in the law is finally achieved, that achievement is more likely to be secure if the public has been schooled to understand the reasons behind the change.

Many of these questions must turn, as I say, on an estimate of the political moment—on the possibilities it offers for teaching the right lessons in public; or, on the other hand, the possibilities for being misunderstood. The man of responsibility who challenges the law would not wish to offer his challenge in a casual or blithe manner, for he would know how morally portentous his act is, even in a good cause. He would speak, at best, in the manner of Viscount Dorte when he was commanded by Charles IX of France to slay all of the Huguenots in his province. The viscount wrote back: "Sire, among the inhabitants of this town, and your majesty's troops, I could not find so much as one executioner; they are honest citizens and brave soldiers. We jointly, therefore, beseech your majesty to command our arms and lives in things that are practicable."[29] There is a manner of speaking to authority that does not call into question the rightfulness of authority itself, but rather reminds people in official power of the moral conditions on which their own authority rests.

IMPLICITLY OR explicitly in these last two chapters, the question has been present as to whether words of this kind might have been spoken properly by Mr. Guy Gillette and others of his persuasion who were opposed to serving in the Vietnam war. That question could not be put directly on its own terms because it was always lurking behind other legal claims, which had to be addressed on other grounds. Those other claims, as it turned out, were not tenable. The claim to "conscientious objection" really reduced to a claim to be exempt from the obligations of law on the strength of personal "beliefs" that could not

[29] Quoted in Montesquieu, *The Spirit of the Laws*, trans. Thomas Nugent (New York: Hafner, 1949), bk. IV, ch. 2, p. 31.

be examined or judged by others. The provenance of those beliefs, whether in "religion" or "sincerity," was beside the point, for neither source could supply a substantive moral argument about the justification or the wrongness of the war in Vietnam. Nor could the case be resolved through an insistence, in the name of "religion," that it was wrong under all circumstances to take human life. A statement that cannot claim coherence as a categorical proposition on its own ground cannot be accorded that standing merely because it is uttered under the authority of a "religious" doctrine.

As we swept away these spurious grounds of judgment, we managed to establish that it must be justified, under certain conditions, to take human life; that people and nations may be justified in going to war for the sake of preserving the terms of principle on which beings with moral judgment deserve to live; and that if nations are justified in going to war at times, they may be justified in committing their own citizens to service in the war. That is to say, it may not only be permissible to take life, but under certain conditions one may be *morally obliged* to risk one's life and possibly take the lives of others. And yet, none of the propositions we have established would rule out the possibility of further argument over the justification for the war in Vietnam. We may be clearer now on the spurious arguments that cannot be used in settling our judgment; but it is still possible for Gillette and others to offer moral arguments with a finer focus in considering whether the particular war fought by the United States in Vietnam was unjustified.

In order to judge that question, it will be necessary to consider the arguments that were raised about the nature of that conflict in particular and the issues it portrayed. Once again, any argument about "justifications" must trace back to principles of judgment, and we discover that arguments about this particular war in Vietnam still draw their judgments from understandings of a more general nature about the things that are right and wrong. They may depend, for example, on the conviction that it is always wrong for one nation to interfere in the internal affairs of another country, even if its engagement may have been invited by the local government. In that event we would again find ourselves in the position of testing the validity of these propositions as categorical propositions, and of clearing away spurious doctrines which cannot properly settle the case.

But the arguments do remain to be considered, along with the facts that may help define for us the character of the war we were asked to judge. I should point out, in addition, that I have so far established only that a nation may be justified in going to war for the sake of preserving the terms of principle on which it deserves to live. The conflict in Vietnam, however, posed no immediate and direct threat to the character of the regime in the United States. It is proper to consider, as a separate question, whether a nation would be justified in going to war not to defend itself (or its regime), but to defend other people and to preserve decent regimes elsewhere. The answer to that question, I think, is already entailed by one of the propositions set forth above, in the section on "first principles." But it is a question that deserves to be raised and addressed separately. If it turns out that a nation may indeed be justified in going to war for the sake of other peoples, it would have to follow, from the reasoning we have reviewed here, that it would also be justified in committing its citizens to the support of such a war. In that case, a nation may actually be justified in creating for its citizens an obligation to fight, not only for themselves and their way of life, but for the lives and freedoms of others.

XI

ON THE JUSTIFICATIONS OF WAR
AND THE TWO VIETNAMS

In 1971, with the war continuing in Vietnam, Professor Michael Walzer offered an essay that asked, "World War II: Why Was This War Different?"[1] No explicit comparison was made to the war in Vietnam, and yet no one could mistake the answer to the silent question, "Different from what?"[2] For anyone concerned about the moral justification of war, the main preoccupation at the time was with the war in Vietnam. The title of Walzer's essay reflected a certain defensiveness: there was a burden of argument to be met by a number of writers and public figures who regarded as patently immoral the American recourse to large-scale bombing, but who were willing to override their moral reservations when it came to judging the same methods of warfare as they had been used against the Nazis.

And so Walzer found it abhorrent for a statesman to put himself in the position of ordering a bombing offensive that he knew would kill a very large and precise number of people—say, 278,966—and to mandate these killings out of a conjecture about a larger evil that might be avoided. Walzer confessed, however, that order the bombing he would. As he admitted, he would have sided with Churchill: Walzer would have committed a "determinate crime" (as he put it) for the sake of averting an "immeasurable evil."[3] Of course, the bombing of German cities could not be considered a "crime" if Walzer really regarded that bombing as necessary and "justified." But the notion of an "immeasurable evil" must be regarded as a matter of no small philosophic significance in Walzer's argument, for it conveys what Walzer, to his credit, understood with perfect clarity: viz., that the

---

[1] *Philosophy and Public Affairs* (Fall 1971), pp. 3-21. Parts of this essay were later carried over into Walzer's book *Just and Unjust Wars: A Moral Argument with Historical Illustrations* (New York: Basic Books, 1977), pp. 253-62.

[2] In *Just and Unjust Wars*, Walzer did suggest some of the considerations that guided his judgment of the war in Vietnam, but the book still did not correct the omission evident in the essay. Neither in the book nor in the essay was there an attempt to judge the war in Vietnam by the same standards that justified, for Walzer and others, a costly war to resist the Nazis. To draw those comparisons explicitly and take matters to their ground of judgment is the object of the pages that follow.

[3] Walzer, in *PAPA*, *supra*, note 1, p. 19; Walzer, *Just and Unjust Wars*, *supra*, note 1, p. 259.

war against the Nazis could never be justified if it were judged solely in a utilitarian way, by making a calculation of the lives lost, balanced against the lives that were saved. Walzer could describe the Nazi regime as "murderous" and "degrading," as "evil objectified," because of the policy of genocide that was carried out against the Jews. And yet, if a moral judgment had to turn on a utilitarian calculus alone, it would have been hard to justify a war that took 30 million lives (in all theaters) for the sake of saving 6 million Jews in Europe, or even several million more elsewhere in the world—or, for that matter, even a few million more Slavs and gypsies. As Walzer rightly remarks, "the human losses involved in a Nazi victory are not losses of life alone, and the gains of war or peace cannot be measured simply in lives saved."[4]

Most wars have not been Carthaginian wars, in which one country seeks to destroy completely the population of another; even in the case of the Second World War, a Nazi victory would not have meant the killing of all people in the conquered countries. Hitler, as we know, was willing to accord a special place in his new "order" to the "Aryan" or "Nordic" peoples. The Anglo-Saxons of Britain and the United States did not have to fear for their physical destruction, and Scandinavians in Minnesota did not have to go to war with the Nazis for the sake of their own self-preservation. Nevertheless, blond children of Scandinavian parents in the United States did risk their lives, and their sacrifice could be explained only by an interest that they shared with others in resisting the imposition of a Nazi dictatorship. They were willing to risk their lives, in other words, for the sake of preserving a certain way of life or certain kinds of political orders that were more justified for human beings.

But when we find that the justification for the war hinged, in this way, on the terms of principle on which a people would live, we are compelled to recognize, as Walzer did, that the evil we sought to prevent was "literally beyond calculation": it had nothing to do with matters of locale or scale or with the absolute numbers of the victims. The wrongness of genocide was indifferent to matters of scale, and in any event the evil of the Nazi regime was evident long before it was expressed in the mechanics of killing in vast numbers. Genocide was only one reflection, among many, of a political order founded on premises that were incompatible with the logic of morals and the principles of constitutional government. Genocide was rooted, we might say, in the character of a certain political regime; and it was in

---

[4] Walzer, in *PAPA, supra,* note 1, pp. 9-10.

the nature of regimes of that kind that they lacked the internal, legal constraints which would make it hard for rulers to carry out policies of genocide.

Once it becomes clear to us that the justification for war turns on the nature of the regime we seek to resist; once we understand that the nature of the evil is indifferent in principle to the size of the country and the race of the victims—once we are clear on these points, we can truly ask: Why indeed *was* the Second World War "different"? Why were the interests at stake in that war different in principle from the interests that were at stake in Vietnam?

WALZER was quite right in recognizing that the justification of a war cannot turn simply on the calculus of lives saved and lost, because he also understood that the polity itself was not merely an alliance for "self-preservation." As he put it, "the social union is something more than a pact for the preservation of life; it is also a way of living together and (inevitably) of living with other peoples and other unions. . . ."[5] What was there about the German "way of living together" under the Nazis which would have made it clear to Western statesmen that they were confronting an "immeasurable evil"? As Walzer understood it, that evil was constituted by "the rule of men committed to the continual use of violence, to a policy of genocide, terrorism, or enslavement."[6] But at the time of the Munich crisis (1938) or the beginning of the Second World War (1939), the Nazis had not launched upon the "final solution" to the "Jewish problem" with the systematic destruction of European Jews. And yet Walzer thinks that what was known to the leaders of Britain and France at the time of Munich should have been enough to counsel their resistance. They knew, as Walzer remarks, "what sort of government the Germans had, what it was doing in its own country, and what it was likely to do in any country it came to rule."[7] The Jews in Germany were removed from the professions, and they were eventually barred from most ways of making a living. They were progressively stripped of their civil rights and finally even of their "natural" rights, as they became the target of lawless assaults in the street, tolerated or even orchestrated by the authorities.

Still, the treatment of the Jews could have been taken merely as the mark of yet another government willing to build support for itself by

[5] *Ibid.*, p. 10.
[6] *Ibid.*, p. 7.
[7] *Ibid.*, p. 8.

cultivating the hostility of the populace toward a local minority. In the American South, blacks were for the most part denied schooling and the possibility for entry into the professions; they were denied their civil rights; and they were quite ofen subjected to a reign of terror that included lynchings and sadistic mutilations. These outrages were somehow "accommodated" within the American federal system, as the national government found it hard to summon the legal authority or the political support that would have been necessary to deal with these injustices. Presumably, however, it would have made some difference to Walzer that this treatment of a minority in the United States ran counter to the principles on which the government itself was founded. The political order in the United States contained within itself the premises that would permit the national government one day to reach these evils and repress them. The violence of the Nazi SS and SA could also have been likened to the rule of thugs and Mafiosi in a number of American cities, and the level of violence in the United States might actually have been higher. But, once again, it made a difference that the violence did not emanate, as it were, from the principles on which the American polity was founded. The structure of the American constitutional order could not have been seen merely as a contrivance meant to further that violence by removing the most important legal barriers which might impede it.

In Germany, on the other hand, the treatment of the Jews arose, comprehensibly, from the perspective set forth by Hitler in his writings and public speeches; and that treatment became part of an intelligible design when it emanated from a government constituted and shaped according to the principles that animated Hitler and his movement. The decisive moral landmark, then, for Western statesmen should have been, as Walzer said, the "sort of government the Germans had." The Nazi regime was itself the most significant mark of the moral character of the Nazi rulers, their commitments, and their intentions. As we saw earlier, genocide, like anything else that is categorically wrong, is incompatible with the very logic of morals. But so, too, is the denial of government by consent and the rejection of all of those requirements which arise out of the character of a government of law. These points, as we have seen, are all connected in principle. And so, even if a political order does not manifest its character in policies of genocide, it is possible to discover, in the founding principles of that polity, the premises that make genocide more legitimate and acceptable. We need not wait, then, for the regime to show a genocidal bent before we may find fault with it: the regime would be offensive on the most fundamental points of principle, and we would be warranted in resisting it even before it acts out its character in policies of wholesale killing. The possibilities for genocide are likely to be strongest in those places where the rejection of the principles of lawfulness and constitutional government have been most radical and thoroughgoing, and it should not be surprising that we have called governments of this kind "totalitarian."

As Hannah Arendt made clear in her classic study of totalitarianism, we do not deal here simply with a more stringent form of the dictatorships or authoritarian systems that have become familiar in the world:

> [A]uthority is not filtered down from the top through all intervening layers to the bottom of the body politic as is the case in authoritarian regimes. The factual reason is that there is no hierarchy without authority and that, in spite of the numerous misunderstandings concerning the so-called "authoritarian personality," the principle of authority is in all important respects diametrically opposed to that of totalitarian domination. Quite apart from its origin in Roman history, authority, no matter in what form, always is meant to restrict or limit freedom, but never to abolish it. Totalitarian domination, however, aims at abolishing freedom, even at eliminating human spontaneity in general, and by no means at a restriction of freedom no matter how tyrannical.[8]

Authoritarian systems have been respecters of traditional hierarchies of authority, and so they have usually been willing to accommodate themselves to the authority that has long reposed in families, churches, private property, and even, in certain cases, the civil service and the judiciary. The ends of authoritarian leaders have often been limited to the preservation of their own power, and they may preserve their power mainly through the expedient of avoiding free elections. So long as the rulers are able to secure the levers of power and quiet the sources of opposition in the press and the universities, they may be willing to leave large areas of society free from their interventions. In many instances, the respect of these regimes for traditional sources of authority has led them to tolerate active dissent and criticism, emanating from sanctuaries within the regime. In 1975 the archbishop of São Paulo denounced the military government of Brazil after a journalist had died under mysterious circumstances in an army prison. The bishops of the São Paulo Diocese joined in a statement read from the

---

[8] Hannah Arendt, *The Origins of Totalitarianism* (New York: Harcourt Brace, 1951), pp. 404-405.

pulpits denouncing the use of torture and unlawful methods in the interrogation of suspects. Their protest was soon echoed by associations of journalists, lawyers, and university students, which called for an investigation into the death of the journalist and the detention of other political prisoners.[9] Around the same time, Eduardo Frei, a former president of Chile, attacked the military government of General Augusto Pinochet in a widely circulated booklet. The booklet was printed and distributed by a Catholic publishing house in Santiago, in defiance of the laws on censorship. In Chile, it was apparently the residual strength of the Catholic Church which provided a shelter of autonomy that could protect political dissenters. In Brazil, under an authoritarian government of less severity, there were many more sources of autonomy, and there was much more freedom then to engage in public criticism of the government.

In totalitarian regimes, we may find occasions when public criticism is permitted, and in certain places the Catholic Church may secure a *de facto* autonomy for itself. That autonomy has been most notable in Poland, and as recent events have shown, it was a sign of a society that became disposed to reject the authority of dictatorship in other spheres as well. If it were not for the hegemony of the Soviets in Eastern Europe, there is little doubt that the Poles would force a movement toward one form or another of "government by consent." It was virtually predictable that the USSR would force a halt to the reforms that were adopted under the influence of Lech Walesa and Solidarity—reforms that had begun to peel back the totalitarian state. For the Soviets are guided by a very precise political science when it comes to preserving a regime of unrestrained, centralized power on the Leninist model. The Soviets may be able to brook, at times, criticism voiced against the government, but when that criticism is broadcast to the public and sets off currents of opposition in the country, and when that opposition seeks its political expression in free trade unions and elections, the Soviet rulers understand that this state of affairs cannot be reconciled with the principles of a totalitarian regime. Beyond that, they are wholly free of the illusion that anything less than a regime based on the Soviet model, and headed by Soviet surrogates, can be counted on to preserve, in Poland, a government "friendly to the Soviet Union."

The Soviets understand that a true totalitarian regime must reject, in principle, any source of authority in society that may rival the authority of the regime in any sphere. In a totalitarian regime, the

<hr>

[9] *New York Times*, November 16, 1975, p. 18.

leadership claims a monopoly of legitimate authority because it claims to represent a monopoly of understanding on the ends and means of justice. That knowledge may take the form of a "scientific" understanding of the "laws of history" and of the social classes whose interests can be counted on to be "progressive" or "reactionary" in history. Or it can be represented by a theory of "race," which may disclose the laws by which races work out their destinies. Either way, the prospect of sharing power must be a prospect of the wise compromising their best judgment by making concessions to the unwise. The progress of history would then be retarded, the attainment of justice would be delayed, and of course justice delayed would be justice denied. For reasons embedded deeply in their character, totalitarian regimes distrust what they do not control; therefore, they cannot make their peace with any limitation on political power or with any source of authority outside the official hierarchy.

There is a risk here in being facile, and we should be careful to note that the offensiveness of totalitarian regimes is not to be found most decisively in their claim to a comprehensive political truth which is universal in its reach. As we have shown, that claim must properly attach to moral propositions in the strictest sense, and if we are in the presence of genuine moral truths, there is no gainsaying their universal sovereignty. As we shall see later, also, the logic of a moral principle must be indifferent to the distinction between the public and the private. Once we understand the ground, say, on which a certain killing may be called "unjustified" and "wrong," the wrongness of the act would be indifferent to the question of whether the murder occurred in a public street or a private bedroom. If totalitarian principles could properly claim the force of moral truth, there would be nothing wrong with their claim to govern within private as well as public spheres.

The critical defect in totalitarian principles lies in their moral substance. The theories that prescribe a totalitarian organization of political power are usually predicated on assumptions that deny the capacity of human beings as creatures with moral autonomy; and they typically fail to comprehend the connection between a regime that claims a moral justification for its existence and a regime that is governed by constitutional restraints. The founders of totalitarian regimes invariably make it the first business of their rule to break down those conventions of law which restrain and discipline the exercise of political power. But if the founders of these regimes understood the implications that arise from their own pretensions to create a morally just political order, they would not see themselves at war with the conventions of lawfulness. They would find in those procedures, rather, an invitation to an exercise they should gladly accept: namely, the task of establishing the *justification* for their policies and demonstrating, at the highest level, their moral claim to govern. Anyone who understands what it means to establish the justice of a political order will know that it is bound up with the possibility of offering reasons, and that nothing can stand as a substitute for the giving of those reasons. The fact that a ruler is drawn from a class of philosophers or proletarians or Aryans cannot be taken to mean that his judgments will be unerring. The proper test for the soundness of moral judgments can never be anything other than a test of the reasons offered in support of those judgments.

A political order that would encourage rulers to offer justifications for themselves would contrive the kinds of institutions that encourage rulers to give reasons in public, to appeal to standards of judgment beyond their own private interests. Experience suggests that the institutions most aptly tailored to that end would be free elections and independent courts. Few things break through the reticence of leaders so well, or induce them more readily to offer an account of themselves to the public, as the need to seek the votes of citizens in a free election. And if a free society should manage to produce a majority concerting in a policy of injustice, the existence of independent courts of law allows even one aggrieved citizen to compel his government to engage in moral discourse: a citizen who goes into court and claims to be injured by the policy of the government may actually compel attorneys for the government to come forward and justify the ground of law on which the government would presume to commit its citizens to that policy. If the complaining citizen should fail to have his judgment vindicated in the courts, he has still another means of withdrawing his acquiescence in the law without choosing a course of lawlessness. He may exercise his right to emigrate to another country and, in that way, he may manifest his unwillingness to consent to the terms on which the government would insist on governing him.

In the *Crito*, Socrates imagines the Laws of Athens taunting him with the prospect of his escape from prison and his gesture of contempt for the laws. Socrates is asked why he would now act out his disrespect for the laws when he has persistently affirmed his acceptance of them in the past. Plato conjures up a scene in which the laws argue to Socrates in this way:

> They would say, Socrates, we have substantial evidence that you are satisfied with us and with the state. You would not have been so exceptionally reluctant to cross the borders of your country if

you had not been exceptionally attached to it. You have never left the city to attend a festival or for any other purpose, except on some military expedition. You have never traveled abroad as other people do, and you have never felt the impulse to acquaint yourself with another country or constitution. You have been content with us and with our city. You have definitely chosen us, and undertaken to observe us in all your activities as a citizen, and as the crowning proof that you are satisfied with our city, you have begotten children in it.[10]

So long as Socrates was free to leave the city, his continuing residence could be taken plausibly as a sign that the condition of the laws, and the moral character of the city, were by and large acceptable to him. For that reason, the freedom to emigrate has been taken as another means by which the individual may manifest or withdraw his *consent* to the laws of the community. When that freedom is combined with the institutions of free elections and independent courts, we have three precise institutional tests by which to gauge whether we are in the presence of a constitutional order. We have, of course, more than three tests. We have all of the implications that arise for political life from the logic of morals—the implications that tell us, for example, why we must have fair trials and make reasoned discriminations between the innocent and the guilty. Beyond that, we have all the implications that arise from the logic of these institutional arrangements—in the way, for example, that independent courts of law may naturally give rise to restraints on the extraction of evidence from suspects through coercion or intimidation. The progressive discovery of these implications marks the refinement of any society as a constitutional order; but even if the refinements have not advanced very far, those countries which are defined by the presence of free elections, independent courts, and free emigration would have to be regarded as morally superior to societies that are wanting in these features. The absence of these legal institutions would signal the division between governments of law and dictatorships. If we find, in the universe of dictatorships, political regimes that recognize no private control of property or respect no sanctuary of privacy beyond the reach of the authorities, we are likely to be in the presence of a political order that reflects, in its institutional life, the premises of totalitarianism.

As I have tried to suggest, no regime could be so persistent in rejecting the conventions of freedom and consent without at the same time rejecting that sense of moral autonomy or moral competence in human beings that makes it morally necessary for them to be governed

[10] Plato, *Crito*, 52b-c.

only with their consent and only through conventions of lawfulness. A political order that rejects those premises will be deflected from policies of genocide or lawless violence only by political prudence or the want of opportunity, for it cannot be restrained by any scruple built into its nature. Once it is assumed that human beings lack the moral autonomy to form their own acts, it remains merely to identify the causes that "determine" certain classes, irredeemably, as criminals or as enemies of the regime. In this way Stalin could assume that any child who grew up as a member of a class of landholding peasants would acquire interests that had to be adverse to the interests of a Communist regime. A Marxist-Leninist society would be at war with the reflexes and freedoms nurtured by private property—hence the necessity of destroying the kulaks as a class. In the Soviet Union, violence erupted when the kulaks resisted the drive, in the 1930's, to expropriate their property and bring them into "collective farms." Some peasants preferred to slaughter their livestock rather than submit to a scheme of collective theft, and the result was a massive famine that was estimated to have taken some 5.5 million lives.[11] The sensibilities of the Soviet rulers were reflected also in their willingness to divert grain from the domestic market during this time of famine for the sake of bringing forth exports which could earn foreign exchange, which in turn could help finance the goods that were needed for industrial development. The deaths that resulted from collectivization and the famine may be charged properly, therefore, to the record of the Soviet regime. The leadership established quite tellingly the cost it was prepared to accept in human lives for the sake of preventing a class of private owners from exercising significant power over any sector of the economy.

Almost regardless of the cost, it was nearly certain that the political interests of a totalitarian regime would impel the rulers toward a war with the kulaks. For the same reason, the experience in the Soviet Union essentially prefigured the collectivization drive and the violence that took place in Communist China and North Vietnam in 1956-57. In the vastness of China the drive to deal with class enemies eventually claimed about a million lives. On the more modest scale of North Vietnam, the terror of the collectivization was estimated to have taken 50,000-100,000 lives. In all cases, the political interests and the governing imperatives were the same. Both sprung from the principles that established the ends of these regimes, along with the structures of power that could permit leaders to act without legal restraint.

But even if the violence of collectivization had been postponed in

[11] Robert Conquest, *The Great Terror* (London: Macmillan, 1968), p. 23.

North Vietnam for a few more years, would it not have been evident as to what this regime was? The size of the territory, as we have said, was virtually irrelevant. The leaders of this government understood themselves to be drawing on the same antecedents as their counterparts in the Soviet Union and China; and, with variations of form to suit the local style, the regime they established in North Vietnam was founded on the same principles as the regimes established by their "fraternal," Marxist-Leninist parties in the USSR and China. They were constituted, in other words, on the same terms of principle that had defined, for Walzer, the "immeasurable evil" of the Nazis.

IMMEDIATELY after the Second World War, a survey of agriculture in Eastern Europe revealed that farms in the Soviet satellite countries were almost entirely in private hands. Before 1948 there was much talk of "separate roads to socialism"—very much like the slogans that have been heard again since the 1960's—and it was suggested that the organization of the economy in Eastern Europe did not have to follow the lines of the Soviet model. In estimating claims of this kind and gauging the true natures of these governments in Eastern Europe, statesmen had to avoid the fallacy of taking mere "behavior" or current conduct as the sole test of character. It made a profound difference whether the tolerance of private agriculture reflected a fundamental revision in the principles of Marxist-Leninist parties—whether it marked an acceptance, in principle, of economic freedom and of private centers of power outside the control of the regime—or whether it reflected merely a prudent compromise accepted in the short run. In the aftermath of the war, the European economies were in disarray; and it could hardly ease the establishment of regimes "friendly to the Soviet Union" if those regimes stirred resistance at once in the countryside and hampered the revival of production. A sober statesman might have predicted that when the rule of Communist parties in Eastern Europe was more firmly secured, private agriculture would be largely eliminated. And he would have been correct. By 1953 the United Nations economic survey told a rather different story about agriculture in Eastern Europe: it reflected the changes wrought by regimes that were beginning to act out their Leninist character and bring all sections of the private economy under the ownership and management of the state.[12]

A similar problem arose in estimating the character of the regime in North Vietnam. In its initial phases, the Lao Dang (or Workers')

[12] United Nations, Department of Economic Affairs, *Survey of Europe since the War* (Geneva: UN, 1953), p. 28.

party of North Vietnam was willing to allow a certain measure of autonomy for the Catholic Church and a number of tribal and religious groups. It did not seek to herd farmers into collective farms and abolish private property. It sought instead a redistribution of land through a scheme of expropriation and partial compensation. But the "reform" of agriculture was carried out in North Vietnam with a wondrously precise system for cataloguing the class standing of everyone in the countryside, and ascribing vast differences in social rank on the basis of minute discrepancies in the holdings of property. In any event, families were soon organized into farming "cooperatives," and by March 1963 those cooperatives encompassed about 88 percent of all rural families. By one report they also accounted for 99 percent of all agricultural production.[13] Whether these farms were "collective" or not, agriculture in North Vietnam soon displayed the notable ineffi- ciencies and failures that were typical of collective agriculture in the Soviet Union. Over half the income for rural families came from "sup- plementary" work—i.e., work invested in the cultivation of private holdings—and the general secretary of the ruling party declared that the "subsidiary family economy is necessary . . . for the society [and] for the state-run economy." Bernard Fall aptly observed that this ad- mission did not necessarily mark any fundamental change in the doc- trine or principles of the ruling party. "It indicates simply," he said, "that when faced with the choice of either starving by the rules of Marx and Mao or eating both its rice and its principles, the North Vietnamese regime preferred the latter."[14] It would have been even more correct, however, to say that the regime was willing to accept the benefits of increased production without formally revising its doc- trine or eating its principles.

But then, how would one gauge the "real" character of the regime? If a statesman in the late 1940's had been dubious about the prospects for free agriculture in Eastern Europe, from what would he have drawn the inference that the preservation of a free economy in agriculture was not enduringly compatible with the character of Leninist regimes? In the same vein, what would have been the source of doubt that the regime in North Vietnam was accepting a free agriculture in principle rather than merely tolerating a partial free market as a necessary expedient?

In the first place, of course, there is the language and logic of prin- ciples. It makes a difference whether a policy is accepted with the

[13] Bernard Fall, *The Two Viet-Nams* (New York: Praeger, 1964), pp. 160-61. Fall neglected to state whether the percentage referred to actual volume or to the dollar value of what was produced.
[14] *Ibid.*, p. 162.

language that describes a regrettable necessity or whether it is put forth as part of a program that arises from a coherent body of doctrine. Rulers may mask their intentions, and it may be part of their purpose to make this distinction obscure. In that event, it would be necessary to disentangle the rhetoric and consider how the policies of political leaders may be reconciled with their previous writings or commitments, and with the doctrines from which they draw their understanding of the ends and uses of political power. In this respect, we remind ourselves that the training and perspectives of rulers must make a profound difference. It does matter, after all, where the leaders were schooled; what "sacred texts" had imparted to them their view of the world; and what models they looked to as examples of political orders that were founded on the right principles and committed to the proper ends.

We have here, in other words, a species of that problem which has long been identified with the sardonic question "Is the pope Catholic?" Was Ho Chi Minh really a Communist? Or was he an agrarian reformer, a Vietnamese nationalist, a Jeffersonian in Indochina? Ho Chi Minh, of course, was educated in Moscow, trained as a committed member of an international movement that found its vital core of leadership in the Soviet Union. The members of that movement have not always been certain about the precise accuracy of all of Marx's predictions, but they have been almost universally impressed with the extraordinary effect of Marxism-Leninism as a strategy for gaining and organizing the most stringent, centralized power. A governing party in its own country will naturally make innovations to suit the politics of the local situation, and so it becomes easy to point to the ways in which communism in Vietnam was "not exactly like" communism in power in the Soviet Union and China. But the questions have to be asked: Did the differences touch the core of fundamental principles? Was the Communist party in Vietnam really revising the principles of Marxism-Leninism in order to make itself relevant to local conditions? If so, what would have been the decisive test of that point? I would suggest that the most patent, obtrusive fact which would provide the touchstone of judgment here would, once again, be the structure of the regime that the party established in its own country. One had to be doubtful about the future of private agriculture in North Vietnam because the regime manifested, in its organization of authority, an unwillingness to accept in principle any source of authority outside the political leadership. In principle, the regime claimed a control over all aspects of society; it had to be hostile, then, to any island of social autonomy outside its reach.

The critical point was not so much that the rulers of Vietnam imitated the Soviet model in the institutions they created for governing the party and the state. The point, rather, was that the regime they sought to emulate was one which rejected the most important features that define a government restrained by law. It went without saying that the "Democratic Republic" of North Vietnam would have no place for free elections, independent courts, or the right to emigrate. And from the absence of these features other marks of a totalitarian state would follow: the absence of any but a rigidly controlled press and radio under the management of the state; the jailing of political adversaries without legal restraint; the imposition of an intricate, inescapable system of surveillance; and the systematic effort to frighten complainers into silence.

In all of these provisions one could find merciful abatements now and then, depending on the exigencies of the time. Over the years, the Communist regime has permitted local elections in which there has actually been a choice of candidates. But those choices have to do with local representation; the regime would never accept the notion that an election might be used by the electorate to change the nature of the regime by replacing one governing party by another. More characteristic was the election that was held in 1945. There was no secret ballot, and since the election was a device for legitimizing the new government under Ho Chi Minh, the avoidance of voting could be seen as an act of disloyalty. The voting cards were ration tickets; the voters were compelled, then, to vote if they would continue to receive food. Under these conditions, Ho Chi Minh managed to "sweep" 98 percent of the vote in Hanoi. Even more remarkable, he amassed 169,000 votes from a population in Hanoi that was listed at 119,000.[15]

After the victory of the North Vietnamese in 1975, the deceptions could finally be dropped. The so-called National Liberation Front was disbanded, and it was made plain—in case there were any lingering doubts—that the NLF had been a front for the rulers of the North in guiding the insurrection in the South. In July 1976 it was announced, with a proper sense of gravity, that the name of the reunified country would be changed to the "Socialist Republic of Vietnam." For those who took labels seriously, the new name marked a regime that was moving beyond the task of establishing independence, unification, and a "people's democracy." The regime, in its new phase, would begin

[15] See Howard R. Penniman, *Elections in South Vietnam* (Washington D.C.: AEI-Hoover Policy Studies, 1972), p. 203. For the following material on elections, the press, and political institutions in Vietnam, I can hardly do better than to rely on this thorough and judicious study.

the "socialist" construction of a new society. As it was reported by "Comrade" Huynh Tan Phat, the deputy from Ho Chi Minh City (formerly Saigon), "the light of Marxism-Leninism is shining in all fields . . .—political, economic, cultural and social." A systematic effort would be made to root out the institutions, culture, and even the "lifestyle" that had been fostered in the past by a society that did not have the guidance of state planning and control in all aspects of its life. And the state which undertook this mission could be nothing other than a "dictatorship of the proletariat . . . relying on the worker-peasant alliance under the leadership of the working class."

Some observers in the West may have been willing to believe that names and labels did not matter—that they were not to be taken all that seriously in revealing the way in which political leaders understood themselves and their commitments. But the people who directed the Vietcong and North Vietnam did not doubt for a moment who they were. They were certainly not *South* Vietnamese nationalists, and to say that they were Vietnamese nationalists was to say simply that they sought to gain control first over the country of their origin. As they soon showed, they were not averse to expanding their control within Indochina, in Cambodia and Laos, wherever weakness existed about them. And they had no doubt about the nature of the regime they would seek to establish within the territory they controlled. It would be a political order established on the principles of Marxism-Leninism as a system for organizing political power, and it would find its main allies in those countries bound together in the "socialist camp."

But then, what of the "other" Vietnam, the regime in the South that was our ally and that defined the alternative to the regime in the North? In the common discourse, that regime was not exactly reckoned to be a bargain. It was considered to have an "authoritarian" aspect even by those who thought the regime had progressed quite far in incorporating the features of a constitutional order. It was charged frequently with corruption and the use of torture, and the conviction took hold in many quarters that the conflict in Vietnam merely offered a choice between two dictatorships. The regime in the South was less efficient than the one in the North, and it was tied to American interests; but for a number of people those characteristics gave a certain ascendance to the moral claims of the Vietcong and their Northern allies. The superior discipline of the Communist forces seemed to promise a larger capacity to "mobilize" the society for revolutionary (and, presumably, "liberating") ends. In a flight of exotic reasoning, moreover, the hostility of that movement to American interests seemed to suggest that the National Liberation Front was directed to ends that were more authentically "nationalist," more shaped to the interests of the Vietnamese themselves. It was rarely contemplated, among the partisans of this school, that the interests or principles the United States was seeking to support in Vietnam were as valid in Asia as in America, and that they might have been at least as beneficial for the people of Vietnam as the ends sought by a movement which found redemptive power in the application of despotic force.

REMARKABLY, the convictions held about the character of the regime in South Vietnam have largely been detached from any specific knowledge about the workings of the political institutions there. It must also be said that ten years of the most intense coverage of the war by the American news media rarely furnished the kind of information that could relieve this general ignorance. It is not surprising that the most telling dimness of vision centered on the question of elections. Some critics were disposed to allow the signs of manipulation in Vietnamese politics to confirm their suspicion that elections in Vietnam were essentially beside the point. In that way, they were able to preserve their view of the regime in the South as an autocracy with a democratic façade. But in their refusal to notice the genuine choices offered to voters in elections that were, indeed, free, they turned away from a recognition of the important differences that separated the two Vietnams.

After the Geneva Accords in 1954, South Vietnam was still under the leadership of Bao Dai, the hereditary ruler who had been established in his position by the French. The redoubtable Ngo Dinh Diem became premier during this perilous phase, when the government of South Vietnam controlled little more than the capital city of Saigon. Diem soon established the authority of the new government by successfully challenging the collection of gangsters, pirates, and gamblers who controlled vice in the Saigon-Cholon area. He gained a reputation as a "nationalist" and as a political man free of corruption, and in 1955 he was able to displace Bao Dai in a referendum which proved quite as one-sided as the election of 1945 in North Vietnam. Most elections thereafter would show a more competitive character, even when an incumbent president clearly held a dominant position. In 1956, there would be elections to a constituent assembly, in which there would be an average of 3.5 candidates per seat. Ten years later, there would be elections to another constituent assembly to frame a new constitution, and there would be an average of 4.5 candidates per seat.[16] Under the two constitutions created by these assemblies, there would be legislative elections in which the degree of competitiveness would typically match or exceed the competitiveness seen in the elections for the constituent assemblies. In the fall of 1963, as the American government was becoming more concerned about the authoritarian tendencies within the government of President Diem, the national elections returned an assembly in which Diem's ruling party failed to secure a majority.[17]

But it was the elections to the presidency that came to be taken as a more significant test of the democratic character of the regime, and once again the most emphatic judgments were usually rendered without the benefit of any precise knowledge of the facts. In the election of 1961, Diem had to be the favored candidate; but even if the election were a setup for Diem, the result in Saigon indicated that the government did not control all the votes. Diem received 64 percent of the vote in Saigon, well below his average in the rest of the country. As a margin of victory, it has been exceeded by many political machines in America, and even by many popular candidates in political orders that could not be called "authoritarian."

In October 1963, Diem was assassinated in a coup that was encouraged by the Kennedy administration. With this move, the administration crossed a critical threshold of American responsibility for events in Vietnam, but without producing a government that was evidently strengthened in public confidence. What followed was a succession of military governments which finally stabilized, in 1965, with the creation of a National Leadership Committee under General Nguyen Van Thieu. Marshal Nguyen Cao Ky would become premier, and together these two men would form one of the most enduring couples on American television. After a new constitution was drafted by the Constituent Assembly, Thieu would become president under the elections held in 1967. Those who had no doubt, in later years, that the Thieu government was authoritarian at its root somehow overlooked the fact that Thieu had run for election in a field that included eleven party tickets, and that the team of Thieu and Ky won with a plurality of only 34.8 percent. That was notably short of the margins by which genuine authoritarian governments usually win elections, if indeed they hold elections at all. Among the opponents of Thieu, the more estimable showings were made by men who had

[16] *Ibid.*, pp. 21 and 36.

[17] *Ibid.*, p. 26. There were independents who were willing to support Diem and the government, but it is nevertheless interesting that a majority of the elected members had not attached themselves explicitly to the ruling party.

established their reputations in national politics. The ticket that came in third, for example, was formed by Phan Khac Suu and Phan Quang Dan, two veterans of the nationalist movement who had been opponents of Diem. This ticket drew strong support among Buddhists and succeeded in carrying three districts (in Danang, Hue, and Thua Thien) where the Buddhist opposition had been militant. In fourth place, with 10 percent of the vote, was a ticket headed by Tran Van Huong, who had been prime minister and mayor of Saigon, and who remained a popular figure in the capital. In fact, Tran Van Huong actually carried Saigon, defeating Thieu by a narrow margin of 137,962 to 135,527.[18]

The runner-up in the election, with 17.2 percent of the national vote, was a ticket headed by a political unknown, Truon Dinh Dzu, a lawyer who had the reputation of operating at the borders of the law. Dzu was the only candidate who ran on a strong "peace" platform, which favored an unconditional end to the bombing of North Vietnam and of the areas held by the Vietcong. Not surprisingly, Dzu found his main strength in areas where the influence of the Vietcong was more pronounced.[19] Dzu was seen, in effect, as the candidate of the Vietcong, and his presence on the ballot allowed the elections to yield a rather clear sense of the state of opinion in South Vietnam. The sentiment that favored an end to the war on almost any terms of accommodation with the Vietcong was rejected by more than 80 percent of the electorate. That majority showed its divisions over a number of issues in the politics of South Vietnam; in its judgment on the war, however, it manifested a firm, though moderate, position. It gave only about 2 per cent to a "hawk" who wished to invade or bomb North Vietnam with the purpose of displacing the Communist regime. The bulk of the vote (about 80 percent) went to candidates who were willing to negotiate with North Vietnam, but who were willing also to persevere in the war if negotiations brought no concessions from the other side.[20]

It was one of the oddities in the American perception of Vietnam that these results of the election in 1967 were not appreciated for what they revealed about the openness and competition of South Vietnamese

[18] Ibid., pp. 68-69, 73.

[19] In contrast, Penniman points out, there was no apparent relation between the presence of government troops and the vote for Thieu and Ky. In the areas designated as I Corps and II Corps, where the fighting was heaviest and where there were larger numbers of troops, the Thieu-Ky ticket ran less well than it did in the South, where the presence of the military was not so prominent.

[20] See ibid., pp. 87-88.

politics, even in the middle of a war. If Thieu could not be branded a despot who arranged 98 percent of the vote for himself, he could be condemned instead as a minority candidate who was imposed on his country with less than 35 percent of the popular vote. Of course, results of that kind are not uncommon in electoral systems in which the victory goes to the candidate with a plurality (i.e., with the largest number of votes, regardless of whether it represents a majority of the votes cast). In the United States, Lincoln was elected at a time of national crisis with a substantial majority in the electoral college, but with only about 39 percent of the popular vote. In this century Woodrow Wilson, Harry Truman, John Kennedy, and Richard Nixon were all elected with less than a majority of the popular vote.

Nonetheless, for the sake of coping with this problem, the electoral laws in Vietnam were changed. In order to avoid the splintering of the electorate, the electoral field was reduced to groups with a broad following. Candidates would have to be endorsed either by 40 members of the National Assembly (out of 197) or by 100 members of the provincial or autonomous municipal councils (out of 554). They could seek their endorsements among one set of officials or the other, but not both. When President Thieu later sought endorsements among both sets of officials—and in that way sought to reduce the number available to other candidates—he was blocked by the Supreme Court. A scheme that was conceived for the purpose of strengthening the legitimacy of the winning candidate would end up producing quite the opposite result. Such a pronounced effect did these electoral rules have in discouraging weak candidates in opposition that they began to appear as a contrivance by an authoritarian regime to keep itself in power. The electoral field soon looked too forbidding even for plausible candidates such as Prime Minister Ky and the ever available General Duong Van Minh. Ky fell short of the number of signatures required for nomination, and it appeared for a while that he would be ineligible to run. With Ky out of the race, General Minh was left in a head-to-head contest with President Thieu which, his own polls confirmed, he had little chance of winning. It was the judgment of observers on the scene that Minh, who was never a model of high enterprise and tenacity, withdrew from the race to avoid embarrassment.[21] In the meantime, the Supreme Court intervened to restore the candidacy of Prime Minister Ky; but with Minh out of the race, Ky's chances were fatally diminished, and so he, too, withdrew. In withdrawing, Ky held a press conference in Saigon to complain that the

[21] *Ibid.*, pp. 138-41.

elections had been "rigged"—a theme that he and Minh had played on heavily in the past. The charges of rigging could bring pressures on Thieu from the U.S. government, as well as encouragement to General Minh to preserve his candidacy. The Americans were deeply troubled by the prospect of an election without opposition, and the problem did not seem to be eased in any way by President Thieu's offer to resign if most of the voters decided to cast blank ballots rather than vote for him.[22]

And yet, the fact of the matter was that Thieu had not forced either Minh or Ky out of the race. The laws and courts in South Vietnam made it possible for opposing candidates to enter the field; but not even the most benign law could assure all candidates an equal prospect of winning. There are many candidates who withdraw from presidential primaries in the United States when the prospects for victory become too meager to justify the effort, and there have been elections to the U.S. presidency (in the cases, notably, of George Washington and James Monroe) when no other candidate had a serious chance. The question of whether other candidates had a good prospect of winning had to be separated from the question of whether the elections themselves were free, and whether the right to compete was supported by legal safeguards. It was the judgment of seasoned observers that, in Vietnam, those possibilities and those legal supports were in place.[23] The strength of the new judicial institutions was still being tested, but the courts were already manifesting independence in their willingness to declare invalid many of the endorsements collected by President Thieu as he sought to secure his nomination and squeeze out other candidates. The critical point is not that the governing party entered the election with considerable leverage, for that may be true of free elections anywhere. The more remarkable fact was that the legal protection of opposing parties was so substantial in a country that was embroiled in a combination of civil war and war of independence. The period of the Revolution in our own country was not one in which dissenters were treated either with tenderness or with the protections of free speech that we associate with the Constitution in time of peace. It was rather unlikely that any prominent person could have accomplished the equivalent of Premier Ky's gesture by calling a conference for the press, domestic and foreign, and denouncing George Wash-

---

[22] *Ibid.*, p. 20.

[23] That was the estimate, very notably, of Professor Penniman, who had considerable international experience as a surveyor of elections. The varieties of evidence to support that judgment about Vietnam are taken up, as a persisting thread, throughout his book on elections in Vietnam.

ington and the Continental Congress. Needless to say, there were no comparable press conferences in North Vietnam, and no comparable denunciations of the government. Nor, of course, were there any comparable elections.

A GOVERNMENT of law is usually enhanced by a system of separated powers, since there will be a possibility of appealing to one branch for the sake of restraining the other. In estimating the vitality of a "separation of powers" and the "constitutional" character of any regime, we would apply some rather simple tests. For example: Is it possible for the executive branch to lose in the courts or to fail to gain its way in the legislature on matters it regards as important? By that measure there were signs that the new institutions in Vietnam were in fact establishing their integrity as separate institutions. In the first place, the executive did not control access to office in the National Assembly and the Supreme Court.[24] The chief justice would be elected for a term of one year; and the first chief justice was Tran Hinh Tiet, a respected minister under Diem, who had been critical of President Thieu.

The selection of Tiet seemed to be a sign that the Court would not be a complaisant tool of the executive branch, and in a few signal decisions the Court did seem to manifest its independence. There was, as a case in point, the decision of the Court to invalidate many of the endorsements that were collected for Thieu's nomination. But beyond that, the Court declared unconstitutional the tax program put forward by the Thieu administration; it rejected the actions of the government against students who struck in protest over the arrest of a student leader; and, even more critically, it declared unlawful a system of military courts which had been established by the government in theaters of military action.[25] In the midst of the American Civil War, the courts had sought to invoke the writ of *habeas corpus* and free civilian prisoners held by the military authorities, but that effort was successfully resisted by President Lincoln. Lincoln's position, I think, was

[24] The members of the National Assembly were elected, with an average of three or four candidates per seat. The nine members of the Supreme Court were elected by the National Assembly without the formal participation of the executive, and the process of nomination was subject to a further filtration through the conventions that guided these nominations. Nominees were required to have legal training and ten years of experience in the law. The nominations were gathered and screened by the Bar Association, the Association of Judges, and the Association of Public Prosecutors before they were sent on to the National Assembly for the final selection.

[25] Penniman, *supra*, note 15, p. 108.

252

the right one, but it is notable that the courts in South Vietnam managed to carve out for themselves a much wider measure of independent authority than the courts in America could claim after seventy-five years of establishing their authority under the Constitution. Not until sixteen years after the establishment of the Constitution would the U.S. Supreme Court claim for itself the authority to declare acts of Congress invalid; and even then, that power was artfully asserted by Chief Justice Marshall on a matter of little consequence, where the executive had no practicable means of blocking the decision.[26] But that same authority was asserted successfully by the courts of Vietnam in the formative period of a new government; it was asserted, also, in matters of political consequence, and under the perilous conditions of war.

It was under the same dangers of war that the National Assembly offered a dramatic demonstration of its own independence from the executive. In the spring of 1972, with the North Vietnamese launching their invasion of the South, the Senate in South Vietnam refused to grant emergency powers to the president. Nor could the president overcome this restraint by flexing an authoritarian control over the House of Representatives: the supporters of the administration failed to command the votes of two-thirds of the members, which would have been necessary in overriding the decision of the Senate.[27] What is altogether remarkable about these experiences is not that the government in South Vietnam should have shown strains of an authoritarian character, but that such a society, in the middle of a war, should have shown so many important signs that the restraints of "constitutionalism" were indeed taking hold.

If there was any doubt about the relative state of freedom between North and South Vietnam, the difference was manifested instantly in the vaster freedom of public discussion and opposition that was present in the South. Even in the United States, certain kinds of inflammatory public speech have been restrained as "seditious," as recently as the Second World War. Judged, then, by the standards of mature democracies, it is not surprising that the authorities in South Vietnam were moved at times to restrain or arrest public figures who sought to build public support for the views of Hanoi or to erode the willingness of the public to persevere in the war. But the noteworthy point, again, is just how free so many people were to attack the government of

[26] I refer, of course, to the case presented in *Marbury* v. *Madison*, 1 Cranch 137 (1803). There the Court craftily decided, on constitutional grounds, not to disturb the judgment reached by the executive.

[27] Penniman, *supra*, note 15, p. 39.

President Thieu and seek its replacement. As we have seen, that free-dom encompassed the possibility of running in a presidential election on a platform that favored ending the war on terms sympathetic to Hanoi. Apart from elections, though, the differences between the two societies could be seen in the press. In contrast to the controlled press in North Vietnam, South Vietnam contained, in the early 1970's, three newspapers publishing in English and twenty-seven in Vietnamese. Where it was possible to discern political leanings, Howard Penniman counted five of these papers as "progovernment" and eight as "anti-government."[28]

There was an attempt on the part of the government to apply cen-sorship, ostensibly for reasons of national security (as in barring the publication of military plans). But the regulations on censorship could also reach articles which treated the Communists in a favorable light or which suggested that President Nixon might abandon the Thieu government. Still, this regimen of censorship was far milder and far less efficient than many schemes of censorship that have been admin-istered by democracies, let alone by authoritarian regimes, in time of war. The government did not have censors sitting in the editorial offices of newspapers, screening out offensive stories. Nor did the government seek to close down newspapers for the publication of articles it re-garded as injurious. The government responded to offending articles only *after* they appeared, and it would take the burden on itself of confiscating from the newsstands the papers that contained these ar-ticles. Nothing in that maneuver, though, prevented the newspapers from resupplying their vendors with more copies of the same issue. And in some instances, the seizure of an edition would become a proud selling point for the paper. One newspaper even ran, on its front page, boxscores of the number of times its issues had been seized.

For some reason, these obvious points of comparison between the two Vietnams have been widely ignored. In a perverse way, the expres-sion of dissent was taken to confirm the defects that were pointed up in the Thieu regime, while the absence of public dissent in North Vietnam seemed to confirm, for many people, the absence of dissat-isfaction with the regime of the North. For a number of people, the regime in the South was marked by the refusal of Ngo Dinh Diem to hold the "first election" scheduled for Vietnam (i.e., the election called for by the Geneva Accords to settle the unification of the country).[29] That election was scheduled for 1956, but neither the government of

[28] *Ibid.*, pp. 159-60.
[29] See Walzer, *Just and Unjust Wars, supra*, note 1, p. 98.

South Vietnam nor that of the United States was a signatory to the Geneva Accords, and neither considered itself bound by the provisions for an election in 1956. Still, that unwillingness of Diem to hold the election was taken as an instance of corruption which established the antidemocratic character of the regime in the South as well as the retrograde motives of the United States in supporting Diem.

For many writers, the character of the regime in the South was foretold by this crisis over the first election, and that impression could not be dislodged even by the continuing evidence of free elections in the 1960's and 1970's. Those who were affected with these views often quoted President Eisenhower's remark that if a free election were held in Vietnam in 1956, Ho Chi Minh would probably have won overwhelmingly. These writers, however, usually fail to quote the rest of Eisenhower's observations: that Ho Chi Minh would have been the likely victor *if* the only alternative were the dissipated emperor, Bao Dai. But beyond that, the writers who cite Eisenhower on this point manage to detach his remarks on the election from his understanding of the radical defects in the settlement of 1954—the defects that would have made a charade out of any scheme to hold "national" elections in 1956 throughout the whole of Vietnam. The Eisenhower administration, after all, held back from endorsing the Geneva Accords because the president objected to any settlement that would accept a partition of the country "without international mechanisms for enforcement."[30] The settlement at Geneva provided that the 1956 elections would be supervised by an international commission, but it is plain from Eisenhower's memoir—and from his refusal to endorse the settlement—that the acceptance of a *de facto* partition would have rendered an international commission ineffectual in supervising elections in North Vietnam.

It was Eisenhower's understanding that once the territory was partitioned, with the Vietminh in effective control in the North, the partition would become a permanent boundary, like the lines that separated Communist and non-Communist states in Germany and Korea. With that structure in place, it did not take much imagination to foretell the character of a "national" election in 1956. There might be "elections" carried on simultaneously throughout the territory of Vietnam, but that would be rather different from a vote conducted under a uniform set of rules nationwide, with the same guarantee of free choice in all sections of the country. A government in North

[30] See Dwight D. Eisenhower, *Mandate for Change* (New York: Doubleday, 1963), pp. 338, 357-58, 371-72.

Vietnam that was both nationalist and Marxist-Leninist would never permit elections to be organized within its territory by the United Nations, or by any neutral, outside authority. Without the guarantee of impartial supervision, no one could have any illusions about the kind of election that would be run by the Communists. The population under the control of the Vietminh could be counted on to be disciplined and unified in its "voting," and if the results were tabulated as part of a single, nationwide vote, it would take but a small increment of support in the South to ensure that the outcome would favor the unification of the country on terms that were congenial to the Communist regime in the North.

At the same time, the awareness of an outcome that was nearly certain would generate incentives of its own that could transform the political situation. People of ambition who could read the political signs would come forward in the South, ready to throw in with the local subsidiary of the winning side. In short, the "election" would be rigged from the start. At best, there would be a free election only in the South, but the overall referendum could not truly be free. It would merely furnish a cover of democratic legitimacy for the transfer of power to Ho Chi Minh and his party.

President Eisenhower was not the only one at the time who recognized this situation for what it was. The junior senator from Massachusetts, John F. Kennedy, called upon the U.S. government to oppose the elections that were stipulated in the Geneva Accords. As Kennedy declared at the time, "neither the United States nor Free Vietnam is ever going to be a party to an election obviously stacked and subverted in advance, urged upon us by those who have already broken their own pledges under the agreement they now seek to enforce."[31] There was no reason to assume that the support of the North for "free elections" represented anything more than an instrumental acceptance of an event that was likely, in that particular case, to serve the interests of the Communist regime. It took a large measure of self-delusion to suppose that the regime in North Vietnam bore any commitment *in principle* to free elections as a means of permitting the people of Vietnam to determine the government that would rule them. And nothing that has occurred since 1956 provides any ground for that assumption. No one who believed in "free elections" in Vietnam for 1956 could have had any reason to believe that they would have marked the beginning of a regime of free elections under the auspices of Ho Chi Minh's party.

[31] Quoted in Guenter Lewy, *America in Vietnam* (New York: Oxford University Press, 1978), p. 13.

That the Thieu regime was plagued by corruption is beyond doubt. In that respect, it suffered from the same maladies that affected all the regimes which preceded it. But there was no telling how that corruption compared, say, to the corruption which became famous in cities like Chicago and Jersey City, or to the corruption that was identified in the American government at the time of Watergate. No one thought to argue that Chicago and Jersey City had become totalitarian states, or that the differences in principle between the American and the Soviet regimes disappeared during the Watergate scandal. No one, that is, would have suggested that America had become so "corrupt" that it was no longer preferable to a totalitarian regime and no longer worth defending.

The goodness or corruption of the officeholders has to be separated from the goodness or corruption of the principles on which a regime is founded. That distinction reminds us of the tiers of wrongs that are encompassed by the term "corruption." In the classic understanding, political orders became corrupt or "perverted" when they were transmuted from associations directed to *public* ends (or a public "good") and converted mainly into instruments for the private interests of the rulers. That understanding certainly could take in corruption in the sense of simple "graft," when holders of office accept bribes and permit their decisions to be governed not by impartial standards of justice, but by the calculus of their own private gain. And yet, that is corruption at its most prosaic and trivial level. Corruption in a much more fundamental sense occurs when the authorities deny the very premises of lawful government, which would oblige them to seek the consent of the governed and offer justifications for their policies to those who will be expected to obey. If the critics who assailed the corruption of South Vietnam could have become clearer on the principles that define the wrong of corruption, they might have been able to recognize the corruption of a wholly different magnitude that was constituted by the totalitarian regime in the North.

ONE OF THE sad ironies of the war was that the corruption which seemed to be a part of everyday life in South Vietnam under Diem and Thieu continued even after a Communist regime was installed. The conventions of corruption were possibly rooted in habits that would not disappear overnight, even with a change to a stringent despotism. But the irony could be seen most tellingly in the case of young Doan Van Toai. In 1970, Toai was a vice-president of the Saigon Student Union, a sympathizer with the National Liberation Front, and a critic of the Thieu regime. In his aversion to the corruption of the government in South Vietnam he toured campuses in the United States,

drumming up opposition to the war. When the Communist government was installed in 1975, Toai was asked to work on plans to
confiscate private property. When he showed a lack of enthusiasm for
the sweep of the confiscations, covering poor and rich alike, he was
imprisoned for twenty-eight months without even a statement of formal charges. During this period, his mother was denied admission to
a hospital because her son was in detention; and she subsequently
died. In November 1977, for reasons that are still not entirely clear,
he was released from prison. By this time, Vietnam itself seemed to
be taking on the character of a vast custodial institution, but Toai was
able to leave the country precisely because his family had retained
some of its original wealth and he was able to bribe his way out. In
other words, Toai became the beneficiary of the same conventions of
corruption, with the same tendencies to favor people with money,
which had marked for him earlier the corruption of the Thieu regime.
But what had stood, in a relatively free society, as the mark of serious
moral defect, would become, in a truly totalitarian society, a benign
source of relief from the oppression of the regime.[32]

THE TEAMS OF observers who went to survey elections in South Vietnam came mainly from the United States. That itself was the reflection
of a rather large truth that had to affect the prospects for constitutional
government in Vietnam: the defense of Vietnam was heavily dependent
on an ally that itself was a constitutional order, and the leadership of
that ally would suffer serious political embarrassment in sustaining
the war if the government in Vietnam seemed to grow more authoritarian. The American government had itself encouraged the coup
against Diem when it saw him growing more despotic. The next time
a government was displaced by a coup d'état, the officers who staged
the coup were given a thorough bawling out by the American am-
bassador, General Maxwell Taylor.[33] Thereafter, the movement to
restore and develop constitutional government was persistently encouraged and pressed by the Americans. If the principal ally of South
Vietnam had been the Soviet Union, it is inconceivable that the South
would have come under the same pressure to establish free elections
and independent courts.

As I have tried to suggest, the vigor of the electoral process, the

[32] The story of Doan Van Toai was told in part in Carl Gershman, "A Voice from
Vietnam," *The New Leader* (January 29, 1979), pp. 8-9. My own account is slightly
augmented as a result of a conversation with Toai.

[33] See the account of General Taylor's conversation with the officers in South Vietnam
in *The Pentagon Papers* (New York: Bantam Books, 1971), doc. #89, pp. 379-81.

range of free discussion, the development of constitutional restraints—
all were rather remarkable for a new government in the middle of a
war. It was reasonable to suppose that the coming of peace would
allow the regime to relax some of the controls that were made necessary
by the war, and the institutions of freedom might have found a certain
breathing space in which to grow. Those prospects would have been
even better if it were assumed, also, that South Vietnam would continue to be incorporated in a system of military alliance and commerce
that was composed mainly of societies with free insitutions. In that
system of alliance, which had the United States as its leading member,
the pressures emanating from the alliance would generally be in the
direction of strengthening constitutional freedoms, rather than abolishing elections and removing legal restraints on the government.

In recent years we have seen three notable cases that confirm again
the difference that can be made by an enveloping structure or alliance
of free countries. The NATO alliance was often embarrassed by the
membership of dictatorial regimes in the Portugal of Salazar, or in
Greece under the military government that came to power in 1967.
And yet, a number of things could be said for keeping these countries
within the web of the alliance. In the first place, they were authoritarian
regimes, which did not restrict freedom with the same extensiveness
or severity as totalitarian regimes. So long as they were incorporated
in NATO they would not allow their territories or resources to become
parts of a rival alliance which could extend the strategic reach of
totalitarian countries, such as those joined in the Soviet camp. At the
same time, these authoritarian regimes did not figure to have the same
staying power as Marxist-Leninist regimes, which had developed their
own political science for the preservation of centralized dictatorships.
No totalitarian regime has yet been displaced by anything other than
a foreign army, but authoritarian regimes come and go and, in many
instances, they are quite brittle. The government of the colonels in
Greece felt the want of its own authority, and it reverted to a civilian
government after a life of only seven years. Franco in Spain and Salazar
in Portugal did hang on far longer; but with the death of Franco and
the enfeeblement of Salazar, their countries were ripe for political
change. When the possibility arose to reform these political orders, it
made a difference that they found themselves enmeshed in a coalition
of free countries. They would not represent a reproach to the principles
of their allies if they sought to move in the direction of democracy.
In fact, they would receive encouragement as they moved toward the
restoration of elections and party government, and each step in their
progress was attended by the readiness of their allies to absorb them

even more deeply into their common intercourse. That Spain and Portugal are today parliamentary democracies, that they have "rejoined," in effect, the Western democracies of Europe and America, must be attributed in large measure to the nature of the alliance that enveloped them when the possibilities for change began to appear.

Of course, polities may decay as well as progress, and with the end of the war in Vietnam the new public morality of constitutionalism might have slackened. The American surveillance might have relaxed, and the country might have fallen into the grooves of a more familiar politics. Yet, there is no gainsaying what South Vietnam had in fact become by the late 1960's. As infirm or fragile as it might have been, it was nevertheless a constitutional order, and it was likely to be incorporated for many years in a system of alliances that would work to preserve free institutions in Vietnam rather than encourage their atrophy.

The two Vietnams represented then, unambiguously, two different understandings of the principles on which political orders may be founded. And those differences in principle had to define the most decisive moral issues that were engaged in the war. For that reason, they constituted the critical ground of principle on which any moral judgment about the war would ultimately depend. There were arguments to be made about war crimes and the scale of force and the propriety of intervention in a civil war, but those considerations (as we shall see) could not finally govern our moral judgment on the war itself. The so-called principle of nonintervention was hardly a principle in any rigorous sense; it was an ancient rule that had its origin in a quite different epoch of international law. It did not express any substantive moral principle, and it could be the source of vast mischief when it was detached from a substantive understanding of the reasons that can make interventions, in certain cases, morally justified.

And if one came to understand the principles that could justify the intervention in South Vietnam, the question of war crimes could be judged with its proper significance. To say that the war in Vietnam was justified was not to say that any atrocity would also have to be accepted as necessary and justified if it were carried out in the mission of the war. At the same time, however, it became necessary to separate the wrong of the atrocity from the question of whether the war itself was in principle wrong. There was no need to deaden our sensibilities to the outrages that were committed by our military. But neither could we let our outrage deflect us from the moral understanding that judges a war on its proper ground and permits our other judgments, on matters of law and prudence, to settle in their rightful places.

XII

THE MORALITY OF INTERVENTION

Within two years after the fall of Saigon, the kind of despotism that was settling on Indochina had become too evident to be ignored even by those people who had opposed the war in Vietnam. In the spring of 1977 an "Appeal to the Government of Vietnam" was signed by Joan Baez, Staughton Lynd, Aryeh Neier, and many others who had been active in the antiwar movement. The signers declared in their appeal that they had hoped the end of the war would bring to Vietnam a government of "reconciliation built on tolerance." But now, they were compelled to speak by "evidence [that was] too specific and persuasive for us to ignore"—evidence of "grievous and systematic violations of human rights by your government." It was admitted even by officials of the government in Vietnam that about 200,000 prisoners were being held in "re-education camps." Some disinterested foreign journalists estimated that the number of political prisoners was closer to 300,000. The signers of the appeal were quite willing to concede to the government a right to punish certain leaders of the former government in Saigon, but they were alarmed by the "arrest and detention of a wide range of persons, including religious, cultural and political figures who opposed the Thieu government despite considerable personal risks."

It was evidently assumed by the signatories to the appeal that people should not be imprisoned without being proved guilty of a crime, and that the lack of full "political" loyalty to the government should not necessarily constitute a crime. These convictions were also thought, apparently, to describe certain canons of justice that should hold true in all places, and that should be treated as valid and binding even by rulers in Indochina. But the signers of the statement seemed serenely unaware that the ground of their appeal and reproach to the government of Vietnam was inconsistent with the premises on which they had conceived their opposition to the war in the first place. For the opposition to the war and to American intervention had depended critically on the premises of cultural relativism. As the familiar argument ran, the United States had no business intervening in the civil war of another country since there were no grounds on which the United States could say just what form of government was in principle better or worse for people in another culture. In this perspective the

261

American resistance to the spread of a totalitarian government was seen, in an odd reverse, as an attempt by the United States to impose its peculiar "values" on the rest of the world. In this particular case, the United States would "impose"on Vietnam the ravages of constitutional government.

But now, with the appeal to the government in South Vietnam, the former votaries of cultural relativism found it necessary to employ a language that was incompatible with their earlier doctrines. When they invoked the claim of "human rights," they appealed to a standard of rights which had been understood in the past to be independent of local cultures. The signers of the appeal suggested, in an ancient voice, that there were indeed rights which arose from the very nature of human beings, and which governments everywhere were obliged to respect. It is illuminating, then, to consider just what wrongs were mentioned in the appeal, for they would reveal the understanding held by the framers of the appeal about the rights that were truly fundamental as "human rights." By the same token, of course, it would be quite as instructive to consider what these advocates chose to omit.

The appeal called first for "a complete public accounting of those detained or imprisoned, indicating, as well, the charges for which they are held." But the document quickly moved from the procedural requirements of justice to the substantive wrongs of the authorities: it called for the release of "any individuals who are held purely because of their religious or political convictions." The appeal noted the self-immolation of Buddhist monks, who protested the restrictions that were placed on their religious practice (restrictions that were also applied more generally to all other religious groups in Vietnam). There was an expression of concern that the government closed down many projects of the Unified Buddhist Church, including programs for the aid of children orphaned in the war. These projects were ended, their "funds frozen and properties confiscated." There might have been a fleeting recognition here on the part of the signers that the control, by individuals and groups, of their own private property was a necessary support to the free exercise of their religion and other personal liberties. At any rate, the appeal called for the release of prisoners who were "held purely because of their religious or political convictions." The appeal, in other words, claimed for the Vietnamese a certain right to the free exercise of religion and to the holding of political views that ran counter to the principles of the regime. "We call," said the signers, "for government recognition of the right to open and free communication."

All of the rights claimed in the appeal were eminently defensible, and yet they were claimed in a context that made them almost comically out of place. The signatories of the appeal had not thought it important, during the course of the war, to insist that any potential government in Vietnam, including a Communist government, would have to show an *institutional* commitment to these human freedoms before it could be regarded as a decent and legitimate government. Instead, as the drafters of the appeal admitted, the leaders of the antiwar movement had been content to rely on the expression of "concern" offered by representatives of the Vietcong and the North Vietnamese, "both in formal agreements and in countless conversations with peace activists." But where had the government of North Vietnam ever manifested a commitment to the legal institutions that were bound up with the protection of those "human rights" mentioned in the appeal?

In the absence of those commitments, the complaints of the former "peace activists" were condemned now to appear preciously innocent. The appeal called for the most rigorous legal scrupulosity in respecting the canons of justice in regard to prisoners; and yet, if there were stringent principles of that kind, would they not have enjoined other conventions that were quite as necessary to a regime of legal restraints? Would they not have required, most notably, the creation of a system of courts independent of the government and vested with certain powers of judicial review? In the same way, how could one insist on the right to "open and free" public discourse on matters of politics without creating the kinds of institutions which protect that right—and whose presence reflects the understanding that public discourse and political competition are indeed legitimate? In other words, how could one insist on a vast body of legal rights for human beings without insisting at the same time on the creation of a "government of law"? And how could one insist on the institutions of a legal order without recognizing that the same premises which enjoin government by law also enjoin government by consent and a regime of free elections?

In our own political tradition—the tradition of the Founders and Lincoln—human rights were identified with those rights which arose from the nature of human beings. As we have seen, those rights were thought to command, in the first instance, a regime of consent and constitutional restraints. That right to be governed by consent under a regime of law was thought to be the most fundamental implication that arose from the notion of "natural rights," and it was understood also that a government of this character was most likely to secure the fuller range of these natural rights. As Hamilton remarked in *The Federalist* #84, "the Constitution is itself, in every rational sense, and to every useful purpose, A BILL OF RIGHTS."[1] There was, in fact, no argument for the legally scrupulous treatment of prisoners or the provision of "First Amendment freedoms" that did not imply, even more fundamentally, a government of free elections and constitutional restraints. But when the signers of the appeal spoke of human rights, they did not think first of a government of free elections and legal restraints. During the war they had never thought it fit to demand that the government of Hanoi establish in North Vietnam, or in Vietnam as a whole, a regime of that kind. And so, what could their complaint have been now? Could they have reproached the Communist leaders of Vietnam for failing to provide the *refinements* of a regime of law when they had never faulted them for failing to provide even the rudiments of a constitutional order? Or had they honestly expected that the leaders of North Vietnam, delivered from the strains of war, would move to establish a parliamentary democracy? But no one of mature years really expected a Communist government in Vietnam to be radically different in that respect from all previous Communist governments the world had seen. What had there been, after all, in the experience of the protestors, or in the principles professed by the rulers in Hanoi, which could have deluded anyone on this point? Apparently the signers of the appeal had been willing to hazard the fortunes of the Vietnamese on the strength of a hope—without precedent, and without foundation—that a Leninist dictatorship would redeem itself through war, transform its own character, and somehow produce a liberal, tolerant political order without the presence of liberal institutions.

And yet the activists might not have been deluded in that way. They might simply have thought it possible that the "human rights" they esteemed could indeed be detached from the structure of constitutional government. But it should be evident that if they had understood the connection between human rights and constitutional government, they would have understood, from the beginning, the principles that were engaged in the war in Vietnam. If they understood why it was proper for themselves, in 1977, to speak across the ocean to another culture and expect the government of Vietnam to honor certain universal requirements of justice, then they would have understood why it was legitimate for the United States in the 1960's to weigh the prospect of a totalitarian regime in South Vietnam and judge it to be quite as undesirable in principle in Asia as it was in America. Or was the Johnson administration still to be reckoned as villainous because it

---

[1] *The Federalist* #84 (New York: Modern Library, n.d.), p. 561.

might have been inconveniently precocious: i.e., because it had the wit to find a totalitarian regime to be quite as abhorrent in 1965 as the signers of the appeal found it to be in 1977? And if there were grounds on which the United States could indeed judge what was better or worse in principle for the people of another country, then the so-called principle of nonintervention would be exposed for what it has ever been: a rule of prudence in international affairs, but hardly a proposition that bears the moral substance of a genuine principle.

THE RULE OF nonintervention became an important doctrine in international law during the eighteenth and nineteenth centuries, but as scholars have pointed out, that rule could have a passing claim to moral intelligibility only because of the international system it reflected at the time. International law is a product of the nations that are important enough to make law, and in the classic period of the "balance of power," the nations that counted in these matters were almost entirely European. These nations pressed their interests at the expense of their rivals; they showed themselves quite willing to fight wars, and yet those wars were rather limited in nature. All of these nations were ruled by monarchies that essentially accepted the legitimacy of one another. A nation might seek commercial or military advantage, and could even seek hegemony in Europe (as in the case of France under Louis XIV); but no nation would ever define its interests in such a way as to require the displacement of monarchical regimes in adjacent territories or throughout the whole of Europe.[2] That state of affairs changed radically with the French Revolution. For now there was, in Paris, a regime whose governing principles were understood to be incompatible with the established order in Europe. The endurance of such a government in France would stand as a reproach, as a persisting challenge, to the legitimacy of all European governments that were not "republican" in character. That government was understood as a threat to other regimes in Europe, and for their own part, the radical leaders of the new French government were disposed to believe that their revolution would not be secure until hostile monarchies were replaced with republican governments. The dynamics of the French Revolution would extend beyond the borders of France, and it quickly became understood that the international system was being transformed. A doctrine of nonintervention no longer carried any moral

---

[2] The connection between the doctrine of nonintervention and the character of the balance-of-power system in the eighteenth and nineteenth centuries is brought out well in Morton A. Kaplan and Nicholas DeB. Katzenbach, *The Political Foundations of International Law* (New York: John Wiley & Sons, 1961), ch. 2, especially pp. 35-37.

plausibility when leaders both inside and outside France could feel so acutely threatened by events taking place outside their borders. After the defeat of Napolean at Waterloo, the victorious powers showed no reluctance about unmaking the regime in France and restoring a revised version of the monarchy.

About a hundred fifty years later, the same problem would present itself, but in a far more portentous way, with the advent of the Nazis. A change in regime in Germany brought to power a totalitarian party that could not take a restrictive view of its interests abroad. To the expansionist designs of Hitler was added the unease of a totalitarian leadership, which distrusted what it did not control. The Nazi movement annexed to itself a network of supranational parties within Europe, and as the interests of the regime were conceived, they required the presence throughout the Continent of governments that were compatible with the Nazi regime in Germany. John Dewey once suggested that the political "community" on any subject ought to be defined by the sharing of extended consequences.[3] In that vein it was apparent to some observers in the early 1930's that the coming to power of the Nazis would have consequences that extended far beyond the borders of Germany, and the argument has been made that the international community had an interest in intervening in Germany as soon as a constitutional government was displaced by a totalitarian regime under Hitler. By 1945 there was no longer any hesitation in asserting that interest. Of course, if the principle of nonintervention were to be honored as a moral principle, then nations other than Germany would have had no legitimate interest in the internal affairs of Germany. The displacement of constitutional government by a dictatorship, and the barbarous treatment of the Jews, were matters, apparently, that could not be judged legitimately by outsiders, if one were guided by the "ethic" contained in the doctrine of nonintervention. The only legitimate concern, in this perspective, was with the harms that the Germans inflicted on others, outside their borders. And so, by the doctrine of nonintervention, the Second World War presumably should have ended as soon as the Allied armies reached the borders of Germany. For at that point the Allies had deprived Germany of the fruits of its aggressions abroad. Under the principle of nonintervention, the Allies were not warranted in doing more unless there were remnants of the German army that still posed a threat to the Allied forces. But with the German armies shattered, the Allies could claim no license, under

---

[3] See John Dewey, *The Public and Its Problems* (Chicago: Gateway Books, 1946 [1927]), ch.1, especially pp. 15-16.

the traditional understanding of "nonintervention," for doing anything more than leaving the Germans, in the midst of their own ruins, to reconstitute their own society.

And yet the crisis merely made plain the moral emptiness in the doctrine of nonintervention. As everyone understood, the war in Europe had been brought on by the Nazi regime in Germany, and the ends of the war would not be accomplished unless the Allies went on into Germany and remade that regime from within. When the Western Allies eventually departed from their zones of occupation in Germany, they left a government constituted on the basis of free elections—a government that could validly claim then to represent the "self-determination" of the German people. Since the time of Woodrow Wilson, the doctrine of nonintervention has received a moral enhancement as a result of being connected with the notion of self-determination: to leave nations free from outside interference was to leave them free to determine the government that would rule them and the ends for which they would be ruled. But "self-determination" was intelligible as a moral concern only as it represented another way of saying "self-government" or the right of human beings to be ruled only with their consent. When that equivalence was understood, it placed rather emphatic limits on the kinds of arrangements that a people would be free to "determine," or on the kinds of ascension to political power that could be accepted as valid exercise of "self-determination." And so it would simply be incoherent to insist that a coup d'état or the seizure of power by guerrillas must be taken as an exercise of self-determination so long as it occurs locally, through the efforts of the natives alone. An outside power that intervened to prevent such a coup and to preserve, for the local population, a government of consent could not then be violating the principle of self-determination.

The justification for acting in these circumstances would be covered by a principle extracted earlier (see Chapter VIII): viz., that any moral principle must be indifferent to the question of who vindicates the principle. As we pointed out earlier, the victim of a lynch mob would derive his right to resist from the fact that he is being assaulted unjustly; in that event, it would be justified for anyone to resist the assault. It would be justified for a third party to step in and vindicate the rights of the victim if the victim is too weak to enforce his own rights. The same reasoning would extend in principle to the interventions that are carried out abroad, and it would be sufficient to establish the moral vacuity of the doctrine of nonintervention. That "principle" cannot be taken to mean that any government, in command of a territory, has a "right" to be sheltered from the intervention of any outside power even if it inflicts on its own subjects a reign of barbarism. As Lincoln reminded us, there cannot be a "right to do a wrong": the doctrine of nonintervention cannot coherently establish a right of rulers to commit atrocities against their own people and be spared interference from the civilized. If there is a principle of nonintervention, it can only mark a claim to exercise self-government under conditions that respect the canons of lawfulness. Thus, if an outside power intervenes for the sake of preserving or restoring an elected government, it would not have violated a moral principle.

In the temper of our times, of course, an intervention of that kind is likely to be denounced as a violation of international law. But that is a measure of how far the understanding of international law has drifted in our own day from its foundations in natural law. It is only when the "law of nations" has been recast to suit the premises of legal positivism that we can be enjoined to regard as equally legitimate—and equally worthy of being insulated from intervention—a government that holds power at the point of a gun and a government that holds power through the votes of its citizens. And it is only when sensibilities have been shaped by the premises of this new international law that the Reagan administration could be denounced for intervening in Grenada, displacing a band of thugs who had ousted an elected government, and "imposing" on the people of Grenada the right to elect their own government once again. The rejoicing of the Grenadians themselves did not alter, for most critics of this move, the immanent sinfulness of the act. It seemed rather to deepen the offense by offering the example of people taking pleasure in vice. For a large portion of the American political class the use of military power to intervene abroad is now regarded as wrong under any circumstances. But it must be curious—and in no small part, portentous—for a republic when many of its leading public figures no longer respect a moral distinction between the use of force for the sake of displacing an elected government, and the use of force for the purpose of restoring a government of consent. The case brings to mind an incident, recalled by John Stuart Mill, of a crisis in Portugal. The "popular party" of the time was on the brink of overthrowing the government, but the British intervened decisively, with their influence, to support the government. Thanks to the intervention of the British, a government of law was preserved. Mill later remarked: "If ever a political act which looked ill in the commencement could be justified by the event, this was; for, as the fact turned out, instead of giving ascendancy to a party, it proved a really healing measure; and the chiefs of the so-called rebellion were, within a few years, the honoured, and successful ministers of the throne against which they had so lately fought."[4]

It may be said, in the voice of prudence, that people will not cherish their own freedom if they do not fight for it themselves. As Mill understood, however, free government may disappear in certain countries not because most people do not cherish it enough, but because the forces that would overturn it may be better armed and disciplined. At these moments, an outside power may be warranted in intervening to supply a deficit in arms that may otherwise imperil a decent government that is not wanting in popular support. The intervention may create dependencies lasting into the future; it may prove inexpedient in a number of other ways. But it could not be regarded *in principle* as wrong. In the case of Vietnam it could be said that, under the government sustained by the United States, even those opposed to the regime and the war had the means of pressing their views politically and gaining support for their ends. If a majority of people in Vietnam really wished to end the war on terms favorable to the Vietcong, they could have begun by offering substantial support for Mr. Dzu in the election of 1967. And yet, that position commanded, at the time, no more than 17 percent of the vote. Whatever else can be said about the American presence in Vietnam, it would be hard to argue that the United States had prevented the Vietnamese from determining their own form of government when it intervened in 1965 to prevent a victory at arms by the Vietcong. It could be argued more accurately that it was only the intervention of the United States which preserved for the people of Vietnam their right to be ruled by a government of their own choosing. The American intervention, therefore, did not violate the principle of "self-determination"; it provided the only means of vindicating that principle.

WHEN THE DOCTRINE of nonintervention is mistaken for a substantive moral principle, it can lead even some of the most urbane people to conclusions that turn the canons of moral reasoning inside out. So it was that Michael Walzer sought to build his case against the American involvement in Vietnam by denying the moral claims of any government that is weak enough to require assistance from the outside. The legitimacy of the government in South Vietnam depended, he wrote, on whether "it could conceivably win the civil war if no external force was brought to bear. . . . [T]he continuing dependence of the new

---

[4] John Stuart Mill, "A Few Words on Non-Intervention," in *Essays on Politics and Culture*, ed. Gertrude Himmelfarb (New York: Doubleday/Anchor, 1963), p. 381.

regime on the U.S. is damning evidence against it."[5] Or again: "A legitimate government is one that can fight its own internal wars."[6] Or, even more emphatically: "a government that receives economic and technical aid, military supply, strategic and tactical advice, and is still unable to reduce its subjects to obedience, is clearly an illegitimate government."[7] In these passages, Walzer was drawing a moral conclusion about legitimacy from propositions that were wholly lacking in moral significance—namely, propositions about the *weakness* of the government. As we have seen (Chapter VIII), moral propositions may be drawn only from the logic of morals itself. A judgment about the legitimacy of the regime in South Vietnam or its *moral* claim to survive can be drawn only on the basis of a *moral* fault in the Thieu regime, which would establish why it did not *deserve* to survive. Walzer would seem to fall here into the fallacy that Rousseau pointed up in the opening pages of *The Social Contract*, when he warned that the mere success of some people in seizing and holding power could not itself justify that power, as though Might were indeed the source of Right. Walzer managed to back precisely into the same mistake by suggesting that the success of the Vietcong in a guerrilla war had to indicate the presence of popular support, while the weakness of the South Vietnamese government in the same kind of contest had to indicate the absence of popular support. If this reasoning is accepted, then the victory of the Vietcong would have to be a measure of a larger public support, and therefore the success of the Vietcong in gaining power by force would indeed be a sufficient demonstration of its *moral* claim to rule. The premises in this argument must turn Rousseau's teaching on its head—for the same reason that it must be incompatible with the first implications that arise from the logic of morals. If the canons of moral reasoning imply anything, they must at least imply that moral conclusions may not be drawn from any condition, such as physical strength or weakness, which has in itself no moral significance.

It is pertinent, in this respect, that Walzer did not consider whether the regime in the South actually *deserved* to be displaced by a totalitarian movement. Strangely missing from Walzer's account was any consideration of elections in South Vietnam or the state of constitutional freedoms in that country. As Walzer himself concedes, an effort was made to undermine the "popular base of the South Vietnamese

[5] Michael Walzer, *Just and Unjust Wars: A Moral Argument with Historical Illustrations* (New York: Basic Books, 1977), p. 98.

[6] *Ibid.*, p. 101.

[7] *Ibid.*, pp. 98-99.

government . . . by a systematic campaign of subversion, terrorism, and guerrilla war, largely directed and supplied from the North."[8] It is entirely possible that elected governments with the support of their populations may still not be a match, in certain instances, for terrorist groups that are disciplined and unconstrained by tender sentiments. Certain populations may also be demoralized or lose their nerve more easily than others when they are faced with systematic terror, and they may be more inclined to buy peace by accepting an accommodation, even with antidemocratic forces. But it should be apparent at the same time that nothing in this catalogue of weakness would affect in any way the *moral* claim of an elected government to survive that terrorism. And in that event, as I think I have shown, the canons of moral reasoning would explain quite easily why a third party would be justified in going to the rescue and supplying the strength that the endangered government cannot summon by itself. Against the necessary force of these moral considerations, the doctrine of nonintervention must be reduced to a formula without moral substance.

THREE YEARS after the fall of Saigon, when the dominoes had fallen in Indochina and Cambodia was being subjected to the reign of murderers, this hard truth about the doctrine of nonintervention finally impressed itself on the mind of the senior senator from South Dakota. George McGovern had established his brief career as a presidential candidate by reviving, in relation to Vietnam, the premises that served Stephen Douglas in his debates with Lincoln: viz., that matters of right and wrong can be known only within the boundaries of a particular culture. In the politics of his time, Douglas was moved to deny the universal validity of the rights mentioned in the Declaration of Independence. And in response to the issues of his own day, Senator McGovern denied that the United States was in a position to say just which form of government was better or worse, in principle, for the people of Indochina. Still, McGovern was apparently persuaded that he himself could render a moral judgment across cultures, when it came to judging the corruption of the Thieu regime in South Vietnam. And as he confronted the record of the new regime in Cambodia, he discovered once again that events in another culture were not always so inscrutable that they defied judgment. What was occurring in Cambodia under the rule of Pol Pot and the Khmer Rouge was genocide. As McGovern recognized, the systematic murder carried out in Cambodia would have exceeded the scale of the Holocaust in Europe, if

[8] Walzer, *supra*, note 5, p. 99.

measured by the proportion of the population which had been put to death. Immediately after taking power in April 1975, the Khmer Rouge government ordered the forced evacuation of the city of Phnom Penh. Within two days, a population of 3 million—including the old, the wounded, and the bedridden—had been swept into a forced march out of the city. Bodies were strewn about on the roads as people died under the rigors of this regimen. The deaths would later be multiplied by starvation and disease as the economy was allowed to sink below the level of subsistence. All of this suited the purposes of the new rulers, who were willing to root out every vestige of the old society, from temples and cities to the people themselves, as though the surest way of obliterating the habits of an established and "corrupted" society was to destroy most of the people who bore the memory of the traditional culture. The first to be destroyed, of course, were the families of anyone connected with the previous regime. From there the revolution moved on with a mindless momentum, slaying the infirm and the educated—those who were too useless to the work of production and those who knew too much to make them obedient. Finally, the revolution began to devour itself as the rulers eliminated members of the party who flagged in their zeal for revolutionary sadism.

It was estimated that the regime carried out between 100,000 and 200,000 executions in its first year. About 400,000 people were thought to have died in the forced marches, and many more were destined to die in the "work villages" or slave camps into which the people of Cambodia were herded. In those camps, people would work long days in digging ditches, clearing trees, or preparing the ground for planting; they would work without breaks for twelve hours and subsist on starvation diets (with meals consisting of half a small can of rice). Any departure from the strict discipline of these camps could lead not merely to reproaches, but to execution. Warnings would be issued over such grievous offenses as flirting, quarreling with one's spouse, talking during work, or fraternizing outside the family. For extramarital sex, for the sin of attempting to escape from the camp, or even for *wishing* to escape, there could be summary execution.[9]

The recognition burst upon Senator McGovern that the kind of butchery taking place in Cambodia could justify the intervention of other nations. In August 1978 McGovern declared, before a meeting of the Senate Foreign Relations Committee, that "we ought not to dismiss out of hand the possibility of the international community

[9] See Carl Gershman, "After the Dominoes Fell," *Commentary* (May 1978), pp. 47-54.

intervening in what appears to be a clear case of genocide." Of course, Senator McGovern had made it his mission in American politics to oppose military intervention in Indochina. But it was his judgment now that military intervention might be justified, after all, in certain "extreme" cases; and he regarded the case of Cambodia as "the most extreme I've ever heard of. . . . Based on the percentage of the population that appears to have died, this makes Hitler's operation look tame."[10] Still, the senator preferred to have any military expedition in Indochina undertaken by a combination of troops from several nations, rather than as an enterprise managed solely by the United States. It was his fear, apparently, that if the United States acted alone, the venture would be tainted by the presence of American interests—as though the interests of the United States were so dishonorable that they would embarrass a legitimate enterprise.

Whether he appreciated it or not, McGovern had conceded the main point in principle: it is possible for a government to do things within its own borders so evil and corrupt, so thoroughly wrong, that another nation would be justified in intervening and even in displacing that government. Once that threshold of recognition had been crossed, the doctrine of nonintervention should have been recognized, in effect, as a slogan without substance, and McGovern's hesitation over the details became just so much moral irrelevance. Once it had been admitted that there is a ground of principle which makes genocide categorically wrong and which justifies an intervention to save the victims, the principle had to be indifferent to the identity of the agents who vindicated the principle. If other countries joined the United States in such a mission of rescue, that joint venture would have reflected an enlarged sense of responsibility in the international community; but in principle any nation would have been justified in going to the rescue, even if it had to act alone.

Senator McGovern's revelation came rather late, and it was also incomplete. McGovern became willing to contemplate intervention because he was compelled to acknowledge, in genocide, a wrong that would preserve its wrongness in all cultures. But with the help of a more strenuous reflection, or with a recollection of the understandings shared by Lincoln and the Founders, McGovern might have discovered that there are other moral wrongs that can be known across cultures. He might have come to recognize that the same premises which establish the wrong of genocide also establish the wrongness of ruling

[10] Senator McGovern's remarks were reported in the *New York Times*, August 22, 1978.

273

human beings without their consent. But if he had acknowledged that point, he would have acknowledged the ground of principle that supported the intervention in Vietnam, and he would have cut the ground out from under the "moral" argument he had made for so many years against the war in Vietnam.

We would remind ourselves, then, that the case of opposing a totalitarian movement in Vietnam did not rest merely on a prediction of the extended consequences that might flow from a Communist victory. It was not hard to predict that there would be vengeance and political executions after the war; nor should it have come as a surprise that the victory of the Communists in Vietnam would strengthen the hands of the Communist factions in Laos and Cambodia and produce Communist regimes in those countries as well. The so-called domino theory, which was so blithely dismissed in many circles, proved soberly accurate. But the "domino theory" could never have furnished, in itself, a proper ground on which to justify the war in Vietnam, and neither could the expectation that terror and genocide would follow the war. Neither of these considerations could properly have been controlling, for as plausible as they were, they still represented nothing more than empirical predictions or *contingent* propositions. The contingency, of course, could have been highly probable, but our judgment of the war did not have to pivot on any estimate of how bloody, precisely, a totalitarian regime in Vietnam would turn out to be. The case for resisting the Vietcong and the North Vietnamese found a sufficient justification in principle once it was possible to recognize the kind of political order they meant to establish.

AND YET, it was often argued that all of these considerations were overborne by the scale of violence wrought by the United States in Vietnam. Even if the war were justified, the argument ran, the United States was employing means of destruction that were "disproportionate" to the nature of the evil it was trying to resist in this small country. As almost everyone would come to know, the United States dropped more bombs, in total tonnage, in Vietnam than it did in the whole of World War II. So massive was the use of ordnance that the duds fired by the United States could have ended up supplying most of the enemy's needs in ammunition. The failure rate in the firing of artillery ordnance was 2 percent, and in the bombs dropped by B-52's the rate was 5 percent. As Guenter Lewy remarked, this "dud rate" would have provided the enemy with more than 800 tons of explosives every month—"more than enough for every mine and booby trap they were willing to make."[11] Added to the bombing was the use of napalm and defoliants, which stirred protests in our own country that the United States was not only using sadistic weapons against the people of Vietnam, but that it was destroying the ecology of the country as well. To the list of these villainies would finally be added the accounts of such atrocities as the killings that occurred at My Lai in 1968. In that infamous case, an American unit, in one of its sweeps, found no enemy forces but gunned down a group of 175–200 villagers, consisting of women, children, and the aged.

When it comes to measuring the scale of violence against the importance of our political ends, we often risk the fallacy of supposing that the "importance" of any country is directly proportional to its size. As we have come to learn, the questions of principle involved in any war may be vastly larger than the territory and assets of the country where the military action is taking place. Michael Walzer grasped a part of this truth when he refused to measure the justification for the Second World War—or the scale of violence employed in resisting Hitler—by reckoning whether the bombing would actually save more lives than it would destroy. But even if we judge the war in Vietnam with nothing more than a simple calculus of that kind, and if we consider the killing that has been carried out in Indochina since the end of the war and the departure of the United States, it should be plain now that the level of force used by the United States was not out of proportion to the evil that was being resisted.

That is not to say that there are no grounds for reservation about the methods used by the United States in fighting the war. Even defenders of the war have been critical of the strategy of employing bombing on a massive scale or fighting the war with the traditional preference of American commanders for large units and heavy firepower. In this latter camp has been Professor Guenter Lewy, who has also come to the judgment that General William Westmoreland must bear responsibility for a certain critical negligence in failing to do more to restrain the crimes of war that were committed in units under his command.[12] And yet, if there were in fact crimes committed by U.S. soldiers and officers, this does not mean that all uses of American force in Vietnam were unwarranted, or that most of the charges leveled against the United States were justified. Once again there was a need to sort out the condemnations that might be made of particular acts

[11] Guenter Lewy, *America in Vietnam* (New York: Oxford University Press, 1978), p. 101.

[12] See *ibid.*, pp. 238-39, 241-42.

on the battlefield, and the judgment that had to be rendered in principle about the war itself. Lewy could condemn the offenses of the American military in Vietnam without disturbing his support for the war because the two issues were separable. It has often been thought that modern warfare, with its willingness to visit destruction on civilian populations, began in the American Civil War with General Sherman's march through Georgia. Those who reacted to the American style of warfare in Vietnam would have found a record of far less constraint on the part of General Sherman, as he prosecuted the war for the Union against a regime of slavery. But they would probably concede nevertheless that the differences in principle that separated the North from the South in the Civil War were not dissolved when Sherman marched through Georgia. The critics might decry the "war crimes" of Sherman, in other words, but they would still be compelled to agree that Lincoln was justified in fighting the war against the Confederacy. In the same way, one might object to the excesses that were committed at different times by American soldiers and their officers, but nothing in these wrongs could efface in principle the wrong represented by the Vietcong and the regime in Hanoi. The apt response was not to take the faults of American arms as offenses which collapsed the differences in principle between the United States and South Vietnam, on one side, and the Vietcong and the North Vietnamese, on the other. It would have been far more coherent to condemn specific wrongs committed by the Americans and South Vietnamese and then enjoin those forces to continue prosecuting, as decently as they practicably could, a war they were well justified in fighting.

As it is, most of the "war crimes" that were charged to the United States in Vietnam do not meet the standards that would mark off, unambiguously, crimes of war or moral wrongs. Whether the condemnations of the American military were offered as legal or moral judgments, they usually turned on the premise that there were no ends which justified the U.S. intervention in Vietnam. Anyone who began with that understanding would of course come more easily to the conclusion that any use of American power in Vietnam was excessive. But when the tactics of the United States are measured by the tests that are typically applied to nations engaged in a war, the United States worked with restrictions that were not only unusual, but often detrimental to the prosecution of the war and the protection of its own forces. American soldiers often found themselves honoring the sanctity of "demilitarized zones" and of hospitals which were the source of heavy hostile fire. One pilot recalled, in this vein, the problems he had in striking at a railroad yard in a town northwest of Hanoi because of a set of buildings nearby which were marked as a hospital, and which were therefore off limits to bombing. "If it was in fact a hospital," he remarked, "it must have been a hospital for sick flak gunners, because every time we looked at it from a run on the railroad, it was a mass of sputtering, flashing gun barrels."[13] Pilots who had struck at targets were not permitted to return instantly to gauge their success and strike again if that should prove necessary. Instead they were compelled to return to the command and receive permission to make a second run. In 1968, Secretary of the Air Force Harold Brown urged the lifting of these restrictions on the bombing of North Vietnam "so as to permit bombing of military targets without the present scrupulous concern for collateral civilian damage and casualties."[14]

With all the furor over the level of violence in Vietnam, it is worth recalling that most of the fighting took place in the jungles or the countryside, well outside the cities of Vietnam. In contrast, the war in Korea had destroyed almost all the major cities in that country. Civilians accounted for about 70 percent of the people killed in the Korean war, while the figure for Vietnam was closer to 30 percent.[15] In Vietnam only around 3 percent of the population lived in areas that were exposed to defoliants, and less than 1 percent lived in areas where crops were destroyed.[16] Of course, both defoliation and the destruction of crops seemed initially to serve a military purpose in exposing the enemy and denying him food. But the destruction of crops often hurt the farmers more than the Vietcong (who were willing to requisition food at the point of a gun). There was no compelling evidence that herbicides inflicted any permanent damage to the soil, but there were enough fears over the long-term effects that the use of herbicides was ended in June 1971, along with defoliation.

There is not sufficient space here to take up, in proper detail, all of the charges of "war crimes" that were made against the United States for its involvement in Vietnam. Guenter Lewy has dealt with these questions carefully, and the reader could do no better than to consult *America in Vietnam*. Lewy concludes that, with the exception of such rare incidents as the shooting at My Lai, none of the charges raised against the United States could be sustained: the actions of the American military were well within the limits of international law, and they were connected to military necessity. If one happens to believe that there was no decent end that justified the use of American force in

[13] Quoted in *ibid.*, p. 404.
[14] Quoted in *ibid.*, p. 403.
[15] *Ibid.*, pp. 450-51.
[16] *Ibid.*, p. 258.

Vietnam in the first place, the limitations of international law may not seem sufficiently demanding as a moral standard. But if the American intervention was in fact justified, then the standards of international law were not trivial as moral tests. For they enjoined, in their essential logic, an imperative that arises from first principles: viz., that one ought to do less harm rather than more; or to put it another way, that one ought to do no more harm than is strictly necessary to the achievement of a legitimate end.

As for the incident at My Lai, it would be hard to make the case that this was characteristic of the American war effort in Vietnam. News of the massacre at My Lai apparently stirred disbelief among other soldiers who had been stationed in other hamlets, and their reactions suggested, even to critics of the war, that the incident was quite far from the experience of most American soldiers. As Daniel Ellsberg remarked: "My Lai was beyond the bounds of permissible behavior, and that is recognizable by virtually every soldier in Vietnam. They know it was wrong. . . . The men who were at My Lai knew there were aspects out of the ordinary. That is why they tried to hide the event, talked about it to no one, discussed it very little even among themselves."[17]

As EDMUND BURKE once remarked, success is the most infallible criterion of wisdom—to vulgar judgments. With the same sensibility, the collapse of the government in Saigon has been taken as a kind of proof that the war in Vietnam had not been merely a mistake but a moral failure. In all strictness, of course, the loss of a war cannot itself prove the moral wrongness of the loser, any more than success at arms would establish the moral rightness of the victor. In the case of Vietnam, the fall of Saigon occurred after the hardest battles had been won. With American help, the Vietcong and the North Vietnamese had been fought to a standoff. The Tet offensive in 1968 was a failure which exhausted the Vietcong, and the attempt in 1972 to stage another major offensive during a presidential election year in the United States proved a decisive failure. Despite the willingness of the American press to overlook the point, the South Vietnamese army developed forces that bore the battles well, took heavy casualties and yet preserved their will to fight.[18] The elections in South Vietnam persistently showed that factions sympathetic to the Vietcong commanded little support

---

[17] Quoted in *ibid.*, p. 327.

[18] This point is documented rather well in Peter Braestrup, *Big Story* (New York: Praeger, 1977), ch. 9.

among the people of Vietnam, and if there was any doubt on that point, it should have been dispelled by the resistance that the South Vietnamese mounted until the very end, even when they were short of ammunition and supplies.

To be sure, a peace agreement had been accepted in 1972 with parts of South Vietnam still under the control of the enemy. But in the arrangement that was finally accepted, the North Vietnamese failed to achieve the principal end they had hoped to gain from a negotiated settlement: they did not induce the United States to displace the government in Saigon; nor were they even able to force the creation of a "coalition government."[19] The Saigon government did not have to compromise its claims to jural sovereignty over its own country; nor was it obliged to cut off relations with the United States or renounce American aid. The government in the South would have been given a decent chance of surviving and strengthening itself if the United States had preserved its own willingness to enforce the peace, with military action if necessary, and to support its ally with arms and supplies. But the advent of the Watergate scandal soon deprived President Nixon of his moral authority to act with vigor overseas in any military action that might stir opposition at home. With the political eclipse of Richard Nixon, the Congress turned away from its responsibility to fund the full level of equipment that was needed in Vietnam.[20] There is direct evidence that the leadership in North Vietnam was very attentive to the effects of Watergate on the presidency; and it guessed, correctly, that even Mr. Nixon's successor would not be able to summon support at home for a renewal of the war if North Vietnam should suddenly bring in new units and raise the stakes.[21]

The bombing ordered by President Nixon in December 1972 (the so-called Christmas bombing, or Linebacker II) was more systematic and precise than any previous application of American force; it delivered a decisive shock that made the North Vietnamese see that they had no alternative but to accept a compromise settlement. At the end

[19] On this point, see Henry Kissinger, *White House Years* (Boston: Little, Brown, 1979), pp. 1344, 1359 *et passim*.

[20] Beyond that, Congress actually strengthened the hands of the adversary by legislating a date for the ending of American military action in Indochina. Kissinger would later recall how this legislative inspiration finally undermined the negotiations to restore Prince Sihanouk in Cambodia and block the ascension of the Khmer Rouge. "What ended the 1973 negotiation," he wrote, "was a Congressionally mandated halt to our bombing in the middle of the year; at that point, certain of victory, the Khmer Rouge lost all interest in negotiations—and Sihanouk's role as balancer was doomed." See *ibid.*, p. 1415.

[21] See Lewy, *supra*, note 10, pp. 204-205, 207-208.

of this bombing, Guenter Lewy noted, North Vietnam found its electrical power supply crippled, its air defenses shattered, and "American planes roamed the skies with virtual impunity."[22] Taking stock later, Sir Robert Thompson estimated that, with the Christmas bombing, the United States had established a military dominance in the war that would have allowed it virtually to dictate the terms of a settlement.[23] Despite the myths that have grown up around the Vietnam war, then, it should be clear beyond caviling that the United States did not lose that war on the battlefield.

IN ONE OF HIS earliest dispatches from Vietnam, after the American combat forces were introduced in 1965, Bernard Fall remarked that the war was not militarily losable so long as U.S. firepower was available. That assessment probably remained quite as true in 1975. But if the war was not so clearly unwinnable, a question has been raised in the name of "prudence" as to whether the interests engaged in the conflict really justified the costs that had to be paid. Some people argued in this vein that Vietnam was simply not important strategically. Some feared, in addition, that we would divert our military resources from Europe and Central America, where there were graver dangers to American interests. And yet, reservations of this kind did not raise any challenge in principle to the war in Vietnam. There were those who held that the United States would be amply justified in resisting a totalitarian movement in Vietnam, but who nevertheless measured the gravity of the danger in any case by the strength of the adversary and the directness of the threat. They regarded the regime in North Vietnam as no more redeeming in principle than the regime in Nazi Germany; but they counted a regime such as Nazi Germany as a danger that merited the resistance of a full-scale war. In the case of Germany, the totalitarian regime of the Nazis stood a chance of controlling the resources of the entire Eurasian land mass. A hostile government in control of those resources and in a position to dominate the seas posed a threat to the United States that could not have been

---

[22] *Ibid.*, p. 412.

[23] As Thompson remarked, "In my view, on December 30, 1972, after eleven days of those B-52 attacks on the Hanoi area, *you* [the Americans] *had won the war. It was over.* They [the North Vietnamese] had fired 1,242 SAMs, they had none left, and what would come in overland from China would be a mere trickle. They and their whole rear base at that point were at your mercy. They would have taken any terms. And that is why, of course, you actually got a peace agreement in January, which you had not been able to get in October." See Sir Robert's comments in W. Scott Thompson and Donaldson D. Fizzell (eds.), *The Lessons of Vietnam* (London: MacDonald & Jane's, 1977), pp. 97-105, at 105. Italics in original.

mounted by a Communist regime in Vietnam, even if it should extend its control over the rest of Indochina.

In the argument drawn from prudence, it might be better not to fight at all: if the United States committed itself to war in a novel setting and lost, unwholesome inferences might be made about the limits of American power, and that itself could hasten the fall of several dominoes. Still, if it were thought necessary to put up an armed resistance in Vietnam, the disposition in this argument was to urge a clear sense of the limits of our own utility: better to get clear in advance that the war was worth a sacrifice, say, of no more than 5,000 American lives or that it would strain other, more valuable commitments if it were allowed to drag on for more than two or three years.

Arguments drawn from prudence must of course hold a necessary place in moral judgment. It could not be irrelevant to know that the pursuit of our ends in any particular case might be self-defeating or that it might impair our capacity, in the long run, to achieve our decent ends. With that kind of sobriety Lincoln understood that the United States did not have the means, in the middle of the nineteenth century, to eradicate slavery wherever it existed abroad, and that any effort on the part of the United States to undertake this mission could lead to the destruction of the republican experiment in the United States. An American intervention in Europe might only invite the more active intervention of Europe in America. And if the United States were destroyed as an independent republic, it would remove from the earth the most prominent example of a government constituted on republican principles. The demise of the American republic would remove that government whose very existence was a reproach to despotic governments and an inspiration to peoples everywhere to throw off the tyrannies that ruled them.

That argument, drawn from prudence, had the force of plausibility because it was governed by right principle—by a correct understanding of the ends that were in principle better or worse for the United States— and it sought to fashion the most practicable means of achieving those ends in the real world. That, we might say, was a proper and accurate invocation of "prudence." But there is also a persisting, legitimate concern that the claims of "prudence" should not furnish a crude license for evading duties borne of principle when it becomes inexpedient to honor them. What must be understood, then, is that prudence, in its proper application, must proceed from a correct understanding of principle, and it must carry at all times the burden of justification.

That burden of justification would instantly complicate the kinds of arguments that might have been made, in the cause of prudence, against the war in Vietnam. For one thing, there would be no tenable ground for any "limits of utility" established in advance, such as a ceiling of 5,000 on the number of lives that may be lost. A president of the United States would not be in a position to explain to the relatives of those 5,000 dead servicemen just why the death of the 5,001st soldier became intolerable, while the lives of the first 5,000 men were not quite so precious. And once our minds were cultivated in the habits of a principled discourse, we would be led to recognize the deeper fallacy of reckoning the "importance" of a country solely by the size of its territory. To take an analogy for a moment from domestic law, we might consider a case in which a person is turned away, on account of his race, from a job as an executive with the most influential corporation in the city, and we may compare that with a case in which a person is turned away, for the same reason, from a job as an assistant in a junkyard. The nature of the offense in principle is no larger or more "important" in the first case than in the second. Whether a case is important depends on the question it raises or the principle it exemplifies—which is why some of the most momentous questions in American law have been expounded in cases involving a kosher butcher in Brooklyn and a family diner in Birmingham, Alabama.

With the same understanding we would be obliged to recognize that the importance of any crisis abroad would not depend solely on the size of the country, but on whether there is a principle engaged in the case. That is not to say that strategic factors are unimportant. It is to say, rather, that in certain cases a country may acquire an importance that extends far beyond its resources or strategic value because it is invested with the significance of a "test case." It may also be threatened with an evil that deserves, in principle, to be resisted by anyone with the capacity to act. Czechoslovakia, in 1938, had a population of only 14.7 million; yet, as a result of Hitler's demands, the crisis at Munich became truly portentous. To acquiesce in the Nazi takeover of that land was to acquiesce in the destruction of a constitutional order. It was to teach the lesson that the honoring of principles may not be worth the cost of war, that the success of Germany would depend less on the justice of its claims than on its willingness to threaten violence, and that statesmen in the West probably did not have the will to resist German obduracy anywhere else. The leaders of Britain and France might have thought that they were backing away out of prudence, and that the "settlement" at Munich did not have to be regarded as a test case. But the meaning of that event could not depend wholly on the meaning given to it by Neville Chamberlain. Whether that settlement would have the standing of a test case would depend also on the construction that *Hitler* was willing to place upon it. A country may be small and impoverished—it may be only an island a mile or two square, with few natural resources and little strategic significance—and yet if it is seized, with manifest injustice, by a totalitarian regime that regards the event as a case that will test the climate for other, similar acts in more strategic places, other countries may have no choice but to treat this hostile move as a test case.

Lest we regard a situation of that kind as too implausible, we ought to recall that the United States went to war in Korea under circumstances that were not too remote from the ones I have described here. In 1950 Secretary of State Dean Acheson marked off the perimeter of American interests in the world, and Korea was not placed within that zone of defense. Edward Luttwak had the occasion not too long ago to list the considerations which lay behind that original judgment. South Korea was a poor, nonindustrial state with little significance of its own. The country was plagued by a constant enemy, North Korea, and since it was part of the East Asian mainland, it could not be defended with air and naval forces alone. Its defense would require, in short, troops on the ground. The situation seemed to offer high costs with few offsetting benefits, and American leaders appreciated at the same time that there was no strong constituency of Korean-Americans in the United States who could exert leverage in Congress. It appeared, then, that the administration could hold back from a commitment to South Korea without encountering political pressures to reverse its judgment.

But then, on June 25, 1950, troops from the North invaded South Korea and the situation was dramatically altered. All of the facts that defined the case were still true, and yet they were dissolved in their significance by this singular, dramatic event. As Luttwak puts it:

> South Korea was still very poor; the peninsula was still irremediably attached to the Asian mainland, and its rescue would now undoubtedly require American troops on the ground; and the number of Korean-Americans ready to write to their Congressman had not appreciably increased. Nothing of relevance to the original decision had changed at all, and yet the policy was utterly overturned, precisely when the North Korean invasion made it operative. For it was then suddenly realized that the United States had become a Pacific power, and since the Pacific is unfortunately empty of significant land masses, the American perimeter would

283

of necessity have to be withdrawn to the shore of Western America unless it rested on the East Asian rim (Hawaii and the islands of Micronesia could be no more than outposts). Finally, it could justifiably be feared that Japan would not allow itself to be held if the United States were to accept the conquest of South Korea without effective challenge: as soon as the end of the occupation allowed it to do so, Japan would extrude an American protector which did not protect. Hence the total and immediate reversal of the decision, and the large war that followed, which a firm American commitment clearly stated might well have averted.[24]

A Communist government in Vietnam posed no direct and immediate danger to the security of the United States. The control of Indochina by regimes hostile to the United States and in league with the Soviet Union was a prospect adverse to our interests; but the importance of Vietnam was marked in the first instance by the principle that defined both the wrong of a totalitarian regime and the evil that would be visited on Vietnam itself in the event of a Communist victory. To the special misery represented by a stringent despotism there was added, for the United States, the prospect of acquiescing in the armed takeover of another country by a Marxist-Leninist power, aided by fraternal parties in adjacent lands. When it became clear that American power would not return to Vietnam, the regime in the North staged a new offensive and finally brought down the government in the South. Camranh Bay would now become available as a port for the Soviet navy. A new population of political prisoners in Vietnam would become transferable as workers to the USSR as a kind of partial repayment for Soviet aid. North Vietnamese pilots would be lent as advisers to the Syrian air force, thus demonstrating that the interests of Vietnamese "nationalists" could coincide in a remarkably precise way with the commitments of the Soviet camp. Vietnam and its satellites in Indochina could be counted on to vote with their Soviet patrons in international forums, and the votes would offer telling measures of the expanding reach of the Soviet network of satellites and allies. As the United States recoiled from its experience in Vietnam, each subsequent crisis would be approached with the assumption that the country had neither the will nor the right to use its military forces. A vocal party could be depended on to insist that there be "no more Vietnams" and to explain, in each case, why Angola or Somalia or Ethiopia or South Yemen or Nicaragua or El Salvador was in itself

---

[24] Edward N. Luttwak, "The Strange Case of George F. Kennan," *Commentary* (November 1977), pp. 30-35, at p. 31.

not very important and not worth the trauma of war. It required the American humiliation in Iran and the Soviet takeover of Afghanistan before the American people could recover an understanding only recently secured and only recently misplaced: that the recession of American power would not bring a diffusion of peace and liberation in the rest of the world. The withdrawal of American strength was likely to result, rather, in a pride of wars and the extinction of freedom.

To anticipate this train of events—these falling dominoes—did not require high powers of foresight. But it was not on the basis of predictions alone that statesmen would have been warranted in committing their citizens to the risks of war. Whether the consequences of a Communist victory worked themselves out fully or quickly was a matter, in part, of happenstance. It was not necessary to wait for all the consequences to take place, however, before it was possible to recognize that the regime being prepared, by force, for the people of Vietnam was a notable evil in itself.

THE RIGHT OF the people of Vietnam to escape that evil could not have depended on whether they had the strength themselves to defend their own interests. As we have established, any third party would have been justified in summoning, on behalf of the Vietnamese, the strength they could not command on their own to vindicate their rights. And if any third party would have been warranted in acting, the United States would have come under the coverage of that principle: this country, *as well as any other*, would have been justified in intervening.

We have established, also, that if the government of the United States were truly "justified" in undertaking any commitment, it would have to be justified at the same time in making that commitment binding for its citizens. (As we have seen, it could not be argued that the United States would be "justified" in having a welfare system, but only if enough people were willing to make voluntary contributions to support the program.) If the United States were justified in deploying its military force in defense of Vietnam, then it would have been justified in drafting its own citizens into the military for the sake of carrying through with that commitment.

Still, a finer distinction might be urged here. It might be agreed that the United States would have been justified in intervening in Vietnam, but a question might be raised as to whether this country had been strictly *obliged* to intervene when the preservation of our own regime was not at stake. And if we were not actually obliged to intervene, would the problem of conscription not become more complicated as a moral question? In the tradition of moral philosophy we have become aware of so-called "supererogatory" acts: literally, acts beyond the domain of what might reasonably be "asked" or commanded—acts "beyond the call of duty." A soldier might be justified in falling on a live grenade for the sake of saving his friends, but it would not ordinarily be thought that he had an *obligation* to fall on the grenade. If the survival of the American republic was not at stake in the war in Vietnam, was it justified to conscript men to fight? Or was conscription under those circumstances rather like drafting a corps of men to do the equivalent of falling on hand grenades? That is to say, these men would be compelled by law to run a much higher risk of giving up their lives for the lives of others.

There is, in fact, something plausible about the notion of "supererogatory" acts, but the concept has been misapplied in recent years, and it has become simply a disguised carrier of Hobbesian premises. The recent understanding of "supererogatory" acts has been built on the assumption that there is a certain core of self-interest that no one may reasonably be obliged to surrender, and that core has been defined most importantly by the interest in self-preservation. For Hobbes, of course, conscription in most cases was tantamount to a policy of coercing people to perform supererogatory acts. When self-preservation was the preeminent interest in our lives, no one could be obliged to fight for any life but his own. To compel a man to fight for the lives of others, or to fight "merely" for the purpose of preserving a certain kind of political regime, was the equivalent of compelling a man to fall on a grenade. It was forcing a man to sacrifice his life— or to run a high risk of suffering violent death—even when his own life might not be imperiled.

But it should be clear that we have indeed obliged men over many years to risk their own lives in war for the sake of others, and those others have included strangers in distant lands. As measured by current understandings, it should be equally clear, then, that we have routinely been compelling men to perform acts that would be described these days as "supererogatory." As we have seen, those commitments have been warranted in point of principle. And so if there is a tension here, we must suspect that the current understanding of "supererogatory" acts contains a serious mistake. In locating that mistake and getting shed of it, I think we would see in a clearer light the ground on which we have properly offered praise in the past for sacrifices directed toward good ends, and obliged even ordinary folk to behave in the manner of saints and heroes. That ground of obligation has been made obscure to us because our laws have been shaped in recent years by a jurisprudence that has sought deliberately to forget the ancient connection between morals and law. It is no wonder that a jurisprudence of that kind has fostered a false distinction between legal and moral obligation—a distinction that tends to reduce moral obligation to the level of a "weak obligation," which becomes no obligation at all. But if we could trace our moral judgments back to their proper ground, we would discover that the obligation to act where we practicably can, even in places like Vietnam, would arise from the logic of "first principles." As it turns out, that obligation would depend on the same core of principles from which the courts have been expanding obligations under the laws of negligence and liability since the early part of the twentieth century. At its furthest reaches, these principles have brought about an expansion in the "obligation to rescue," or in the duty to render help where there is a special competence and a compelling circumstance for offering that aid.

It may be no surprise that the same principle would stand behind the argument, often made today, that the United States is obliged to go to the rescue of the hungry in the world. Ironically, the people who make this argument are willing to contemplate an intervention in the politics of other countries if that were necessary to the humanitarian mission of bringing food to the starving. Without much awareness, the spokesmen for this persuasion have themselves absorbed Hobbesian premises: they assume that the preservation of life is a purpose that must override all others and transcend political differences. Paradoxically, then, they would blind themselves to the question of whether the lives they would save are imprisoned, in effect, in regimes that are despotic and murderous, and whether the aid they would render would actually work to strengthen those regimes. The question, in that event, is whether the principle that enjoins an obligation to rescue would also entail a commitment to do far more than preserve the lives of the victims. Might we not also be obliged to deliver people, where we can, from regimes of oppression, and establish the kinds of government that are more fitting by nature for human beings? I will set out this problem a bit more fully in the next chapter, in tracing it back to the principle that is ultimately at work here. If that principle is recognized, and if the partisans of humanitarian aid can be redeemed from their Hobbesian premises, then the remaining pieces in the argument would fall into place. The principles that enjoin our obligation to act where we reasonably can to reduce starvation and suffering abroad, even at the risk of political intrusions, would be quite sufficient to enjoin, at the same time, the obligation that was accepted by the United States when it intervened in Vietnam.

287

XIII

THE OBLIGATION TO RESCUE AND
SUPEREROGATORY ACTS

Over the last decade we have witnessed a series of earthquakes which
have wrought destruction and suffering in Pakistan, Guatemala, Italy,
and other countries. In each instance, the United States offered help
in the form of food, medicine, and materials for shelter. The aid was
either administered directly by the American government or distributed
indirectly, through international agencies. Immediately after the Second World War, the United States had been content to make its contributions abroad through the United Nations Relief and Rehabilita-
tion Administration (UNRRA), but the government moved away from
this "multilateral" aid when it became evident that no foreign aid was
"apolitical." The scheme of multilateral aid was designed partly in the
hope of insulating humanitarian aid from political manipulation in
the service of separate national interests. The commitment to save life
and relieve distress was conceived as a purpose which could be shared
by all nations, and which transcended political differences. What the
United States discovered, however, was that the aid worked to
strengthen the government in power, and when that government happened to be hostile to American interests, the United States found itself
in the irritating position, for example, of sending supplies to Yugo-
slavia at a time when that country was shooting down American planes
that strayed over its airspace. When the Marshall Plan was created in
1948, the United States had come to the recognition that if aid was
going to confer political benefits, those benefits ought to be distributed
in ways that supported the interests of the United States and its allies.[1]

The natural disasters that struck Pakistan, Guatemala, and Italy
confirmed again the lessons that were learned thirty years earlier. A
natural disaster may test the character and cohesion of a people, but
it also tests the government in a demanding and dramatic way. An
incompetent and corrupt administration will find its weaknesses exposed quickly. The initial effort to organize medical aid and provide
shelter to the victims may be delayed through administrative bungling.
Supplies brought in from the outside may fail to move through the

[1] The account of this change in the perspective of the United States is offered in Arkes,
Bureaucracy, the Marshall Plan, and the National Interest (Princeton: Princeton University Press, 1973), pp. 44ff.

288

administration and reach the stricken population. Or the aid may be distributed in ways that serve the political interests of the party in power. In Guatemala, for example, the ruling party in 1976 had its base in the countryside, and the government was determined not to channel aid to the cities through the municipal councils, which were dominated by the opposition. Instead, as the *New York Times* reported, "food distribution in the slums has been left to a hard-working Mexican field kitchen, while most clothes, blankets, tents and construction tools have been dispatched to the provinces." In Joya de Senahu, where none of the shacks had running water, the communal water tap had run dry, and despair seemed to deepen when women and children would climb a steep ravine to the emergency tank, only to find it empty. For the residents, the experience seemed to magnify the impoverishment of their lives, and it deepened their cynicism about their own government. As one local official said, "The earthquake allowed people to see many problems that have always existed."[2]

It should be apparent, then, that these natural disasters are not politically neutral events, and no aid supplied to governments in such circumstances will be barren of political significance. The provision of aid, along with able administrators, may prop up a weak regime that might otherwise strain its last thread of credit with its own people. If this were also an offensive regime, which on the whole deserved to perish, a position of detachment by outside benefactors might give Providence a helping hand and bestow on the country a much better gift than medicine. The alternative might well be to firm up the hold of a bad regime over its own population by making its rule more salutary. In any event, we should harbor no illusion that aid can be rendered for the sake of saving lives without representing an "intervention" in the politics of the receiving country. One way or another, that aid cannot help but affect the balance of political forces and perhaps even the survival of the regime itself.

But as we know, there is a strong appeal in the notion of acting where we can for the sake of saving lives, quite apart from the political regime in which these lives may happen to be caught. My own reservation is not with the desire to render aid, which stems from imperatives that are grounded in first principles. My concern, rather, is that the argument for supplying aid is morally truncated. The principle

---

[2] *New York Times*, February 22, 1976. Nearly ten years later, precisely the same account emerged in the aftermath of the earthquake in Mexico City. See "Earthquake Aftermath Points Up Weaknesses of Mexican Leadership," *Wall Street Journal* (October 15, 1985), pp. 1, 10. The subhead in the story read: "Citizens Score Ruling Party for Inaction, Inefficiency; Big Boost for Dissidents."

that impels us to this aid might suggest itself more clearly if the problem were approached as follows. *Would the capacity to affect the outcome in any case confer a certain responsibility for the results?* If the United States had the means of sending medicine, food, and helicopters after the earthquake in Guatemala; if the United States decided instead to hold back from that course; and if, in holding back, lives were lost; would the United States bear any responsibility for the lives that were lost through its temporizing?

In putting this question to people, I have found a uniform inclination to say that the United States would indeed bear some responsibility. In the common reckoning, the United States would have had an obligation to act, provided that it did have the means to relieve suffering and that it would not have caused any comparable suffering for our own people by going to the rescue. Along the same lines, one recent commentator has even argued that the United States should be obliged to reduce its standard of living to the subsistence level if that condition must in fact result from a commitment on our part to prevent starvation in the world.[3] The capacity to affect the outcome, then, is apparently understood by many people as a source of an obligation to act. What is involved here, of course, is the relation between the "can" and the "ought." As we have seen, the first principles of morals must imply the "can" as the precondition for the "ought" (see Chapter VIII). We may not cast moral judgments on people for acts they were powerless to affect. A man who is unable to swim would not be obliged to plunge into a river and rescue a person who is drowning. Where the "can" is not present—where there is no capacity to affect the outcome—there can be no obligation. But when the "can" *is* present, does the "ought" follow? Would there be an obligation to act?

In the *Groundwork of the Metaphysics of Morals* Kant writes, as if in passing, that "to help others where one can is a duty."[4] These words are set forth without a hint of equivocation, because the conviction here arises from the logic of morals itself. We saw earlier that the logic of morals obliges us to regard the good as higher than the bad: the "good" is that which people ought, universally, to seek to do, and the "bad" is what people, universally, ought to refrain from doing. In following out the chain of reasoning that emerges from this point, I offered (in Chapter VIII) a further implication of first principles: since we are obliged, by the logic of morals, to do what is good

[3] See Peter Singer, "Famine, Affluence, and Morality," *Philosophy and Public Affairs* (Spring 1972), pp. 229-43.

[4] Immanuel Kant, *Groundwork of the Metaphysics of Morals* [1785], trans. H.J. Paton (New York: Harper & Row, 1964), p. 66; p. 398 of the RPA ed.

and refrain from what is bad (provided that it is within our means) we are obliged, where we can, to do more good rather than less, and to do less harm rather than more.

This was the principle that enjoined us to follow a rule of proportionality—to inflict as little harm as possible as we seek our decent ends. But if that principle enjoins us to avoid doing harm, it must also oblige us, where we can, to do good. If it is within our power to relieve the suffering of the innocent, this principle would at least oblige us to offer reasons as to why we did not act. If we could not have acted without creating comparable dangers for other innocent people (including ourselves), the act of holding back becomes comprehensible and justified. But if one held back from a good act for reasons merely of convenience or self-interest or even of indifference, then one would neglect to do a good for reasons which cite no countervailing interest or harm, and which may therefore claim no comparable moral weight.

If it were within the means of the United States to act in other countries for the purpose of saving lives, then we would be enjoined to do what reasonably could be done. And yet, it could not be irrelevant to any judgment here that what we do in the cause of saving lives may actually strengthen the hold of a local despotism. Let us suppose that an earthquake had struck not in Italy or Guatemala, but in Nazi Germany or Stalinist Russia, on the sites of concentration camps or slave labor colonies. A presumptive interest might have arisen for the United States in sending supplies abroad for the sake of aiding the victims. But could there really have been an obligation on the part of the United States to save lives and restore the victims to health, when the act of healing meant restoring these people to lives of slavery and advancing the ends of a totalitarian regime? The root problem with the arguments for so-called humanitarian aid is that their understanding of the "humane" rules out a sense of those needs which are most distinctively human. They fasten merely on the interest in physical survival which human beings share with animals. In the spirit of Hobbes, they give precedence to the interest of self-preservation, while subordinating a concern for the terms of principle on which those lives are led.

Let us suppose that the United States had somehow been able to act in 1978 on the revelation that came to Senator McGovern: let us assume that it had been within our power to stop the genocide in Cambodia, either by intervening with military force or by using sources of leverage apart from the military. Once the killing had been stopped, would we have reached the moral limits of our intervention? Would we have been obliged then to withdraw from the scene and leave the

291

people of Cambodia once again in the hands of their local totalitarian regime? Again, we would have to ask, by what truncated moral understanding are we furnished with a warrant for resisting genocide, but somehow denied the capacity to judge the regime that produced the genocide?

Those who would save lives with food and medicine in all countries, those who would protest the extinction of "human rights" in countries other than our own, and those who would press their humanitarian concerns even when they know they would be intervening in the politics of other countries have all acknowledged the most decisive principles that sanctioned the American intervention in Vietnam. For they would have recognized certain rights that hold true across cultures, and they would have acknowledged the force of the principles that enjoin us to act, even at the cost of intervention. And if we can be obliged to intervene abroad for the sake of saving lives, then the principles of moral judgment would establish quite as clearly that we would be obliged to act where we can to secure, as much as practicable, the kind of lawful government that human beings, anywhere, deserve.

BUT HOW MUCH was the United States "reasonably" obliged to do in honoring any obligation it might have had to act in Vietnam? The measures employed in judgments of this kind have been made more precise for us over the years through the analogies that have been worked out in our tort law in cases involving negligence, liability, and the obligation to rescue. The trend of the law, from the early part of the twentieth century to our own day, has been marked by a steady expansion in our understanding of "obligation." That trend becomes comprehensible only when it is recognized as a gradual filling out or discovery of the principle we have set forth here: namely, that the logic of morals enjoins us, wherever practicable, to do good where we can and refrain from what is hurtful. The changes in our law have been dramatic, and it should be noted that they have been carried out for the most part without statutes. These changes have come about as courts have taken cases under the common law for "wrongs" inflicted among private parties. The expansion that the courts created in legal obligations did not require a statutory source, for it represented a course of drawing out the implications that arise from the logic of morals or from the very idea of law.

The nature of the change that has taken place in our law becomes more revealing if we recall for a moment the perspective contained in the law as it was. The state of legal sensibilities under our earlier doctrines has never been conveyed more vividly than in Justice Carpenter's opinion for the New Hampshire court in the case of *Buch* v. *Amory* in 1898: "Suppose A., standing close by a railroad, sees a two year old babe on the track, and a car approaching. He can easily rescue the child, with entire safety to himself, and the instincts of humanity require him to do so. If he does not, he may, perhaps, justly be styled a ruthless savage and a moral monster; but he is not liable in damages for the child's injury, or indictable under the statute for its death."[5] The case Justice Carpenter was addressing involved an 8-year-old boy who had visited a mill that employed his older brother. The boy was there to observe the working of the machinery, with the hope of learning enough to secure a job himself, but as a result of his curiosity one of his hands became caught in the gears. The boy had not been invited into the factory, and he had been directed to leave the premises by one of the overseers, who had been aware that the machinery was dangerous. But the overseer was unaware that the boy did not understand English, and he did not apparently grasp that his words of warning were not being absorbed. The court argued, however, that an 8-year-old had "sufficient reason and discretion to appreciate the particular risk of injury that he incurred and to avoid it." Even if the boy did not have enough wit to observe more caution, the court did not see that the owners of the factory bore any responsibility for a trespasser on their property. An effort had been made to warn the boy, and the court found it hard to see how the company could have been *obliged* to do very much more in preventing a heedless person from injuring himself. As Justice Carpenter put it, in a passage that would be widely quoted, "The defendants are not liable unless they owed to the plaintiff a legal duty which they neglected to perform. With purely moral obligations, the law does not deal."[6]

In our own day, of course, no mere "warning" would be taken as sufficient to stay the curiosity of an 8-year-old and absolve the owners of a factory from their responsibility for accidents taking place in their own plant. In an age when even burglars may sue for damages against proprietors who shoot and wound them, the manufacturers of candy, for example, would be obliged to take the most stringent precautions in order to keep children from jumping into their vats of chocolate. As late as the 1930's it was assumed that a shopper who fainted in a department store could be left there without liability for the store so long as no one stepped on her.[7] In our current law, however, it would

---

[5] *Buch* v. *Amory*, 44 Atlantic Reporter, 809, at 810 (1898).

[6] *Ibid.*, 810.

[7] See *Zelenko* v. *Gimbel Bros.*, 287 N.Y. Supp. 134 (1935), cited by Charles Gregory,

be assumed that the management would at least have a responsibility to call for help. Even if the store would not be obliged to pay the medical expenses, it may at least be expected to cover the victim with a blanket or provide some brand of first aid.

The difference between the law expressed by Justice Carpenter and the law of our own time is marked by a larger imagination in seeing the reasonable acts forgone in so-called acts of omission. There is, no doubt, a notable difference between wrongs done directly and wrongs permitted to take place through indifference or inaction, but judges in recent years have refused to agree that the gross distinction between acts of commission and acts of omission marks a difference in the capacity to act. As in the case of the 2-year-old near the railroad tracks, there might be instances in which a passer-by may be able to render aid—and do an immeasurable good—with hardly more than the cost of an inconvenience to himself. At those moments, it becomes pertinent to ask just what interest deflected the passer-by from the commission of such a good service. It simply does not suffice for the man to answer that the question is unreasonable because he was not himself responsible for the presence of the child near the tracks. That response pales as an adequate moral response precisely because we recognize the responsibility that must arise presumptively whenever the capacity to act is clearly present.[8]

That logic was apparently accessible to John Stuart Mill and Jeremy Bentham, both of whom favored a legal obligation to rescue in some cases. Since Mill and Bentham have been important figures in shaping the liberal jurisprudence of our time, their positions seem to indicate that the sensibility shown by Justice Carpenter did not have to flow, necessarily, from the teachings of liberal jurisprudence. It is one thing to hold that people should be restricted in their freedom only when they cause immediate, material injury to others; it is quite another to insist that people bear no responsibility to help, where they can, in

---

"The Good Samaritan and the Bad," in *The Good Samaritan and the Law* (New York: Doubleday, 1966), pp. 23-41, at 25.

[8] Honoré has commented aptly on this point: "It has been urged that there is something peculiarly irksome in requiring people to take positive action as opposed to subjecting them to mere prohibitions. Why this should be so is a mystery. Perhaps we have a picture of Joe lounging in an armchair. It is more effort for him to get up than to stay where he is. But this is not how the law operates. Prohibitions are usually imposed because there is a strong urge or temptation selfishly to leave others in the lurch. Certainly there are important spheres, for instance, taxation and military service, where the law does not shrink from demanding positive action. Why should it do so in the law of rescue?" Anthony M. Honoré, "Law, Morals, and Rescue," in *The Good Samaritan and the Law, supra,* note 7, pp. 225-42, at 240-41.

averting serious injury to others. Still, it is worth noticing that the source of Carpenter's problem lay in his tendency to assume that the difference between acts of commission and acts of omission coincides with the difference between the legal and the "moral" realms. He fell into his mistake because he assumed, in the first place, that the domain of morals was to be separated, grossly and emphatically, from the domain of law. And that assumption was a central part of the project in liberal jurisprudence that Justice Holmes had helped to advance. As Holmes put it, the aspiration of this jurisprudence was to bring us to the point at which "every word of moral significance could be banished from the law altogether."[9]

The courts would gradually come to recognize that the responsibility to act finds its source in the simple capacity to act with effect. But before the judges could arrive at that point of recognition (if, indeed, they have arrived at it even yet), they would work their way through a series of cases in which they would find the origin of responsibility in special relations. They would move from the special responsibility of parents or spouses to the responsibilities of professionals, until finally the law could be brought to the threshold of an enlarged sense of obligation on the part of any person who could have acted, without danger or strain, in saving another from injury.

It is taken now as an understanding beyond question that parents are obliged to furnish help to their children in peril or distress. That obligation holds even if the parents were compelled to forgo their convenience, spend their money, or waive their religious objection to certain forms of medication. And what can be said in this respect for parents in relation to their dependent children can be said also in relation to spouses. In a noted case in Australia, in the 1930's, a couple had sat quarreling at the edge of a swimming pool. The wife, in a fit of anger, jumped into the pool, a gesture that was all the more dramatic since she could not swim. But the husband, in vengeful detachment, sat watching her thrash about in the water until she drowned. The husband was eventually convicted for criminal homicide.[10]

Certain occupations are understood to be vocations of "helping," and so it is implicit in the definition of the job that policemen, firemen, and first-aid teams will go to the rescue when they are called. But even when a profession is not devoted to the rendering of care in emergencies, there may be situations arising in the course of ordinary com-

[9] Oliver Wendell Holmes, "The Path of the Law," in *Collected Legal Papers* (New York: Harcourt Brace & Co., 1920), p. 179.

[10] *Rex* v. *Russell*, 1933 Victoria Law Rep. 59, cited by Gregory, *supra*, note 7, p. 24.

mercial transactions in which clients have made themselves dependent on people in positions of official responsibility, and that responsibility may carry special obligations. The captains of ships (and, presumably, the pilots of commercial aircraft) would bear a special responsibility for the safety of their crews and passengers. The headmaster of a boarding school would bear a special responsibility for his students. Even a baby sitter, in case of an emergency, would be obliged to do more than seek his own safety; if there were a fire in the house, we would expect a baby sitter to provide for the safety, also, of any child placed in his charge for the evening. Those expectations would arise even though the baby sitter was not bound to his clients through a formal contract, and even though he would be the practitioner of no highly specialized profession. The responsibility, in other words, would emerge from the nature of the job, and it would emerge precisely because the sitter is one who is understood to possess the capacity to act for the care of his charges. But then, it becomes more evident that the source of the responsibility lies in the combination of a special competence and a unique opportunity to help, and those ingredients may be present even when the potential rescuer is not tied to the potential victim through a contractual relationship. Charles Gregory has raised the question, in this vein, of whether the case of the Australian couple by the pool would have been different if the man and woman had been lovers, rather than two people connected through a contract of marriage. Would it have been different, he asks, if their legal marriage had been dependent on a Mexican divorce which turned out to have been illegal?[11] In other words, once it had been established that the man could swim and that he was the only person who could have rendered aid, would his obligation have been any less if he had not been bound to the woman through marriage—or, indeed, if he had not known her at all?

It is only by this logic, I think, that we can explain the statutes in several states that oblige doctors to stop and render aid if they pass the scene of an accident. On the same principle, obligations have been legislated in certain places for lifeguards, even when off their "watch," to go to the rescue of swimmers in distress. Insignia worn on swimming trunks may designate people who have been certified as lifeguards and who would be called upon in an emergency. It goes without saying, of course, that no comparable obligation may be established for non-swimmers, and that no penalty should have been imposed on the Australian husband had he not been able to swim. At the threshold of obligation the first test is the capacity to act, but there must also

[11] Gregory, *supra*, note 7, p. 25.

be a principled reckoning of the interests being risked and the end to be achieved. If a man were drowning and the only one in a position to rescue him were a stranger with almost no ability as a swimmer, we could not enjoin the second man to attempt the rescue of the first, and our judgment would not be governed simply by the claims of "self-preservation." The decisive point, rather, is that on the basis of what we know, there would be no evident ground of principle on which we could say that the life of one innocent person should be sacrificed for another. There is no ground on which to say that one life is less worth preserving than another, or that one life commands the sacrifice of another.

But the circumstances might not always support this conclusion. To take a case similar to one that arose in the American law, a woman might be driven into hysteria as the result of a rape and fling herself into a river. The rapist would probably be held responsible for her death, and if his ability as a swimmer gave him only a fifty-fifty chance of rescuing his victim, we might still be more inclined to hold, in his case, that he was obliged to make the attempt. The peril that threatened her life arose only because of his criminal act, and it may not be unreasonable to impose upon a guilty, responsible man a risk quite as grave as the danger facing his victim.

We would be recognizing here shadings and degrees of responsibility, but there is nothing subjective or inscrutable about the standards that are being applied. Responsibility would be measured by the same tests employed in other cases where we seek to gauge blame or bestow credit. And when we assess the reasons people have for holding back from a rescue, we would judge them by the same principles we use in other cases when we judge whether their reasons (or interests) justified their acts. In that case cited earlier from Chicago, there was no trouble in judging that it was unwarranted to take the life of another merely because that person "ate the last piece of pizza." There was nothing arbitrary or subjective about that judgment; it flowed from principles which enjoin us to observe a rule of "proportionality" between the offense and the punishment (see Chapter VIII). If these principles offer us comprehensible standards of judgment, the task of weighing justifications is not altered in any significant respect when we come to judge the reasons that are offered for acts left undone.

Let us return, for example, to the case Justice Carpenter suggested in *Buch* v. *Amory*: A man, "standing close by a railroad, sees a two year old babe on the track, and a car approaching. He can easily rescue the child, with entire safety to himself." If he held back from rescuing the child, Carpenter thought he might be "styled a ruthless savage and a moral monster," but he had no doubt that the man was beyond the reproach of the law. That Carpenter could think it fit to label the man a "ruthless savage and a moral monster" implies that the judge at least thought there was a ground on which he might be justly condemned. Carpenter was expressing a moral judgment, and if he had been alert to the moral foundations of law, he might have recognized that the same grounds which permitted him to find fault with his hypothetical savage and call him a moral monster would have justified the reproach of the law as well.

Let us suppose that the man had been asked why he did not rescue the child, and that his answer was, "I was on my way to a movie and I would have missed the beginning." Or: "I had to get home to finish the last piece of pizza." Or: "I simply didn't care to." In all these instances, he would have been willing to see a life destroyed without alleging any cost to himself that was in any way comparable to the injury at stake for the child. He would have been deflected from the doing of a patent "good" for the sake of interests that were incontestably trivial by comparison.

On the other hand, the man might have explained that at the same moment he had also become aware of two infants, quite distant from one another, who were both approaching the railroad tracks. He recognized one child, and since he could not save both, he acted upon the sentiment that bound him to those he knew. In this case, he would have held back from saving one life because that was a necessary consequence of his commitment to save another innocent life. If he had been given a choice between Idi Amin and Mother Teresa, there were principles that could have helped him make the choice. But in a comparison of two lives equally innocent, equally deserving of rescue, there was no ground of principle that could have established why it would have been wrong, in this case, to rescue one victim rather than the other.

These cases, in short, would be judged with the same principles of judgment that we would use in other cases in which people suffer death or serious injury. There would of course be many borderline cases of baffling intricacy, but there are many borderline cases, also, of homicide and assault. The point, though, is that the principles of judgment we use in weighing justifications would remain the same regardless of whether we are dealing with so-called acts of omission or acts of commission.

None of this need imply that the penalties prescribed for the failure to rescue ought to be staggering—that the "moral monster" who fails to pull the child away from the railroad track should receive capital punishment or life imprisonment. The precise penalty that is fixed would convey the sense of the community as to how seriously it regarded the injury and the neglect of duty. If the penalty for negligence in failing to save a life were placed, say, at the level of the average parking ticket, this would suggest rather eloquently that the community did not attach very much value to the life that was lost or the duty that was neglected. But the severity of that punishment, as I say, is a matter to be worked out along the scale of outrage, with an awareness of the kinds of measures that would be needed to make an impression on the sensibilities of the community. The critical threshold is crossed, however—the main point in principle is conceded—if one simply acknowledges that it is reasonable, in cases of this kind, *to ask for justifications*. If it is legitimate to confront the man who held back from rescuing the child and compel him to give us reasons—to explain what pressing interest of his own deflected him from that important task—then we are assuming that the capacity on his part to affect the outcome must generate, at least presumptively, an obligation to act. He may in fact overcome that presumption by offering compelling reasons as to why he was warranted in holding back. But in responding to our question he would confirm the principle that allows us to ask for a justification and to judge the validity of his reasons.

WE WERE LED into these questions about the obligation to rescue as we followed out the threads of judgment about the war in Vietnam. The existence of the American republic was not directly threatened by a Communist takeover in Vietnam, and so it was necessary to consider whether the U.S. intervention in Vietnam was really a "supererogatory" act for the United States. Was America *obliged* to intervene, or was the military effort on behalf of South Vietnam strictly beyond the call of duty? I have argued that the logic of morals itself would establish a presumptive obligation to act in those instances where there is a capacity to affect the outcome and where the act of going to the rescue would be in principle justified. In that respect, the same principles that would apply to the "obligation to rescue" in domestic policy would apply with comparable force in international affairs. Obligations would be generated by the same principles, and excuses would have to be judged with the same canons for measuring justifications. As in the case of domestic law, the first question we would have to ask is whether the capacity to act was present. If the United States had been powerless to affect the situation in Vietnam, if it were predictably condemned by the logistics of the situation to fight a long, costly war with inconclusive results, our "capacity to affect the outcome" would have been in serious question; and any obligation on our part to intervene would have been diminished in its moral force. The question of our capacity to achieve our ends in

Vietnam has been subject, as I have noted, to serious dispute. But before the Watergate affair made it impossible for President Nixon to secure the settlement he had gained, the record in Vietnam was sufficient to establish that American arms could be used with effect, and that they could preserve a government that was notably better than a totalitarian regime.

In other words, the United States was not in the position of the nonswimmer contemplating a drowning man; nor was its position analogous to that of the man who must risk the loss of his singular life in order to save another singular life. It is precisely because the existence of the American republic would not have been threatened directly by a Communist regime in Vietnam that it becomes untenable to argue that we were risking "our life" for "theirs." What was risked, of course, were the lives of America's sons, and 50,000 of those lives were lost. Was that too high a price to pay? In the nature of things, as I have suggested, the principles at stake could not be converted into equivalents of their "worth in lives." If we weigh those 50,000 lives in a balance with all the lives that have been lost in Vietnam and the rest of Indochina, then of course the loss to the United States was far exceeded by the losses that were suffered by the people of Indochina, both during and after the war, at the hands of the victors. For citizens who are bound together in the same polity through ties of conviction and sentiment, the lives of 50,000 may be thought more important than the lives of several million people in Indochina. But if the matter had to be judged on strict grounds of principle, it would be hard to say that those 50,000 American lives were in fact "worth more."

Many considerations, then, of prudence and calculation might have deflected the United States from the path of intervention in Vietnam. But it should be clear that the conditions were quite sufficient to establish a presumptive moral obligation on the part of the United States to act in Vietnam and, at the very least, to offer some compelling reasons as to why it should not intervene. Whatever might have been said at that moment by American statesmen, their moral burdens were enlarged by this one, ineffaceable point: they might offer their hunches about logistics and their dark conjectures about the Fates that govern wars; but they could not have offered any proposition with the standing of a principle to explain why it was unjustified for the American people to make sacrifices at war for the people of Indochina.

THE NOTION OF "supererogatory" acts, of acts beyond the call of duty, has been with us nearly as long as moral reflection itself. Yet, if it is employed in a casual way, it runs the risk of being detached altogether from the canons of moral judgment. In recent years the place of "supererogatory" acts within moral philosophy has been defined in J.O. Urmson's widely cited essay, "Saints and Heroes," and it was Urmson's explicit intention to use the example of these acts "beyond the call of duty" for the sake of altering our understanding of the foundations of moral judgment. His concern ran back to the logic of morals itself, as that logic was understood by many utilitarians as well as by Kantians and other moral philosophers: to say that an act was "good" was to say that it was universally good—that anyone in a position to perform that act should indeed have performed it. This logic leads to the recognition of a duty to do what is good or just and to refrain from what is bad or unjust. Kant and the utilitarians might have been separated in their understanding of the sources of moral judgment, but they shared, at least, the recognition that nothing may be called morally good or bad without implying a principle which defines the nature of goodness or badness; that the force of a principle would be to establish, universally, a duty to do what is right and avoid what is wrong.

What Urmson sought to argue, however, was that there are certain acts—acts of an heroic or saintly character—which have "full moral worth," but which people could not be *obliged* to perform.[12] They might include the act of the soldier who falls on a live hand grenade in order to save the lives of his friends, or they may encompass the devotion of a St. Francis in undertaking a ministry to birds. In any event, these acts involve a denigration of self-interest or a disdain for self-preservation that could not be commanded in the name of duty.[13] As I remarked earlier, this persuasion really depends on concealed Hobbesian premises, and it is evident that Urmson's argument depended on the assumption that it is immanently unreasonable to establish, for mortal men, obligations that run counter to the commands of self-interest or self-preservation. In truth, of course, it is precisely the logic of moral principles that they do override the claims of self-interest and, on occasion, they supersede the commands of self-preservation. Urmson made his break from Kant, as well as from other utilitarians, by confounding questions of prudence with questions of principle. The business of ethics, for Urmson, was not merely to consider what was right or wrong, but what "worked"—what most people were *willing to accept* in the domain of obligations:

> If we are to exact basic duties like debts, and censure failure, such duties must be, in ordinary circumstances, within the capacity of the ordinary man. It would be silly for us to say to

[12] See J.O. Urmson, "Saints and Heroes," in A.I. Melden, *Essays in Moral Philosophy* (Seattle: University of Washington Press, 1958), pp. 198-216, at 206-207.
[13] *Ibid.*, pp. 200, 202.

ourselves, our children and our fellow men, "This and that you and everyone else must do," if the acts in question are such that manifestly but few could bring themselves to do them, though we may ourselves resolve to try to be of that few. . . . The basic moral code must not be in part too far beyond the capacity of the ordinary man on ordinary occasions, or a general breakdown of compliance with the moral code would be an inevitable consequence; duty would seem to be something high and unattainable, and not for "the likes of us.". . .[14]

It was understood in the past that the spirit of a people may not be in harmony with the commands of moral duty, and that the task of the law, as Aquinas said, is to lead people to virtue, not suddenly but gradually. Still, it was understood that the requirements of moral duty are drawn from principles having their own integrity as principles. What is done in the name of prudence to moderate the demands of the law was not to be taken as a modification or debasing of the principles themselves. And yet, that is the prospect Urmson has in mind when he would urge us to form moral principles in part through a canvass of popular opinion: moral principles would have to be "adjusted" or scaled down in accord with a sense of what most people could "bring themselves to do." The justification for ethics, in this perspective, is not that it enjoins what is in principle good, but that it helps men "live together in society."[15] Just why it is good to "live together" is a question that must be persistently embarrassing to writers of this persuasion: they cannot explain why their ends are "good" in any case without appealing to principles that define goodness and badness, and those principles, of course, cannot depend merely on what most people accept. If most people in our society were to accept a notion of "living together" which included policies of repression toward a racial minority, it is doubtful that utilitarians like Urmson would be willing to find the goodness of all acts in their tendency, overall, to preserve a society built on *this* notion of a good way of life.

In typical Hobbesian form it was assumed by Urmson that it is easier to oblige men not to kill or injure others than to oblige them to forgo their self-interest or risk their self-preservation. From that assumption he went on to regard acts not merely as estimable, but as "saintly" and "heroic," when they show a disregard of self-interest and self-preservation. Urmson apparently took it for granted that any

[14] *Ibid.*, pp. 211-212.
[15] *Ibid.*, p. 214.

acts which met this description could be considered "good." In that way, however, he detached our estimate of these acts from the principles of judgment that alone could tell us whether any of these acts was in fact right or wrong, justified or unjustified, in the context in which it occurred. In the case of the soldier falling on the grenade, it could not have been simply the disregard of self-preservation that marked his act as good or noble. It was also important for our judgment of the event that he sought to save innocent lives. Suppose Pope John XXIII had gone on a mission of conversion to a convention of Mafiosi; a live hand grenade was thrown into the midst of this group; and John fell on the grenade in order to save the lives of Vito Genovese, Sam Giancana, and the other cutthroats who were assembled. We would have to say that the act had indeed been undertaken with a thorough disregard of "self-preservation." But we could not also say that the act had been "good." For we could not bring ourselves to say, as a universal proposition, that any other innocent person, in the place of John XXIII, should have performed the same act of sacrifice in order to save the lives of the Mafia cutthroats.

The fallacy involved here is, once again, the fallacy of offering a spurious categorical proposition by drawing a moral conclusion from nonmoral attributes of the act. As the point was expressed earlier, "No moral conclusion can be entailed merely by facts or by factual propositions of a nonmoral nature" (see Chapter VIII). In the case of Urmson and supererogatory acts, the fallacy comes in offering a proposition of this kind: "Acts are 'good' (they have 'moral worth') when they are undertaken with a disregard for self-interest or a disdain for self-preservation." This proposition is exposed as a spurious categorical proposition in morals in the same way that other spurious propositions are usually exposed: we recognize that it is possible for people to satisfy the proposition even while they are engaged in the service of evil ends. In the case of Urmson's proposition, we would be made to reflect on whether it would really be good, under all circumstances, for a person to subordinate his own interests to the interests of others. We would realize then that this act of sacrifice would be good only when the interests of the agent are less worthy than the interests of others, or when he would trade his own advantage for the benefit of many. But there could be no justification in subordinating a decent interest of his own to the corrupt interest of the many. For the same reason that John XXIII should not throw his body on the hand grenade to save the Mafiosi, he would not be acting in a commendable way if he subordinated his own purposes to those of the gangsters. Tocqueville once celebrated the moral instruction that was offered through

303

participation in civic associations, because, as he said, people "learn to surrender their own will to that of all the rest and to make their own exertions subordinate to the common impulse."[16] He assumed, however, the most important point that deserved to be made explicit: viz., that the "common impulse" would be governed by a legitimate end. If the common impulse ran in the direction, say, of racism, a citizen would not offer an example of moral restraint at its highest level if he laid aside his own reservations about racism and deferred to the sensibilities of the multitude.

In setting forth his argument, Urmson penned a few lines that should have alerted him to what was most problematic in his own analogies: "It seems clear that there is no action, however quixotic, heroic, or saintly, which the agent may not regard himself as obliged to perform. . . . He alone can call . . . an action of his a duty, and then . . . only for himself and not for others. . . ."[17] This passage might have alerted Urmson instantly to what was immanently questionable in labeling acts of this kind as "moral" acts. If there is no ground on which it could be said that *anyone else, in the same situation, would be obliged to perform the same act*, then we are apparently not in a position to say that the act is "moral" in the strictest sense. In that event, we would have to call into question the ground on which the act could be regarded as morally right, even for the person who is styled a "saint" or a "hero." A soldier may tenably hold back from falling on a hand grenade because he may recognize that there is no ground of principle that would make his life less worth saving than the lives of everyone else around him. *That* is why we would say he is not obliged to sacrifice his life—not because a life is at all times too much to sacrifice. If, in spite of this recognition, the soldier still falls on the grenade in an act of sacrifice, we may find traces of nobility in his willingness to sacrifice for others; but we could not be sure that what he had done was "right." If the soldier had been an officer in the Wehrmacht, his act of sacrifice might not have been directed solely to the good of saving the lives of his men, but advancing the mission of Hitler's army.

We may admire, then, the willingness of a soldier to fall on a grenade, but unless we have a ground on which to say he was right or justified in sacrificing himself in that way, we cannot be sure that his act was governed by moral understanding. If the act of sacrifice was not animated by a justified end, which the soldier himself at least roughly

---

[16] Alexis de Tocqueville, *Democracy in America* (New York: Knopf, 1945), vol. II, p. 124.

[17] Urmson, *supra*, note 12, p. 204.

understood, it is not clear that his act would have moral standing, or that we should commend his example to others. We ought to remind ourselves that there is nothing novel about this understanding. It can be found in its rudiments in Plato, especially in the *Laches*, which anticipated the kind of problem that Urmson would later be raising.

The question in the *Laches* concerned the nature of courage. As the dialogue advances, Socrates leads his interlocutors to see that courage cannot be defined through formulas that have nothing to do with moral purpose. It is quickly agreed, for example, that courage could not inhere simply in staying at one's post and not running from the enemy. Courage could not be merely endurance in bearing adversity, for as Socrates points out in the dialogue, there may also be a "foolish endurance."[18] The leader who stays obdurately at his post in a futile engagement, or who leads his men up a hill in a reckless charge without hope of success, may simply be squandering lives.

At one point in the dialogue, Nicias rejects the argument that certain animals, such as lions and leopards, display a courageous nature: "I do not describe as courageous animals or any other creatures which have no fear of dangers because they are devoid of understanding, but only as fearless and senseless. Do you imagine that I should call all little children courageous, who fear no dangers because they have no understanding?"[19] The lion, which cannot deliberate about ends, and cannot know why any act is justified, may show spirit, but we could hardly call him "courageous" and single him out for *moral* commendation. "Courageous" is, after all, a term of moral commendation rather than a term merely of description. But no act can properly be called moral if it does not proceed from an understanding of the principle that makes the act morally desirable or necessary. When the question is raised, then, in the *Laches* as to what kind of wisdom or understanding ought to govern the act of courage, the answer is offered initially that it is wisdom in knowing the "grounds of fear and hope." As it is soon pointed out, however, that standard could be satisfied by a "soothsayer." And yet, as Nicias recognizes, the wisdom that directs courage must be able to establish whether "suffering or non-suffering . . . will be best for a man," and that wisdom clearly does not fall within the "science" of the soothsayer.[20] For it is not a matter of prediction; it is a matter of establishing the grounds on which any sacrifice would be justified. The wisdom that governs courage must

[18] Plato, *Laches*, 190d-e, 192b-d.
[19] *Ibid.*, 197a-b.
[20] *Ibid.*, 195e-196a.

be a wisdom in understanding whether certain ends are indeed worthy of the commitment of decent people, and whether they would justify the risk of death.

In the annals of warfare, few armies have fought with as much cohesion as the German Wehrmacht in the Second World War, and that cohesion was preserved largely through the commitment and leadership of German officers in the fighting units. Those men risked their lives and offered examples of dedication to their cause; yet, could we regard them as "courageous"? As I have suggested, we could not call them "courageous" unless we were prepared to commend them, and we could hardly commend people who chose to expend their valor, risk their lives, and inspire the sacrifice of others in the service of ends that were thoroughly evil.[21] "Courage" can be known then properly as courage only when it is directed by an understanding of the principles that define what is truly just and unjust, and the same thing must be said of any activity we would commend on moral grounds. The wisdom that is required in directing bravery or recognizing courage can be nothing less than the wisdom of the moral philosopher. As Socrates states the matter at the end of the *Laches*, "Courage, like the other sciences, is concerned not only with good and evil of the future, but of the present and past, and of any time."[22]

MY POINT, again, is that we cannot mark off a class of "supererogatory" acts that are beyond moral judgment altogether. We may honor selfless acts as heroic or saintly only if they are in fact directed toward good ends. If we cannot say that an act was morally justified, then

---

[21] General Grant recalled in his memoirs that he had been jubilant when he received General Lee's note, accepting his invitation to surrender. When he encountered Lee at Appomattox, however, they reminisced about their service together in the old army at the time of the Mexican War, and as Grant took in the full presence of the defeated general—his dignity and bearing, enlarged, as they had to be, by the record of Lee's accomplishments in the field—Grant's pleasure was touched by sadness. There was a pity to be felt, as Grant said, for "the downfall of a foe who had fought so long and valiantly, and had suffered so much for a cause." But he was quick to add—"though that cause was, I believe, one of the worst for which a people ever fought, and one for which there was the least excuse." Grant's respect for valor could not be detached from the principles of moral judgment on which respect was properly offered. He could not extend the final measure of his respect, therefore, unless he were willing to blind himself to those ends for which Lee was willing to expend his valor. Grant fit Plato's understanding, in the *Laches*, of the true general, for he reflected seriously on the ends which justified war and which determined whether "suffering or nonsuffering . . . will be best for a man." For Grant's observations on Lee, see *Personal Memoirs of U.S. Grant* (New York: Charles Webster & Co., 1894), pp. 629-630.

[22] Plato, *Laches*, 199b-c.

306

we cannot say with any confidence that it was good or desirable. But if we can call a selfless act good or justified, that is because it flows, comprehensibly, from the logic of a moral principle. And if any act is enjoined by a moral principle, it is entirely possible that, under certain circumstances, someone may be *obligated*, legitimately, to perform that act.

It is one of the enduring ironies in the history of moral reflection that the celebration of saintly and heroic people has led us to disparage the realm of "ordinary" acts that are performed out of a sense of duty. In a curious diversion, we have often turned away from noticing the strength—perhaps even the heroic and saintly qualities—that may be shown by ordinary people who respect the claims of duty. The conceptual lens that identifies, for our vision, "supererogatory" acts also distorts the moral dimensions of these acts, which are thought to stand beyond the call of duty: it offers, for a special claim on our esteem, the reckless captain who leads his men into exploits of combat that may be as unnecessary as they are daring. At the same time it diminishes, in comparison, the man with a deep aversion to violence, with an unshakable fear of battle, who nevertheless came forward to serve in the war against Hitler because he recognized the awful danger that obliged him, and others like him, to take up arms. But our examples need not reach the scale of global war. One may also think of the young mother, widowed or divorced, who may feel the overpowering weight of her troubles, but who nevertheless preserves her hold on life, manages to earn a living, and does, in short, all the things that must be done for the sake of supporting her children. In either case, personal inclinations could move these people toward a course that is less demanding and traumatic for themselves. Yet, they accept a special discipline and sacrifice out of their sense of obligation to others. Their example may simply remind us of an old and necessary truth: that there can be nothing "higher," or more worthy of admiration, than the good act performed out of a sense of obligation. The act may be performed purely out of a concern for the well-being of others, or out of a simple respect for the commands of justice.

The person who is animated by these motives cannot be regarded as a lesser person, morally, than the soldier who, say, hazards his life for the sheer love of battle. There are men, we know, who are drawn to battle by their love of excitement and by a fascination with the spectacle, even the aesthetics, of war. They cannot be accorded a stature more "heroic" and elevated than the men who accept the dangers of war reluctantly, out of a sense of obligation. The celebration of the dramatic, then, has often blinded us to the heroism implicit in

307

the quiet honoring of obligations. One recalls here George Eliot's final commentary in *Middlemarch* on her heroine, Dorothea Brooke: her life bore out the fact that "the growing good of the world is partly dependent on unhistoric acts, and that things are not so ill with you and me as they might have been, is half owing to the number who have lived faithfully a hidden life, and rest in unvisited tombs."

We remember the more dramatic cases, and we may remember for the wrong reasons. The man who tangles with thugs in the street, while others turn away from the crime and the victim, claims a place in our memory. In our language of praise, we would honor him today for risking himself in a rescue he was not obliged to try. But that understanding, I think, is wrong: it may be more accurate to say that we honor him because he was the only one who recognized that he was obliged to act where he could to avert a wrong. His excellence, in other words, did not come from attaining a state of goodness beyond the rules of morality. His distinction inhered in the fact that he alone recognized his obligation and summoned the strength to pursue it.

When this understanding is brought back to the problem of Vietnam, we remind ourselves that the prospect of risking ourselves in war for other peoples is not enough to establish that these exertions abroad must be regarded as "supererogatory." Nor is it sufficient to remove acts of intervention from the domain of our obligations. At the same time, though, it cannot efface the heroism of the Americans who fought in the war if we recognize that many of them went to Vietnam only because their government called upon them, legally, to go. They acted, finally, out of a sense of obligation to the laws of their country. There were others, of course, who did not go. In refusing, they made it clear that a choice was before them, and that the men who respected the summons of their government were acting quite as consciously as the men who chose a kind of exile. There is a difference, of course, between "legal" and "moral" obligation: there is a difference between the man who obeys the law merely because it is the law, or because he fears the punishment for disobedience, and the man who obeys out of a respect for the moral maxims that lie behind the law. And yet I think it can be said that the men who entered the army and knowingly risked their lives did not make themselves less admirable to us—or less worthy of our moral esteem—because many of them joined the military only out of a sense of obligation to the laws of that country in whose service they fought.

XIV

THE MORAL CASE FOR WELFARE, THE TROUBLED CASE FOR REDISTRIBUTION

Once we understand that acts of neglect may be judged with the same standards that govern other judgments, we can restore to the realm of judgment many acts and public policies that have claimed our endorsement over the years under the misleading label of "acts of benevolence." That description has been used in the past precisely because there was thought to be no ground on which these acts could be commanded by law and treated as matters of obligation. And so, a program of welfare support could be understood, at best, as a measure of the generosity or "humanity" of a community, in the provision it was willing to make for its needy members. When the claim to welfare was put forth as a "right," there was remarkably little effort made to explain the moral foundation of such a right. Whether the rendering of welfare was understood, then, as a provision of benevolence or the satisfaction of a "right," the question was usually placed beyond the realm in which justifications are offered and assessed. It was not assumed in either case that the argument for this financial support could be traced back to a ground of principle and judged true or false. But once we understand that there can in fact be an obligation to help others, that there are principles which make it possible to judge the claim to receive help and the obligation to furnish it, we would be in a position to speak more precisely about the grounds of principle on which we would finally establish this commitment to those who cannot sustain themselves.

We may consider, as a case in point, the problem of providing financial support for people who are disabled. Let us assume that we are dealing with paraplegics who have no means of support apart from their own possibilities for earning a living. If they happen to be professionals, their prospects may not be impaired by the fact that they do not have use of their legs or that they are forced to spend most of their time in wheelchairs. But outside the professions, the job market may be rather constricted for people with these disabilities. The question would be posed under the terms of the obligation to rescue: would the community be obliged to act where it can to provide support to disabled people who cannot find support for themselves? If the only

309

thing we knew of these people was the nature of their disability, we would know nothing of moral significance, which could establish why these people *deserved* to perish. And therefore it would have to be unacceptable in principle to permit them to perish because of their disability, or because of the current state of the market for paraplegics. We could never say, for example, that a man thrown off a ship deserves to drown if he cannot swim; nor could we say that people deserve to die if they cannot find jobs in the constricted market available to paraplegics. If the community should withhold aid and permit the paraplegics to die, it would be implying that there was no injury here which deserved to be resisted; that the weakness of the crippled, or their failure in the marketplace, was sufficient to justify the misery they would suffer. And that, as I say, is a proposition in which the community could not acquiesce for a moment.

The state, of course, could never be expected to redeem every life and relieve every injustice; it would be obliged to do only what it practicably and decently could. If the needs, say, of a paraplegic were being met, in any instance, through acts of private beneficence, the government would not be faced with the prospect of acquiescing in the death of the disabled, and it would not come under the same necessity to act in the name of the community. On the other hand, the community would not be on strong moral ground if it held back from the provision of aid merely because it was suspected that private charity would come forth in offerings large enough to provide, for the paraplegics, the kind of support that the taxpayers refuse to furnish. The difficulty here is that the judgment would turn on an empirical prediction or a contingent propositon ("If public aid is withdrawn, private charity will take its place, and the disabled will still be supported"). Whether the prediction is true or not, it must remain problematic, and it cannot displace the commitments that arise from these propositions: (1) paraplegics face destruction for reasons that have no standing as moral justifications (see Chapter VIII); and (2) we are obliged to act where we can to avert harm to the innocent.

As we have seen, though, the obligation to rescue must always be affected with a sense of the interests that are risked in the rescue. There may be no ground of principle that obliges one innocent person to risk his own life, in a dangerous and doubtful mission, in saving another innocent life. The rescuer may be faced with a choice of saving one innocent victim or thirty; if he cannot do both, he may choose to do more good by saving the thirty. In the same way, we must assume that the community measures its capacity to save paraplegics. If we are dealing with an impoverished community that can barely support itself, there may not be sufficient surplus to support the disabled. Or the community may have to make a decision to provide for the care of one class of victims rather than another. It may turn out, for example, that the same expenditure of money could save far more lives if it were committed to the purchase of dialysis machines for people with failing kidneys. Or it might be calculated that a far greater number of lives may be saved overall if the same amount of money were invested in schemes for preventive medicine.

As we enter upon considerations of this kind, the task of judgment is suddenly taken up with empirical reckonings and estimates about outcomes. A critic may even suspect that the enterprise of principled judgment is being displaced now in favor of low arts of prediction, directed toward a series of ends whose goodness may merely be contingent on a variety of conditions that are highly mutable. And yet, there is nothing in these reckonings or calculations which alters in any way the principles that govern our judgments. We are simply reminded that the task of moral judgment requires the application of principles to concrete cases. Statesmen who understand the sources of moral judgment know things that are unchanging. But they also know that there can never be a substitute for the arts of prudence or for that worldliness which allows them to deal with intractable dilemmas and find more sensible ways of achieving what their principles enjoin them to do.

If the relief of the poor were established as an obligation flowing from the capacity to help, the question would be set up for us in a way that directs our attention at once to the moral considerations which must govern the assessment of responsibility. When the matter is viewed from the perspective of the "obligation to rescue," we would recognize in the first instance that we are not speaking about the kind of responsibility that is assigned to a particular person through a finding of fault. If a man became a paraplegic as a result of an automobile accident caused by the negligence of a particular driver, the victim may single out the responsible driver and sue him separately in an action for damages. If the paraplegic must look beyond this lawsuit for additional sources of support, or if his condition did not result from harms inflicted by others, the claim he makes for the support of the community implies a different understanding of responsibility. This is not a responsibility that implies "fault" on the part of the community or its members. The responsibility flows, rather, to the community as a whole by virtue of its character as a political association. Citizens who are joined together in a relation of polity bear a special responsibility for the well-being of their members, and their highest task, in this respect, is to cultivate the moral understanding of the community. A polity that would teach something to its members about the requirements of justice would be obliged to make its members attentive to those duties which arise when people have the means to save the innocent from injury.

In measuring the commitments of the community, it would be quite proper for the government to make exactions upon its citizens in proportion to their capacity to pay, but those exactions must be subject in turn to principles of equity. And in strict justice the argument can be made that only a consistent "proportionate" tax would be morally defensible in this case. The proportionate tax would tailor the contributions of any citizen to his capacity to pay (a levy, say, of 1 percent would yield a far larger contribution from a person with an income of $1 million than it would from a person with an income of $25,000). To go beyond that measure and introduce "graduated" rates, which become higher as incomes grow larger, would no longer be drawing revenue from citizens as a function of their "capacity" to pay. The moral problem inherent in this scheme may reveal itself more clearly if we suppose for a moment that the community sought to fund its obligations through a flat fee rather than a proportionate tax. Let us suppose that the community simply charged every taxpayer the same amount—say $100—and that it was able, in this way, to cover the cost of its services to the poor and needy. But we would recognize instantly that a tax of $100 would represent a larger portion of lower incomes than of higher incomes: instead of being geared to the capacity to pay, the tax would impose, in effect, a higher rate on those people with lower incomes, who have a lesser capacity to pay. This assignment of burdens would be comprehensible only if it could be assumed that people with lower incomes were somehow "more responsible" for the condition of the needy than were people with higher incomes. In the aggregate, of course, we cannot know any such thing. As I have already pointed out, the move toward a *communal* responsibility must mark a recognition that no one in particular bears a moral fault for the disability or impoverishment that we encounter in any given case. If that were not true, then the relief should come in part through a lawsuit directed at the person who is responsible. When responsibility is diffused through the community, however, it suggests that the members of the community stand on a plane of equality in bearing that responsibility: none is more at fault than another; none is less responsible. People with lower incomes cannot bear any larger moral responsibility, as a group, for the miseries that the community would seek to relieve.

312

But by the same token, neither would the wealthy, as a group, bear any larger moral responsibility or partake of any moral blame, and the community could not be warranted in departing from a standard of equality as it establishes the liability, in taxes, of its wealthier citizens. The standard of equality would be satisfied by a proportionate tax, which applies the same rate to everyone. That standard would make no false assignment of blame or responsibility; and it would take more from those with more, while extracting less from those who have less. What we may not justly do is use the tax system for the purpose of assigning moral "faults" and responsibilities to aggregates of people who are defined simply by their income and property. Once again we would find ourselves assigning penalties and benefits to people, not on the basis of their own acts, but merely on the ground of their membership in groups that are set apart from one another by differences that are wholly lacking in moral significance.

These kinds of considerations have largely been obscured in the movement toward "progressive," or graduated, taxation. That is not to say that the literature on this question has been unaffected with moral reasoning. When the proposals for the graduated tax on wealth were raised in the eighteenth and nineteenth centuries, economists were quick to recognize that this scheme of taxation would generate discouragements for work and investment. But political economy at that time was closer to moral philosophy than it is today, and the objections of the economists were offered even more emphatically on moral grounds. As J.R. McCulloch wrote in 1845, "The moment you abandon . . . the cardinal principle of exacting from all individuals the same proportion of the income or their property, you are at sea without rudder or compass, and there is no amount of injustice or folly you may not commit":[1]

> Having said that a man with 500£ a year shall pay 5 per cent., another with 1000£ 10 per cent., and another with 2000£ 20 per cent., on what pretence of principle can you stop in your ascending scale? Why not take 50 per cent., from the man of 2000£ a year, and confiscate all the higher class of incomes before you tax the lower? . . . Graduation is not an evil to be paltered with. . . . The savages described by Montesquieu, who to get at the fruit cut

[1] J.R. McCulloch, *Treatise on the Principles and the Practical Influences of Taxation and the Funding System* (London, 1845), p. 142, quoted in Walter Blum and Harry Kalven, Jr., *The Uneasy Case for Progressive Taxation* (Chicago: University of Chicago Press, 1953), p. 45 and n. 115.

down the tree, are about as good financiers as the advocates of this sort of taxes. . . .

As McCulloch and his contemporaries recognized, the graduated tax was tied from the very beginning to notions of "redistribution" and the removal of inequalities in wealth. On that plane, the case for progressive taxation encountered an insuperable problem in establishing a moral ground of justification. What is remarkable about the history of the graduated tax is that the scheme achieved its ascendance largely without facing this serious moral challenge. As Walter Blum and Harry Kalven showed, the cause of progressive taxation was won almost absent-mindedly, without the benefit of debate. The scheme was introduced for the sake of raising revenue, often in time of war, and it was usually "justified" on the basis of theories of finance which were both highly dubious as empirical theories and quite divorced from any moral consideration that might supply a ground of justification.

As Blum and Kalven pointed out, the most influential argument for progressive taxation was found in the theory, advanced quite seriously by a number of economists, for the "diminishing utility" of money.[2] The common sense of this theory was that satiety may be counted on, at some point, to diminish excitation or at least soften the intensity of interest in money as well as anything else. For the man worth several millions, the seven-millionth dollar may be a matter of indifference; presumably it would not matter to him as much as the tenth or even the first dollar would to a man in poverty. But even if this proposition about the diminishing utility of money were true some of the time or even most of the time, it would still be true only contingently or statistically. It could not be true as a matter of necessity, and it therefore could not be true at all times. As a proposition, it deals with things that induce feelings of pleasure, and as Kant wisely remarked, even if rational beings were unanimous in the kinds of objects that induced feelings of pleasure or pain, "the unanimity itself would be merely contingent. The determining ground would still be only subjectively valid and empirical, and it would not have the necessity which is conceived in every law, an objective necessity arising from a priori grounds. . . ."[3] We would still be dealing, in other words, with an empirical account of the distribution of pleasurable feelings, and the distribution of feelings may change over time, as rational beings come

---

[2] *Ibid.*, p. 42.

[3] Immanuel Kant, *Critique of Practical Reason* [1788], trans. Lewis White Beck (Indianapolis: Bobbs-Merrill, 1956), p. 25; p. 26 of the RPA ed.

to find their pleasure in other objects. Whether people who have more and more money take less and less pleasure in it is not something we can reliably and enduringly know. But even if we knew it, there is nothing in the logic of morals which could tell us why any particular distribution of pleasure or income is the right or just distribution. From the logic of morals we can know, as an *a priori*, necessary truth, that people may not be held blameworthy for acts they were powerless to affect. But we cannot establish, in the same way, a *logical* connection between the notion of morals itself and any particular distribution of income (say, "$30,000 a year for a family of four," or a "parity of incomes, with departures in a range of plus or minus 5 percent"). And since there is no ground of principle which can establish the right allotments of income and pleasure, there can be no *moral* ground for taking more money in taxation merely because some people have more money or feel less pleasure. Nothing in these attributes would define anything of moral significance, which could establish why certain people *deserve* to be taxed at a higher or lower rate.

Blum and Kalven have collected, in all its improbable variety, the full inventory of these arguments, which were advanced in support of "progressive" taxation. And like the argument over the diminishing utility of money, each of the arguments was fashioned out of a combination of dubious psychologies and contingent propositions. As a descriptive account of the world that awaited their redeeming justice, these theories bore, at their best, a problematic connection. But even if they made a more substantial contact with the world we inhabit, nothing in them provided the foundation of a moral theory. Typical of these arguments was the speculation, put forth by the economist Sir Roy Harrod, that the amount of effort exerted in earning money declines as income advances to high levels.[4] Starting with this assumption, it may well seem immoral not to tax higher incomes at higher levels, because people with lower incomes would be working correspondingly harder to meet their tax bills, while the wealthy would be permitted to retain the money they earn through little effort.

Even a modest measure of experience should be enough to establish that there is no such evident or uniform association of higher income and lesser effort. It should be apparent that these assumptions about the "facts" of the world are bound up with primitive notions of manual labor which measure the worth of work according to the expenditure of calories. They cannot comprehend, then, the worth of that work provided by the practiced surgeon at a research hospital, who may

[4] Cited in Blum and Kalven, *supra*, note 1, pp. 47-49.

315

diagnose a rare illness accurately in seconds. The time he needs to spend on the patient seems insignificant; he does not need to lift anything heavy or undergo physical strain. And yet, even though the patient pays more for the benefit of this experienced eye, the service may be worth far more to him than a cheaper diagnosis, rendered by a local practitioner, for a judgment that cannot claim the same accuracy. The worth of work must turn on estimates as various and complicated as the range of experience that produces, for people, needs that are various and complicated in the same measure.

But even if it were true that some people make money in work that is less onerous and perhaps even more satisfying, it is not clear why the community would be more justified in taxing income earned in that way. In place of a moral argument we may simply find a public policy animated by a puritanical temper. We may find conclusions emanating from the suspicion (as H.L. Mencken put it) that someone, somewhere may be happy: that it is nearly sinful for a man to earn money through work he enjoys while others must work at unsatisfying jobs in order to earn a living. Yet, if taxation is drawn to support the moral commitments of the community, it must be tailored to its moral ends and it should not be confounded with matters as unfathomable (and as morally beside the point) as the distribution of pleasure. Workaholics may not suffer pain as they are forced to work harder in supporting their taxes; but it should be clear that nothing in the psychological attributes of workaholics would justify the law in taxing them at a higher rate than it would apply to other people earning the same income. Some ethnic groups may have a tendency to work harder, even under higher taxes, and yet we would not provide a ground of justification, say, for taxing Orientals at a higher rate because the higher taxes will not discourage them from working or reduce their overall pleasure. There is no principle that can prescribe the proper distribution of pleasure; and no contrived formula, purporting to balance the "utilities" of the public, can supply that principle or provide, at last, a moral justification for such schemes of taxation.

BLUM AND KALVEN decorously considered, in turn, each of the arguments brought forth to support the graduated tax on income, and they pointed up in a gentle way why each specimen of nonsense was incapable of carrying the argument. Their own recognition was that the case for the graduated tax would have to stand or fall on whatever moral ground could be extracted from a principle of "equality." But that case, they admitted, was at best an "uneasy" one. Their disposition was to look kindly on the possibility of a corrective to the "amoral" distributions that were brought about in the marketplace. It was no surprise that people often achieved worldly success and prosperity for reasons that had little to do with moral virtue, and through a want of material success people were often denied the standing they might rightfully have commanded by the strength of their character. To the extent that the market obscures, to those dim of vision, the figures who properly merit their esteem, the market, in its uncorrected state, can distort the moral understanding of a people. Blum and Kalven entered their own limited, emphatic avowal: "We rebel at any notion that the society is foreclosed from second-guessing the market. The ultimate appeal of the progressive tax may then be that it is the only attractive way of doing this without interfering too much with the operation of the market. Progression then would be an assurance by the society that the answers of the market were not taken with absolute finality."[5]

And yet, their refusal to accept the allocations of the market as the ultimate standard of justice was virtually in accord with the argument I offered earlier about treatment of the paraplegic: we could not accept the notion that the paraplegic forfeited his claim to live merely because he was paraplegic, or because no job had been yielded for him in the restricted job market for paraplegics. In either instance, a moral conclusion would be drawn on the basis of facts that are lacking in moral significance. The distress of paraplegics called forth the response of the community to deal directly and precisely with the injustices which threatened these people. But nothing in this commitment to relieve the condition of paraplegics implied the necessity of a graduated income tax. It called, as I argued, for a levy on the public which reflected the sense of responsibility that was shared by all members of the community in proportion to their own capacity to bear the burden of support. The market could be corrected—the injustice threatening the paraplegic could be averted—without the need to provide, as an added, gratuitous measure, a scheme that "redistributes" money from one *healthy* group to another, for reasons that have nothing at all to do with paraplegics.

The problem, then, for Blum and Kalven was that their argument took a leap here and it rested, in its conclusion, on no evident moral foundation. We can weigh, for example, the wrong or the harm suffered by paraplegics or by other disabled people, and we can draw a firm argument in principle to relieve the suffering of the innocent. But it is notably different to move to the conclusion that people who are

[5] *Ibid.*, p. 84.

317

wealthier, precisely because they *are* wealthier, deserve to keep less of their own money than people with lower incomes. Let us suppose we have a policy of taxing everyone at a rate of 25 percent, except for Orientals, who are taxed at a rate of 50 percent. We should have no trouble in pointing out that there is nothing in the simple fact of being an Oriental which could possibly establish why these people deserve to be taxed at a higher rate than the one applied to everyone else. We would recognize at once that race or ethnicity cannot furnish a moral ground of discrimination, which could explain why one group of citizens deserves to be treated differently from others. But now let us suppose that we have a policy that taxes everyone at a rate of 25 percent, except for those with incomes over $60,000 a year, who are taxed at a rate of 50 percent. We should be able to recognize, in the same way, that when we divide people into two classes—those with incomes above $60,000 per year and those with incomes below that figure—we say nothing of moral significance about these two groups. We furnish no reason for supposing that those with higher incomes have gained them unjustly, or that those with lower incomes have been victims. We offer no ground for concluding that one group deserves the penalty of steeper taxation, while the other deserves the benefit or compensation of a lower rate. We establish, in short, no fact which could explain why we are justified in applying different rates of taxation to these two groups, especially when these people are being taxed to support commitments in which they are equally concerned and equally responsible.

As we came to recognize earlier, the notion of "equality" could never enjoin an equality of rewards and punishments, as though the innocent and the guilty, the virtuous and the vicious, the industrious and the slothful, stood on the same plane. Not everyone, I pointed out, has the same claim to our affection and respect; and things could never be equal in that sense unless we suspend all moral judgment. The principle of equality can be understood in its proper sense as a principle only when it is connected to the logic of morals: our claim to "equality" is our equal claim to be treated morally or justly—by standards that apply to us equally because they apply *universally*.

There is nothing very novel about this point, and one would think that confusions should have been dispelled by now, after twenty-five hundred years of reflection on the subject. And yet, there has been a persisting assumption in our public discourse that there is something immanently unjust about a situation in which there are major disparities in wealth. Whether the point is made explicit or not, our

discussions are often governed by the assumption that a healthy democracy ought to show a progressive tendency to reduce the inequalities of income which separate its members. But in the abstract—
without knowing anything about the persons or the cases or how the
inequalitites came about—it is not possible to say anything about the
"justice" of any distribution of income.

Imagine for a moment a distribution that is worked out in a restricted
population of, say, 60,005. The 5 happen to be the Rolling Stones,
and the 60,000 constitute their audience for one evening in Yankee
Stadium. At the end of the evening the Rolling Stones will probably
have made several hundred thousand dollars. Each member of the
rock group will probably have made more in that one evening than
most members of the audience will be able to make in a few years. If
this population is viewed as some economists would view it—not as
a group of performers and a collection of their admirers, but as a
population revealing a distribution of income—it becomes plain that
the events of the evening will have brought about a vast skewing of
wealth. A group of five people would be standing at the apex of a
pyramid, vastly distant, in their incomes, from the population below
them. This would be the kind of disparity which is routinely considered
a mark of the injustice of "capitalist" society, and which has been
thought to justify the remedy of requiring people with higher incomes
to give back most of those incomes in taxes. But, of course, the inferences that seem to leap out at people from an abstract profile of
the incomes apparently have not impressed themselves on the awareness of the Rolling Stones and their audiences. After all, if there were
something morally wrong in the distribution of income they were
creating, then it should have been wrong for all the participants to
will the arrangements that would produce these results. It should be
wrong for the Stones to perform on these terms, and it should be
wrong for the members of the audience to attend voluntarily when
their patronage will produce an immoral result.

And yet there is a lesson contained in the fact that the participants
do not seem aware of anything so morally portentous in their decision
to come together. Neither the Rolling Stones nor their fans have any
awareness that the Stones are doing anything unjust. The audience
has not apparently been disturbed by the notion that the Stones would
extract a large fee for appearing. Many younger members of the audience will probably spend the preceding night sleeping in their places
in line at Yankee Stadium in order to buy tickets in the morning.

For their part, the Rolling Stones have probably not suffered any
sensation that they came by their earnings dishonestly. There is not

likely to be any trouble in filling the stadium with people who would come of their own volition and who would be pleased to pay for the pleasure of seeing the Stones perform. If the 5 Rolling Stones had constituted, instead, the Dalton gang, and the 60,000 had been their victims in robbery, then the skewed distribution of income would in fact have been unjust. And it would have been unjust not because of the wide disparities, but because the money would have been extracted through theft, in particular and provable cases. It is for such cases that we have laws on theft; for other cases in which money is taken unjustly, through deception or fraud, we have other laws tailored to the precise character of the crime. But where there is no wrong engaged in the process by which the money has been obtained, no "wrong" would suddenly emerge when disparities of income are plotted on a graph and reveal—to no one's surprise—an unequal distribution. The Stones might rightly have wondered why they should be forced to surrender 70 percent or more of what they earned that evening, as though they had done something improper in luring an audience to Yankee Stadium. Some of them, in fact, have reacted to the moral presumption implicit in the tax—to say nothing of the loss of cash— by removing themselves to tax havens outside the British Isles.

The moral mistake involved in the graduated tax, and in policies of redistribution generally, was marked in Chapter VIII:

> No moral conclusion can be entailed merely by facts or by factual propositions of a nonmoral nature. Moral propositions are grounded ultimately in facts or truths, but they can be derived only from the necessary truth which affirms the existence of morals or explains its essential logic.

No one will gainsay that it would be wrong to extract money from people in a manner that harms them without justification. But the simple fact of having more—even vastly more—than others does not describe any state of affairs which inflicts harm, of necessity, on others or which reflects an intention to injure. And of course, that state of having more defines no "wrong" in principle, which derives from the logic of morals. To say that it is morally wrong for some people to have more while others have less is to fall, once again, into the fallacy of extracting a moral conclusion from facts that are barren of moral significance.

It is a revealing oddity that the partisans of redistribution, who are usually so sensitive to the inequalities of American life, have routinely failed to mention the extraordinary, outsized incomes that have been earned by such groups as the Rolling Stones, who have become celebrated as entertainers. Bob Hope and Frank Sinatra have made fortunes that place them among the wealthiest men in the land. John Lennon, at his death, had accumulated holdings that rivaled those of the Queen of England. Baseball luminaries such as Pete Rose and Reggie Jackson have attained annual incomes surpassing the annual earnings of many corporation presidents. During the late 1960's, Barbara Streisand was making $100,000 for a night or two of singing in Las Vegas, at a time when an assistant professor at an established Ivy League college might be making the respectable sum of $10,000 a year (a comparison I recall with a vivid personal interest). If the market were to be taken as a measure of worth, then two nights of Streisand's performances apparently counted as the equivalent of ten years of preparing lectures, commenting on student papers, writing articles and books. And yet, how would this disparity be corrected? Would the entertainment industry be "nationalized," so that performers like Barbara Streisand would be given no more than the salary available to civil servants? Some writers have argued that entertainers are moved by more than the prospect of wealth, that they thrive on the excitement of being celebrities and the satisfaction of receiving applause. Perhaps, but people like Streisand might also lose the incentive to invest much time in what they do, to say nothing of giving up their evenings and weekends. (They might come to conclude, with Oscar Wilde, that the problem with socialism is that it requires altogether too many evenings.) Nor is it beyond reckoning that a corps of entertainers under the control of the government will have to mute their social commentary and, after a while, they may show the same level of inventiveness and initiative that we associate with other nationalized industries.

But then—to follow out this vision—what if the imposition of uniform salaries is not enough to suppress the inequalities of demand and support that are still present in the market? What if her loyal fans offered Barbara Streisand special fees beyond her civil service salary, at small, private gatherings? What if they insisted on showering upon her flowers and gifts and cash tips, all of which might raise her total compensation well above the plane of a senior economist in the Department of Agriculture? To respect the premises that underlie the policy of equal distribution, the power of the government would have to be called in to repress these outpourings of private generosity. This sort of suppression is, of course, unmanageable, especially in the framework of a constitutional order, and no serious socialist has proposed such a scheme. And yet, why is it thought more fitting to subject to a similar regimen the executives who manage oil companies and steel plants, and who might be converted into civil servants running nationalized industries? Is it thought that the skills and creativity of these men are so trifling that the society would lose nothing if they were discouraged from using those aptitudes at their highest pitch? Is it thought that these men might somehow be improved by political controls—that their efficiency would be enhanced, that their inventiveness would be unimpaired?

The willingness to overlook these evident comparisons has been with us for a long while. More than thirty years ago, Bertrand de Jouvenal remarked on the picturesque way in which this tendency manifested itself in the Communist party of France. The party stood as the most militant adversary of bourgeois society, with a hostility in principle to all signs of inequality; yet the members warmly drew on their own money to provide an expensive automobile to their leader, Maurice Thorez, and to convey their affection with a continuing supply of gifts. For Jouvenal, the sentiments at work here were comparable to those shown by working people, in Britain and other countries, who were willing to support the dignity of their monarchs with furnishings and properties that were suitably lavish.[6] If the monarch elicited the affection and respect of the working people, they were not grudging in their support of the sovereign with their taxes. And for the same reason they would not be resentful of the wealth attained by an Edith Piaff or a Frank Sinatra, who made their fortunes, after all, by pleasing the multitude. Perhaps the difference lay precisely there: people persistently "elected" Piaff and Sinatra in the marketplace through the suffrage of their own purchases. Piaff and Sinatra were never imposed on them. Their willingness to pay for the pleasure of hearing Piaff and Sinatra was a manifestation of their own choice, and it dissolved any ground of complaint.

But people have not felt that they possess the same degree of choice when it comes to purchasing electricity or heat or automobiles. They may derive fully as much pleasure from these goods as they derive from Piaff and Sinatra, but in a strange way they may resent far more powerfully the men who make their fortunes by providing the public with the "necessities" of their daily lives. Those contributions may be even more fundamental than the contributions supplied by Piaff and Sinatra, and it may make a profound difference for the standard of living of the many that a small number of inventive men have expended their genius in making these goods and services accessible to a mass

---

[6] Bertrand de Jouvenal, *The Ethics of Redistribution* (Cambridge: Cambridge University Press, 1951), pp. 79-80.

public. No small part of their accomplishment has been that they have schooled the public to regard as "necessities" goods and services that were available only to the aristocracy at the beginning of this century.[7] But this may simply be to recognize again that it is hard to establish a moral ground of discrimination here, and for that reason the partisans of redistribution cannot begin to distinguish between the outsized fortunes they find objectionable and the accumulations of wealth they are content benignly to overlook.

That selectivity of vision is not without its political uses. It manages to conceal the fact that, behind the insistence on "redistribution," there may be no moral ground of justification, but rather a mean, unredeeming truth: the persistence of a spiteful envy. In *The Princess Casamassima*, Henry James has his young protagonist, an aspiring revolutionary, make his first, extensive trip through France and Italy. As the sights unfold, they reveal the depths of an historical experience that was previously foreign to him, and they stir the most serious reflection. In Venice, the young man recalls a friend, a revolutionary of sterner commitment, who "wouldn't have the least feeling for this incomparable, abominable old Venice. He would cut up the ceilings of the Veronese into strips, so that everyone might have a little piece." James went on to have his character admit, "I don't want everyone to have a little piece of anything and I've a great horror of that kind of invidious jealousy which is at the bottom of the idea of redistribution."

Remarkably enough, so have many others described as "working people," who are supposed to be the beneficiaries of these policies of redistribution. Many of them have expressed the concern that they or their children, one day soon, might have an income sufficiently comfortable that politicians will be itching to redistribute it. Many of these working people have sensed the presence of some serious questions of equity, and they have not begrudged earnings well beyond the average for those who generate, through their uncommon effort, a wealth that others can share. In New York one evening, a friend and I went to the Carlyle Hotel to take in a performance by the redoubtable Bobby Short. When we arrived, the waiter eagerly offered us our choice of any table in the house, since the room was empty. On inquiring, we learned that Bobby Short was not working that night. As we departed, we told the waiter that we would be back on a night when Short was performing. The waiter was evidently disappointed, but not surprised.

[7] See Stanley Lebergott, "How to Increase Poverty," *Commentary* (October 1975), pp. 59-63.

323

Nor, one imagines, could he have been very resentful of the fact that Bobby Short earned an income far higher than his own. For without Bobby Short, he knew, there were no patrons to be waited on, no tips to be earned.

George Gilder recalls the story of Intel, a small firm which began with 12 employees in 1968. Three years later it developed the microprocessor, and five years later it was the leading producer of these devices, with 8,000 employees.[8] One hardly imagines that the people who benefited from new jobs in this business of advanced technology could resent the higher rewards that went to the inventor and the directors, whose efforts—and whose willingness to take risks—had created these new jobs. People may not have much trouble in grasping the essential justice of unequal salaries when they are able to perceive a direct relation between the efforts that produce the income of the wealthy and the operations that produce employment for themselves. The harder thing to comprehend quite often is that the holdings, even of the idle rich, may not themselves be idle in supporting investment and production. And yet, the security of property rightly acquired and rightly held would depend on the same understanding that supports other kinds of rights. That security is less apt to be established in the long run merely by convincing people of the utilitarian payoffs to themselves of respecting the claims that other people have to their own earnings. Those claims are more likely to be secured by a recognition, more instant and less labored, that people offend no principle simply because they have more than others, and that there is no moral ground on which it could be determined that their money belongs properly to anyone else.

It has not been my purpose to suggest that the socialist perspective has been without any plausible moral concern. There was a recognition, expressed by R.H. Tawney, that the distribution of wealth may cloud the moral understanding of a people. Among a people without cultivation, success may be taken as a sign of moral virtue, and there may be a disposition to accord little moral weight to those who have not impressed themselves on the consciousness of the community with the show of wealth.[9] But it is not clear that this problem finds its proper remedy in a policy of redistribution, even if a policy of that kind had any moral foundation. It would be more appropriate to take

[8] For this and similar accounts, see George Gilder, *Wealth and Poverty* (New York: Basic Books, 1981), p. 81 *et passim*.

[9] See R.H. Tawney, *Equality* (London: George Allen & Unwin, 1931), pp. 143-44.

measures that are aimed more precisely to offset the wrongs and slights produced by the market: libraries can be built; the children of workers can be provided with higher education; scholars of Greek can be rescued from penury; families can be sheltered from the financial devastation of catastrophic illness. A state of mind that becomes sensitive to defects of justice is likely also to encompass the understanding that wealth and success are not, after all, the only measures of worth or the only qualities that bring esteem in this world. The man of wealth may still not command the respect of his neighbors or the love of his family. He may be without influence on his government or his relatives; he may be disregarded in life, unmourned in death. He may possess, in short, a fortune in assets and yet be impoverished, in his own reckoning, in the things that really matter.

For all of these inequalities, in their fuller sweep, there is no practicable authority in politics that can furnish a corrective. With their blind clumsiness, totalitarian regimes may seek to deny people the freedom to bestow unequal rewards by patronizing, in a free market, the people and services that please them. But these regimes cannot eradicate the differences in nature which make some people more competent and appealing, and which continue to attract to these people a measure of deference and affection that is not uniformly shared with the rest of the population. For these inequalities, even the most obdurate totalitarian regime can furnish no cure. As Samuel Beer once remarked, the socialist regime which fancies that it has brought down the old social hierarchies, with their invidious distinctions of wealth, may find itself confronting hierarchies quite as rigid and invidious, with distinctions based on social esteem. Even if the esteem were rightly apportioned and the inequalities were morally justified, they may be felt with the same sting of resentment and the problem would be insoluble; for if a socialist order conveys its own ethic, and if it holds up for emulation a New Man, who disdains acquisition and selfishness, it will have to esteem the unselfish man and offer reproach to the selfish.[10] In its own way, it will have to elevate its own "best" men to positions of standing and power, while it denies place and importance to those who do not embody the ethic of the new social order. And yet, these disparities in esteem and privilege may be felt as intensely and as bitterly as any of the inequalities produced in a free economy.

The beginning of wisdom, of course, is to recognize that the problem

[10] See Samuel H. Beer, *British Politics in the Collectivist Age* (New York: Knopf, 1967), p. 238.

remains intractable because it cannot claim moral standing as a "problem." So long as morals continue to exist, they must imply rankings. Equality can be manifested properly only in our commitment to treat everyone with justice. Therefore, statesmen who begin by assuming that the inequality of wealth is morally wrong, regardless of how it was brought about, are statesmen who begin in error. When they find that the malady will not yield to their remedies—when they discover that inequalities persist—they are likely to be driven to measures even more radical and sweeping, which can be counted on to be quite as useless and destructive.

The only means of removing ourselves from this spiral of bootless tinkering is to restore the understanding that discriminates between the genuine and the spurious in moral problems. If we understand the moral grounds on which we are obliged to relieve suffering and harm, when we have the capacity to help, we will have opened a vast field of possibility for seeking, where we can, to remedy all species of wrongs. At the same time, we would address those wrongs on grounds that permit us to understand the principles which define them as wrongs, and which oblige us to act.

The world could have been spared a large measure of misfortune— and no harmless train of moral blundering—if it had turned away from policies of redistribution in the way that the French finance minister Jacques Turgot turned away from one of the early proposals for a graduated tax on income. With his cultivated judgment, Turgot managed to sense at once that the scheme was as morally doubtful as it was economically ruinous. "One ought," he said, "to execute the author and not the project."[11]

---

[11] Quoted in Friedrich A. Hayek, *The Constitution of Liberty* (Chicago: University of Chicago Press, 1960), p. 308.

XV

PRIVACY AND THE REACH
OF THE LAW

As I have sought to show in these pages, the logic of morals must override claims of personal preference or private choice, and before the law may claim to bind, it must be founded on propositions that are authentically moral and categorical. Only a proposition that establishes what is right or wrong for everyone—what is right or wrong universally, as a matter of necessity—can properly claim to supersede the liberty of personal choice. The requirements of morals and law, then, are very demanding: unless we can trace our judgments back to categorical propositions, we would not be warranted in invoking the language of morals and interfering with the freedom of individuals. But when we begin with the moral ground of the law, we remind ourselves also of the ground on which claims to privacy and personal choice must justify themselves. We may then understand more readily that privacy cannot be justified coherently—as the attempt is made so widely to justify it these days—as a source of insulation from the law, a shelter in which we become free to do things the law may condemn. As Lincoln taught us, we cannot have a "right to do a wrong." By the same logic, privacy cannot be morally *justified* in the name of a freedom to do things that are *unjustified* and wrong.

In a strict moral perspective, the claims of privacy are arrived at indirectly, through the assurance that these claims are indeed *rightful*. If we cannot say that any particular act is in point of principle wrong, then we must restrain ourselves from using the language of condemnation; we must hold back from invoking the authority of law; and we must leave individuals free to pursue their own, private choices. If we cannot say that it is in principle wrong to prefer an evening of bowling to an evening of Beethoven, we must leave people free to decide how to spend their evenings, without the restraint of the law and without the presumption of moral disapproval. It is not, then, that there is a "right" to bowl or to listen to Beethoven: there is simply a right not to be restricted in pursuing ends that are innocent and legitimate—ends that cannot be condemned by any proposition which has the standing of a moral principle. When the requirements of a moral principle can be met, our condemnation may apply, with a universal sweep, to all acts that come within the terms of the principle.

At all other times, however, people would have to be considered free to make their own private choices in that vast universe of *legitimate* choices which is properly open to them.

In this understanding, privacy and private rights are affected with the moral claim that attaches to activities we recognize as legitimate in their ends and means: "privacy," then, embraces in its moral coverage only those activities which are indeed legitimate. And without this connection to standards of moral judgment—without this conviction that privacy is directed to legitimate ends—the claims of privacy would not have the moral standing we usually accord to them.

Yet, in the liberal jurisprudence that has been dominant in our own day, the understanding of private rights has been the reverse of what I have set forth here: it has been assumed that there is a core of private or intimate relations that the law may not penetrate, precisely because those relations *are* private or intimate. In this perspective, the law begins only where privacy ends, as though moral judgment itself becomes pertinent only outside the household or some inner zone of privacy. The fallacy engaged here is one of the most common we have encountered. It involves, once again, the tendency to reach moral conclusions on the strength of facts or conditions that are wholly lacking in moral significance: in this instance, it is assumed that private quarters are somehow the bearers of moral significance; that merely because an activity takes place in a private establishment, it ought to be insulated from the reach of the law. It is as though there were something in architecture itself which guarantees the irreproachable nature of everything that takes place behind private doors. But that is a judgment which can be reached only when we consider the activities themselves, and not when we are merely told that they are taking place under the shelter of privacy. If our moral judgments find their ground in the "logic of morals," or the laws of reason, the walls of a house cannot mark off a domain outside the province of logic. If it offends the laws of reason to punish a person for acts he was powerless to affect, there is nothing in the features of a private building that would suspend these laws or alter the axioms of our judgment. What makes the act wrong in principle, wrong of necessity, would make it wrong wherever the laws of logic remain intact.

If we could become clear on these points, we would become clear, at the same time, on the standards that must govern the reach and limits of the law. We have law, as we have seen, only because there are, in fact, moral principles that can define for us the things which are wrong and which ought to be forbidden. By implication, of course, the things that are not forbidden must be permissible. The principles that tell us, with the force of necessity, of the things that are wrong must also mark off for us, with a decent clarity, that vast domain of things which are morally indifferent or morally right. And with the things that are not wrong, the law should have nothing to do. The limits to the law can be defined, then, only by the limits to our moral principles themselves. Only the principles which can tell us of the substantive things that are right or wrong can determine for us the things that the law must condemn and the things that must stand beyond the proper reach of the law.

IN HIS NOTORIOUS opinion in *Buch* v. *Amory* (see Chapter XIII), Judge Carpenter was apparently guided by a distinction that is commonly made in our public discourse even today. He referred to the case of a man who could rescue a 2-year-old child from a railroad track without any serious risk to himself, but who nevertheless refuses to go to the rescue. As Carpenter commented, the man "may, perhaps, justly be styled a ruthless savage and a moral monster; but he is not liable in damages for the child's injury, or indictable under the statute for its death." The man could be censured on "moral" grounds, but that was quite separate, in Carpenter's understanding, from an obligation to act which could have been enforced at law. Carpenter was assuming, in other words, a distinction between moral and legal obligation which has become a conventional part of our public discourse. A man might borrow money from a relative, but if the two of them fail to sign a contract, it would typically be said that the man has only a "moral" obligation to repay the loan. For one reason or another, a decision was made not to establish the duty to repay as an obligation enforceable at law.

But when "moral obligation" is understood in this manner, in contradistinction to "legal obligation," what does it mean? Apparently, it would be reduced in its import to mean "soft" or weak obligations— i.e., obligations that are not to be considered binding or enforceable. They are "obligations" that will be honored only so long as the parties are willing to honor them; and yet, that is to say that they are not obligations at all, in the strictest sense. We must remind ourselves that the root of "obligation" is *ligare* (to bind). An obligation arises only when there is a principle that enjoins a commitment. In the case of a contract, an obligation would arise only if the contract were valid and binding; and if it were, it would have to be respected even when the honoring of the contract no longer suited the interests or inclinations of one of the parties who made the agreement. To put it plainly—and literally—an obligation that does not bind cannot be an obligation. If the distinction between legal and moral obligation seems plausible to modern jurisprudence, it is only because that jurisprudence has restricted the meaning of "morals" to matters of subjective belief or personal taste. In that understanding, as we have seen, morals would entail no obligations because they would imply no propositions of universal validity which compel respect and commitment.

It is well known that Kant made a distinction between moral and legal obligation, but his distinction was notably different from the one that prevails in our own time. Kant simply pointed up a difference in the incentives or reasons that led people to obey the law. If they obeyed the law only because it *was* the law (or because they feared punishment), then they were manifesting only a sense of *legal* obligation. But if people obeyed because they understood the moral proposition which made the law necessary and justified, then they obeyed out of a true sense of "moral" obligation. For Kant, only the second kind of obedience was affected with moral significance. As we have seen, an obedience that arises from fear or coercion alone could not be rendered as an "obligation." The obligation to obey can be entailed, in the strictest sense, only by a moral principle, which articulates a proposition we are logically obliged to respect. We have laws—and therefore *legal obligations*—only after we come to recognize certain *moral* propositions which entail obligations for us. Whether we speak of legal duties or ethical duties, both are duties; and "all duties," said Kant, "simply because they are duties, belong to ethics."[1]

If we speak seriously of any obligation, then, we must imply a moral source of that obligation, and we must assume that the obligation would be expressed also in a legal commitment—if it were, in the most literal sense, an "obligation." If a man should have a "moral obligation" to pay back a loan from his relative, that obligation would be enforceable and binding. If not, then we can only suppose that the parties had not really intended to treat the commitment as binding in the most stringent and literal sense, and that turns out, quite often, to be the case. For one reason or another, the parties wished to establish commitments, but not the kind that would require intervention of the government into their affairs. There is no limit to the kinds of accounts that may be put forward in explaining why it is desirable to preserve a certain insulation for the family from the intrusions of government;

---

[1] Immanuel Kant, *The Metaphysical Elements of Justice* [Part I of *The Metaphysics of Morals* (1797)], trans. John Ladd (Indianapolis: Bobbs-Merrill, 1965), p. 20; p. 219 of the RPA ed. For a slightly more extended discussion of this issue, see Arkes, *The Philosopher in the City: The Moral Dimensions of Urban Politics* (Princeton: Princeton University Press, 1981), pp. 390-91.

but most of those explanations are essentially unnecessary or inapt. They are unnecessary because, in the absence of wrongdoing, the government has no more right to interfere in the family than in an ice cream factory, and nothing more need be said in explaining why the government would not be warranted in intervening. If the explanation seeks to go much beyond that, it is likely to offer nothing more than a collection of empirical predictions or conjectures about the wholesome trends that might work themselves out in the family if the government stays its hand. (For example, the members might take more responsibility for one another; they might learn the lessons of caring for others, including people who are not in the family; and they might then go on to become better citizens.) But even though many of these conjectures are no doubt true, they represent nothing more than a collection of contingent propositions and, therefore, they cannot supply the ground of a justification. None of them could stand then as decisive arguments in any case against the intervention of the government when the family becomes a theater of injustice, a scene for acts that are deeply wrong in principle.

If, for example, we have a case in which sadistic parents are systematically torturing their small children, the law would be obliged to vindicate the wrong that is occurring here and now. It is possible to find sociologists who would urge the law to hold back and respect the "autonomy" of this family, on the theory that its members will develop a sense of responsibility and self-confidence and that the results may be more salutary in the long run. But the law may not be distracted by speculations of this kind. In the face of acts that are patently wrong in principle, mere conjectures must give way. For those who would defend an absolute autonomy for the family as a kind of repository of extraterritorial rights, the philosophic problem at its root is one we have encountered earlier. The argument for this autonomy must be stated in the form of a "justification," which must explain why it would be *good* or *justified* to respect such an absolute power in the family. In other words, it could not be argued that the family must be accorded a station beyond the reach of moral judgment and legal control, because the argument necessary to establish that case must itself be a moral argument. The proponents of this argument would be in the position of trying to establish that it is *morally good to withhold moral judgment* from acts that take place in the privacy of the family—an argument which dissolves into nonsense as soon as it confronts events within the family that are thoroughly vicious. The advanced thinker who would defend the "right" of parents to mistreat their children would find himself backing into the fallacy exposed by Lincoln; he would be arguing, once again, for "a right to do a wrong."

The logic of morals cannot yield a license for that kind of accommodation. It would enjoin us to condemn and vindicate wrongs where we find them, and it would be a matter of indifference as to *where* those wrongs are found, whether in a park or a palace, in a delicatessen or a private household. If it is wrong to inflict torture on small, innocent children—or on large, innocent adults—then the principle which establishes the wrong of that torture is utterly indifferent to the question of whether the torture takes place in public or in private. A murder—an unjustified killing—would be quite as wrong whether it takes place in Times Square or in the privacy of a bedroom, and we seem to have no trouble in recognizing that the law would be wholly justified in reaching that crime. It would be well within the claims of the law to enter the bedroom for the sake of preventing the murder, or to punish people later for the events which took place within these private quarters.

If we would detach ourselves for a moment from the reigning clichés of our own day and account for our reactions to these cases, I think we would recognize that the decisive consideration for us, in working out the jurisdiction of the law, is not where the borderline is between the public and the private—whether it begins at the edge of the garden or at the bedroom door. The decisive consideration, rather, is whether we can tell that we are in the presence of a wrong:

> A child may be sent to bed one night without his supper—and sent, as it turns out, unjustly. But the wrong that was done might have been the product of an honest error on the part of the parent. And yet if the parent keeps the child in his room for a month without food, or if his spanking one day moves across a threshold to serious injury, a design of malice may become evident, a firmer judgment may finally be shaped, and the law would not be obliged to hold back. The difference ... does not turn on degrees of privacy, but on the clarity of evidence that tells us that there is an intention to hurt, and that a harm is being inflicted without justification. And in certain instances, as we know, the law may go so far as to remove a child from the family.[2]

Just after this passage was written, a case arose involving a minister in upstate New York who took his 15-year-old daughter across his

---

[2] Arkes, *supra*, note 1, p. 358. The surrounding pages contain further discussion on this general question of the reach of the law.

knee and administered a severe spanking with a cedar shingle. The father explained later that the daughter had been disobedient. From the report in the press it was not clear that the hurt inflicted by the father reflected anything like the injury or malice that was suggested in my hypothetical case of the parents who lock up their child for a month. And yet, social workers in Syracuse argued that the spanking had bruised the child's buttocks; that the parents were guilty at least of neglect, if not assault. On the strength of this evidence, the social workers obtained a court order that removed the daughter to a foster home. The spanking had taken place in April 1978, and the daughter returned to her family in January 1979. Apparently, the daughter returned more willing to govern her own conduct according to the code established in the family.[3] But the incident made plain just how easy it may be, even under our current laws, to intervene in a family for the sake of redressing "wrongs" that are less than momentous.

We ought to remind ourselves, also, that there are instances in which the legal authorities are actually invited into the sanctuary of the family by one of the members, who may be threatened with a grave injury or injustice. The police logs nationwide are filled with accounts of policemen who are called in to mediate in families when disputes erupt over matters as various as drunkenness, infidelity, and the stubborn refusal to switch channels on the television. When family members fear for their own safety at the hands of their relatives, or when they summon sufficient outrage, they implicitly recognize the imminence of a wrong so emphatic that they would be justified in breaking the unity of the family and calling to their own side the weight of the law.

I suggested earlier the informal "contracts" that may be worked out among relatives in the borrowing or lending of money, when they wish to avoid any entanglement of the family with the law. But these same relatives—with the same aversion to the law—may nevertheless end up suing one another in disputes over the inheritance of property. Even when there is no legal will to be interpreted, relatives have not been loath to sue one another in public courts over injuries they have regarded as serious. In 1979, a judgment was won in a New York court by a woman who claimed that her father had reneged on an agreement he had made to pay for her sophomore and junior years at Adelphi College. The promise had been made on condition that the young woman would continue to live at home and commute to school in a car that her father would purchase for her. But the father reneged on the agreement after his daughter took the side of her mother in

---

[3] *New York Times*, February 18, 1979.

disputes that arose from the divorce of the parents. The daughter claimed that her "offense" could not justify the revocation of the promise and the financial burden that was placed upon her. She apparently convinced the jury, and she was awarded $6,700.[4]

Cases of this kind may open our awareness to a point that has been unaccountably overlooked when commentators have addressed the question of limits to the reach of the law. There seems to be conjured up a notion of statutes spelling out the things that may not be done, even in the privacy of the household or the bedroom; of police invading homes in the middle of the night, with or without warrants; of citizens receiving criminal penalties for intimate acts performed in the privacy of their homes. But this sense of the problem overlooks the fact that the hand of the law does not make itself felt only through the criminal law, with prosecutions directed by the state. There is also the civil law, in which private individuals may sue one another. The courts that hear these suits are still, after all, courts of law; the judgments they hand down are *legal* judgments, which must be connected to principles of law; and the penalties they impose may be as serious as anything administered through the criminal law. In 1950, Joseph Beauharnais was fined $200 for distributing, in the streets of downtown Chicago, pamphlets that defamed blacks as a racial group.[5] At the same time, in civil suits on defamation, offenders were faced with assessments for the "damages" suffered by their victims, and those assessments could often exceed $1 million. When fines are not paid in civil cases, the judgments of the courts may be enforced by sending the guilty parties to jail, and we have every reason to suspect that the jails are every bit as confining in these cases as the jails to which people are assigned after criminal trials. Through civil actions of all kinds the law may apply its judgments to the most intimate matters of private life, which we never suppose we could reach through a criminal statute. And the sanctions applied may be more draconian than the typical fines and punishments that are levied in the criminal law. They may involve such extraordinary measures as removing children from the custody of a parent or denying a person the right to be quit of a marriage and to be free, legally, to marry again.

It seems to be taken for granted today, for example, that statutes forbidding adultery are simply not enforceable in the moral climate of our age, and that the statutes would not be defensible in point of principle. But there may be a tendency here to confuse the main issue

---

[4] *New York Times*, July 25, 1979.
[5] See *Beauharnais v. Illinois*, 343 U.S. 250 (1952).

in principle with the nightmares we might well imagine if adultery were made the object of a criminal statute and if it excited the interest of zealous prosecutors. Once again, we conjure up a vision of the government conducting surveillance of intimate quarters and of the police crashing into bedrooms in their eagerness to root out wrongs. And yet, adultery could elicit the sanction of the law without involving *criminal* statutes or prosecutions or any regimen of surveillance conducted by the state. The issue of adultery could be raised by a spouse in the course of a legal proceeding in which adultery is thought to bear some relevance to matters that the court must decide: e.g., in granting a divorce, assigning blame and responsibility, or settling the custody of the children. In these cases, the practice of adultery has been taken by the courts to reflect adversely on the character and claims of the person who had the adulterous affair. If this judgment of the law is plausible, then there would have to be a ground of principle on which the law would be justified in considering adultery, in some cases at least, as wrong. And if we could define, with the proper fineness of distinction, the grounds on which adultery, under some circumstances, might be regarded as wrong, it is not unthinkable that this same, qualified understanding of the offense might be incorporated quite as tenably in the criminal law.

Of course, the "wrong" of adultery may simply be effaced in matters of divorce through the device of "no fault" divorce. Under this legal regimen the problem of adultery is simply legislated away: there is no assignment of moral blame, no judgment on rights and wrongs, no need to *justify* a divorce. But even if adultery can be removed as a concern of the law in cases of divorce, it is not likely to be eliminated altogether from cases involving the custody of children. Even the courts of our own day, in one of the dark ages of jurisprudence, are likely to discover that families are not concerned simply with protecting the physical health of the young. Judges are likely to recognize also that families must have a responsibility for the moral education of children. And so, if parents are involved in a communal life of crime, if they are schooling their children in burglary or preparing them for prostitution, the courts may intercede and remove the children from that family. If the courts must award custody of children by choosing between parents, the courts will have to be attentive to those habits of life that may stamp one of the parents as irresponsible or corrupt, incapable of providing care for the children or giving them the benefit of a decent example. And in this setting, judges who would not think of enforcing a statute on adultery may nevertheless be forced to consider in a serious way the question behind the issue of adultery. Are there certain instances in which a disposition to persistent, casual sex, unenveloped by love or commitment, with partners known well or hardly at all, may not in fact betray a want of character? Might it define a condition that would justify reproach?[6]

In one case on assigning custody of children, a court in Oregon reached an adverse judgment about a mother who exposed her child to her sexual involvements, and who ordered the child to fetch beer one day when she and her paramour were in bed.[7] In another case, *Mullinex* v. *Mullinex*, a mother carefully shielded her three children from knowledge of her sexual relations with her lover. She had also been, by most counts, a conscientious mother, very attentive to the needs of her children. In that sense, there was a strong contrast with her estranged husband, who had put in long hours as an executive in a pretzel factory, and who had never been able to give much time to his children (including the time necessary to share a vacation with them). The husband and wife had been joined mainly by their problems with drinking and their morbid interest in combat with one another. In the reckoning of the court, the mother had demonstrated a larger measure of experience and competence in managing the children; but the court could not bring itself to ignore entirely the evidence of her adultery, and the conduct of the mother was still taken as a reflection on her character. And so, while the court granted her custody of the children, it granted that custody on conditions that had to be regarded as quite sobering. As Judge Turnbull put it, the custody of the children would be granted to Mrs. Mullinex, but "with the specific, rigid provision that she must not at any time, in any way have anything to do with Mr. McCloskey [her lover], or he with her . . . ; and the children shall in no way, at any time, at any place or under any circumstances, except by accident, passing him on the street, or something of that kind, be exposed to his company."[8]

Even for people tutored in the law it might seem bizarre to imagine that two adults, innocent of a crime, may be forbidden by the law to meet and to have sexual intercourse with one another. And yet, that is precisely what was ordered here with the full authority of the law. Of course, adultery was against the law in the state of Maryland, where the case arose; but since there was no prosecution for adultery in this case, the court had to reach its judgment on separate grounds, which could take into account the "wrong" of adultery, even though

---

[6] See Arkes, *supra*, note 1, pp. 406-413.
[7] See *Shrout* v. *Shrout*, 224 Ore. 521, 356 P. 2d 935 (1960).
[8] *Mullinex* v. *Mullinex*, 278 A. 2d 674, 678 (1971).

there was no criminal prosecution. It was evident, then, that Mrs. Mullinex was being forbidden the company of Mr. McCloskey as a kind of punishment for the act of adultery, and the award of the court was put forth on the condition that this "wrong" not be committed again. The penalty for disobeying the court would be quite as palpable as a fine or a prison term: the punishment would be, for Mrs. Mullinex, the loss of custody over her children. As Judge Turnbull summed up the ruling, he reflected with chilling plainness the authority he exercised over the life of this woman: "It will be her choice to make," he wrote; "if she is determined that she would rather have McCloskey than the children I will accommodate her, because I will quickly move to take custody away from her, upon any properly presented evidence that she has failed to comply with this order."[9]

At the time this decision was handed down, it was probably taken for granted by most people that the state would no longer prosecute cases for adultery and annex criminal penalties for acts of sexual intercourse among consenting adults. And yet, in other parts of the law, there was no hesitation in vindicating the "wrong" of adultery with penalties quite as severe as any fine or imprisonment that was likely to be imposed for the same offense under the criminal law. By overlooking these applications of the civil law, however, many commentators have been able to preserve a serene assurance that the law may not reach matters as private and intimate as sexual relations.

In December 1978, a family court in Providence, Rhode Island, removed two young children to a foster home because their parents, who were producers of pornography, persistently held "group sex parties" in their home. The court stipulated at the end of the month that it was willing to grant temporary custody to the maternal grandparents of the children once certain conditions were met. Included in those conditions were a requirement of psychiatric counseling for the parents and a commitment not to hold any more "group sex parties."[10] It was an open question as to whether the courts in Rhode Island would sustain a statute that forbade "group sex parties" among consenting adults. Nor would the courts have been likely then to order compulsory psychiatric treatment for those people who engaged in acts that the law did not condemn. It is conceivable, however, that the courts might have reached a different judgment about the staging of those spectacles of group sex in the presence of minors. If parents managed to draw these rituals into the social routine of the family, it

---

[9] *Ibid.*, at 678.
[10] An account of this case appeared in the *Boston Globe*, December 20, 1978.

was not so unthinkable that judges might begin to wonder whether those parents were mature enough in their judgments to manage the moral demands of raising children. But if it were legitimate for a court to act on these understandings in civil cases, it could not be illegitimate to incorporate the same understanding in the criminal law: that is to say, it would not be inconceivable to have a statute which forbids the staging of group sex in the presence of minors. Law of any kind, whether criminal law or civil law, must find a principled ground of justification; and if there is a ground on which adultery or group sex may be regarded as wrong for the purposes of the civil law, that ground of principle must preserve its validity for the criminal law as well.

In January 1980, another American court barred an adult man and woman from having sexual intercourse with one another, and this time the couple were forbidden to see one another for at least ten years. In this particular case, the order of the court in Stafford, Virginia, was explicitly backed with the prospect of a *criminal* penalty if the couple did not comply. The man in question was a 20-year-old marine who had spent his childhood in a foster home. At age 19, the young man was reunited with his natural mother, a woman 41 years of age, and their attraction for one another came to express itself intensely in a sexual relationship. Their rare connection came to the attention of county officials when a welfare worker heard one of the woman's small daughters refer to her stepbrother as "Daddy." An inquiry later showed that the couple had been married. They were subsequently tried and convicted for incest and illegal marriage. The son/husband testified at the trial that he could not possibly restore the relation of a son to his mother, that he regarded his mother, irrevocably, as "a girl friend, a wife, a companion."[11]

If statutes on incest are legitimate, and if they may be applied legitimately to adults of the age of consent, then this order of the court in Virginia could not be implausible. I do not have the space here to take up the question of incest in its proper complexity. The literature on the subject, including the academic literature, has routinely been innocent of the distinction between principles and empirical predictions; and so, while I think there is, in the matter of incest, a genuine moral concern which justifies the interest of the law, the rationales for the law have not been drawn from any proposition that has the standing of a principle.[12] The concern of the law is at its strongest when it

[11] *Washington Post*, January 9, 1980.

[12] I discuss at length the problem of establishing a principled foundation for these laws in my essay, "The Question of Incest and the Properties of a Moral Argument,"

deals with incest between adults and very small children; it stands at its most problematic level when it deals, for example, with a mature aunt and nephew, or a stepfather and a grown stepdaughter. I would simply point out, however, that so long as we preserve our law as it is, the law would indeed interfere with the most intimate sexual relations of adults. It can impose penalties on incestuous couples; it can bar them from the company of one another; it can forbid them the right to marry; and it can deny them custody of children. The law can also deny the rights of legal marriage to people of the same sex, and though the matter is continually under litigation these days, it may restrict the right of homosexuals to have custody of children.

I do not suggest that all of these provisions are legitimate simply because they have been incorporated in Anglo-American law for generations. It is arguable, I think, that the statutes on adultery have been rather grossly drawn, for they would usually treat, as a categorical wrong—without any recognition of shadings or circumstances—every instance of sexual intercourse outside the context of marriage. On the other hand, the context of marriage and commitment cannot be irrelevant to the meaning of sexual intercourse. Nor is it impossible that people may manifest, in their sexual conduct as in other phases of their lives, an instability in character and a want of judgment that may raise the most serious questions about their fitness for other responsibilities. At those moments, a court which finds itself with responsibility for assessing character may not be able to blind itself to this evidence. The result, however, is that the law may have no choice but to issue mandates that reach into the most private recesses of family life.

The law reaches these kinds of cases because it is compelled to deal with real wrongs or injustices, and when a case arises that manifests, unmistakably, the need for the law, we not only fail to object, but we may even fail to notice that the courts are invading the zone of sexual relations within the family. And so there is no protest against the intrusion of the law when a father forces his 13-year-old daughter to lie on a pool table and have sexual intercourse with him while he rests a gun on the table near her head.[13] For this offense the father was prosecuted and convicted.

In 1976, in the case of *Bateman* v. *Arizona*,[14] Justice Rehnquist refused to stay a judgment of the Supreme Court of Arizona which

in Nahman Greenberg (ed.), *Incest: Toward an Understanding* (Washington D.C.: U.S. Department of Health & Human Services, 1985).

[13] *Hill* v. *State*, 480 S.W. 2d 670 (1972).

[14] 50 L. Ed. 2d 32 (1976).

upheld the conviction of a husband for forcing his wife to commit fellatio. The statute in Arizona proscribed sodomy, along with other acts deemed "lewd and lascivious," but it allowed the charges to be rebutted with a showing of "consent." As the Supreme Court of Arizona interpreted the law, the statute would be "construed to prohibit nonconsensual sexual conduct," even between spouses.[15] In that respect, the statute was connected in principle to the statutes which have been enacted recently to recognize a crime of rape even in the context of marriage. One statute of this kind, in the state of Oregon, produced a celebrated prosecution in the case of John Rideout and his wife, Greta. The prosecution failed in that case, in large part because of the complicated task of decoding the patterns of aggression and forgiveness that may form the relation of a husband and wife and make it harder to judge matters of consent. The equivocal nature of the motives at work was confirmed after the trial, when the Rideouts were reconciled, only to break up again a short while later.[16]

The question of consent is obviously complicated in the case of married couples who have already committed themselves to one another or consented, publicly and legally, to the closest sexual relations. To detect a coerced sexual act is of course harder in this setting than it would be in an encounter between strangers. But even if the matter may be difficult to judge, and even if the cases within the reach of the law may be very few, the question in principle must remain: we seem able to understand, with no particular strain, that the consent offered in marriage cannot encompass a consent to be assaulted without justification. If the law can detect battering and abuse in the relations between husbands and wives, the same arts of reason may detect assaults, in certain cases, when they take the form of sexual humiliations. In those rare cases where the motives are unambiguous and the evidence is compelling, the law would be quite as warranted in acting as it would be in any other case in which one spouse suffered injury or assault at the hands of another.

Again, the main point to be made here is that there is nothing about the notion of the family, or of relations as private and intimate as sex within the family, which can mark off a sphere of freedom insulated entirely from the reach of the law. Claims of privacy can be respected only on the grounds on which respect is offered to any association or activity: viz., that the shelter of privacy is sought in order to preserve a decorous screening from public view of acts which are thoroughly

---

[15] *Ibid.*, at 34-35.

[16] An account of this case appeared in the *Boston Globe*, December 31, 1978, and the story was carried by many other newspapers at around the same time.

legitimate and which may require, for their integrity, a certain measure of intimacy. But the presumptive walls of privacy must give way in the face of genuine wrongs or evils, and the force of principle compels the law to invade these precincts, if it must, for the sake of redressing wrongs.

AND YET, anyone familiar with the recent experience of our law would be aware that many lawyers and jurists have sought to write as though our law had become settled in a radically different understanding. Many legal briefs and judicial opinions have been written recently with the assumption that there are in fact "zones of privacy" that are virtually beyond the reach of the law. The incentive to establish that understanding apparently enlarged during the early 1970's, when the state laws on abortion were subject to a campaign of challenge in the courts. The challengers sought to establish a freedom or "right" to abort, unencumbered by the restrictions of law, and so it was only natural that they would try to assimilate abortion to a cluster of intimate, private activities that ought to be insulated, in their privacy, from the reach of public law. From this perspective, there was a strong temptation to argue that the Supreme Court had already recognized these zones of privacy, on one substantive matter after another, from marriage and procreation to the raising of children. And from there it seemed but a short, additional step to attach the decision on abortion to this domain of "private" acts. The argument was accepted by a number of courts with an astonishing ease, and Justice Douglas would later recall, in part, the litany that was so facilely adopted, along with the understandings which were attached to each case: *Meyer v. Nebraska* (1923) and *Pierce v. Society of Sisters* (1925) were taken to mark "the liberty to direct the education of one's children"; *Skinner v. Oklahoma* (1942) signified "the right of procreation"; *Loving v. Virginia* (1967) stood for "the liberty to marry a person of one's own choosing." And, most important of all, *Griswold v. Connecticut* (1965), which tested a law on contraception, was held to establish "the privacy of the marital relation," especially the privacy of spouses in conducting their sexual relations.[17] Years later, the plaintiffs in *Doe v. Bolton* would argue that these cases formed a design of privacy which could easily encompass—as the district court put it—"the right of a woman to terminate an unwanted pregnancy in its early stages, by obtaining an abortion."[18]

[17] See Justice Douglas concurring in *Doe v. Bolton*, 410 U.S. 179, at 212-13 (1973).
[18] *Doe v. Bolton*, 319 F. Supp. 1048, at 1054 (1970). In his concurring opinion in *Doe v. Bolton*, Justice Douglas cited this passage, but reported, incorrectly, that it expressed the views of the district court in Georgia. See 410 U.S. 179, at 210 (1973).

In all strictness, however, the Supreme Court had never established, in *Griswold* and its related cases, any new classes of "rights"; nor did it create zones of privacy that were beyond the reach of the law. For that matter, the Court had never acknowledged anything like a "right to one's own body." As we shall see, the Court did not even create such a right in *Roe* v. *Wade*, when it struck down virtually all the laws in the country that forbade abortions. And if the court never confirmed for any person a "right to one's own body," which could be exercised outside the claims and restraints of law, it was hard to see how that string of earlier cases could have established a "right" to carry out a lethal operation on *another* body—i.e., the body of that separate being contained in the womb of a pregnant woman.

On the latter question I shall have much more to say in the next two chapters. For the moment, however, I simply wish to recall, very briefly, the question raised in some of those earlier cases and to suggest, again, why those cases could not have established the kinds of "rights" that their interpreters would later claim for them. None of these cases marked off classes of acts that were cut off from the regulation of law, and it should be plain that none of them could have established precedents for anything as portentous as a "right" to take the life of an unborn child without the restraints of law or without the need to render a justification.

THE CONFUSION that has grown up around the cases on "privacy" may be attributed in large part to that confusion, which has been cultivated more broadly in the legal profession, on the difference between principles and those cases or instances in which principles are manifested. For example, once we came to understand the principle that defined the wrong of racial discrimination, it really should not have mattered as to where that wrong in principle was manifested, whether in schools or swimming pools, in restaurants or inns or cinemas. When the Supreme Court struck down segregation in the public schools in *Brown* v. *Board of Education*, it suggested that the wrong of segregation inhered in an injury that was being inflicted on black children through their education in segregated schools.[19] When the judgment of the Court was cast in these terms, scholars of the Constitution could be forgiven for wondering how the Court made the transition between schools and public accommodations. If the Court had been clear in the first place on the principle that defined the

---

[19] See 347 U.S. 483, at 494-95 (1954).

"wrong" of racial segregation, there would not have been so much puzzlement about the reach of its holding.

Imagine a case, for example, in which there are public tennis courts with a sign listing the regulations, along with the hours at which the courts will be available. Imagine also that the courts have been declared open to everyone, but that "Armenians may not play on Tuesdays and Thursdays." A case of this kind, hardly momentous in itself, nevertheless engages a moral principle. The principle is, of course, the same one that makes it wrong to assign benefits or disabilities to people on the basis of their race or ethnicity. If the principle were vindicated in this case, it would not establish a "constitutional right to play tennis." Nor would the issue be that the regulations impaired the right of Armenians "to travel," by preventing them from entering certain public quarters. Armenians would be wronged in this case because they were treated in accord with the same unjust principle that is engaged in the cases of racial discrimination. That principle would be manifested here in a rather prosaic case, but it is the violation of a moral principle that makes any case morally and legally significant; and most cases *are* prosaic until they emerge as instances in which principles are being engaged and violated. The principle that bars discrimination on the basis of race was tested in relation to public accommodations in the landmark case of *Katzenbach* v. *McClung*,[20] and yet the "right" engaged in that case was evidently more than a right on the part of black people to have access to the exotic offerings of "Ollie's Barbecue" in Birmingham, Alabama.

If these strands can be disentangled, if we can avoid the temptation to confound principles with the instances in which they are manifested, then it may be easier to avoid the confusion that has been wrought in the cases on privacy. In the case of *Loving* v. *Virginia*,[21] for example, the state of Virginia had an "antimiscegenation" statute, which prohibited "interracial marriages involving white persons." The assumption had been shared, even by the framers of the Fourteenth Amendment, that legislation of this kind would be permissible because it bore equally on blacks as well as whites.[22] But the Court was compelled to challenge that older view with a more demanding standard. Chief Justice Warren argued, for the Court, that the statute could not be spared that "very heavy burden of justification which the Fourteenth

[20] 379 U.S. 294 (1964).

[21] 388 U.S. 1 (1967).

[22] See Charles Fairman, "Does the Fourteenth Amendment Incorporate the Bill of Rights?" 2 *Stanford Law Review* 5, at 18 (1949), and the *Congressional Globe*, 39th Congress, 1st Session (1866), pp. 598, 604, 606.

Amendment has traditionally required of state statutes drawn according to race."[23] Before he finished, Warren did deliver himself of a grand flourish in which he wrote of marriage as "one of the basic civil rights of man." But apparently he did not regard a "basic civil right" as beyond the restriction of the law, for he conceded that "marriage is a social relation subject to the State's police power."[24] The statute on miscegenation might be constitutionally invalid, but that did not mean that marriage was so private that it could not be legitimately regulated by the law. Nothing in Warren's decision would imply that the states were on doubtful ground when they barred the marriage of fathers and daughters; when they refused to issue marriage licenses to people of the same sex; or when they established an age of consent for the sake of ensuring that the parties to the marriage were competent to contract for themselves.

The critical point in the decision, as Warren recognized, was that the state of Virginia was "restricting the freedom to marry solely because of racial classifications." The statutes implied that there was something in the nature of being black or white that made the members of each race undesirable or unworthy as prospective partners in marriage for the other. Therefore, it should have been a matter of irrelevance as to whether the case concerned the freedom to marry or the freedom to own and operate a delicatessen. In fact, let us suppose for a moment that a case of this latter kind did arise. Let us assume that there was a statute which forbade partnerships between members of different races in the operation of retail establishments dealing with the public. And let us suppose, further, that a case was brought by partners of different races who were prosecuted for violating the law in their operation of a delicatessen. (We might call this case "*Zabar's* v. *Virginia*.") We can assume that the Court would have struck that statute down for the same reasons that were controlling in *Loving* v. *Virginia*, and "*Zabar's*" would have taken its place among the precedents of the Court. If the occasion arose later for the Court to refer back to "*Zabar's* v. *Virginia*" and apply its logic to a current case, is it really conceivable that the Court would have concluded that the case had established "a fundamental right to own and operate a delicatessen"? Or is it more likely that the Court would have recognized that "*Zabar's*" merely marked another instance in which the judges had vindicated the right not to suffer disabilities on the basis of race; that the same principle could have been engaged in a case involving

[23] *Loving* v. *Virginia*, *supra*, note 21, at 9.
[24] *Ibid.*, at 7.

a drugstore or a dry-cleaning establishment; and that the nature of the enterprise (a delicatessen) was irrelevant to the principle of the case? With a judicial mind suitably cleared on these points, it would become evident that the precedent constituted by *"Zabar's"* would bear on other cases, involving disabilities based on race, even if they did not involve delicatessens. In the same way, I would suggest that it misses the point quite as lavishly to look back at *Loving* v. *Virginia* and conclude that the case established a "constitutional right to marry."

For the same reason, it would have been a mistake to say that *Meyer* v. *Nebraska*[25] and *Pierce* v. *Society of Sisters*[26] established an inviolable right on the part of parents to provide, in any manner they choose, for the education of their own children. The *Meyer* case involved a statute in Nebraska that forbade the teaching of any language but English to students who were still in grammar school. The measure was aimed at fostering a sense of common citizenship, and it was applied in this case to a man who was teaching German. In *Pierce*, a statute in Oregon required students between the ages of 8 and 16 to attend the public schools. In this particular case, the measure was having a devastating effect on a group that operated private elementary and secondary schools having a Roman Catholic character. The opinion of the Court was written in both cases by Mr. Justice McReynolds, who found in both of them an unwarranted attempt by the state to interfere with the liberty of parents in directing the upbringing and education of their children. McReynolds even went so far as to declare that "the fundamental theory of liberty upon which all governments in this Union repose excludes any general power of the State to standardize its children by forcing them to accept instruction from public teachers only. The child is not the mere creature of the State; those who nurture him and direct his destiny have the right, coupled with the high duty, to recognize and prepare him for additional obligations."[27]

But apart from these sweeping sentiments, which swept, I think, somewhat further than the terms of the decision, Justice McReynolds was a bit more precise in fixing the ground of his holding. In both cases, he emphasized that there was nothing "inherently wrong" with the activities being banned. There was nothing about private education or the teaching of German that was harmful in itself; and for that

---

[25] 262 U.S. 390 (1923).
[26] 268 U.S. 510 (1925).
[27] *Ibid.*, at 535.

reason the state could have no tenable ground for interfering in this way with the presumptive freedom of parents to arrange for the education of their children. And yet, McReynolds was far from denying that the state had a legitimate claim to regulate either parents or the education they furnished for their children. In the first place, he did not look upon the public schools merely as a service provided by the community for parents who wished to use them. The establishment of public schools marked an *obligation* of parents to provide education for their children. That obligation would be manifested, of course, in public commitments, supported by taxes legally drawn from the public. Not everyone would be compelled to use the public schools, but apparently McReynolds thought it legitimate for the law to compel all parents to arrange in some minimal way for the education of their children. And precisely what that minimum would be, either in its technical or moral character, would not be left entirely to the discretion of the parents. As McReynolds wrote, the state had a legitimate claim to regulate *all* schools, public and private; to inspect, supervise, and examine their teachers and pupils; to require attendance at school; to ensure that teachers are of "good moral character and patriotic disposition." The state could rightly insist, also, that "certain studies plainly essential to good citizenship must be taught, and that nothing be taught which is manifestly inimical to the public welfare."[28]

When this list was added up, Justice McReynolds was evidently conceding that the education of children could be "standardized" quite legitimately after all. By the sweep of his argument he would have conceded, also, that the state had a legitimate claim in certain cases to override the judgments made by parents about the education of their own children. What he seemed to affirm in *Meyer* and *Pierce* was that parents had a residual, presumptive authority for the education of their children. But nothing in his opinion would have obliged the state to hold back if the parents sought to enroll their children in Mr. Fagin's School of Pickpocketry or in a vocational academy cultivating the trade of prostitution. The state would not be obliged to grant accreditation or even legitimate standing to "schools" of this kind, and it might remove children from the custody of parents who were converting their families into schools for vice. It would also have been consistent with McReynolds's opinion for the state to refuse to hire committed Nazis or Communists as teachers and to refuse certification to those parents who wished to tutor their children at home in the curricula of Hitler and Lenin. And so, whatever was established

[28] *Ibid.*, at 534.

in *Meyer* and *Pierce*, those cases did not create an inviolable wall around the privacy and authority of the family. They did not deny in any way the responsibility of the state to ensure that the authority of the family was exercised in a manner compatible with its moral purposes. And for that reason, they did not deny the moral claims of the law to intervene in the family for the sake of protecting the rights of members too weak or immature to defend their own interests.

A CLOSE READING will show, in a similar way, that the Supreme Court did not create an inviolable shelter of privacy even on such matters as procreation and sexual intercourse between spouses. The so-called right to procreation has been attributed by lawyers recently to the redoubtable case of *Skinner* v. *Oklahoma*,[29] which was decided by the Supreme Court in 1942. The case involved a statute in Oklahoma that provided for the sterilization of "habitual criminals," people who seemed to be driven irresistibly to commit felonies of "moral turpitude." For the purposes of the law, the conviction and imprisonment three times for such felonies would be taken as the test of an habitual, incorrigible disposition. Crimes of "moral turpitude" could be constituted by almost any felony, but expressly deleted from the list were embezzlements, political offenses, and violations of the tax laws. The latter crimes, in the judgment of the legislature, were apparently not genetically transmissible and therefore open to "remedy" through sterilization. As the law was applied in this case, sterilization was ordered for a man who had been convicted twice for robbery and once for stealing chickens. Justice Douglas, who seemed to have an habitual, incorrigible disposition to invoke the Equal Protection Clause of the Fourteenth Amendment, pounced at once on the disparity created in the legislation between embezzlers and chicken thieves. The laws of Oklahoma commanded sterilization for the chicken thief but they left unsterilized the embezzler, who might steal property of much larger value and do, withal, much vaster injury. "[When] the law," said Douglas, "lays an unequal hand on those who have committed intrinsically the same quality of offense and sterilizes one and not the other, it has made as invidious a discrimination as if it had selected a particular race or nationality for oppressive treatment."[30]

Of course, the Equal Protection Clause operated with a majestic neutrality toward the substantive things that were being distributed equally. In this instance, it fell to Chief Justice Stone to point out the

---

[29] 316 U.S. 535.
[30] *Ibid.*, at 541.

moral awkwardness of settling the case through the Equal Protection Clause. As Stone aptly remarked, the moral defects in this legislation would hardly have been cured if the legislature of Oklahoma had gone on, with a proper sense of symmetry, to provide for the sterilization of the embezzlers as well as the chicken thieves. The Chief Justice went on to twit Douglas for quibbling over the details after he had already conceded the main issue of principle: if the Court allowed that the legislature knew enough, in the first place, to define the criminal tendencies that were genetically transmissible, then "we must likewise presume that the legislature, in its wisdom, knows that the criminal tendencies of some classes of offenders are more likely to be transmitted than those of others."[31]

Stone rightly suspected that the science of genetics could not yield any such knowledge about the heritability of dispositions toward criminal acts, any more than it was likely to reveal genetic tendencies to buy excessive amounts of life insurance. Stone preferred to cast his argument, however, as a concern, born of "due process," for the appropriateness and the adequacy of the evidence. Skinner had been given a hearing for the sake of considering whether sterilization would adversely affect his health. But he was given no hearing for the purpose of determining whether his own "criminal tendencies" could have been inherited. As Stone argued, then, the problem in the case was defined by a "wholesale condemnation of a class" to a restriction of personal liberty "without opportunity to any individual to show that his is not the type of case which would justify" these restrictions or punishments.[32]

Chief Justice Stone surely must have realized that the state had no chance of proving its case in hearings of this kind, and in that event we are led to wonder why he did not simply say that the state had no substantive justification for the policy it was enforcing? Why did he pretend instead that the defect in the case arose from an inattention to matters of evidence and procedure? Stone might have had several reasons for avoiding an argument about the "substantive" defects in the legislation; but in skirting that argument he caused the least disturbance to earlier precedents of the Court, and he preserved the possibility that the state, under different circumstances, could be justified one day in ordering sterilizations. By forming his argument as he did, Stone left undisturbed the decision in *Buck* v. *Bell*,[33] in which

---

[31] *Ibid.*, at 544.
[32] *Ibid.*; see also at 545.
[33] *Buck* v. *Bell*, 274 U.S. 200 (1927).

the Court had sustained another law on sterilization, in Virginia. The statute in that case applied to mentally retarded people in state institutions, and the law had no more scientific justification than the statute in Oklahoma. *Buck* v. *Bell* offered Justice Holmes the occasion to pen his famous aphorism that "three generations of imbeciles are enough." As it turned out, the "facts" supporting the assessment of imbecility were shockingly casual and infirm, but Holmes succeeded once again in deciding a case on the strength of a slogan.

That was the ruling, in any event, which Stone was pleased to leave unchallenged, and in preserving it he managed to preserve the possibility that the state might have a valid reason, at some other time, for carrying out sterilizations. Even very recently there has been a willingness among urbane commentators to accept the sterilization of retarded people who seem unable to manage their sexual activity. One wonders, of course, why the same evidence that established the incompetence of these people to control their sexual activity might not recommend measures of supervision and governance, which might restrain their activity without the need for compulsory surgery. Nevertheless, people of liberal disposition have shown a willingness, even today, to accept, in certain cases, sterilizations ordered by the state. Chief Justice Stone apparently sought to write an opinion in the *Skinner* case that would not close off these possibilities. By casting the judgment in this way, he also established this notable point: that the only comprehensible opinion for the Court in the *Skinner* case did not articulate any "right of procreation," which would be wholly beyond the reach or restriction of the law.

At the same time, the ground of Stone's judgment in *Skinner* was not tied distinctly to the act of procreation. The heart of the problem, as Stone said, was the "wholesale condemnation of a class." A drastic punishment was imposed without an opportunity for the condemned man to show that he would not be classified properly in the group being picked out for punishment. Presumably, the same objections would have been decisive in this case if the punishment had not been sterilization but "psychosurgery" (for the purpose, say, of "pacifying" the tendencies toward criminality). In his opinion for the Court in *Skinner*, Justice Douglas did list marriage and procreation among "the basic civil rights of man," but it would be hard to find, in the operative sections of the opinion, a distinct right of procreation, inviolable against the regulations of the state. Almost forty years later, prisoners in the United States would be invoking the Civil Rights Acts and petitioning the federal courts for "conjugal visits" with their wives or girlfriends. With counsel inspired by a casual reading of the law and seized with the spirit of "rights," they would claim a "right to pro-creation" that was being restricted by the confinement of prison. Their arguments might have carried a larger residue of plausibility if pro-creation represented a fundamental right, which would be wrong at all times to restrict. The fact that the argument was not accorded even a slight measure of plausibility is a reflection once again of the fact that the Court had declined, in the *Skinner* case, to convert a slogan into a right.

In *Griswold* v. *Connecticut*[34] the Court was faced with a statute in Connecticut that forbade the use of contraceptives and provided pen-alties, in addition, for people who would counsel or aid others in the use of contraceptives. Griswold was the executive director of the Planned Parenthood League in New Haven, which offered information and advice to married couples on the means of preventing conception. The Supreme Court struck down the statute on contraception, but it split into several opinions. In essence, all of the opinions for the majority regarded the statute in Connecticut as an unwarranted intrusion into matters that were properly left to personal choice. The disagree-ment arose over the section of the Constitution to which the argument would be appended. But this was a dispute, in fact, without substance, since the argument to be made here could have been made under any number of headings within the Constitution.

Of course, if one looks upon the Constitution as an inventory of rights, instead of a collection of principles, then it can indeed be baffling to consider whether the freedom to use contraceptives should be at-tached, say, to the right of association (in the First Amendment) or to the right to be free from unreasonable search and surveillance (under the Fourth Amendment). An inventive lawyer, with the right client, might even be tempted to use the Commerce Clause. Justice Douglas chose to argue that the freedom engaged in this case did not have to be mentioned specifically in the Constitution or even drawn as a precise analogy to any rights that had been extracted by then from different parts of the Constitution. He argued, rather, that the provisions in the Bill of Rights had "penumbras" which ran beyond their literal terms; these penumbras were "formed by emanations from those guarantees that help give them life and substance."[35] There had been no mention in the Constitution of a right of procreation or a right to educate children, and yet those "rights" had been drawn as implications of

[34] 381 U.S. 479 (1965).
[35] *Ibid.*, at 484.

the Constitution through cases such as *Meyer* v. *Nebraska* and *Skinner* v. *Oklahoma*. Just how long Justice Douglas had been seeing these penumbras he did not say; nor did he disclose whether he had ever been visited by one. But he was convinced that they disclosed a comprehensible design, rather like Henry James's "figure in the carpet"; and what they created, he thought, were "zones of privacy" beyond the interference of the law. If there were such zones of privacy, then it seemed evident that the freedom of spouses to engage in sexual intercourse should not be encumbered by the surveillance and restraint of the law. As Douglas put the question, "Would we allow the police to search the sacred precincts of marital bedrooms for telltale signs of the use of contraceptives? The very idea is repulsive to the notions of privacy surrounding the marriage relationship."[36]

It was by no means clear, however, that this was after all the proper question. As I have suggested, there is a danger in these cases in confusing the principle behind a policy with the most intrusive form in which the policy may be enforced. Whether a policy can be practicably enforced—or enforced in a less intrusive and more artful way— is quite separate from the question of whether the policy of the state is in principle justified or unjustified. For all of their differences with Justice Douglas, it was the same kind of problem that afflicted Justices Goldberg and Harlan as they offered separate arguments to support the judgment of the Court. Goldberg was left uncomfortable by the notion of "penumbras" floating easily overhead, unattached to any particular section of the Constitution. He proposed to make Douglas's argument in another way, by invoking a right of "privacy" that he found, along with a variety of other claims, conceived and as yet not conceived, in the vast residuum of the Ninth Amendment. That rarely used amendment simply stated that "the enumeration in the Constitution, of certain rights, shall not be construed to deny or disparage others retained by the people." The Ninth Amendment, we know, was added to the Constitution for the sake of those with an overly literal mind, who might have been tempted to conclude that the people possessed no other rights under law apart from those which had been anticipated by the Founders and set down in the Constitution. But Goldberg made use of the Ninth Amendment now as a repository of all "rights" which could be drawn plausibly as implications of the Constitution, but which could not be attached easily to any of its other sections or amendments. It might have been said then that the Ninth Amendment was, for Goldberg, one huge "penumbra" in which he

---

[36] *Ibid.*, 485-86.

could find the same rights of "privacy" which—he and Douglas were both convinced—were lurking somewhere.

Wherever the penumbras finally settled, it was the assumption of Douglas and Goldberg that the provisions in the Bill of Rights would be binding in their entirety on the states. Or, as the saying went, those provisions would be applied to the states as a result of being "incorporated" in the Fourteenth Amendment. Justice Harlan persisted in his opposition to such an uncalibrated application of the Bill of Rights to the states. He agreed with Cardozo and Frankfurter that the federal Constitution would impose on the states only those restrictions that arose from the character of constitutional government itself or from the requirements of administering "justice." In the parlance of the Court, it became common to refer here to "fundamental values" that were "implicit in the concept of ordered liberty"—which is to say, implicit in the very idea of a government of law.

Of course, Harlan and Douglas would often achieve the same result, and it was their enduring delusion that they arrived at the judgment from different premises or from different routes of argument. In fact, only the labels differed. As Harlan and Douglas went about locating "wrongs" and working out justifications for their judgments, the propositions they employed were utterly identical in their underlying form. And so, in the *Griswold* case, Harlan was convinced, no less than Douglas and Goldberg, that the policy of the state represented an intrusion "without justification." Precisely why that policy was "without justification" Harlan did not linger to explain, any more than Douglas and Goldberg. Like his colleagues, Harlan was distracted by the matter of "privacy": it was apparent to him that this legislation touched the most intimate relations in the private life of a family, and he thought it axiomatic that a regime of law implied a separation between the public and the private. A government "limited" by the Constitution would have limits to the reach of public law, and if those limits were not to be found in the sanctuary of the marital bedchamber, then where were they plausibly to be found? Five years earlier, another case had tested the Connecticut law on contraceptives, and Harlan had argued that

> the most substantial claims which these married [plaintiffs] press is their right to enjoy the privacy of their marital relations free of the inquiry of the criminal law. . . . And I cannot agree that their enjoyment of this privacy is not substantially impinged upon, when they are told that if they use contraceptives, indeed whether they do so or not, the only thing which stands between them and

being forced to render criminal account of their marital privacy is the whim of the prosecutor.[37]

To Harlan, evidently, the marital relation commanded a privacy so secure that it was virtually obscene for the law to address that relation in any way. His argument turned, then, on a distinction between the public and the private which he regarded as so patent that it hardly needed a defense. And yet, the moral ground of that distinction remained unexplained. Once again, one of the most urbane members of the Court was so distracted by the standard sentiments about "privacy" that he was willing to settle the case on the basis of a formula which could not entail any moral or jural conclusion, and which could not even account for the body of law that he and his colleagues had been shaping over the years through their other decisions. The formula of "privacy" settled no case because, as we have seen, it is irrelevant to any substantive moral issue. If it is wrong to kill without justification, and if the law may reach that wrong, the wrong remains even if the killing is performed inside a private home. If it is wrong to inflict serious bodily harm without justification, that assault is quite as wrong when carried out by a husband against his wife, even if it occurs within the sanctuary of the marital bedchamber. Douglas, Goldberg, and Harlan knew, quite as well as any battered wife within a ghetto, that the walls of the marital bedchamber offered no legitimate barrier, in that respect, to the reach of the law. When faced with cases of this kind, the judges would not have drawn lurid pictures of a public surveillance that penetrated the bedroom. They would not have permitted themselves to become distracted with these prospects, because they would have understood that the cases could be brought to the attention of the law in a number of ways which did not involve any surveillance of that kind. The complaint, as we have seen, could have been brought by the wife or by another member of the family, or even by a social worker who noticed the injuries of the wife. The cases could be brought within the reach of the law, in other words, quite as easily as cases that involved incest between a father and a small child. The fact that cases on incest involve sexual activity within the privacy of the family has not prompted lawyers and judges to declare that there is something about sex within a family which is so manifestly

---

[37] See Harlan in *Poe* v. *Ullman*, 367 U.S. 497, at 536 (1961); for his opinion in *Griswold* v. *Connecticut*, see 381 U.S. 499-502 (1965). Since spouses could not testify against one another, prosecutions were unlikely, but even so, Harlan thought that the statute would impart quite enough offense if it merely required married couples to defend themselves in courts of law for their use of contraceptives.

private, so irreducibly intimate, that it cannot be addressed by the agents of a constitutional government. And if all of this should have been apparent at the time of *Griswold* v. *Connecticut*, it should be even more apparent today, when the Court has refused to overturn laws against forced sex within a marriage.[38]

In the world of the judges, the law could apparently reach the intimate sexual relations involved in incest and rape, but it could not reach the intimate sexual relations involved with the use of contraception. The difference—it should have been plain—could not have turned on the presence of intimate, sexual relations. The difference could have turned only on the reasons which led judges to regard incest and rape as wrong, but which made them far less certain that the use of contraception was unjustified and wrong.

To put the matter another way, it was not the problem for the Court in *Griswold* to work out a distinction between the private and the public, or to tell us with the precision of architects and engineers just where we were to locate the threshold of the private home or the marital bedroom. The problem before the Court was not an empirical question of working out descriptions, but a moral question of working out justifications. The moral question was not whether it would be justified at times for the law to intervene in the privacy of sex and the family, for the answer to that question was unequivocally *yes*. The more precise moral question in this case was whether the law was justified in intervening *for the sake of preventing married couples from using contraceptives*. The substantive moral question in the case was whether it was morally wrong to use contraception and whether the law would be justified then in forbidding its use. *That* question—nothing more, and certainly nothing less—defined the *only* issue of principle in this case.

The only member of the Court who seemed to grasp this point was Mr. Justice White. He did not quite manage to lead the Court back to the philosophic root and consider the fundamental grounds on which contraception could be said to be right or wrong. But his opinion did have the virtue of framing the correct issue and exposing the proper vulnerabilities of the statute in Connecticut. His was also the only opinion that bothered to consider the reasons behind the statute. As White pointed out, there had been no serious contention by the state that "the use of artificial or external methods of contraception [were] immoral or unwise" in themselves—an implicit concession that was quite significant. The purpose of the statute, as it was professed in public, was to discourage "all forms of promiscuous or illicit sexual

[38] See *Bateman* v. *Arizona, supra*, note 14.

relationship, be they premarital or extramarital," a purpose that White was willing to regard as "permissible and legitimate."[39]

But even if the end were legitimate, the means were clumsy and inappropriate. A ban on contraception for married couples could hardly advance the concern of the state for sexual intercourse carried on outside a context of love and commitment. Beyond that, the statute had virtually fallen into disuse. Contraceptives were widely available within the state, they were not seized as contraband, and no effort was made to challenge the sale of contraceptives in certain cases when they were sold, ostensibly, for the purpose of preventing disease. As White commented, "the only way Connecticut seeks to limit or control the availability of [contraceptives] is through its general aiding and abetting statute whose operation in this context has been quite obviously ineffective and whose most serious use has been against birth-control clinics rendering advice to married, rather than unmarried, persons."[40]

It did not take much wit, then, to recognize that the enforcement of the law had fallen into a pattern that inverted the original purpose of the statute. White, we should note, did not wholly rule out the possibility that the Court might sustain a statute on contraception which was focused more precisely: we might imagine, for example, a statute that barred the sale or distribution of contraceptives to minors. But the current statute, in White's judgment, swept far too broadly and restricted, without warrant, the freedom of married persons. Precisely why that restriction was unjustified is a question that could not have been answered by anything in the body of White's argument. In all strictness, his conclusion could have followed only if he could have explained why there was nothing wrong in principle with the use of contraceptives. What he had established, though, was that the state of Connecticut had brought forth no principled justification for the banning of contraceptives, and in the absence of any demonstration that the practice was wrong, married people could properly claim the freedom of their personal choice. White did not settle the ultimate rights and wrongs of contraception, but he had the distinction at least of being the only member of the Court who recognized what the main question in the case really was.

I REMARKED earlier, in what may well have been a cryptic passage, that the limits to the law could be found only in the limits to the moral principle which underlay the law. We are in a better position now, I

[39] 381 U.S., at 504.
[40] *Ibid.*, at 505-506.

think, to make that observation more readily graspable. When we speak of limits to the law, we must be speaking of moral limits: we must be speaking of a perimeter in which the law would be warranted in acting, and we must be implying that the law would not be *justified* in reaching any matter beyond that perimeter. But then, it should be clear that the presence or absence of a moral justification cannot be furnished by any act or condition that is itself without moral significance (see Chapter VIII). As we have had occasion to remind ourselves, there is no moral significance in the brute physical presence of a wall or a door. No moral wrong loses its character as a wrong if it is enveloped by walls or placed behind doors. For the same reason, no doctrine about the limits of the law can be founded merely on the distinction between the public and the private, or on any other distinction without intrinsic moral significance. The limits to the law can be established only with the same principles that allow us to tell the difference between the things that are right and wrong, on the one hand, and the things that are morally indifferent, on the other. If, as we have said, there is no ground of principle on which it would be wrong for people to bowl in the evening rather than listen to Beethoven, then the choice between bowling and Beethoven stands outside the limits of the law. If it is wrong for husbands to subject their wives to sadomasochistic rituals without their consent, then their acts of assault are within the reach of the law even if the husbands initiate these rituals with sexual intercourse. If it were in principle wrong to prevent new lives from coming into being by using contraception, then it would be within the reach of the law to forbid the use of contraceptives. But if the matter were subjected to the most demanding scrutiny, and if we could not establish any ground of principle for regarding contraception as morally wrong, then the law would have to recede. The use of contraception by mature or married couples would have to be placed outside the limits of the law.

Once again, I would stress that we are not speaking here about religious beliefs, but about grounds of moral principle and the establishment of categorical propositions. As we have seen, no statements of religious faith or private belief can take the place of moral propositions as the foundation of law, and no cultivated school of religious reflection should have it otherwise. For any serious understanding of religion and nature would have to respect the province of moral reasoning in the universe; and that understanding could not permit a casual resort to claims of "revelation" for the sake of overturning the maxims of law. The only proper way for the question of contraception to be faced *as a matter of law* is to determine whether the case against contraception could be established on a ground of principle, which would hold true of necessity for others as well as ourselves. My own judgment, again, is that it could not have been, and that the matter was best placed—as the Court in the *Griswold* case finally placed it— outside the reach of the law. But to range over the considerations that arise here, to survey the tradition of religious teaching and test the arguments in a principled way, would furnish work worthy of our supplest minds, and it would leave an intellectual record far more enriching than the collection of writings left to us in the *Griswold* case. And whether or not the sitting members of the Court were capable of weighing the question in these terms, it must nonetheless be said that these were the only terms on which the issues of principle in that case could properly have been settled.

THROUGH CASES like *Meyer, Loving, Skinner,* and *Griswold,* the Court schooled lawyers and judges to a rather coarse understanding of questions of privacy, rights, and the limits of law. If the exertions of the Court are judged here in a demanding way, they offer a melancholy portrait of the quality of mind cultivated by the Court on the road to *Roe* v. *Wade.* The Court which finally met the issue of abortion had not been prepared, either by its predecessors or by its profession, for a level of reflection that was adequate to the seriousness of the question it would have to address. Citing the usual litany of cases, Justice Blackmun would declare, as a fact long established, that "a right of personal privacy or a guarantee of certain areas or zones of privacy does exist under the Constitution."[41] Still, Blackmun was sufficiently aware of those earlier cases to know that "the Court's decisions recognizing a right of privacy also acknowledge that some state regulation in areas protected by that right is appropriate. . . . The privacy right, therefore, cannot be said to be absolute."[42] But if "rights" of privacy did not rule out all regulation by the state, Blackmun and six of his colleagues were nevertheless convinced that this "right of privacy" established in the earlier cases was "broad enough to encompass a woman's decision whether or not to terminate her pregnancy." The Court, in those earlier cases, had never articulated a "right" to do anything which was unjustified, and it certainly had never created an abstract "right to privacy" detached from the right to do something in particular (e.g., the "right" to provide one's children with an education in legitimate subjects). But now there was thought to be a

[41] *Roe* v. *Wade,* 410 U.S. 113, at 152 (1973).
[42] *Ibid.,* at 154.

presumptive "right" to an abortion, without any consideration of the question of whether abortion itself might be justified or unjustified. Justice Blackmun did of course concede, in a gesture of judiciousness, that the right was not unlimited: "[A] State may properly assert important interests in safeguarding health, in maintaining medical standards, *and in protecting potential life*. At some point in pregnancy, these respective interests become sufficiently compelling to sustain regulation of the factors that govern the abortion decision."[43]

But in no subsequent case would Blackmun vote to uphold any effort on the part of a state to protect "potential life," and it is arguable that his response to these cases was already foretold by the fact that he chose to define the life of the fetus as nothing more than "potential life." In the contest between the interests declared by a woman (an "actual life") and the interests asserted on behalf of a fetus (merely a "potential life") the enduring disposition of Justice Blackmun was to subordinate the interests of the "potential" life. Blackmun's decision was predicated, after all, on the premise that the beginning of human life was an inscrutable religious question. On that premise, the law was incapable of knowing whether the being within the womb was a human being, who had all the claims to the protection of law that vested in human beings. How, then, could Justice Blackmun let the interests of a *real* person be outweighed by the interests of a "being" whose nature, he professed, he could not know?

If one began by assuming that an abortion did not do harm to any "person," then it was far easier to conclude that there is a presumptive right to an abortion, just as there would be a presumptive right to have cosmetic surgery or any other medical operation that was morally indifferent. But that assumption was governed by the premise that the fetus is no more than a "potential" life, and the critical question was whether that premise itself could claim any principled ground of justification. For Blackmun, the question "When does human life begin?" was ultimately a religious question and, therefore, it was a question he could place beyond the domain in which evidence and argument may be judged by the canons of principled reasoning. Since he knew no better, that conclusion was his destiny. But for those who have been tutored in a more demanding school, the question is, What judgment do we reach on the matter of abortion when we come to that problem with an awareness of the difference between religious faith and *moral* argument? How do we judge the decision of the Court in *Roe* v. *Wade* if our understanding is informed—as the understanding

[43] *Ibid*. Emphasis added.

of the Court was not—by an awareness of the properties and requirements of a moral proposition? Those who have had the patience to follow me through these pages will discover, I think, that every implication we have drawn from the logic of morals bears on this matter of abortion in one way or another, either in framing the question properly, as a moral question, or in bringing it finally to the point of judgment.

XVI

THE QUESTION OF ABORTION AND THE
DISCIPLINE OF MORAL REASONING

Anyone in America who writes these days about abortion must take account of the landmark decision of the Supreme Court in *Roe* v. *Wade*;[1] and in estimating the "quality of mind" manifested by the Court, he would have to regard that profundity which stands near the beginning of Justice Blackmun's opinion for the majority: "Pregnancy often comes more than once to the same woman, and . . . if man is to survive, [pregnancy] will always be with us."[2] One becomes aware instantly that one is in the presence of no ordinary mind. Justice Blackmun's opinion reached, with this memorable passage, its philosophic acme. In the balance of the opinion—which is to say, in the parts that sought to settle the substantive rights and wrongs of the issue—Blackmun's opinion achieved that distance from any rigorous philosophic and moral reasoning which has become typical of the Supreme Court in our own time.

Blackmun's judgment rested on the conviction that the Court "need not resolve the difficult question of when life begins. When those trained in the respective disciplines of medicine, philosophy, and theology are unable to arrive at any consensus, the judiciary, at this point in the development of man's knowledge, is not in a position to speculate as to the answer."[3] Within the space of five lines, Justice Blackmun managed to incorporate three or four fallacies, not the least of which was the assumption that the presence of disagreement (or the absence of "consensus") indicates the absence of truth. That particular fallacy hinged in turn on his assumption that the question of when life begins—or, more accurately, the question "What is a human life, and when can it claim the protection of the law?"—is an inscrutably religious or "theological" matter. Blackmun reflected here the tendency in our public discourse to equate moral questions with matters of religious faith or private belief, which cannot be judged finally as true or false. It was as though the matter of abortion, as a profound moral question, was somehow cut off from the prospect of weighing evidence and testing arguments by the canons of principled reasoning. Justice

[1] 410 U.S. 113 (1973).
[2] *Ibid.*, at 125.
[3] *Ibid.*, 159.

Blackmun, at any rate, never subjected to the test of principled reasoning his own assumptions about the nature of the fetus and its standing in the eyes of the law. But if the arguments over abortion were tested in that way, we would discover that almost all of the "first principles" we have managed to extract here from the logic of morals would come to bear on that issue. And as they did, they would move us decisively to a judgment radically different from the one arrived at by Mr. Justice Blackmun in this case.

IT IS NOT surprising that the most prominent cliché in the public dispute over abortion would have been exposed as a fallacy by the very first step we took in drawing out the implications that arise from the logic of morals. The first thing that had to be understood about a moral proposition was that it is distinguished at the root from statements of merely personal, subjective taste: it is not consistent with the logic of morals to say, for example, that "X is wrong" and yet to insist at the same time that "people must be left free to do X or not, as it suits their own pleasure." This incompatibility between the logic of morals and the claims of personal preference was precisely the point that Lincoln brought out in his debate with Stephen Douglas:

> [W]hen Judge Douglas says he "don't care whether slavery is voted up or down," . . . he cannot thus argue logically if he sees anything wrong in it; . . . He cannot say that he would as soon see a wrong voted up as voted down. When Judge Douglas says that whoever, or whatever community, wants slaves, they have a right to have them, he is perfectly logical if there is nothing wrong in the institution; but if you admit that it is wrong, he cannot logically say that anybody has a right to do a wrong.[4]

Apparently, the moral lessons that were taught in the debate between Lincoln and Douglas have not become part of the education of political men and jurists of our own generation. And so it has become common for public figures to declare in public that they "personally disapprove" of abortion, but that abortion is a "deeply religious and moral question," and *therefore* that the laws should not impose an official policy on this matter. It may be, in most cases, that our public men and women have failed to recognize their own fallacies, but that recognition has not been lost on their constituents who have been opposed to abortion, even if they have not been schooled in moral philosophy.

---

[4] *The Collected Works of Abraham Lincoln*, ed. Roy P. Basler (New Brunswick: Rutgers University Press, 1953), vol. III, pp. 256-67. See also, *supra*, Chapter II, *passim*.

They have had wit enough to understand that their politicians would not be likely to declare that they are "morally opposed," say, to the torture of children, but that they are disinclined to interfere with the religious or moral views of parents. "It is not," they may aver, "that we are in favor of torture, but that we are 'pro-choice.' " That argument is not likely to be heard because its incoherence would be understood instantly: one could be "pro-choice" on the torture of children only if there were nothing in principle wrong or illegitimate about the torture of innocent people. The point is not grasped so quickly in relation to unborn children because they are not viewed as children, or "persons"; and so long as it is possible to mask from view the nature of the fetus, it is possible even for the most decent people to settle their judgments on abortion on grounds they would be too embarrassed to apply to any other question of consequence.

But the nature of the fetus is a problem that must be judged with the discipline of principled reason, and once again Lincoln would offer the best example of the way in which the question ought to be addressed. I had occasion earlier to recall that fragment which Lincoln had written for himself, in which he questioned an imaginary proponent of slavery about the grounds on which the slavery of black people could be justified:

> You say A. is white, and B. is black. It is color, then: the lighter having the right to enslave the darker? Take care. By this rule, you are to be slave to the first man you meet, with a fairer skin than your own.
>
> You do not mean *color* exactly?—You mean the whites are *intellectually* the superiors of the blacks, and therefore have the right to enslave them? Take care again. By this rule, you are to be slave to the first man you meet, with an intellect superior to your own.
>
> But, say you, it is a question of interest; and, if you can make it your *interest*, you have the right to enslave another. Very well. And if he can make it his interest, he has the right to enslave you.[5]

By the force of principled reasoning, in other words, there was nothing which could be said to justify the slavery of black men that would not apply to many whites as well. In the same way, it would be found that there is nothing which could be said for the sake of questioning the human nature of the human fetus that would not also disqualify, as "human" beings, many people who are moving about outside the womb. And if we find that there is no ground of principle

[5] *Ibid.*, vol. II, p. 222.

on which an unborn child can be regarded as anything less than a human being, then the arguments offered in favor of abortion will have to be judged by a far more demanding standard. For with the force of the same principled reasoning, the arguments that would now be required to justify the taking of fetal life would have to be at least as compelling as the kinds of arguments we demand on other occasions to justify the taking of human life. At that point, we would discover that arguments which have been regarded as quite plausible by large sections of our public may be exposed as either vacuous or embarrassing once they are framed explicitly as justifications for the taking of *human* life.

BEHIND THE disposition in our own time to be more tolerant of abortion there seems to be an intuitive sense that the fetus, after all, does not really "look" like those beings around us we typically identify as "human"—the creatures who deliver lectures, repair plumbing, or run to first base. The fetus, in other words, does not speak; it does not work with its hands—indeed, at a certain stage it does not even appear to have hands—and it is not able to walk about on its own. But if the fetus lacks the power of oral expression, so do deaf mutes. If the fetus lacks arms or legs in its early stages, there are many people who have lost one or more of their arms or legs or who were born without power over their limbs. And yet, no one would suggest that these people lack features essential to their standing as human beings or that they have forfeited their claim to live. The fetus, of course, would not have an articulate sense of itself, and it would not display those stable habits which reveal the mark of a distinct "character." But there are also many adults who are not in possession of themselves, as we would say, and who are not competent to manage their own interests. Their condition does not seem to elicit contempt in our society; if anything, their infirmity seems to call out for a special concern and protection.

There are children, as we know, who were born with flippers where their arms should have been, and so it is arguable that they do not "look" the way human beings are supposed to look. But this example serves to remind us that "looks" are thoroughly irrelevant to the question in principle here. There was a time, not all that long ago, when many Americans did not think that blacks "looked" like real human beings. As Roger Wertheimer recalls, even men who were otherwise decent and educated regarded the black slave as "some sort of demiperson, a blathering beast of burden,"[6] somewhere between a

---

[6] Roger Wertheimer, "Understanding the Abortion Argument, *Philosophy and Public Affairs* (Fall 1971), pp. 67-95, at 84.

human being and a monkey. The question, however, is not what the organism "looks" like, but what it is. The embryo may not look like the average undergraduate—some people may even think it looks like a tadpole—but it is never the equivalent of a tadpole even when it "looks" like one. That apparently formless mass is already "programmed" with the instructions that will make its tissues the source of specialized functions and aptitudes discriminably different from the organs and talents of tadpoles. This "tadpole" is likely to come out with hands and feet and with a capacity to conjugate verbs. Fortunately, our knowledge of embryology has advanced beyond the state at which it was left by Aristotle, and it is no longer even quaint to suppose that the human offspring begins as a vegetable and becomes an "animal" before it ascends to the condition of a "rational" being. Over the last twenty years, embryology has shown us just how clearly it is possible to recognize, in the zygote or embryo, the genetic composition that defines a unique being. But these recent advances have merely confirmed the ancient recognition that human beings cannot give birth to horses, cows, or monkeys. As we were reminded by André Hellegers, the late, noted fetologist, all species are identified biologically by their genetic composition, and by that measure the offspring of *Homo sapiens* cannot be anything other than *Homo sapiens*. Daniel Robinson has remarked on this point that

> for a being to be a human being, it is necessary that its genetic composition be drawn from the gene-pool of homo sapiens. It is further necessary that this genetic composition be of such a nature as to sustain that form of biological maturation which culminates in the unique biochemistry and gross anatomy of homo sapiens. Neither of these necessary criteria is satisfied by ducks or fish. The first criterion may be met by certain kinds of "growths," but not the second. . . .[7]

The fetus may be a *potential* doctor, a *potential* lawyer, or a *potential* cab driver; but he cannot be considered merely a *potential* human being, for at no stage of his existence could he have been anything else. That is also why it is futile to pick out phases in the development of an embryo or fetus and suggest that the offspring is more human, say, at nine months than it is at nine months and a day. The process

[7] Daniel N. Robinson, "Reflections on the Rights of Fetuses and Other Animals," paper presented at the meetings of the American Political Science Association, Washington D.C., September 4, 1977, p. 6. The argument set forth in that paper has been published in part of Professor Robinson's book, *Psychology and Law* (New York: Oxford University Press, 1980), ch. 6.

of development is continuous; each step along the way will bring a further articulation of what is built into the nature of the offspring. But at no point will the fetus *acquire* features that are essential to its standing as a human being. The force of that proposition seems to strike us more fully after birth, for we are not inclined to suggest that people cease to be human when they suffer the loss or impairment of these faculties. People may lose their breath with the collapse of a lung, or lose their consciousness with a blow to the head; they may even suffer a permanent loss of memory and speech. But our inclination has been to revive these people and remedy their disabilities where we can, and we have presumed all the while that we are ministering to injured humans, not merely to creatures who have suddenly become subhuman.

The stages in fetal development cannot be taken, then, as landmarks along the path by which a nonhuman creature turns into a human. What we have come to know more precisely about the maturing of the embryo and the fetus tends to point up for us just how early the offspring manifests those properties which are widely identified with its human nature. Between the eighteenth and twentieth weeks of pregnancy, the fetal heartbeat can be heard with a simple stethoscope. After only twelve weeks, the structure of the brain is complete, and the heartbeat can be monitored with electrocardiographic techniques. By this time, as Bernard Nathanson has pointed out, the fetus is "a fully developed, functioning human body in miniature, 3 inches in length. . . . Its fingerprints and sole and palm lines are by now unique for each individual and remain for permanent identification throughout life."[8] At the ninth or tenth week, the fetus has "local reflexes," such as swallowing or squinting or moving its tongue. At the eighth week, fingers and toes are discernible (which would indicate, by recent records of performance, that the fetus would have about all the equipment that is necessary to manage the investment portfolio of my college). But if we go back as far as the second or third week after the fertilized egg has been implanted in the uterine wall, when the embryo is merely an elongated substance about one-third of an inch long— and when, as Paul Ramsey remarks, the woman may begin to wonder whether she is pregnant—the most important "decisions" have already been made. In rudimentary form there is already a structural differentiation of head, eyes, ears, and brain, digestive tract, heart and bloodstream, simple kidneys and liver, and two bulges where arms and legs will appear.

[8] Bernard Nathanson, *Aborting America* (New York: Doubleday, 1979), p. 203.

365

From the earliest moments, therefore, as Paul Ramsey has written, we become aware of the presence of "immanent principles and constitutive elements." Not only is the humanity of the offspring established, but the genetic uniqueness of the individual has been determined. "In all essential respects," says Ramsey, "the individual is whoever he is going to become from the moment of impregnation. . . . Thereafter, his subsequent development cannot be described as his becoming someone he now is not. . . . Genetics teaches us that we were from the beginning what we essentially still are in every cell and in every generally human attribute and in every individual attribute. . . ." For that reason, Ramsey adds, "any unique sanctity or dignity we have cannot be because we are any larger than the period at the end of a sentence."[9]

At this point, of course, the argument against abortion would summon a large measure of moral imagination. Left to a common sense untutored by principle, it would be hard to treat the microscopic zygote as a "human being" having the same claims upon our concern as the humans we see all about us. Could the fetus, after all, have the same "moral presence" in our lives as an Immanuel Kant or a Mother Teresa? And yet, we must be clear that there is no disposition to claim for the fetus the special esteem that may be won through professional achievement and good works; nor is there any effort to claim privileges or rights that are unsuitable to the condition of an embryo. No one would suggest that a fetus could have a claim to fill the Chair of Logic at one of our universities; we would not wish quite yet to seek its advice on anything important; and we should probably not regard him as eligible to exercise the vote in any state other than Massachusetts. All of these rights or privileges would be inappropriate to the condition or attributes of the fetus. But nothing that renders him unqualified for these special rights would diminish in any way the most elementary right that could be claimed for any human being, *or even for an animal*: the right not to be injured or killed without the rendering of reasons that satisfy the strict standards of a "justification." Our society already prescribes punishment for the wanton killing or torturing of animals, and as Daniel Robinson has argued, we may condemn the sadistic killing of animals—the willingness to inflict pain for nothing more than one's own pleasure—quite as surely as we may

[9] Paul Ramsey, "Reference Points in Deciding about Abortion," in John Noonan (ed.), *The Morality of Abortion* (Cambridge: Harvard University Press, 1970), pp. 60-100, at 66-67.

condemn the taking of human life for the sake merely of pleasure or convenience.[10]

In this elementary claim not to be injured or killed "without justification," the moral claim of the fetus cannot be less than that of any other person. The parity of its claim would be quite indifferent to distinctions in intellectual or physical development that would separate the fetus, say, from an Immanuel Kant or a Dick Butkus. No one should suppose that the tall and articulate are somehow "more human" than those who are short and cryptic; nor may it be supposed that any rights we may have to the protections of the law may be proportioned to our height or to the breadth of our vocabularies. Of course, we could hardly expect that any creature in its formative stages would be as dignified or impressive, as cultivated or attractive, as the same creature in the flowering of its maturity, when it is established in its competence and in command of its powers. But if we understand that our fundamental claims in the law are not proportioned to our size or to our gifts of language—that our right not to be harmed without justification is unaffected by our weakness or strength, by our "normality" or eccentricity, or even by our thoroughgoing disability— then we are compelled to judge the taking of a nascent life with the same severity of principle by which we would measure the justifications that are brought forth for the taking of other human lives. Our senses, we know, may resist at first the comparison of this nascent life with the mobile figures, endowed with mass and wit, whom we see around us. And yet, we would have then but another occasion in which a cultivated understanding of principle must summon our imagination to correct the untutored judgment of our senses.

I am reminded of a scene from Graham Greene's *The Third Man*, where the two protagonists meet in a compartment on the big Ferris wheel in Vienna. It is immediately after the Second World War, with the city under military occupation, and one of these men, Harry Lime, is being sought by the military police for his part in a ring selling adulterated penicillin on the black market. His friend, Rollo Martins, has been pressed by the British police to lend them his help. Through an intermediary, Martins has been able to arrange a meeting with his friend at an amusement park, and when they are alone together in the cabin of the Ferris wheel, Martins asks, "Have you ever visited the children's hospital? Have you ever seen any of your victims?":

Harry took a look at the toy landscape below and came away from the door. . . . "Victims?," he asked. "Don't be melodramatic,

[10] See Robinson, *supra*, note 7.

Rollo. Look down there," he went on, pointing through the window at the people moving like black flies at the base of the Wheel. "Would you really feel any pity if one of those dots stopped moving—for ever? If I said you can have twenty thousand pounds for every dot that stops, would you really, old man, tell me to keep my money—without hesitation? Or would you calculate how many dots you could afford to spare?

For that distance in space between the top of the Ferris wheel and the ground, one could substitute the distance in time that separates the embryonic "dot" from the offspring that comes out of the womb. And almost as surely as one dot will turn into a visible child when the wheel completes its circuit and the cabin returns to the ground, that embryonic "dot" will turn into a being that we would see, quite surely, as a child. In over eighty percent of all cases, barring abortion, a pregnancy will come to full term, and the infant, when it emerges, cannot be anything but a child.

BUT IF the offspring of *Homo sapiens* cannot be anything other than human, we would still not establish that it would be wrong under all circumstances to take the life of a human fetus. As we have seen, the proper form of the categorical proposition here is not that "it is always wrong to kill," but that it must be wrong, under all conditions, to kill "without justification." Killing may find a ground of justification when it is undertaken as a necessary effort to resist an unjustified, lethal assault. In the case of abortion, however, that ground of justification is almost entirely absent, since the fetus can be the source of no intended harm to its mother. The child is without intention or malice; it is animated by no *mens rea*, or "guilty mind." Its presence may be perceived by many people as a threat to the interests of the mother, and it cannot be gainsaid that the advent of a child, at an awkward time, may bring severe costs, financial and psychic. But neither can it be gainsaid that the child is wholly and inescapably "innocent"— innocent of any intention to harm, and innocent of any responsibility for creating the "problem" that inspires the interest in abortion.

That ineffaceable fact cannot help but burden the case for abortion even in those cases—exceedingly rare today—where the life of the mother might be threatened by the pregnancy. In those instances, at least, the life of the fetus is posed against the life of the mother; the interests at stake are on the same plane of gravity. This is not so evidently the case, however, in most of the abortions that are now performed, in such massive volume, in the United States. That is not to say that there is anything trivial about the interests that seem to be threatened by an unwanted pregnancy. It is to say, rather, that those interests must be gauged with a new severity when they are weighed seriously as grounds of justification for the taking of human life.

No one could deny, for example, that the addition of another child to a household may strain the circumstances of a poor family or impose serious costs on the "psychological health" of the parents. No one who has seen a mother drawn to her limits by the demands of raising children would make light of the physical costs and emotional burdens that an added child may bring. Nor could one doubt the resentment that may be fostered in a family by the advent of an "unwanted" child. But we need not close our eyes to these things—or belittle in any way the hardships they may involve—in order to recognize that they cannot stand on the same plane with the kinds of justifications we demand in other instances for the taking of human life. The finances of the family or the psychological condition of the parents may be ravaged just as much by the addition of aged relatives to the home, or by the crashing arrival at puberty of the children who are already on the scene. The condition of the family could obviously be eased in these instances by "doing away with" the aged relatives or the spirited teenagers, and from the standpoint of strict justice, I suppose, one might be more justified in removing the 13-year-old who has already become the terror of the household rather than the offspring who has not had a chance yet to show any malevolence.[11]

A child may not be "wanted," but we have never thought, on other occasions, that people lose their claim to live when they become unwelcome or unwanted. By that measure we would have lost Harold Stassen in his leaner years, to say nothing of Charles de Gaulle and Billy Martin. Not too long ago a court in Connecticut noted with sympathy that, as a result of bearing a child, "the working or student mother frequently must curtail or end her employment or educational opportunities," and the unmarried mother may be condemned to suffer shame.[12] In the estimate of the court, those interests were apparently

---

[11] The same answer in principle would have to be offered in response to the so-called population problem—a "problem" regarded with apocalyptic vision by some biologists, but which most economists do not seem to take seriously. A telling statement as to why economists do not treat this matter as a genuine "crisis" can be found in Julian L. Simon, *The Ultimate Resource* (Princeton: Princeton University Press, 1981). But even if the population crisis were more pressing, there is no ground of principle that could command us to solve the problem by killing the newest members of the population rather than the oldest.

[12] *Abele v. Markle*, 342 F. Supp. 800, at 802 (1972).

grave enough to warrant the freedom to choose an abortion. And yet, if the proposition were put to us explicitly, as a matter of principle, we would not consider for a moment that people may have a license to kill those who stand in the way of their education or the advancement of their careers. As for the matter of taking life for the sake of avoiding embarrassment or shame, the mere statement of the claim should be enough, among people of ordinary sensibility, to generate its own reproach.

The willingness to entertain arguments of this kind reflects a certain distraction of mind; and yet, with the recent doctrines of the courts, distraction has been converted into a medical condition, which becomes the source of even more extravagant claims. Justice Blackmun declared, for the Supreme Court, that the interest of the state in protecting "potential life" may be overridden, at any stage in the pregnancy, "when it is necessary . . . for the preservation of the life or health of the mother."[13] But he made it clear very soon that the "health" of the mother would encompass what has loosely been described these days as mental or "psychological health." As Justice Blackmun was to put it, the health of the mother would have to be estimated in a medical judgment that took into account "all factors—physical, emotional, psychological, and the woman's age—relevant to her well-being."[14] As John Noonan aptly remarked, it would be a rare case in which a physician willing to perform an abortion would not be persuaded that the "well-being" of the patient would indeed be served by an abortion that she herself had requested.[15]

The sovereign consideration, then, in cases of abortion was whether the woman simply "wanted" one. With this kind of license there would be no obstacle to carrying out abortions, not only past the first trimester, and not only up to the moment of birth: it would become clear very soon that a child who survived an abortion could legitimately be destroyed *if the presence of the living child would be a cause of distress for the mother.* In one way or another, the courts would manage to render ineffectual legislation which forbade the abortion of fetuses that might be viable or which established an obligation for physicians to preserve the lives of children who survived the abortions.[16] In *Floyd* v. *Anders*, Judge Haynesworth refused to regard as a "viable" child,

---

[13] See Blackmun in *Roe* v. *Wade*, 410 U.S. 113, at 164-65.

[14] *Doe* v. *Bolton*, 410 U.S. 179, at 192.

[15] John T. Noonan, Jr., *A Private Choice* (New York: Free Press, 1979), p. 12.

[16] See *Commonwealth* v. *Edelin* (Mass.), 359 N.E. 2d 4 (1976); *Floyd* v. *Anders*, 440 F. Supp. 535 (1977); *Planned Parenthood* v. *Danforth*, 49 L. Ed. 2d 788 (1976); and *Colautti* v. *Franklin*, 58 L. Ed. 2d 596 (1979).

within the protection of the law, a fetus of seven months who had been treated and operated upon for twenty days after he had survived an abortion. For Judge Haynesworth, the medical facts about "viability" were dissolved by the legal premises established in *Roe* v. *Wade*: a fetus that was not wanted by its mother would not be considered "viable" because it would not be regarded as a "person" with claims to the protection of the law.

In other words, the right to an abortion would be taken to mean *the right to a dead fetus*, not merely the removal of the child from the womb. After all, the prospect of giving a child up for adoption has always been present, and there has been no want of people in recent years who have been willing to come forward and adopt even children who are supposedly "hard to place" (children who may be black or retarded or infirm). If the right of the mother entailed nothing more than the right to be rid of a child she did not "want," then the solution to an unwanted pregnancy could have been found rather easily without the need for a lethal operation. But there would be women who would find unsettling the prospect of carrying a child to term and then giving over the fruit of their own bodies to someone else. In this paradoxical morality there was a curious assertion of "property rights": it was somehow easier to kill the fetus in the womb than to give away to others what was recognizably a child—and recognizably, also, a child of one's "own." The indulgence that has been accorded to this argument is a measure of how far the law has receded from moral judgment for the sake of honoring the claims of psychological "distress."

We discovered in an earlier chapter why the teachings of utilitarianism could never supply the substance of a genuine categorical proposition in morals. What is good or just can never be equated with "that which makes most people happy." The doctrine of the "greatest happiness of the greatest number" merely added another item to the inventory of spurious categorical propositions in morals, and it can be exposed as a spurious proposition simply by considering whether it is possible to satisfy the maxim even while engaging in acts that are in principle unjust. The argument over "psychological health" now offers an obverse statement of the same fallacy which afflicts utilitarianism. In this case, the spurious proposition would be that it is wrong or unjust to do that "which causes anyone distress or unhappiness." And the proposition would be embarrassed by the same recognition that it is possible to comply with its terms while performing acts that are irredeemably wrong. There are people, as we know, who find sadistic pleasure in the torture of humans and animals. They may even

371

feel an intense frustration and psychic pain if their cravings here cannot be satisfied. And yet it could not be the responsibility of the law to gratify their appetites. As Daniel Robinson remarked, "A man who has a need to torture and destroy has an *inhuman* need which it is society's task to eliminate, not to satisfy."[17]

For that reason, it could not settle any question about abortion to report that the birth of a child would induce the most severe distress and that it would impair the "psychological health" of the mother. The decisive question in principle must be whether the mother would have a justification on other grounds for taking the life of the fetus. If she does not, there is nothing in her state of distress that would supply that justification. Even if she were subject to an enduring depression, we would still have to know whether the despair she feels arises from the fact that she is being frustrated in her desire to take a life that she has no justification otherwise for taking. If her despair can be relieved only by destroying a life that she has no warrant in destroying, that is a despair the law cannot be obliged to remedy.

On this problem we often find pertinent stories in the advice columns of the daily newspapers. Not too long ago Ann Landers carried a report of a young man who had fallen into a deep depression—and even suffered serious acne—when his girlfriend broke off their relationship. The mother of the girl reported that her daughter was being harassed continually by the former boyfriend's mother, who was naturally alarmed about the state of her son. In his depression, the young man was wasting away, and it was not beyond reckoning that he would move himself to the edge of suicide. The mother warned the former girlfriend that she would be responsible for the "consequences" if she remained adamant in her rejection of this lad. Ann Landers wrote back to the mother of the young woman and declared, quite aptly, that her daughter was not to be used as a skin remedy: she was not to be assigned against her will to this fellow, even if he were suffering the deepest psychological torment and even if he threatened suicide. That he might be willing, in his distraction, to take his own life for a trivial reason could not furnish a justification for abridging the freedom of the woman and making her the possession, in effect, of this young man. If those conclusions are inescapable, why should the same point not be equally clear in the matter of abortion? If the prospect of death was radically insufficient to justify the restriction of liberty in the case of the former girlfriend, why should the "distress"

[17] Robinson, "Reflections," *supra*, note 7, p. 10. Emphasis in original.

of a pregnant woman be sufficient not merely to restrict the freedom of the fetus, but to justify the taking of its life?

THE COMMON THREAD of fallacy that runs through most of these arguments for abortion is that people are willing to accept, as a justification for destroying fetal life, "facts" that have no bearing on whether the fetus *deserves* to live or die. That is to say, we find in most of these arguments an expression of the problem that was addressed in Chapter VIII:

> No moral conclusion can be entailed merely by facts or by factual propositions of a nonmoral nature. Moral propositions are grounded ultimately in facts or truths, but they can be derived only from the necessary truth which affirms the existence of morals or explains its essential logic.

The fallacy addressed by this passage is perhaps the most common mistake in moral reasoning, and in the argument over abortion it keeps expressing itself in a succession of forms. Apart from the instances I have already reviewed, it may be found in the inclination to argue that human life begins when certain vital attributes are first manifested: e.g., the onset of "quickening," in which the mother may feel the movement of the child within her (usually between the twelfth and sixteenth weeks); the detection of electrical activity in the fetal brain (as early as the eighth week); or the threshold of "viability," when the fetus can be kept alive outside the womb of the mother.

André Hellegers once said of "quickening" that it is "a phenomenon of maternal perception rather than a fetal achievement."[18] The child is the source of its own movement two or three weeks earlier. The child may become a more vivid presence to the mother when she feels its movement, but nothing in that feeling marks any transformation in the nature of the fetus itself. Only thirty years ago the conviction was still held in the medical profession that there was no electrical activity in the fetal brain through most of gestation. But in 1951, two researchers in Japan managed to take electroencephalographic (EEG) readings on fetuses between three and seven months; in the late 1950's, studies in the United States produced EEG tracings as early as forty-three days.[19] It should be plain, on reflection, that it is not the nature of the human fetus which has been changing over the past thirty years:

---

[18] André Hellegers, "Fetal Development," *Theological Studies* (March 1970), pp. 3-9, at 8.
[19] Nathanson, *supra*, note 8, p. 199.

fetuses are not developing activity in their brains earlier than they had in the past. The change, rather, has been in the sensitivity of the electronic equipment that has made the measurements possible. With further refinements, we may receive readings even earlier, but that will not mean that fetuses are becoming "human" much earlier.

It has been assumed altogether too casually that an ineffable something called "consciousness" is necessary to the definition of a "person." Those who have proffered this standard have not been luminous in explaining what precisely this "consciousness" is supposed to be "conscious" of, but they seem to be sure—without any testing—that everyone running about the streets, well outside the womb, is in ample possession of this "consciousness." But there are many young people (to say nothing of adults) who have not yet come to an understanding of the principled ground of their own acts and motivations. If we were to measure the "humanity" of "persons" by the degree to which they have attained "consciousness" of the highest implications of their own natures—their natures as *moral* beings—we would find that a large portion of our population would fail to qualify as persons. If we were to test for the presence of this "consciousness," it would be appropriate to establish whether the subject had an awareness of the rudiments of moral reasoning. We may assume that the fetus lacks that awareness, but we would not be warranted in assuming that everyone else is in command of it. To be strict about the matter, we would have to apply the test to the putative "persons" who are ordering and performing abortions. Women in a comatose state have given birth, and in those situations, as Daniel Robinson has pointed out, the pregnant mother would display fewer "psychological attributes" than those already found in prenatal human beings. If the test of personhood is to be found in "consciousness," we cannot infer consciousness from the condition of being pregnant; therefore, we cannot conclude, on the evidence of pregnancy alone, that a pregnant woman is a "person" who is competent to order surgery for herself or others.[20]

---

[20] See Robinson, *Psychology and Law, supra,* note 7, p. 186. Cf. L.W. Sumner, *Abortion and Moral Theory* (Princeton: Princeton University Press, 1981), pp. 197-98. Even some of our most accomplished writers may fail at times to recognize the same fallacy when it is arrayed in other terms, and it is curious in this respect to see the same mistake reproduced by a scholar as seasoned as Alan Gewirth. Gewirth has offered a defense for abortion on the assumption that the pregnant woman is a "purposive agent" (though, as Robinson has shown, that kind of inference could not be drawn from the mere fact of pregnancy). Gewirth assumed, with the same license, that a fetus must lack purpose while it lacks a "physically separate existence." On the strength of these premises Gewirth concluded that the fetus has no rights which can be protected against the mother, because the interests of a "purposive agent" would be "drastically subor-

Of course, the point of these exercises in our public discourse has not been to arrive at an "empirical" measure of when the fetus makes a transition from nonhuman to human. As we have already seen, there can be no serious problem about the genetic provenance of this offspring. The dispute really is a *moral* one about the point at which a fetus is sufficiently close to the nature of an "authentic" human being that it can claim those protections we accord to human beings. Once we are clear on the nature of the question, it should be clear to us that none of these markings or attributes, none of these readings from the brain or heart, can be invested with that kind of moral significance. Whether a fetus *deserves* the protection of law, whether it may be killed without the need for a justification, cannot depend on anything as lacking in moral significance as the current state of the art in amplifier science.

---

dinated [in that case] to a minimal possessor" of purposes. There is, of course, a difference between the presence or absence of purposes. But what is there, in that difference, which establishes a *justification* for the taking of life? By neglecting to raise that question, Gewirth joined a long tradition of writers who have been willing to draw moral conclusions—in this case, moral conclusions with lethal results—from facts that are wholly lacking in moral significance. Professor Gewirth has constructed the groundwork of a moral philosophy with painstaking care, and yet nothing in that structure of reason apparently made it relevant to consider whether the life being taken in abortion was "innocent" life, or whether it "deserved" to be destroyed. Did it make a difference, after all, if the fetus posed no threat to the life or health of the mother, or if it were animated by no intention to harm? And does a "purposive agent" establish, preeminently, his claim to "rights" when he places himself serenely beyond these kinds of moral questions? See Gewirth, *Reason and Morality* (Chicago: University of Chicago Press, 1978), pp. 142-43, 159-60.

What is said in this vein would have to raise similar doubts about the argument offered by Professor Bruce Ackerman in *Social Justice and the Liberal State* (New Haven: Yale University Press, 1980): viz., that a fetus cannot be a person within the protection of the law because the fetus cannot be a "citizen of a liberal state." In order to be a citizen of a liberal state, a person must be able "to play a part in the dialogic and behavioral transactions that constitute a liberal polity" (p. 127). It is one thing to note the capacity for moral reasoning that distinguishes human beings; it is quite another to say that the right of any person to live or die must depend on his "articulateness." By that measure, we might imperil the steelworker who is content to sit mute by his television or, for that matter, anyone who does not show a facility for participating in the public discourse on politics and law. We may reduce the circle of protected human beings mainly to professors and cab drivers. Ackerman admits, by the way, that a day-old infant has no more capacity than a fetus to engage in the dialogue of a liberal state. But it is revealing that he would not seek to protect the infant on any ground that depends on the dignity or worth of the child itself. Ackerman would allow infants to be protected by the state only because the failure to protect them might deprive certain "infertile" people of the pleasure of having children through adoption (p. 129). In this curious twist, however, the infant would be protected only by treating it as a commodity or an article of property that certain consumers might be deprived of unjustly.

375

What can be said in this respect about the tests of "quickening" and brain waves can be said in equal measure about the standard of "viability." In *Roe* v. *Wade*, Justice Blackmun suggested that the fetus becomes "viable" somewhere between the twenty-fourth and twenty-eighth weeks, and he indicated that the state would have a stronger "logical and biological justification" to act, at this point, for the sake of protecting "potential life."[21] He would subsequently make clear, however, that this "justification" would never be sufficiently compelling in any case to override the interest of the mother in having her abortion. In marking off the stages of pregnancy, it would appear that Blackmun's concern was not to guide legislatures in protecting fetal life, but to establish a period, early in pregnancy, where the interest of the state in protecting nascent life could be denied altogether. With the standard of viability, Blackmun could declare—as a kind of judicial assertion of fact—that the fetus does not have "the capability of meaningful life outside the mother's womb," and therefore it cannot claim the protections of law. At the same time Justice Blackmun was handing down his pronouncements on biology, Dr. Bernard Nathanson was a member of the board of the National Abortion Rights Action League (which he had helped found in 1969) and a former director of the largest abortion clinic in the world. Nathanson, a trained gynecologist, had presided over an estimated 60,000 abortions before his reflection moved him to weigh the arguments on abortion much in the way we have weighed them here and he came to the judgment finally that he had been mistaken. Writing later about *Roe* v. *Wade*, Nathanson observed that Blackmun's benchmark of twenty-four weeks was "a line unknown to obstetrics." It was evident to an observer like Nathanson that Blackmun and his colleagues had framed a momentous decision without even bothering to draw on the most informed technical understanding available to them. As Nathanson pointed out, the words of the Court were "not only inaccurate but obsolete even as they came out of Mr. Blackmun's typewriter. The concept [of viability] is fluid and is constantly being pushed backward."[22]

And in fact, not long after Blackmun's opinion for the Court, doctors at Georgetown University Hospital and the medical school of the University of Colorado made some notable gains in advancing the point of viability. Through the application mainly of more intensive care, and with little help from new technology, the staff managed to improve dramatically the survival rate for fetuses weighing 1,000 grams (less than 3 pounds). Up to that time, only about 10 percent

---

[21] 410 U.S. 113, at 160, 163.
[22] Nathanson, *supra*, note 8, pp. 207-208.

of these premature children had survived, but now doctors were saving 60-75 percent of these infants. At last report, they were seeking to extend the same rate of success to babies weighing 800 grams (less than 2 pounds). Within the next five to ten years, it is regarded nearly as certain that premature babies may be sustained outside the womb at a weight of less than 500 grams. Beyond that, the new technology may make it possible to nurture infants of 100 grams (1/4 pound) and 50 grams (1/8 pound). As Nathanson has commented, "This is no Huxleyan peyote dream; this is a medical certainty." What stands behind this certainty is technology, which has produced new equipment, along with the specialty of "neo-natology" in caring for the newborn. Nathanson has ticked off the mechanical supports for this new system of care: "sophisticated incubators with efficient oxygenators, humidifiers, temperature controls, cardiac-monitoring systems, artificial respirators, ventilators, methods for determining arterial blood gases, complex new intravenous feeding solutions and equipment for administering them, and an infinite variety of new diagnostic techniques such as ultrasonography and computerized X-ray scanning. . . ."[23]

If the definition of "human" life were to depend, then, on the point of "viability," we would again fall into the technological fallacy: in this case, the definition of a human being would be made to rest on the current state of the art in incubator science. And if *Roe* v. *Wade* really accepted the notion that fetuses may be protected by the law when they are "viable," then that decision contains the grounds for its own dissolution as our technology makes it possible to rescue these threatened fetuses almost at the very beginning. Work has already been done toward the development of artificial placentas, and Nathanson sees the possibilities for the rescue of embryos prefigured in the remarkable advent of fiber optics and microsurgery: the blastocyst has been sighted at the point of implantation, and its age and health identified; with microsurgery, "the tiniest of blood vessels can be repaired, the gossamer strands of the retina can be woven together, and the tiny pituitary gland and its vessels can be explored and manipulated."[24] What remains, then, as far as the embryo is concerned, is the development of "an instrument of sufficient delicacy that it can be threaded through the hysteroscope . . . and can then pluck [the new being] off the wall of the uterus like a helicopter rescuing a stranded mountain climber."[25]

Would these new developments make some pregnant women more

[23] *Ibid.*, pp. 280-81.
[24] *Ibid.*, p. 282.
[25] *Ibid.*

amenable to obligations they have resisted in the past? What if it were possible to remove the embryo in the first few weeks of pregnancy, with a thoroughly safe operation, when the being removed from the mother may not impress her so vividly as a "child"? But if the law could ask that much, why could it not reasonably ask her to carry the fetus to the current threshold of viability? The law could tenably invoke the principle of the "obligation to rescue" and point out that the mother has a unique capacity to preserve the life of a separate, living human until others would be able to take over the responsibility for nurturing the child. Of course, that is precisely what the law had done when it expected the mother to carry the child to term, even though she might later have been moved to give the child up for adoption. If Mr. Justice Blackmun and his colleagues saw no justification for imposing this obligation on the mother, they are not likely to alter their judgment if technology merely makes it possible to rescue the child earlier. They are more likely to follow the lead of Judge Haynesworth and regard the medical evidence as a collection of facts that must simply be blocked from judicial view by the presence of a new, decisive jural postulate: viz., the "right" of the mother to dispose of the fetus for any reason she regards as sufficient.

It would be a mistake to suppose, then, that the standard of "viability" invoked by the Court ever really depended on biological facts. Behind the standard of viability stood nothing more than an immense political fact or a political persuasion which could be stripped to this proposition: that the fetus could not claim the dignity of a human being and the protection of the law until it could establish itself as a separate being, independent of its mother. Legions of citizens unadorned with judicial robes have managed to figure out for themselves that the child who emerges from the womb is still very much dependent for its care on those around him. The man on the street has often had the wit, also, to recognize that dependency has never been a justifiable ground for homicide. Apparently without even being aware of the proposition they were affirming, Justice Blackmun and his colleagues inverted the lesson taught by Rousseau: Might would indeed be the source of Right. The fact that the mother had power over the child—the fact that the child was dependent and at her mercy—was enough to invest the mother with the authority to do with this nascent life what she would. Now, contrary to Rousseau, power *was* the source of its own justification, and strength generated its own moral warrants. Once again, the Court fell into the fallacy of drawing a moral conclusion (the right to take a life) from a fact utterly without moral significance (the weakness or dependence of the child).

The Court discovered, in other words, that novel doctrines could be wrought by reinventing old fallacies. And the Court turned out to be more revolutionary than even Justice Blackmun suspected. For one thing, it sought to overturn the moral understanding that had been settled for generations in regard to the weak and infirm. The restraints of the law had been extended to parents in the past precisely because children were powerless and dependent, and therefore vulnerable to the strength of their parents. Their relative helplessness, then, provided the occasion for their defense. But now, by the explicit holding of the Supreme Court, the dependence and weakness of the offspring established its lack of dignity as a separate being and its lack of standing to receive the protection of the law.

In reversing the ancient understanding of Might and Right, the Court was striking at the logic of morals itself, and this new teaching of the courts could be secured only when the public discourse safely purged itself of any lingering attachment to the habits of moral reasoning. The "progress" of the public in accepting abortion could be measured, then, by the extent to which the public seemed to absorb certain "neutral" or "practical" arguments which promised to resolve the question on grounds that were divorced from any convictions of a "moral" nature. Two of the most prominent arguments in this vein were the argument for "leaving people free to follow their own moral convictions" and the plea, offered in the name of prudence, to rescue women from the hazards of illegal abortion by allowing physicians to perform abortions legally.

The first argument, of course, fell into the most fundamental error concerning morals—the reduction of moral questions to matters subjective belief or private taste. It became common, in our public discourse, to equate moral judgments with religious convictions, which could not be regarded as true or false for anyone but the person who held them. Justice Douglas once quoted approvingly a version of this argument, put out in the name of a group of psychiatrists. For all its reliance on the expertise of psychiatry, it could have been written just as well by a team of podiatrists. "We submit that [the issue of abortion] is insoluble, a matter of religious philosophy and religious principle and not a matter of fact. We suggest that those who believe abortion is murder need not avail themselves of it. On the other hand, we do not believe that such conviction should limit the freedom of those not bound by identical religious convictions. . . ."[26]

[26] "The Right to Abortion: A Psychiatric View," 218-19 (Group for the Advancement

If one were to indulge here the possibility that the lives taken in abortion are human lives, the preceding argument would reveal its own defect. If we found a group of parents who were willing to engage in the ritual sacrifice of their children, would we really have the law hold back from interference so long as the parents were claiming to act under the command of "religious" beliefs? This problem was actually addressed by the Supreme Court over a hundred years ago, when the Court refused to accept the right of a religious sect to engage in the far less lethal practice of polygamy. The case involved the Mormons, and after upholding legal restrictions on plural marriages, the Court went on to illustrate its point:

> Suppose one believed that human sacrifices were a necessary part of religious worship, would it be seriously contended that the civil government under which he lived could not interfere to prevent a sacrifice? Or if a wife religiously believed it was her duty to burn herself upon the funeral [pyre] of her husband, would it be beyond the power of the civil government to prevent her carrying her belief into practice?[27]

As we have already seen, there are compelling reasons in principle why we cannot permit an exemption, on the basis of religious belief, from the obligation to obey a valid law. Ironically, there has been much alarm of late about the emergence in our politics of groups like the Moral Majority, who bring an explicitly religious perspective to their judgment of public issues. But, for all the fears that have been stirred, none of these groups has sought to establish in the law a premise as radical as the one that has already been emplaced by the proponents of abortion: namely, that people may take the life of a human being, without any need to render a justification, if they merely profess their "belief" that the being is not human.

And yet, even the most zealous partisan of abortion would not give license to people to commit homicide at will, so long as they declared, as a matter of "religious belief," that Armenians or redheads or people with low scores on the Law School Aptitude Examination are not really "alive." Why, then, should we treat as any more plausible the claims of those who concede that they are destroying a *living* being, but who profess to "believe" that an offspring conceived of human parents is not "really" human while it is still in the womb? The dif-

---

of Psychiatry, vol. 7, pub. no. 75, 1969), cited in *Vuitch* v. *United States*, 401 U.S. 62, at 78-79n (1971).

   [27] *Reynolds* v. *United States*, 98 U.S. 145, at 166 (1878).

ference surely lies in the uncertainties that arise for many people about the life in the womb: we are evidently willing to honor professions of doubt about the offspring in the womb that we would never take seriously for a moment in regard to people who have moved beyond that dwelling. But then it should be even more apparent that this question does not pivot on religious belief. It must turn, instead, on the facts or considerations that make us more or less willing to regard the child in the womb as a human child. And if that is indeed the decisive point, it can be addressed only with the discipline of a principled argument: those who "believe" that the fetus is less than clearly human would have to bear the same burden of argument we would assign to anyone who would invoke the same kind of belief in regard to redheads, landlords, or auditors from the IRS.

THE PREEMINENT "practical" argument on abortion seeks to detach the issue from any moral ground of judgment and to recognize the practice of abortion as an irresistible "fact." In this view, there are several hundred thousand women in America who will be seeking abortions each year and who will have those operations regardless of what the law might forbid. If they are compelled to seek abortions covertly, the wealthy may be able to arrange, at a proper price, an operation performed in a respectable hospital by an established physician. Those who cannot afford the price may have to settle for the ministrations of paramedicals and midwives in the notorious "back room" abortions, where they may be hazarding their own lives. At one point, the partisans of legal abortion claimed that as many as 10,000 women each year lost their lives in these clandestine abortions. In short, then, the plea was that the law should not pass moral judgment in the face of a need so intensely felt and so desperately pursued. Rather, it should withdraw its prohibitions for the sake at least of saving the women who would be driven, incorrigibly, to risk their own lives in defiance of the law.

The answers that must be offered in response to this argument would arrange themselves in tiers, for they would raise a critical challenge over questions of fact as well as considerations of principle. The first thing that must be recognized is that the form of the argument advanced here would be instantly rejected as untenable if it were offered on any other matter of moral consequence. It might be contended, for example, that the laws which ban discrimination on the basis of race in the sale of private dwellings are very difficult to enforce, that many violations escape the notice of the law, and that the rich have more devices for evading the law than people who are not so well off. And yet, the response to this record has not been to seek the repeal of a law which large numbers of people seem determined to disobey, and which, as a practical matter, is enforced less strenuously on the wealthier classes. The response, rather, has been to demand ever more stringent laws and larger budgets to support the prosecution of these cases. The intractable question, of course, is whether there is a principle that justifies the laws on the books. If there is, then the *validity* of that principle cannot be affected in any way by showing that the laws are being widely disobeyed. At the most, statesmen would be cautioned to be prudent in enforcing the law until they could tutor the public in a more demanding sense of justice. But the flouting of the law cannot itself provide a moral justification for repealing the statute and pretending that the wrong we once condemned has ceased to be wrong.

Nor can our understanding of right and wrong be reduced, in principle, to that collection of maxims which the wealthy will find themselves powerless to evade. To turn the problem around, it requires a radical misunderstanding of the notion of "equality"—or a critical detachment of "equality" from any substantive moral sense—to claim on behalf of the poor an "equal right to do a wrong." Even apart from its moral incoherence, though, the argument for "equality" here would carry implications that have to be untenable for the American polity. As soon as Japan and Sweden, for example, had legalized abortion, American women were flying abroad for the purpose of having abortions. At that moment, the rich were enjoying an access to legal abortions which were not available to the poor. Would we have been obliged then, in the name of "equality," to have swept away all U.S. statutes and ordinances that made abortion any more restrictive than it was in Japan and Sweden? When its logic is carried through, this morally untethered sense of "equality" would ultimately deny the right of the American government to legislate on any subject with more restrictiveness than exists in legislation anywhere abroad—*if* these differences in legislation would create advantages that are more likely to be exploited by the rich.[28]

As for the number of deaths caused by illegal abortions, these portentous estimates have as much reality as any other set of figures that has been politically inspired. Christopher Tietze, an expert on population and a firm advocate of legal abortion, weighed the estimate of

[28] For a fuller consideration of this issue of "equality" with respect to abortions, see my essay, "On the Public Funding of Abortions," in James T. Burtchaell (ed.), *Abortion Parley* (New York: Andrews & McMeel, 1980), pp. 239-64; reprinted in *The Human Life Review* (Winter 1980), pp. 86-107.

10,000 deaths per year and branded it "unmitigated nonsense." His own estimate put the figure at 500-1,000 before *Roe* v. *Wade* made abortions legal. John Finnis has reported other studies which place the figure, more realistically, between 400 and 600 deaths each year, and probably closer to 400.[29] The figure of 5,000-10,000 had been used by the National Abortion Rights Action League when Bernard Nathanson was one of its directors. "I confess," he would later write, "that I knew the figures were totally false, and I suppose the others did too if they stopped to think of it. But in the 'morality' of our revolution, it was a *useful* figure, widely accepted, so why go out of our way to correct it with honest statistics?"[30] In reckoning the number of deaths resulting from illegal abortions, Nathanson came close to Finnis, putting the figure at around 500 each year.

Tietze had estimated that there were about 600,000 illegal abortions every year, and many supporters of abortion argued that its "legalization" would merely bring these operations into safer settings, without adding to the volume of abortions. That argument was quickly embarrassed however by the news—reported by Tietze—that by 1974 the number of abortions had risen to 900,000 per year, 53 percent above their level in 1972, one year before *Roe* v. *Wade*.[31] By 1977, the annual number of abortions had risen to 1.2 million,[32] and by 1982 it was well over 1.5 million.[33] Clearly, then, the laws were not merely accommodating the abortions that would have been performed illegally; the laws were also teaching new lessons about the propriety of abortion, and it should not have been surprising that people who were taught to regard abortion as a legitimate medical procedure should be encouraged to make use of that operation when it seemed to suit their interests. The figures were altogether staggering, and the "practical" argument for legalizing abortion became all the more bizarre as soon as the possibility was seriously considered that what these figures were measuring was the taking of human life. In other words, for the sake of saving about 500 women who might die each year from illegal abortions, the law was asked to permit a practice that would take 1.5 million lives each year. With a simple calculus

---

[29] John M. Finnis, "Three Schemes of Regulation," in John T. Noonan, *The Morality of Abortion* (Cambridge: Harvard University Press, 1970), p. 186, n. 45. For Tietze's estimates, see the *New York Times*, January 28, 1968, and Tietze and Sarah Lewit, "Abortion," *Scientific American*, vol. 220 (1969), pp. 21, 23.

[30] Nathanson, *supra*, note 8, p. 193. Emphasis in original.

[31] *New York Times*, February 3, 1975.

[32] *Boston Globe*, July 4, 1979.

[33] *New York Times*, July 12, 1984.

that compared the number of lives saved to the number destroyed, the argument should have revealed, instantly, its own vacuity. But with a serene willingness to believe that these abortions did not involve the taking of human lives, novel possibilities for "newspeak" sprang up overnight. Only in this spirit—with this high-minded filtering of the reality behind the figures—could the *New York Times* report the assessment of the city's administrator of health services: that the legalization of abortion had helped "to bring . . . infant mortality to an all-time low."

Bernard Nathanson has pointed out that, as a result of new technology, the number of deaths from illegal abortions each year might not be as high as 500 even if abortions became illegal again. One notable "advance" here was the introduction of suction curettage in 1970. With this device, it was no longer necessary to scrape the lining of the uterus with a sharp instrument. The nascent being in the womb— the "material" in the uterus—would be drawn out with a vacuum, and a curette would slice up the "tissue" that emerged. As Nathanson has remarked, "one can expect that if abortion is ever driven underground again, even non-physicians will be able to perform this procedure with remarkable safety. No woman need die if she chooses to abort during the first twelve weeks of pregnancy."[34] Later in pregnancy, the legendary "coat hanger" would be replaced by prostaglandins, which will be available in the form of vaginal suppositories. With this step, the wonders of technology will have made possible a "do-it-yourself" abortion. The prostaglandins bring on contractions and cause the fetus to be expelled; and suppositories would leave no evidence to suggest that the woman suffered anything more than a spontaneous miscarriage.[35]

It is just that much more unlikely today, then, that a restrictive policy on abortion would produce many casualties from illegal operations. In fact, it is entirely possible that the number of women killed in abortions under a policy of legal restriction would be far less than the number being killed now each year in legal *and* illegal abortions. It seems to come as a surprise to many people that illegal abortions persist even after most of the legal restraints have been removed. But the dynamics of "legalization" have now become familiar on matters like gambling as well as abortion, and illegal abortions would be sustained by the same tendencies which account, say, for the persistence of illegal gambling even in such places as Las Vegas, where gambling is not only legitimate but a local industry.

[34] Nathanson, *supra*, note 8, p. 194.
[35] *Ibid.*

In the case of abortion, the logic may express itself in this way. Once the courts have swept away the moral inhibitions which used to restrain people from seeking abortions—once they school people to the notion that there is nothing wrong with abortion itself—it simply becomes a matter, for many women, of finding the establishment that will provide the abortion at the lowest price. A lower price can usually be provided by the unlicensed practitioner or midwife, and the underground service can be especially attractive to the woman who does not wish to inform her husband or her parents, and who, for a number of weighty reasons, does not wish to leave a record behind. If a woman is also led to believe that abortion involves her sovereign "right over her own body," she may invest herself as the sovereign judge of the risks she is willing to take with her body. She may be even more inclined to take that risk if her legal "right" to an abortion is hedged in with procedural restrictions that induce delays and raise the cost of the operation. Those effects may be generated, for example, if the woman and her physician are required to appear before boards of review in order to justify a "medical need" for the abortion, or if the operation must take place in facilities inspected and licensed by the state.

These restrictions may interpose only the slightest barriers, and prevent no one from obtaining an abortion, and yet they may still be enough to encourage a movement toward illegal operations. In the late 1930's, as a case in point, Denmark and Sweden allowed abortions to be performed legally. But the legislation provided for medical boards of review to receive applications, and the boards refused to accept as a justification any claim of danger to the "mental health" of the pregnant woman. Almost half of the applications were rejected, and the result was a steady rise in the number of illegal abortions even under a regime of legal abortions. In 1964, Denmark registered 3,936 legal abortions, against an estimated 12,000-15,000 illegal abortions.[36] In Britain the laws on abortion have been far more permissive—as a practical matter, virtually any abortion performed by a qualified physician may be regarded as legitimate—but the volume of illegal abortions seems to have remained the same. According to recent testimony from Dr. Margaret White, the number of people discharged from British hospitals for the effects of nonlegal abortions held steady between 1964 and 1972 at a level of 50,000.[37]

In the United States, of course, review committees and most other serious impediments were swept away by the decision of the Supreme

---

[36] Finnis, *supra*, note 29, pp. 183, n. 31, and pp. 191-92.
[37] *Obstetrical and Gynecological News* (March 15, 1977), p. 38.

Court in *Roe* v. *Wade*. The Court indicated at the time that it might be willing to accept certain restrictions "reasonably related to maternal health," and with that understanding it subsequently upheld a statute in Connecticut that required abortions to be performed only by licensed physicians.[38] That judgment made it clear that the decision in *Roe* v. *Wade* could not have been predicated on any "right" of the mother to do whatever she wishes with her own body. For if that premise were accepted, it would be hard to see how the Court could deny to any woman the right to take whatever risks with her own body she might regard as acceptable—including the risk of having her abortion at the hands of an unlicensed practitioner. But so long as restrictions are preserved in the law, there is likely to be an incentive to seek out illegal abortions: the price of legal abortions can always be undercut by paramedics and inspired amateurs, who are able to operate without the expensive overhead of a professional facility. And the market being what it is, there will always be "customers" who are willing to take more risks for the sake of a lower price.

We cannot say at the moment just how many illegal abortions are performed in the United States every year, for a decision has apparently been made, in the highest official circles of the medical profession, to "eliminate" the problem of illegal abortions simply by refusing to collect evidence on the point.[39] We can expect, however, that there will always be some illegal abortions, especially, as I say, if the "right" to an abortion is burdened with any restrictions. But apart from this matter of underground operations, we have had dramatic evidence recently that the atrocities identified with illegal abortions have simply been removed from the infamous "back rooms" and reenacted in scores of shoddy abortion clinics which have sprung up legally since *Roe* v. *Wade*. These establishments thrive on high volume and quick turnover; they are, one might say, the medical equivalent of McDonald's, but without McDonald's integrity and quality control. These businesses have become the legal version of abortion mills, and the character of their practice was brought to light in a series published by the *Chicago Sun-Times* in 1978. In the rush to achieve a high turnover in customers and perform more abortions each day, the operations in these clinics were carried out in as little as five minutes. They were often performed *before* the anesthetic had taken effect; at

[38] *Connecticut* v. *Menillo*, 46 L. Ed. 2d 152 (1975).

[39] The omission was quite noticeable in a study of legalized abortion that was published under the auspices of the National Academy of Sciences; see Institute of Medicine, *Legalized Abortion and the Public Health* (Washington, D.C.: National Academy of Sciences, 1975).

times they were done without an anesthetic; and on a few occasions they were performed on women who were not even pregnant! (The clinics had neglected to administer pregnancy tests.) The investigators reported twelve deaths that were attributable to four abortion clinics in their sample.[40] Those twelve deaths—from only four clinics— amounted to nearly half of the deaths that were reported officially for abortion in the nation as a whole.[41] And if, as we may suspect, the experience in Chicago can find even a modest replication in New York, Detroit, Los Angeles, and elsewhere, the total deaths from legal abortion may now exceed the number of deaths that were thought to occur each year as a result of illegal abortions.[42]

The casualties from these operations do not seem to register in the official statistics because the hospitals manage to report the proximate, rather than the ultimate, cause of death. A woman with a perforated uterus may be described later as suffering the effects of peritonitis or of a pelvic abscess. There are known cases in which the deaths resulting from abortions have been attributed to anesthesia or to "abnormal uterine bleeding"; and one physician in Los Angeles, who had a higher quotient of inventiveness than of shame, was willing to report that his patient died of "spontaneous gangrene of the ovary."

Even on its own terms, then, the "practical" argument for abortion fails. A policy of legalized abortion will not eliminate illegal abortions, and it is not likely to reduce, overall, the number of women who die from abortion. In fact, it is likely to make matters far worse by the simple fact of enlarging the total volume of abortions. Ironically, there are likely to be far more maternal deaths and serious injuries under a

[40] See the *Chicago Sun-Times*, November 12 and December 6, 1978; and the special edition on "Abortion Profiteers," December 1978. For a more recent account, in the same vein, of an enterprising gynecologist in Virginia, arrested for performing "abortions" on women who were not pregnant, see the *Washington Post*, July 27, 1984.

[41] The most recent figures are reported in *Vital Statistics of the United States, 1975* (Washington D.C.: Government Printing Office, 1977), vol. II (Mortality), pt. A, p. 1-73.

[42] Bernard Nathanson recalls a report he received from a founder of an abortion clinic in New York, complaining about the standards of performance in the clinic. As the founder scolded the managers of the clinic, she provided a telling portrait of the level of professionalism that prevailed at this *legal* facility: "[H]alf of [the doctors] don't even wash their hands anymore before doing an abortion, let alone scrubbing. They refuse to use masks or caps, and their moustaches are dragging into the suction machines. I swear, one of these days we're going to lose one of those guys right into the suction trap and the lab is going to tell us the tissue is pregnancy tissue and the abortion is complete. One guy refuses to take the cigar out of his mouth while doing the abortions. Even the counselors aren't *that* crazy." Quoted in Nathanson, *supra*, note 8, p. 99.

policy of legalized abortion than under a regimen in which abortion, once again, is legally restricted.

But, of course, the question cannot be settled mainly as a "practical" matter of reducing the risks facing women who wish to destroy their fetuses. The issue cannot be abstracted from the question of whether human lives are taken in abortion, and whether anyone has a justification for taking those lives in the first place. But so long as the courts are free to insist, as a matter of judicial fiat, that human fetuses are not human, it is clear that the interest of an unborn child in preserving his or her life will not be accorded any weight against the interest that would move a pregnant woman to destroy that life, no matter how transient or even trivial her interest may be. Hence the state of affairs in which families decide to "interrupt" a pregnancy that would interfere with the "vacation out West" they were planning for the following summer. Or the situation in which an abortion is decided upon because it is discovered that the fetus is a girl and the parents wish to have a boy. In the sensibility that has been shaped in our culture of abortion, it is now possible for a human being to be destroyed for nothing more than the offense of being female.

In a burst of judicial novelty, Justice Blackmun and six of his colleagues created, in the law, a class of human beings whose lives may be taken virtually without the need to render a justification. Our current situation might be compared to one in which the law holds back and permits members of a certain minority group to be assaulted and murdered at will, in public settings or private. If 1.5 million members of any minority were being killed in that way each year, it is scarcely believable that the public would fail to notice; and if this carnage were taking place during a presidential election year, it would very likely be regarded as an issue at least as urgent as unemployment or inflation. Nor would there be any doubt that we were in the midst of a crisis that touched the moral premises of the political order itself. As Lincoln understood, it is a portentous act for a people to take upon itself the franchise of determining that human beings may be regarded as less than human and treated as "only the equal of the hog." For when those humans are denied the protections of law that attach, by nature, to human beings, then (to paraphrase a venerable passage) the government will have become destructive of those ends for which governments are instituted among men.

But in this instance, the new laws on abortion have not been adopted at the urging of the people; rather, they have been imposed against their resistance and protest. And instead of acquiescing in the moral teaching of the new laws, a majority of the American public has become

388

ever firmer in its opposition to the decisions of the courts and to the premises on which those decisions have been founded. The opposition of the public has been reflected in the most pronounced way in those branches of our government which are most sensitive to local opinion: it has been strongest in the state legislatures and in the House of Representatives; it has been weaker in the Senate, and weakest of all in the federal courts. This opposition has not enjoyed a course of continuous success; it has been stymied at several points where it has searched for a political breakthrough. And yet its influence, overall, has held steady or grown stronger. It succeeded in removing most of the public funding of abortion from the federal government and from many of the states. It helped to persuade the American government to withdraw from programs of foreign aid that promote abortions; and it may induce Congress to remove public grants and tax exemptions from private groups that sponsor abortions. It failed in its drive to overturn the holding in *Roe* v. *Wade*, and by a narrower margin it fell short in its effort to revise that decision through an act of ordinary legislation (the "Human Life Act"). But the movement has also helped bring to power a national administration that explicitly proposed to the Court the overruling of *Roe* v. *Wade*. And it may yet accomplish its end through the steady efforts of the administration in appointing new judges to the federal courts. The existence of this movement represents far more than a *political* threat to the doctrines established by the courts. The very extent and persistence of the opposition pose a serious challenge to the premises on which the Supreme Court itself defined the ground of its own decision on abortion. For as the Court came to the question of whether a human fetus constituted a human life, it had two sources from which an answer could be drawn:

(1) The Court might have recognized that it was facing a rather old question—namely, whether it is possible to know the things in nature that are human. The institutions of a constitutional order were founded on the premise that it is indeed possible to know human things and the differences between the human, the sub-human, and the superhuman. If that question were inscrutable, then there could be no government by consent, no regime of law, no courts dispensing justice. The Court might have concluded, then, that the question before it was a question which had to lend itself to a "true" answer. And since the question concerned the things that are in nature, true or false, right or wrong, the answer could not depend in any way on the shape of public opinion or the state of the local culture.

(2) Alternatively, the Court could have argued that the question of human life is a question whose solution resides wholly in the domain of belief, and which therefore admits no "true" answer. In that event, the sense of what constitutes a "human being" would depend on the evolving sense of the culture, on the conventions and the collective perceptions of a people. For that reason it would have to depend, finally, on whatever the community might *choose* to consider a human being. And yet, if an authoritative answer to the question had to be found in the opinions or conventions of a people, then the decision of seven judges could not claim a sovereign authority. The opinions having a preeminent claim to authority—the opinions most likely to represent the dominant views within the culture—were the opinions held by a majority of the population.

The Supreme Court decided, of course, that the question of human life could not depend on any proposition that had the standing of truth. It understood the question as one that had to be answered, perforce, through the authority of "opinion." With those premises, however, the Court established the ground for its own undoing if it failed to persuade a majority of the public to its own views. For once it established, as the ultimate ground of judgment, that ground on which majorities are most sovereign, to what standard could it appeal if the majority came to a judgment that differed fundamentally from the understanding held by the Court?

As it turns out, the opinion of the public has in fact settled in an understanding that differs notably from that of the Court on the nature of the fetus as a human being and on the justifications for abortion. A majority of the public has remained steadily opposed to the notion of abortion "on demand," and yet that opinion of the public has been formed from different streams of conviction. For the public has not been uniform in its understanding of the grounds on which abortion ought to be regarded as wrong, and this uncertainty about the ground of judgment must complicate the task of the statesmen who would frame a law that could at once tutor the public and gain its assent. Even when the public is convinced that abortion in general is wrong, it may be divided over the "exceptional" cases in which abortion might be justified. Would abortion be permitted to save the life of the mother? Would it be sanctioned in cases of rape or incest, or when the baby is likely to be "deformed" or retarded?

In its judgments on these matters, the public has mixed its reasons with its passions. It often shows a willingness to accept abortions in cases that could hardly be warranted if people were clear, in the first place, about the grounds of principle on which their opposition must rest. The statesmen who would frame laws for such a public cannot be heedless of these passions. It is the challenge of their art to help the public get clear on the main principles that must underlie its opposition to abortion. After that, they must find a prudent way of accommodating the passions of the people, while permitting those passions to recede over time. In the end, political men will have performed their highest service if they have helped the people to discover the fuller implications of the principles they have willed in the law, for themselves and for others. But before statesmen can deploy their arts in that task, they will have to come to a judgment themselves on the "exceptional" cases in which abortion may—or may not—be justified.

XVII

ABORTION AND THE FRAMING
OF THE LAWS

Within a decade after the ruling of the Supreme Court in *Brown* v. *Board of Education*, the teachings of the Court on racial segregation had been very widely absorbed into the public understanding. The Court had done nothing less than reshape the opinions of the majority; and as it did that, it stirred the political movements that would complete, in legislation, the alteration of the law that the Court had begun. More than a decade after *Roe* v. *Wade*, the Court has once again prompted a political movement of vast breadth and power, but this time the movement has been one of a dramatically different stamp. Instead of molding the opinion of the public to its principles, the Court has seen the public grow more adamant in its opposition. The passage of time did not confirm for the public the soundness of the reasons put forth by the Court; but rather, quite the opposite occurred. With further experience and reflection, the public began to reject the premises from which *Roe* v. *Wade* had been fashioned. Four years after the decision of the Court, those premises were rejected by a majority of the American people and the opposition was even firmer among women than among men.

The evidence for this steady disposition of the public has been offered in a variety of places, but never has it been brought out more tellingly than in 1977, when it was reported in detail by an academic who has been an emphatic supporter of abortion. Professor Judith Blake, a sociologist at the School of Public Health of the University of California, drew her findings on abortion from a survey she had commissioned from Gallup. These findings did not leave her entirely without hope, but plainly she could not have found them very cheering. The "advanced" feminist position accepted abortion right up to the time of birth, but 70 percent of American women in 1975 were opposed to abortion beyond the first trimester. Why they should take such a constricted view of these new possibilities in civil freedom rather puzzled Professor Blake. But "one reason," she said, "appears" to be that people "regard the fetus as a 'human life,' or a 'human person,' very early in the gestational period."

Just how early they placed the beginning of human life would be gauged by a question in which the respondents were given a choice among certain critical points for the beginning of life. The inventory would include conception, quickening, viability, and birth. In 1973, the modal response in the sample (the answer that was given most often) was not "quickening" or "viability," but "*conception.*" Two years later—two years, that is, after abortion had been made legal by the Supreme Court—this response was no longer merely a modal response, but the conviction held by a majority of women. Fifty-eight percent of all women in the United States held to that view, and the number of men sharing that position had risen substantially, to 43 percent.[1] In contrast, only 15 percent of the men thought that life began at "quickening," and 14 percent thought life began at "viability."

These findings reflected a pattern that has been evident for more than a century: despite all the claims for abortion as part of the liberation of women, the opposition to abortion has come mainly from women. On the other hand, abortion has had an evident appeal to the self-interest of men—especially upper-class whites, who might be particularly vulnerable to a loss of social standing as a result of the inconvenient pregnancies that could arise from their liaisons with women of another class. Men of this background have ever been in the vanguard of the movement for legalized abortion.[2]

As we might suppose, Catholic women were somewhat more inclined to think that life began at conception (75 percent of them held to that view), but that understanding was also shared by 52 percent (i.e., a majority) of women who were not Catholic.[3] Beyond that, most women disdained a franchise that feminist ideology and the Supreme Court would insist on settling upon them: namely, the exclusive right to destroy their unborn child without seeking the consent of the father.[4] Fifty-eight percent of married women under the age of 45 did *not*

---

[1] Judith Blake, "The Supreme Court's Abortion Decisions and Public Opinion in the United States," *Human Life Review* (Winter 1978), pp. 64-81, at 72-73; published originally in *Population and Development Review*, vol. 3, nos. 1-2 (March and June 1977), pp. 45-62.

[2] Bernard Nathanson recalled a meeting with Lawrence Lader during the formative days of the National Association for the Repeal of Abortion Laws. Lader complained about the scarcity of women in the leadership of their movement, . . . and he remarked: "We've got to keep the women out in front. . . . Why are they so damn slow to see the importance of this whole movement to themselves?" Nathanson, *Aborting America* (New York: Doubleday, 1979), p. 53. See also John T. Noonan, Jr., *A Private Choice* (New York: Free Press, 1979), pp. 49-51.

[3] Blake, in *HLR, supra*, note 1, p. 74.

[4] The Court's insistence on this "right" came in *Planned Parenthood* v. *Danforth*, 428 U.S. 52 (1976).

think that "a woman should be allowed to have an abortion if her husband opposes it." And yet, that level of rejection, recorded in 1975, represented a noticeable decline from the level of opposition registered in 1970, three years before the decision of the Supreme Court in *Roe v. Wade*. At that time, 81 percent of married women under the age of 45 refused to accept an exclusive right on the part of a married woman to order an abortion.

After scanning the trends in these surveys over the years, Judith Blake concluded that the decisions of the Court had largely failed to impress the public with a more favorable attitude toward abortion.[5] But one must wonder whether the teaching of the Court might not be related, after all, to the erosion of conviction that has been seen on such matters as the right of a woman to abort her child without the consent of the father. Blake discovered that a firm majority of Americans remained opposed to what she called "elective" abortions, by which she apparently meant abortions that were not strictly necessary to preserve the life of the mother. Among the justifications put forth for elective abortion were the "health" of the mother (broadly conceived, apparently, to include "psychological health"), the embarrassment of an illegitimate pregnancy, and the financial stress that might be caused by an additional child in the family. In 1977, 63 percent of the respondents in a Gallup survey were opposed to abortions under these circumstances. But in 1968, 81 percent of the public had been opposed.[6] With artfully phrased questions, it has been possible to entice as many as 40 percent of the respondents, in some surveys, to support "elective" abortions. But the sobering fact for Judith Blake was that this 40 percent seems to mark the hard outer limit of support for those premises which are necessary for the "abortion liberty" as Professor Blake and Justice Blackmun would wish to define it. Unless those premises are accepted—unless most Americans come to regard abortion as legitimate under any circumstances, whenever a woman is moved to "elect" one—the liberal regime of abortions established by the Court cannot be secured.

What Professor Blake knows is that the obduracy of most Americans on the matter of "elective" abortions is part of a series of judgments on abortion that have remained stable for years in their main outlines.[7] Most Americans, it is now clear, have been opposed to "abortion on

---

[5] Blake, in *HLR*, *supra*, note 1, pp. 75, 76.

[6] *Ibid.*, pp. 68-69.

[7] For a recent confirmation of this stability, see *American Medical News* (September 12, 1980), p. 7. This report, on the results of a Gallup survey, was recounted in other newspapers at around the same time.

demand"—abortions accepted under all circumstances, for any reason. Most people have no doubt that the being in the womb is human and that it is a child. For that reason, they think abortions should be restricted by the law to those cases which are truly grave or pressing. Most have no trouble deciding that an abortion would be justified when another human life is at stake—when the operation would be necessary to save the life of the mother. They also seem disposed to think that abortions could be justified in those instances in which the mother might be threatened with a serious and lasting impairment to her health. Beyond that, the same public which remains hostile to the notion of "abortion on demand" apparently suffers little strain in accepting abortion in cases of rape or incest, or when the child is likely to be "deformed."

This ensemble of responses represents, as I have said, a mixture of the judgments and passions of the people, and it is a mixture that must be reckoned with as statesmen try to frame new laws on abortion. For if the matter is viewed in a rigorous light, most of these exceptions simply cannot be reconciled with the recognition, shown by most of the public, that life begins at conception and that abortion involves the taking of human life. It may be that most people have not yet grasped the *principle* which underlies their responses or the canons of reasoning which connect their recognitions to their moral conclusions. So long as they remain unclear about the principled ground of their judgments in these separate cases, there must be a serious question as to whether they really understand the ground of their opposition, in general, to abortion.

IN CASES OF rape or incest, we react with outrage to the offense, but our outrage may blind us to the proper assignment of guilt and punishment. However gravely we regard these offenses, the children who may be conceived through these acts cannot partake in any way of the guilt attached to the crimes. No one could pretend that the fetus, in these circumstances, would be anything other than the innocent issue of the act. What remains to be explained is why so many worldly people are willing to visit on this innocent party a punishment far more astounding than the punishment they see fit to impose on the assailant himself. People who would never sanction capital punishment for the rapist are nonetheless willing to inflict a lethal operation on the innocent issue of the rape.

Of course the passion for abortion in the case of rape or incest has little to do with any sober assessment of the guilt or innocence of the fetus. The child is seen as a lingering monument to an injustice, and most often the abortion is probably sought for the sake of relieving the pregnant woman of embarrassment or trauma. But these arguments have all the same defects in principle that would make it unjustified to perform an abortion for the sake of avoiding the embarrassment of an illegitimate birth or the psychological distress suffered by the mother. Once again, we need not turn coldly away from the anguish that people may feel—we should extend all the support that our compassion and inventiveness may inspire—but we would be obliged to point out that the injuries in prospect for the mother cannot possibly stand on the same plane as the injury that would be inflicted on the fetus through an abortion.

As for the matter of "deformities," it has been aptly remarked that our language changes in a revealing way with the transition from pregnancy to birth. After a birth, we say that the child has a "handicap," not a deformity. Handicaps elicit our sympathy; they do not imply any flaw in the person himself that affects his moral claim to live. They may even suggest that the rest of us should be prepared to show a larger measure of compassion and patience in helping people cope with their handicaps. "Deformities," on the other hand, bring to mind an image of "defective" goods, produced in a factory, and which probably ought to be discarded. The shift in language marks, once again, the difference between the human and the nonhuman, and if we remind ourselves that we are dealing with human lives, the question of "deformities" will have to be put in a more demanding way. Would we say that the *actual presence* of handicaps (or deformities) in people outside the womb is sufficient to justify a policy of putting those people to death? But if we would not order the destruction of people for the "offense" of being mentally retarded or for being born with flippers rather than arms, how could we justify the destruction of infants in the womb on the *chance* that they might bear the same disabilities?

Our medical records bring persisting reports of "therapeutic" abortions carried out to prevent the birth of "deformed" children, only to find that most of these children had no apparent "abnormalities." One of the main incitements to these kinds of abortions has been the prospect of rubella, or German measles. When contracted by a pregnant woman, this disease has been responsible for infirmities in children ranging from deafness and impairment of vision to mental retardation. The risks are far graver when rubella has been contracted within the first twelve weeks of pregnancy (in some studies, the probability of producing these infirmities has been as high as six in ten); but the risks drop markedly after the first trimester. At any rate, the calculation of probability must include an estimate of whether the disease was contracted in the first twelve weeks. But beyond that, our experience suggests that, even during epidemics, the likelihood of bearing children with handicaps has been notably exaggerated. In 1954, for example, during a major outbreak of rubella, a survey of more than 6,000 pregnancies turned up only 54 cases (less than 1 percent) with an onset of the disease within the first twelve weeks. And in 37 of these 54 cases, the children were born without serious infirmities. In the remaining 17 cases, the handicaps of the children were generally not severe enough to keep them from leading what are called "useful" lives (though, of course, we would not reckon the dignity of any human being by the "use" he may provide to others). One British study sought to gauge, with the usual standardized tests, the "intelligence" of children born under similar circumstances, and it was found that the children scored at the average level for the population as a whole.[8]

What we must notice, then, is a willingness to carry out lethal operations on the strength of nothing more than contingent propositions—to justify abortions on the basis of the *possibility* that a child might be handicapped. And yet, *even if predictions were replaced with certainties*, enough has been said by now to establish that none of the "facts" which describe the infirmities of the fetus can have any relevance to the moral question of whether a fetus deserves to live or die.

WHEN THE CONTINUANCE of the pregnancy would pose a threat to the life of the mother, we would finally reach a point at which the interests that may be in conflict stand at least on a common plane of gravity. Many Catholics have had no trouble accepting abortions in those cases where the life of the mother may be endangered, and this "exception" has been incorporated in many proposals for a constitutional amendment to protect fetal life. Yet even here, where abortion receives its widest acceptance, the need for the "exception" is notably less than urgent, and the moral justification is not really so compelling as it may appear. In the first place, the interests of the fetus and the mother are not in conflict in the same way they were in the nineteenth century, when childbirth itself was significantly more dangerous to the pregnant woman. But under the current state of medical science, there is almost never a case in which the life of a mother may be threatened by the continuance of a pregnancy. Even Alan Gutmacher, who became a celebrated advocate of abortion, conceded that "it is possible for almost any patient to be brought through pregnancy alive unless she

[8] See Germain Grisez, *Abortion: The Myths, the Realities, the Arguments* (New York: Corpus Books, 1970), pp. 88-89.

suffers from a fatal illness such as cancer or leukemia; and if so, abortion would be unlikely to prolong, much less save life."[9] When he was the director of the Margaret Hague Hospital in New Jersey, Dr. Joseph Donnelly presided over a facility that delivered 115,000 babies between 1947 and 1961, not once needing to perform an abortion to save the life of the mother. With an awareness of the medical facts, Dr. Roy Heffernan of the medical school of Tufts University stated flatly that "anyone who performs a therapeutic abortion is either ignorant of modern medical methods or unwilling to take the time and effort to apply them."[10]

The removal of the fetus would be necessary, of course, in those instances in which a cancer or tumor requires the removal of the uterus, or in which there is an ectopic pregnancy, with the embryo lodged in the Fallopian tube. In the first case, the danger to the mother would not be created distinctly by the pregnancy; therefore, the removal of the fetus would be an ancillary, regrettable effect of a procedure that is necessary on its own grounds to save the life of the woman. In either case, as Catholic theologians have pointed out, the intention would not be to destroy the fetus. And as we advance our technical means for preserving the lives of fetuses and embryos from the earliest moments, it should become even clearer that the decision to remove the child is not a decision to take its life.

A more common hazard arises in those cases in which the pregnancy might be a source of strain for a woman who is already suffering from a serious disease. This problem will not be entirely dissolved, but it has been compressed, along with other mortal dangers, by recent advances in medicine. In contrast to the situation twenty or thirty years ago, it is now rare to see an abortion carried out because the mother has heart disease. Pulmonary tuberculosis was once regarded as a justification for abortion, but it is now recognized that pregnancy does not worsen the disease and abortion does not contribute to its cure. Kidney disease may be substantially worsened as a result of pregnancy, but here, too, improvements in treatment have considerably reduced the need for abortion. In cases where the kidneys of a pregnant woman are deteriorating, however, a regimen of treatment may not always be enough to avert the danger to the mother. In this, as well as in other cases, there may still be moments in which a woman absorbs serious risks for herself by carrying her child to term, and it

[9] Alan Gutmacher (ed.), *The Case for Legalized Abortion* (Berkeley, Calif.: Diablo Press, 1967), p. 9.

[10] Quoted in Thomas J. O'Donnell, *Morals in Medicine* (Westminster, Maryland: Newman Press, 1960), p. 159.

is at those moments that we must consider, in a demanding way, the principles that must govern our judgment.

If the matter were indeed judged in a rigorous way, we would discover that the interests of the mother could not claim any clear moral preference over the interests of the fetus. But even before we reach a point at which those interests are set in balance against one another, we must be impressed with a notable disparity in the dangers facing the mother and the child. For the fetus, the abortion will almost always mean death, and in most cases the operation is chosen precisely for that reason. The question must be considered, then, of whether the threat to the mother is equally certain or whether it remains, at most, a probability. Even with a high probability of danger, we are still faced with the balancing of a probability against a certainty, and in that kind of reckoning there are compelling reasons to choose the risk rather than the certainty. There are compelling reasons, that is, if we understand that we are faced here with a balance between two human lives, and that the child does not deserve to die any more than the mother. And if we should have to weigh, in our calculus, the certainty of death for the child against the risk of permanent damage to the health of the mother, we would presumably recognize that death represents a graver injury.

If we conceal these imperatives from view, that is most likely because we engage our sympathies with the person we know vividly rather than with the being who is not yet known to us. But in point of principle, a newer life has no less a claim to live than an older life, and it would be a perverse notion of "seniority" to suggest that, in a choice between two lives, we must assume that older persons are more human and have a higher claim to live. That assumption would be as untenable in principle as its converse: that the older generation should always be sacrificed to the younger.

Faced with the choice, then, of saving one of two innocent lives, the hard fact of the matter is that there is no ground of principle on which to choose. We might have a presentiment that the loss of the mother would be agonizing for a family grown dependent on her love and care; but in these cases we find ourselves regarding the potential victims as means rather than ends. Our decision would hinge on a calculation or comparison of how useful either party is likely to be to the interests of other people. In certain instances, calculations of that kind may be justifiable: finding, on a battlefield, that there is a choice between saving one of two people who are equally "worthy" (shall we say) of being saved, there may be a good reason to save the doctor, who in turn may be able to save other lives. Perhaps that analogy comes into play here, but in any case we are dealing with empirical predictions which are at best problematic, and at worst quite tenuous. For all we know, the mother may soon desert her family; the newborn child may grow up to be the source of stability and affection, holding the family together and providing its main financial support. Altogether, then, doctors were on far firmer ground when they refused to take up the franchise of making life-and-death decisions on the basis merely of social predictions—an enterprise supported by no science, and for which doctors could claim no more authority than anyone else. Doctors practiced their arts on a more defensible moral ground when they simply sought, as much as they could, to save both of the lives that were placed in their hands.

To make the problem here even more difficult, the choice before us cannot be eased in any way by annexing to the interests of the mother the claim of "self-defense." The notion of self-defense carries a moral sanction because it implies the presence of an assailant. And yet, in any strict reckoning, it could never be said that we have an assailant here. There is no *mens rea*, to use the language of the law—no "guilty mind," no intention on the part of the fetus to inflict a harm. The mother may seek her self-preservation, but her moral problem is complicated by the fact that, in this instance, she would have to seek that "self-preservation" at the expense of an innocent being. The claim to kill, in these cases, would represent, at most, a claim to the "rights of the strong"—which, as we have seen, is no *moral* claim at all. Of course, in certain rare cases it is possible for a person to become an assailant even without the intention to harm. He may carry a weapon while sleepwalking; he may be placed in an hypnotic trance and, in a diabolical plot, he may be used unknowingly to carry out the evil designs of another. In either event, he would be the inadvertent or unknowing agent of harm, and he might take life unjustly unless his own were taken first.

Though the analogy to abortion might be strained, let us suppose that the situation of the fetus might be quite as rare as the predicament of the person caught in a hypnotic trance. In both instances, an innocent being may become the source of mortal danger to another, and we would think that the victim has the right to resist. But the analogy begins to weaken precisely as we recognize what is different about the situation of the fetus. The physician attending the mother and her fetus would not be aware of anyone in a trance "setting upon" another; he would not discover any docile agent carrying out the designs of another. He would notice two innocent beings, and if asked, he could not say just which of these two beings was "threatening" the other.

400

The mother, in this instance, represents as much a danger to the fetus as the child represents to the mother. If life may be taken in the interest of "self-preservation," without the need to render a justification, that claim may be advanced on behalf of the child as easily as it may be asserted on behalf of the mother. If the mother claims that the child has become an unknowing agent threatening her life, it might be said in that respect that the child is in a more defensible position morally than the mother. For the mother at least *does know* what she is willing; she is consciously choosing death for her own offspring. The mother may be driven by her interest in "self-preservation," but the physician who must carry out the operation can claim no such interest himself. If he had to justify his decision, he could not strictly explain why he sought to remove the danger posed to the mother by the fetus, *rather than the harm threatened to the fetus by the mother*. The physician may be the agent here only if there is a principle that justifies one course of action rather than another. If there is a principle that supports the mother in her claims of self-defense, that same principle will furnish a justification for the doctor in carrying out the abortion. But if the doctor is lacking in a justification, that is because the mother in turn has no principle on her side to justify the sacrifice of her child.

I once thought that the most sensible way of resolving this problem was to recognize that if there is no principle justifying the sacrifice of the fetus, neither is there a principle compelling the mother to sacrifice her own life for the unborn child. In that event, the mother would be faced with the possibility of performing a "supererogatory" act—an act literally beyond the call of duty. She might well decide to risk her life for that of her child, but she could not be *obliged* to make that sacrifice. And yet, I do not think this argument would finally hold: it would be eroded by the same considerations that call into question the coherence of supererogatory acts.[11] If we could show why the child in the womb would merit an effort to save its life, or why a pregnant woman would be "justified" in risking her life to save her child, we would probably establish at the same time why a pregnant woman would be *obliged* to take risks in order to save the child in her womb, a human being whom she is in a position, uniquely, to save.

What philosophers strain to understand, many pregnant women seem able to grasp with the same recognition that tells them what they are bearing in their own bodies. It is precisely because the justification for sacrificing the child is as doubtful as it is that we find so many women who refuse to claim the franchise which the law has long been

[11] See Chapter XIII.

willling to grant them. And if women have been willing to take these risks on behalf of nascent life, then why should the rest of us fear to incorporate, in our public understanding, the things these women have grasped? Why should physicians be any more tremulous about bearing again the responsibilities they once accepted under their oaths: to inflict no harm, to administer no abortifacient, to dedicate their arts to the saving of lives, to save any life they practicably can, and, when they cannot save two imperiled lives, to save the life they have the best chance of saving.

THE CONVENTIONS of our medical practice have long permitted doctors to take the life of a fetus when the life of the mother is in danger. Those conventions have been followed even when the laws on abortion have not been explicit on this point, and today it is hard to imagine a law on the subject which would not be understood to incorporate that "exception" for the life of the mother. Without the assurance of such an exception, it seems unlikely that a law on abortion would gain the assent of the public. As a matter of prudence, therefore, this exception will have to be accommodated in the law even though it may be hard to justify with any strict moral reasoning. But if this exception is to be accommodated, it matters profoundly that it would find its place within a body of law which recognizes the human standing of the fetus and which sets the obligation of all parties in the direction of saving the life of the fetus wherever a rescue is practicable. A public that absorbs the moral premises contained in laws of this kind is also a public that may be encouraged to reason on correct premises and work its way to conclusions which are more compelling morally than anything the laws may be able, quite yet, to embody.

Doctors may be more reluctant then to assume a casual license for the destruction of unborn children, and some mothers may feel freer to follow their moral sense and take risks for their own babies. For those women who encompass, with their large natures, a vaster sense of commitment to their unborn children, the law should be the source of no embarrassment or reproach: if women are willing to risk themselves out of a generous spirit and a more demanding sense of justice, the law should avoid the gratuitous impression that it might prefer a different result. The law cannot help but teach lessons when it makes a special point of mentioning that abortions will be regarded as legitimate when they might save the life of the mother. A provision accepted in the interest of prudence may be understood, falsely, as a judgment that proceeds from a necessary principle. And if the principles of the law vouchsafe for us all the "rightness" of abortions

402

under these conditions, how could people not begin to doubt whether a different course of action could be quite so defensible or plausible? It seems better, therefore, that the law remain silent on the subject, especially at the national level, and especially in any constitutional amendment on abortion. It would be bad enough for an exception born of prudence to be given the standing of a principle in the law; it would be far worse if it were to be incorporated, in effect, as a principle of the regime itself.[12]

The same thing may be said with equal force on the "exceptions" for rape and incest. The public has not yet schooled itself to the temper of justice that would protect children conceived in these circumstances, and if it becomes possible for the states to legislate again in restricting abortions, the laws in most places will probably make allowances for cases of rape and incest. The passions of the people would seem to make these provisions politically necessary, but the gratification of those passions may be a small price to pay for the sake of securing the commitment of the public to laws that express the principled grounds of its opposition to abortion. As it turns out, the number of pregnancies resulting from rape in this country is minuscule. Before *Roe* v. *Wade*, the laws in California permitted abortions in cases of rape and incest, and in one year (1970), less than one-tenth of 1 per cent of abortions in the state were performed for those causes. At around the same time, a study of hospitals in Minneapolis–St. Paul showed that, over ten years and 3,500 cases, there was not one instance of pregnancy resulting from rape. A similar study in Buffalo a year earlier revealed no record of a pregnancy arising from rape over a period of thirty years.[13]

Even if we suppose that some rapes went unreported, the numbers

[12] As Senator Jesse Helms has pointed out, it is not necessary for a constitutional amendment to spell out "exceptions" on abortion, because the common law of the states has long incorporated the notion of a "choice among evils," which has made it legitimate to save the pregnant mother while sacrificing the fetus: "State criminal laws have long recognized the legal principles of self-defense and necessity or choice-of-evils without their specific incorporation into the Constitution. Certainly, they form a part of the American legal tradition which predates the Constitution itself. At times these doctrines have been held to be contained within the due process clause of the Constitution; but the silence of the Constitution on these principles has not detracted from their vitality. There is no reason to suppose that a similar resolution of the propriety of procedures to save the life of the mother would not be developed by the States." See Helms, "A Human Life Amendment," *Human Life Review* (Spring 1977), pp. 7-42, at 29.

[13] B.M. Sims, "A District Attorney Looks at Abortion," *Child and Family* (Spring 1969), pp. 176-80.

still do not figure to be very large. In the first place, the probability is only .165 that the rape will take place at a time when the woman is able to conceive or when the sperm could live in her body. Rapes, moreover, are directed at females of all ages, from the infant to the elderly, and many of the victims are not able to bear children. Of those women in the population who are able to bear children, many are using forms of contraception that would prevent pregnancy during a rape. In addition, the fear induced by rape may interrupt the normal operation of hormones in the body of the woman, which in turn may prevent ovulation and conception.[14]

Altogether, then, the incidence of conception arising from rape promises to be rather low. The disposition to resort to abortion in these instances is rooted in a passion that will not easily be dissolved by sedate reflection, and so we can probably assume that the volume of these abortions is as vast, or as contracted, as it is likely ever to be. Still, it is not inconceivable that the reflexes of people in such cases may be affected by the climate of opinion. In certain places—such as BETA House in Los Angeles—a local community can provide a reservoir of sympathy and support for unmarried pregnant women, who may be encouraged to carry their pregnancies to term rather than abort their fetuses. It is not beyond the wit of a community to create the kind of enveloping cushion of sympathy in which an unmarried mother, or a woman made pregnant in rape, could be made to feel the commendation and support of the community—could be made to feel that she is doing an admirable thing—if she should decide to preserve the life of the child rather than destroy it. In that kind of setting the incidence of abortion, even in "exceptional" cases, may be substantially compressed. But this climate of opinion is more likely to be encouraged if the law begins again to teach lessons of this kind, and the law will not teach these lessons until it is once again settled—though settled more clearly—on the right principles.

WHAT, PRECISELY, might a law or a constitutional amendment on abortion say? A constitutional amendment would provide the foundation of all other laws on abortion in the country, and if it were necessary to have one, I would suggest that it be confined to those propositions which are incontrovertible: viz., that the offspring of *Homo sapiens* cannot be anything other than a human being; that the human fetus must have the same claims to the protection of the law

[14] Noreen Connel and Cassandra Wilson (eds.), *Rape: The First Sourcebook for Women* (New York: Radical Feminists, 1974), p. 98.

that attach to other human beings. If these premises were established in the fundamental law of the Constitution, it would become the responsibility of the Congress and the legislature of the separate states to reconcile their legislation with those premises. If certain states wish to permit abortions in cases of rape or incest, they would be free to make those provisions, but they would be constrained from permitting abortions in a blanket way, without regard to circumstances. For the grounds on which they allow the destruction of fetal life would have to be reconciled with the grounds on which they would permit the taking of human life generally. And so, for example, if the states do not usually permit their citizens to kill people who stand in the way of their careers, they will be hard put to explain why they would permit a pregnant woman to destroy the child in her womb solely because the untimely birth might interfere with the plans of the family.

This need to reconcile the provisions of the law with a new set of premises would impart its discipline to the courts as well. The courts should be prevented, then, from rendering the kind of judgment that the Supreme Court of California was able to produce in the celebrated case of *Keeler* v. *Superior Court*.[15] In that case, a divorced couple encountered one another on the road, and the erstwhile husband discovered that his former wife had become pregnant by another man. Her pregnancy was in the seventh or eighth month, and the sight of her moved the man to rage. As his anger flared, he said, "I'm going to stomp it [the child] out of you." He then shoved her against the car, kicked her in the abdomen and hit her several times in the face.

As a result of this trauma the baby died, and the former husband was prosecuted for murder. Under the laws of California, he was charged with the killing of the human being within the womb. As Justice Mosk wrote for the Supreme Court of California, the case had to turn on the question of whether the fetus of seven or eight months was a "human being" within the meaning of the statute. In a rare feat of interpretation, the majority of the court decided that when the legislature had proscribed the killing of a "human being" it meant that term to apply only to "a person who had been born alive."[16] With that reading of the law, Keeler could not have been charged properly with murder, because it had to follow from the divinations of Judge Mosk that there had been no human being to kill. As Mosk noted, in applying this logic, the laws of California would have given no "no-

---

[15] 470 P. 2d 617 (1970).
[16] *Ibid.*, at 618-19, 622.

405

tice" to the petitioner "that the killing of an unborn but viable fetus was prohibited."[17]

In a conceptual world that existed, so far as one could tell, only in the chambers of the court, Mr. Keeler apparently had no understanding of what he was destroying. By his own declaration, as Judge Mosk pointed out, he signaled his intention to "stomp out" an "it," and nothing in his acts would apparently support the assumption that Keeler knew anything about the nature of the "it" he was destroying. Of course, if the "it" were anything other than a human being, one can only wonder why Keeler's outrage had been ignited. The event was comprehensible, in other words, only because Keeler knew precisely what he was doing: he was not merely assaulting the mother; he was striking at a life separate from that of the mother, a life conceived by his former wife in congress with another man. It was only through the most radical detachment from *natural* understanding, and from the language in which that understanding was expressed, that the court was able to produce a judgment as strained—and as immured in nonsense—as the judgment rendered in the *Keeler* case.

No case would provide a more vivid example of the benign effect that a constitutional amendment could have in rescuing the courts from a kind of juridical imbecility. For with the advent of a constitutional amendment, the premises of Justice Mosk and his colleagues would be swept away. Whether the legislature of California had understood in 1850 that an unborn child was a "human being"; whether the courts in the past had treated the killing of a fetus as a crime of "murder"—these would be matters of no consequence. The new premise of the law would be supplied by the Constitution, and with that premise, every decision on abortion reached by a legislature, court, or administrative agency would have to incorporate the understanding that the destruction of a fetus is the taking of human life.

A NEW constitutional amendment would protect life from the point of conception, but a mild dispute could arise over the question of when conception should be said to begin. In an amendment proposed by Senator Jesse Helms, human life would come under the protection of the law from "the moment of fertilization."[18] Bernard Nathanson and others would regard that as slightly premature; they would not accord the sanctity of human life to the zygote until about one week after its formation, when the blastocyst becomes implanted in the wall of the

[17] *Ibid.*, at 628.
[18] For the text of the proposed amendment, see Helms, *supra*, note 12, p. 23.

uterus. Nathanson points out that the union of the sperm and egg will not always produce what we consider a human being, even when the organism has forty-six chromosomes: there is the hydatiform mole, which is usually a degenerated placenta having a random number of chromosomes; the choriocarcinoma, a "conception cancer"; and the "blighted ovum," a conceptus having forty-six chromosomes, but "which is only a placenta, lacks an embryonic plate, and is always aborted naturally after implantation."[19] But a "premature" policy of protecting nascent life will run no risk of protecting a blighted ovum, since nature will dispose of this conceptus quickly. As for the others, there should not be a serious problem—and I suspect that Dr. Nathanson would not encounter any difficulty himself—in distinguishing between a human being and a tumor. As Daniel Robinson observed, in the passage I quoted earlier, we identify as a "human" that being whose maturation "culminates in the unique biochemistry and gross anatomy of homo sapiens. . . . The first criterion may be met by certain kinds of 'growths,' but not the second."[20]

Nathanson finds a special significance in "implantation" because at that moment the new being "establishes its presence to the rest of us by transmitting its own signals—by producing hormones. . . . The [pregnancy hormone] is discovered by the mother, doctor, and society when it enters the mother's blood and urine and is picked up via the use of immunological techniques."[21] Waxing mystical—or at least sociological—Nathanson suggests that the "essential element" in humanity is "an interface with the human community and communication of the fact that [the offspring] is there." But, of course, the embryo is not really "communicating" in the sense of intending to convey meaning, and Nathanson admits that his argument here may be no more than another variant on the contention offered by proponents of abortion that "life is not protectable until we 'see' it." Nathanson is wise enough to know that this argument, in either of its forms, has no moral foundation. The reticent and the recluse, the shy and the misanthropic, those people who would rather avoid, altogether, "an interface with the human community" at cocktail parties, do not have less standing as human beings than their more sociable contemporaries.

As Nathanson himself recognizes, his understanding betrays serious flaws as soon as the prospect arises of nourishing a zygote in a test

---

[19] Nathanson, *supra*, note 2, p. 214.
[20] See Chapter XVI, note 7.
[21] Nathanson, *supra*, note 2, p. 214.

tube or culture dish before it is "re"-implanted in the mother's womb. Nathanson appeals to literary license and contends that the zygote is "implanted" when it is in the dish, and since we are aware of its presence, it has "established the nexus with the human community."[22] Literary license, however, will not convert a dish into a uterus, and it cannot obscure the fact that the humanity of the offspring would still depend, in Nathanson's argument, on the question—utterly lacking in moral significance—of whether the rest of us are aware of its presence.

As a practical matter, the issue of abortion arises in most cases only after a woman becomes alert to the possibility that she may be pregnant—and at that time, of course, implantation has already taken place. The sanctity attached to the zygote takes on more importance when we ask whether intrauterine devices (IUD's) or "morning after" pills would work as contraceptives by destroying zygotes or by preventing them from reaching the uterine wall. On this question, as I say, even the most committed opponents of abortion have held back. To some of them, it has simply seemed impracticable for the law to protect every union of a sperm and egg. Nature, it appears, has provided its own method of reducing the number of fertilized eggs that may be implanted, and there may be a practical wisdom in working with the implanted zygotes that nature has provided. This persuasion, however, would suffer embarrassment over the case of fertilized eggs nourished outside the womb, on behalf of parents who apparently do not have many fertilized zygotes to spare. It is not a natural process that places the zygote in a petri dish; and yet, once it is there it differs from a normal zygote only in its method of nourishment. Between the embryo nourished in the petri dish and the embryo sustained in the womb there is no difference of moral standing that would permit us to discard the embryo from the dish for reasons any more trivial than the reasons we would demand before we detached the embryo from the uterus. It should be clear, then, that any obligations which arise to protect nascent life must be focused on the human organism itself; those obligations cannot be affected by the *location* at which the organism is nourished, and they must be wholly indifferent, in principle, the question of whether this new being has yet reached, in its travels, the uterine wall.

The late André Hellegers suggested that the zygote cannot claim the respect we typically accord to human offspring until it reaches at least the "chimera" stage, where it is incapable of splitting and forming

[22] *Ibid.*, p. 217.

identical "twins." At that stage, also, it is incapable of recombining—
or *merging* with another zygote—to form again a singular being. Until
this stage is reached, the question put by Hellegers is whether we can
be sure that the new offspring has yet become "irreversibly an individual, since it still may be recombined with others into one new, final
being."[23] Imagine, for example, two men—we will call one "Billy,"
the other "Martin"—and let us suppose that when their shoulders
touch they merge to form a single being of incomparable character,
whom we may then call "Billy Martin" (and who, so far as we know,
has no duplicate anywhere in the civilized world). The question is
whether we can assume that "Billy" and "Martin" had much reality
or integrity as separate beings before they merged to form "Billy Martin." If the new being, "Billy Martin," cannot combine any further
when he meets the shoulder of another creature, we might be inclined
to think that he has more genuine standing as a separate being than
either of his former selves (or, as we might say, either of his former
"constituents").

But if we work with this analogy, it is proper to raise another
question. What if "Billy" were killed on the street by an assailant
before he had ever met "Martin" and consummated his destiny? Would
the assailant be exonerated of any crime because "Martin" was incomplete or uncombined and therefore less than a fully human being
with the right to be protected from unjustified assaults? We could
hardly think so, and if the analogy were applied to zygotes, I am afraid
that we would simply be faced with another variant of the problem
expressed by the refrain "A funny thing happened to me on the way
to the uterine wall." Once we are clear on the being who is the object
of protection, his moral claims are not affected by the fact that he is
in transit to a place where he would find it easier to make himself
known and to call for protection. In fact, if we were to create rights
and entitlements with the same comic inventiveness that has seized
the Supreme Court in recent years, we might suggest that the person
who employs devices or chemicals for the sake of preventing the human
zygote from reaching the uterine wall has interfered with his "right
to travel."[24]

---

[23] André Hellegers, "Fetal Development," *Theological Studies* (March 1970), pp. 3-
9, at 4-5.

[24] And if the Fourteenth Amendment may not apply to this private act of obstruction,
we have plenty of assurance by now, from our most learned jurists, that the Commerce
Clause would probably suffice. The zygote, after all, if he makes it to the uterine wall,
may one day journey along our national highways, patronizing restaurants and motels
along the way, inducing each of the businesses in turn to order food and furnishings

There seems to be a tendency, in some quarters, to settle this question backwards. It is assumed that IUD's and "morning after" pills must be beyond moral challenge, for they are—are they not?—devices for contraception. And if the protection of human zygotes would rule out these popular devices, that prospect seems to establish, on its face, that there must be something absurd about the notion of protecting humans from the point of conception. But these assumptions would have to dissolve if the question were addressed in a demanding way, and if it were arranged with first matters first. Once we are clear that a human being is present from the moment of conception, and once we understand that its claim to the protection of the law does not depend on its size or verbal ability, then it makes no difference in principle as to whether the offspring may be killed by a bus or a surgeon, by a pill or a coil. It is not for us to remove protections from human beings just because these protections interfere with the use of IUD's and "morning after" pills. If IUD's and "morning after" pills work as abortifacients, then it is the responsibility—and the humane opportunity—of the users of these devices to choose among other, legitimate forms of contraception which do what contraceptives may properly do: prevent the creation of new life rather than destroy a separate, unique being who has already been created.[25]

But as a practical matter, there would be no way for the law to reach the abortions that might be effected by IUD's, just as the law could not prosecute a dilation and curettage (or "D and C," as it is widely known) performed on the "morning after." If the lining of the uterus were removed before the fertilized egg had been implanted, it would be impossible to prove that the woman had been pregnant. It would be impossible, also, to distinguish this procedure from the D and C's performed on women who are not even thought to be pregnant. In neither case would there be any way of knowing that an "abortion" had taken place. In any event, the questions involved here are far more refined and intractable than the main issues that must be addressed on the matter of abortion, and the amendments that have been proposed on abortion would not make it necessary for the law to roam the countryside searching for these undiscoverable abortions. The language I suggested in my own version of a statute or constitutional

---

from other suppliers. This vision, which I of course offer in a sardonic vein, has been anticipated by constructions quite as satiric—even if unintentional—on the part of the Supreme Court. See above, Chapter V, note 11.

[25] In the case of IUD's, a more meticulous moral judgment would have the advantage also of turning women away from a form of conception that has many hazards, and which would be better to avoid.

amendment simply stated that the offspring of *Homo sapiens* cannot be anything other than *Homo sapiens*; that the human fetus must have the same claims to the protection of the law that attach to other human beings. It would say nothing about the precise point at which the embryo is protected. But if the offspring of *Homo sapiens* cannot be anything other than human, then the amendment would have to recognize, implicitly, that the offspring must be human from the moment it comes into being.

John Noonan, who has traced, in maddening detail, the moves of tendentious judges, has been far less willing to risk the absence of explicitness. Some federal judges have cultivated a new sport of steering around restrictions on abortion, and that sport is not always practiced with the highest subtlety. Such judges might accept, as a new premise in the law, that the human fetus must be regarded as a "person," but they might hold nevertheless that human persons are not protected by the law *at all moments* of their development. And so, Noonan sought to foreclose these possibilities through an amendment he proposed to the Senate Committee on the Judiciary. His amendment would have made the point explicitly that unborn children may be protected by Congress and the states "at every stage of biological development, irrespective of age, health, or condition of dependency."[26]

That language may go even further toward securing the ends of the law, but even with its added explicitness, it still does not foreclose the kind of dispute that André Hellegers and Bernard Nathanson preserved among those who would oppose abortion. Noonan's amendment would still permit the dispute to continue, and with further discourse we might finally be able to settle the question of whether the zygote will be protected from the very beginning or only from the moment of its arrival at the uterine wall. In the meantime, however, proponents of abortion have little reason to fear that zealous sheriffs and prosecutors will be seeking warrants to inspect wombs throughout the land, in search of fertilized ova to protect. That kind of hysteria should be beyond the reckonings offered by the urbane as they ponder the substantive question here. It is plain that there will be grounds of dissatisfaction on both sides. The defenders of abortion would have the disappointment of seeing abortions outlawed even at the earliest stages; the opponents of abortion would have no hope of restraining every clandestine move on the part of doctors to insert an IUD or issue a "morning after" pill, and no doubt many zygotes will be ambushed

---

[26] See Noonan, *supra*, note 2, p. 185 *et passim*.

on the way to the uterine wall. But the problems lingering here, as I say, are rather refined and intractable; nor are they, after all, the most pressing aspect of the problem constituted by abortion in America. For the sake of settling this particular question beyond peradventure, it cannot be defensible to put off the settlement of the main points in principle, which would save an overwhelming majority of the 1.5 million lives taken each year in abortions. And on the settlement of those points of principle, the dispute over the zygote, between its first day of life and its seventh, will have little bearing.

For the proponents of abortion there is a profitable constriction of vision in a discourse that would focus the entire dispute on a point at which the defense of human life must appeal persistently to the most sensitive moral imagination—the kind of imagination that would summon sympathy and protection for microscopic dots—while the advocacy of abortion can appeal to a stronger, "natural" sympathy for beings we can readily see—the beings who are convinced that their lives can be rescued only by having abortions. At the same time, our eyes would be diverted from the plain, grisly killing in the bulk that forms the routine experience of abortion in America for anyone who has eyes to see.

AFTER HER OWN abortion, Professor Magda Denes, for one, was willing to direct her eyes and look again, in a close, extended way, at the kinds of operations performed in cases like her own. Her study of an abortion clinic produced an account that was rare in its detail and candor, and it encompassed a telling description of the tools and methods that are employed in abortions. During the first trimester, the most common technique for abortion is dilatation and curettage. The cervix is dilated, and then the curette goes to work. A curette is a cutting instrument; it may be used by hand, or it may spin at the end of a vacuum pump that draws material from the uterus. But even when the vacuum pump is used, it is necessary to explore the cavity of the uterus with a curette, and any insertion of a sharp instrument into the uterus carries risks for the woman. As John Noonan has remarked, when the curette is "improperly used, the knife will cut the mother. Properly used, the knife will cut the unborn child." Noonan cites a description of the procedure as set forth in a medical text, *Techniques of Abortion*:

> The suction machine is turned on, and a finger is used to block the handle until a small amount of suction is obtained. ... A vacuum is created in the uterus. [The curette is rotated.] At any

point that material is felt flowing into the tube, motion is stopped until the flow stops. Then the slow up-and-down gradual rotation pattern is continued. Bloody fluid and bits of pink tissue will be seen flowing through the plastic tubing during the entire suction curettage. However, the procedure should be continued until the entire endometrial cavity is covered at least twice. . . . If no more tissue is obtained and the endometrial surface gives a consistently gritty resistance to the sharp edge of the curet, the procedure is finished.[27]

In a clinic studied by Magda Denes, this method was applied in one case to a woman carrying a fetus of about fifteen weeks in gestation. As the physician in charge remarked, "It's really too advanced a pregnancy for suction to work at the start, but I do it routinely anyway. There is nothing to lose and it often clears the way for the forceps." The figure identified as "Dr. Holtzman" further explained that "up to twelve weeks the machine gets everything out, but beyond that the pieces are too big to come through the tubing unless I take it apart with the large ovum forceps." What this procedure was like when carried out was portrayed in vivid detail by Denes:

> Holtzman begins to vacuum deep inside the patient. The tubing is transparent, and I see thick blood swirling and flowing toward the glass jar. "God-damn," Holtzman says, "I am getting nothing." It does not look like "nothing" to me. There is blood everywhere. The floor is spattered, the table drips, pools spread on Holtzman's green gown, tinting it purple. The glove hanging from the speculum [and collecting blood] has grown into a full sized inverted red hand, which now, through overflowing, itself bleeds into the wastebasket below.
> [The assistant] turns the machine off. Holtzman withdraws the suction tip, . . . and holds out his right hand. "Forceps please." Mr. Smith slaps into his hand what looks like over-sized ice-cube tongs. Holtzman pushes it into the vagina and tugs. He pulls out something, which he slaps on the instrument table. "There," he says. "A leg. You can always tell the fetal size best by the extremities. Fifteen weeks is right in this case." I turn to Mr. Smith. "What did he say?" "He pulled a leg off," Mr. Smith says. "Right here." He points to the instrument table, where there is a perfectly formed, slightly bent leg, about three inches long. It consists of a ripped thigh, a knee, a lower leg, a foot, and five toes. I start

[27] Quoted in *ibid.*, p. 166.

413

to shake very badly, but otherwise I feel nothing. Total shock is passionless.

"I have the rib cage now," Holtzman says, as he slams down another piece of the fetus. "That's one thing you don't want to leave behind because it acts like a ball valve and infects everything." Raising his voice and looking at the nurse, who stands next to Dr. Berkowitz, he says, "The table is a little bit too high. I am struggling." The nurse jumps to crank it lower. "That's better," Holtzman says. "There, I've got the head out now. . . ."[28]

When it comes to fetuses that are well into the second trimester, the most frequent method of abortion involves the injection of a saline solution into the amniotic fluid that surrounds the child. Within two hours, the child has been poisoned and its heart has stopped. At the same time, contractions begin for the mother and the fetus is expelled. In the clinic attended by Magda Denes the products of these operations were collected separately in buckets before they were discarded. Professor Denes visited the room containing the buckets and she began, with a mild presentiment of the fearful, to open the buckets and inspect the contents:

> I look inside the bucket in front of me. There is a small naked person in there floating in a bloody liquid—plainly the tragic victim of a drowning accident. But then perhaps this was no accident, because the body is purple with bruises and the face has the agonized tautness of one forced to die too soon. Death overtakes me in a rush of madness. Oh yes, I have seen this before. The face of a Russian soldier lying on a frozen snow-covered hill, stiff with death and cold. . . . Who says you can't go home again. A death factory is the same anywhere, and the agony of early death is the same anywhere.[29]

What Professor Denes has described, in chilling effect, are the operations that the Supreme Court has now freed people to "elect," without the need to show a justification or even the faintest comprehension of what occurs in this "elective surgery." In fact, the Court has even struck down local ordinances that required the patient to receive very precise information about the nature of the operation and the development of the fetus. Nothing in the decision on *Roe* v. *Wade* should have been incompatible with the notion of "informed consent"—that the patient understand the surgery she was electing, and

[28] Magda Denes, *In Necessity and Sorrow* (New York: Basic Books, 1976), p. 222.
[29] *Ibid.*, p. 60.

that she might even be made to reflect about the grounds on which surgical procedures may be justified. The Court rightly sensed, in these local statutes, an attempt to discourage people from choosing abortion. And yet, that animating purpose behind the statutes was quite separable in principle from the question of whether it is proper to ensure that patients have at least some rudimentary knowledge about the nature and consequences of the surgery they "elect." There have been cases, after all, in which women have changed their minds about an abortion as soon as they were made aware of some of the most elementary facts about the fetus they would abort. But what the Court seems to be saying now is that this interest in the informed consent of the patient cannot be honored if the consequence is to establish even a slight impediment to the exercise of the "right" to an abortion.[30]

The judges have also shown a special zeal to ensure that this freedom will be available even to minors and, in many cases, they have seemed insistent that this "choice" be pressed upon young teenagers who may not be as sure as the judges that an abortion would really serve their best interests. For young people, however, the world may become a more terrifying place once they come to understand the extraordinary, awful powers that Justice Blackmun and his colleagues have settled upon them. I recall here the reactions of a young woman, 19 or 20 years of age, who happened to be my own student. She had written a paper on abortion and had reviewed, with clarity, the arguments that were raised on both sides of the issue. She conceded the difficulty she had in forming a defense of abortion, but as in many other cases I had seen, she went on to say that her "feelings" would lead her to have an abortion if she herself became pregnant: at that moment she would become aware of a possible tension between the commands of moral judgment and the measures that would serve her "personal interests."

Of course, there was nothing novel in the discovery that what is morally necessary might not coincide with the things that serve our interests. The response of my student had become, by now, a rather routine evasion. At this moment, however, when she had created for herself a vivid sense of how she would feel, poised at the edge of a decision, with interests pressing on her from either side, she expressed an understanding which has eluded many of our better jural minds: "But isn't that," she asked, "why we have laws?" We have laws, that is, precisely because we cannot leave the vindication or avoidance of wrongs to the commands of self-interest. When our obligations collide

---

[30] See *Akron* v. *Akron Center for Reproductive Health*, 76 L. Ed. 2d 687 (1983).

with our "interests," even men and women with the best of intentions may need an additional support to firm them up in their strength to choose what is right and avoid what is wrong. The law could never expect that a 19-year-old, left to her own resources, would somehow manage to reconstruct, through her own wit, the moral understandings that were accumulated over many generations on the question of abortion.

When the law proscribed abortion, it was informed by an understanding far more impressive than that which most 19-year-olds—or, for that matter, most adults—could summon for themselves. When it forbade abortion, it made the procedure rare, clandestine, and subject to embarrassment. It enveloped the event, in other words, with an understanding that signaled its portentousness to anyone who might be tempted to resort to abortion for the most casual or thoughtless reasons. To the extent that the law discouraged young people from taking life for reasons that were casual and self-serving, it saved them from an experience that would enduringly haunt the thoughtful. For those who would never suffer the strains of serious reflection, the law spared them from the arrogance of believing that their own, untutored reflexes on a matter like abortion was as good—and as worthy of respect—as any other reflection that had been produced on the subject.

In Robert Bolt's play *A Man for All Seasons*, Thomas More argues to a young member of his family that "this country's planted thick with laws from coast to coast . . . and if you cut them down . . . d'you really think you could stand upright in the winds that would blow then?"[31] Thanks to Justice Blackmun and his colleagues, the restraints of the law have been swept away on the matter of abortion, and my student, along with many other young people, now found herself on the unshielded plain that was left, without the benefit of those laws which furnished guidance and shelter. They were freed from the obligation to consult or even inform their parents, and they were armed with a license to take life for reasons that could be entirely frivolous. In the name of "freeing" women, the courts have created burdens that most people—and especially most young people—should never be asked to carry by a compassionate law.

FOR THE UNBORN children who will be destroyed every year in this country, for the people of all ages who will harm themselves in choosing and performing abortions, it would be a benign, merciful service if the law would again teach the proper lessons and become the source

---

[31] Robert Bolt, *A Man For All Seasons* (New York: Random House, 1962), p. 66.

of rightful restraint. As I have already noted, efforts have been underway to pass a constitutional amendment that would override the decision of the Supreme Court in *Roe* v. *Wade*. But it is arguable that the laws may be changed decisively by Congress and the president through an act of ordinary legislation, without the need to amend the Constitution. At this writing, the possibility of a legislative remedy was being tested through a bill called the Human Life Act.[32] With this legislative project, the Congress would address itself directly to the question that Justice Blackmun and his colleagues professed they could not resolve: viz., the question of when human life begins. The congressional sponsors of this measure intended to provide the reasoning that the Court did not supply in *Roe* v. *Wade*. They intended to collect the evidence which established, as a necessary fact, that the offspring of *Homo sapiens* could not be anything other than human. From there, presumably, they would seek to show why the fetus could not be regarded as anything but a "person" in the eyes of the law—or why living, unborn children could be given the protection of the law, quite as much as terriers and sandhill cranes, even if they were not "persons."

If a bill of this kind became law, it would accomplish many of the same ends as a constitutional amendment: it would furnish a new premise for the courts and for the legislatures of the separate states, and it would permit the legislatures to protect unborn children, as most of them sought to protect these children before the Supreme Court overturned the laws on abortion. But this manner of addressing the legal problem has not been without controversy. A number of scholars of the Constitution (including some who had reservations about *Roe* v. *Wade*) see a danger of bringing about a radical alteration of our constitutional arrangements. Their concern is that the "constitutional" decisions of the Supreme Court should not be overruled through acts of ordinary legislation, for that arrangement would recognize, for the Congress, an authority to overturn at will the judgments that the Court arrives at in creating the "fundamental law" of the Constitution. These fears, I think, are surprisingly overstated. Scholars of the Constitution must know that if the Supreme Court fails to find the Congress persuasive, the Court may strike down the new legislation and the opponents of abortion may then find it necessary to seek a constitutional amendment. For some unaccountable reason, opponents of the Human Life Act seem unhinged by the prospect that this dispute

---

[32] The case for such a statute has been set forth by Stephen H. Galebach, who also participated in the drafting of the bill. See Galebach, "A Human Life Statute," *Human Life Review* (Winter 1981), pp. 5-33.

might be settled well short of such a confrontation between Congress and the Court—that the Court may in fact be persuaded by the reasoning produced by the Congress, and that it may be moved to change its mind.

Even if we set these considerations aside, however, the "dangers" projected here are dangers only if one accepts the constitutional theory held by opponents of the new bill. That constitutional theory, as it turns out, is in principle faulty; it is also historically mistaken. In point of fact, the architects of the Human Life Act would not revise the constitutional relations of the branches. They would restore the understanding that had been present from the beginning, an understanding shared by the Founders and by Lincoln: namely, that Congress and the president have quite as much standing as the Courts to act, in their own spheres, as interpreters of the Constitution. The understanding of the opposition rests on an assumption that the Supreme Court must be the final and unchallengeable authority on the meaning of the Constitution (apart, of course, from the authority of the people themselves in amending the Constitution). Hence the surety we find among judges that there is, beyond question now, a constitutional right to abortion, which came into being as soon as the Supreme Court articulated that right in *Roe* v. *Wade*. And for that reason, it has been assumed that any attempt on the part of a legislature to call that right into question must itself be unconstitutional.[33]

So far as I can see, this understanding has been enunciated only by men in judicial authority, or by lawyers outside official authority, who have connected their own sentiments and interests to the authority of the courts. But the Constitution is utterly silent on any doctrine of that kind. It seems to be assumed today, even by justices of the Supreme Court, that this authority of the Court was established in the landmark case of *Marbury* v. *Madison*. And yet, no such understanding was set forth in that decision. Chief Justice Marshall argued compellingly that the Constitution had to be regarded as "fundamental law," and in that event, "those who apply the rule to particular cases, must of necessity expound and interpret that rule. If two laws conflict with each other, the courts must decide on the operation of each."[34]

This "judicial duty," as Marshall described it, was modestly drawn. Marshall simply recognized that the judges had an obligation to be governed by the Constitution as they sought to settle the particular case that was submitted for their judgment. As Professor Herbert

---

[33] See, as a clear case in point, Judge Jon Newman (Connecticut) in *Roe* v. *Norton*, 408 F. Supp. 660 (1975).

[34] *Marbury* v. *Madison*, 1 Cranch 137, at 177, 178 (1803).

Wechsler would later observe, "Federal courts, including the Supreme Court, do not pass on constitutional questions because there is a special function vested in them to enforce the Constitution. . . . They do so rather for the reason that they must decide a litigated issue that is otherwise within their jurisdiction and in doing so must give effect to the supreme law of the land."[35] In that sense, nothing was claimed for the judges that could not have been claimed for other officers of the government: If, for example, the president were faced with an act of Congress that drafted into the military service only members of a minority race, would he be obliged to judge the measure only on grounds of utility? Or would he be warranted in considering whether the legislation offended a principle rooted in the Constitution? And if he thought that the legislation was incompatible with the Constitution, he would be obliged, quite as much as any judge, to give primacy to this question of principle in the cases that came before him.

This was the understanding held by Thomas Jefferson and Andrew Jackson, as well as by Lincoln, and without that understanding, Lincoln's resistance to the *Dred Scott* case[36] could not have been comprehensible. In that infamous case, the Court "established" that blacks could not have the standing of citizens to sue in the courts, and that no man could be deprived of his property in slaves, even if he brought that property into territories in which slavery had been forbidden by Congress. In the spirit of respect for law, Lincoln was willing to respect the disposition made by the Court in settling the fate of Mr. Dred Scott in this particular case. But he and his party would "oppose that decision as a political rule which shall be binding on the . . . members of Congress or the President to favor no measure that does not actually concur with the principles of that decision."[37]

Lincoln was willing, that is, to accept the judgment as "binding in

[35] Herbert Wechsler, "The Courts and the Constitution," 65 *Columbia University Law Review*, 1001, at 1006 (1965). On the Court itself, the same point was made quite precisely by Justice Sutherland in *Adkins* v. *Children's Hospital*: "From the authority to ascertain and determine the law in a given case, there necessarily results, in case of conflict, the duty to declare and enforce the rule of the supreme law and reject that of an inferior act of legislation, which, transcending the Constitution, is of no effect and binding on no one. This is not the exercise of a substantive power to review and nullify acts of Congress, for no such substantive power exists. It is simply a necessary concomitant of the power to hear and dispose of a case or controversy properly before the court, to the determination of which must be brought the test and measure of the law." 261 U.S. 525, at 544 (1923).

[36] *Dred Scott* v. *Sandford*, 19 Howard 393 (1857).

[37] *The Collected Works of Abraham Lincoln*, ed. Roy P. Basler (New Brunswick: Rutgers University Press, 1953), vol. III, p. 255 (debate with Douglas at Quincy, October 13, 1858).

any case, upon the parties to a suit, as to the object of that suit, . . . [and] limited to that particular case."[38] What he was not obliged to accept was the *principle* or the broader rule of law that the Court was trying to create in the case. As Alexander Hamilton remarked in *The Federalist #78*, the Court had no control of the sword or the purse— it had "neither force nor will, but merely judgment; and must ultimately depend upon the aid of the executive arm even for the efficacy of its judgments."[39] The power of the Court would ultimately depend, then, on the force of its reasoned argument. With that sense of the matter, Lincoln insisted that other officers of the government could not be obliged to accept any new "law" created by the Court unless they, too, were persuaded by the force of the Court's reasoning. In Lincoln's judgment, no other understanding could be reconciled with the logic of the American Constitution in its separation of powers. To hold to the contrary would be to accept the possibility that "the policy of the government, upon vital questions, affecting the whole people, [could] be irrevocably fixed by decisions of the Supreme Court, the instant they are made, *in ordinary litigation between parties, in personal actions.*" And in that event, "the people will have ceased, to be their own rulers, having, to that extent, practically resigned their government, into the hands of that eminent tribunal."[40]

If we apply this understanding to the current problem of abortion in the law, the situation would be viewed in this way: the Supreme Court alone has propounded a constitutional right to an abortion, but the president and Congress have not been persuaded by the Court. Under these conditions, it cannot be assumed just yet that any legislation which restricts abortion would be unconstitutional on its face.

It has not been regarded as unthinkable, in other words, that Congress may take a different view on a matter of constitutional interpretation from the view taken by the Court, and that the Congress need not be obliged to recede in favor of the Court. In recent years, there have been occasions when this understanding has been applied by liberals as well as conservatives. In the case of liberals, there was a willingness, in 1965, to have the Congress set aside, in a casual way, the literacy requirement for voting in New York State, even though the Supreme Court had not found that requirement to be unconstitutional.[41] As for the conservatives, there was a continuing attempt

---

[38] *Ibid.*, vol. IV, p. 268 (First Inaugural Address, March 4, 1861).

[39] *The Federalist #78* (New York: Modern Library, n.d.), p. 504.

[40] Lincoln, *supra*, note 37, vol. IV, p. 268. Emphasis added.

[41] See *Katzenbach* v. *Morgan*, 384 U.S. 641 (1966). The Court acquiesced in this move, but Justice Harlan pointed out the implications of the decision in his dissenting opinion. See 659-71, especially 666-68.

throughout the 1970's to restrain the disposition of the courts to order busing and "racial balancing" in the public schools. But, leaving these recent cases aside, there is a more dramatic precedent to support this power on the part of Congress to act, along with the president and the Court, as an interpreter of the Constitution. In June 1862, Congress abolished slavery in all existing territories of the United States, and from all territories that might be formed or acquired in the future. As Professor James Randall would later write of this legislation, "Congress passed and Lincoln signed a bill which, by ruling law according to Supreme Court interpretation was unconstitutional."[42] What the president and Congress had done, in the most explicit and direct way, was to counter the decision of the Court in the *Dred Scott* case.

And yet, even before this legislation was passed, the administration was compelled to face the implications of the *Dred Scott* case—and the question of constitutional authority—in a number of administrative decisions. During the first year of the Lincoln administration, a black man who was an inventor applied for a patent in Boston, and he was refused by the Federal Patent Office on the grounds that, according to the ruling of the Court in *Dred Scott*, he was not a citizen of the United States. That same year (1861) a young black man from Boston applied for a passport to study in France, but the State Department refused to issue the kind of passport that it extended to U.S. citizens. Once again it was assumed that the case would be governed by the *Dred Scott* decision. It is worth noticing that in neither case were the circumstances even remotely similar to the ingredients that described the *Dred Scott* case. The blacks were not former slaves; the rights they sought to exercise did not depend on their sojourn in a territory of the United States; and there were no former owners seeking to vindicate their rights of property in slaves. The executive agencies in these cases were doing precisely what Lincoln argued need not, and ought not, be done: they were applying what they took to be the *principle* in the *Dred Scott* case to situations quite far from any circumstances present in that case. *That* Lincoln was committed to resist, and the administration reversed both decisions: both the patent and the passport were issued. A year later the administration firmed up the legal grounds for its acts when the attorney general published his legal opinion that free blacks born in the United States were to be regarded as citizens.[43]

---

[42] James G. Randall, *The Civil War and Reconstruction* (Boston: D.C. Heath & Company, 1937), p. 136.

[43] These cases are recorded in *The Work of Charles Sumner* (Boston: Lee & Shepard, 1880), vol. V, pp. 497-98; vol. VI, p. 144. See also the opinion published by Attorney

But if we hold to the view of constitutional authority that has become dominant in our own time—the view held by opponents of the Human Life Act—these decisions by the Lincoln administration would have to be regarded as unconstitutional. They can be regarded as plausible and constitutional only on the basis of the understanding held by Lincoln about the authority to interpret the Constitution: that the separate branches were warranted in applying, in their own spheres, in the decisions that came before them, their own understandings of the Constitution. If the acts of the Lincoln administration may be regarded as justified in these cases, then it must follow that it would be quite as proper today for the administration and the Congress to apply, in their own spheres, their own judgment about the constitutional authority to restrict abortions.

It is true, of course, that the administrative and legislative acts of 1862 would later be supported by the Thirteenth Amendment—much in the way that a Human Life Act might one day have the additional support of a Human Life Amendment. But in the absence of such an amendment, the legislation that protects unborn children would stand on the same plane as the legislation signed by Lincoln before the advent of the Thirteenth Amendment: it would represent an attempt by the administration and Congress to engage the Supreme Court in a continuing dialogue on the question of what precisely the Constitution commands. If the Court finds this legislation unacceptable, it may strike it down and force the matter to be settled through a constitutional amendment (or through the appointment of judges who share the perspectives of the administration and Congress). On the other hand, it is not inconceivable that the Court might be persuaded by the Congress on the one decisive question it managed to avoid in *Roe* v. *Wade*: On what ground of principle may the human fetus be reckoned as anything other than a human being? As the Supreme Court ponders the evidence and arguments offered by the Congress, it may be induced to consider just why it is being forced to keep addressing these questions—just why, in the years since *Roe* v. *Wade*, a majority of the public continues to be unpersuaded by the reasons offered by the Court. In this spirit—the spirit of a government of shared powers and reasoned exchange—the Court may be encouraged to take a sober second look at what it has done and to consider, with detachment and modesty, that it might have been mistaken.

General Bates under the heading of "Citizenship" (November 29, 1862) in *Opinions of the Attorneys General*, vol. X, pp. 382-413.

XVIII

CONCLUSION

In a recent article appearing in a reputable journal of ethics, a sociologist reviewed two books which sought to marshal the evidence and the reasons that would argue against abortion. Rather than address the substantive arguments in these books, the reviewer hit upon the ingenious device of denying that reasons had any meaning or consequence in matters of moral dispute. "So long," he wrote, "as all reasons are created equal, abortion will remain a form of birth control like any other."[1] In the *Encyclopedia of Bioethics* (by any reckoning, a respectable, scholarly enterprise), two writers sought to explain why it is "impossible today" to say that suicide is wrong and that the government would be justified in intervening to prevent a person from taking his own life. That understanding has been rendered untenable, they thought, by certain "facts" which were apparently more accessible to the modern age. First among those facts was "the moral pluralism of Western society":[2]

> Acts of self-destruction will be described and evaluated differently by different people, probably on the basis of their education in diverse . . . communities of moral discourse. If Western societies at the end of the twentieth century agree on basic moral principles, these are quite abstract and general. If perception, description, and evaluation of acts of self-destruction lead to little consensus, it is even more difficult to come to consensus on the morality of interference with such acts.

Had these statements been overheard in a parking lot or in the stands at a baseball game, or had they been offered by a reflective waiter, there would have been nothing remarkable about them. They would have been but further examples of the understanding of morals that has become current in our public discourse. One reason that our public discourse may be so philosophically untutored, however, is that statements of this kind can in fact be made routinely, not by salesmen on holiday, but by professional commentators on ethics, who would

[1] In case the point might have been missed, the review essay bore the title "Abortion and the Equality of Reasons," *Hastings Center Report* (June 1980), pp. 44-45.

[2] "Suicide," in *Encyclopedia of Bioethics* (New York: Free Press, 1978), vol. IV, pp. 1618-26, at 1624.

423

ordinarily be in a position to shape the minds of public men if they had a subject to teach. But if we were to accept the premises underlying these statements, there literally could not be a discipline of ethics or moral reflection; there would be no point in writing extended articles *to reason* about moral questions; and certainly there would be no rationale for journals of ethics. To say that "all reasons are created equal," is to say that, in morals, no reason is better than any other— which is to say simply that there is no truth in matters of morals. If there were, then statements which embody truths would have, after all, a compelling claim to be regarded as more valid and authoritative than propositions which are either false or uncertain. The assertion that all reasons are equal is comprehensible only if it is taken to mean that moral judgments reduce finally to matters of personal or subjective feeling, which cannot be judged true or false. With this understanding, as I have sought to show, there cannot strictly be any such thing as morals, for there would be no ground on which we may condemn any act done by another person which that person himself happens to approve.

But if morals do not involve judgments about the things that are universally right or wrong, justified or unjustified, then what is it that we do when we seek, in portentous and tangled essays, to discuss the rightness and wrongness of such things as abortion? Are we simply seeking to discover whether the people who have abortions genuinely approve of what they are doing, or whether they are acting without an awareness of the "moral" views established within their respective "communities of moral discourse"? The study of morals would have to dissolve, then, into an aimless exercise of survey research, in which we merely document the varied and exotic notions of morality held by different tribes in our society. In that case, the discipline of morals would never involve an attempt to establish the justice of any matter— to determine the things that people *ought* to do or refrain from doing regardless of what their personal beliefs or feelings inclined them to do.

As for our commentators on suicide, they are victims of the same self-inflicted fallacies. The root fallacy, of course, is ancient and fundamental: viz., that the absence of agreement or consensus establishes the absence of truth. We have already had the chance to consider this proposition at length. It must be exposed as soon as one comes to the recognition that in morals, as in mathematics, our knowledge must be founded ultimately on certain first principles or necessary truths, and if those truths are indeed true, then their validity cannot be affected in any way by the presence or absence of a consensus. Their universal truth is guaranteed by their own necessity, and that truth must be indifferent to the question of whether it is universally recognized. Surely it did not require the advances of the modern age to discover that people often disagree on questions of right and wrong. What is novel in our day is that we now have scholars who are apparently unable to recognize that they stand at the threshold of contradiction whenever they assert that knowledge must be rooted in agreement. These scholars must ever make themselves hostage to the churlish critic who is prepared, in turn, to assert that this fundamental premise, this ground of all their convictions in matters moral, is one that does not command *his* agreement. At that moment, our modern relativists may discover that their conviction about the relativity of moral truth is a conviction they treat as nothing less than a necessary truth, which retains its validity in all places, even in the face of disagreement.

If it were correct that the presence of disagreement marks the absence of truth, then it would have to follow, again, that there could be no morals. It could never be possible to condemn, in principle, the acts performed by another, for there would obviously be a disagreement between the person who performs the act and the person who does the judging. And in the presence of disagreement, so we have been told, there can be no moral truth. Therefore, there can be no basis on which we may judge or restrain another person when he happens to approve of what he is doing. Once again, if we were to ask, "What does it mean, then, to deliberate about the rightness or wrongness of any act?" the answer would have to be that we simply establish, as "moral anthropologists," the views people hold about the nature of what is just or desirable. We should be hard put to explain, however, precisely what is meant by "just" or "desirable." With an investment of about two minutes, the average schoolboy can be made to understand that his words are incomprehensible unless he understands by "just" or "desirable" the things which are right or wrong, good or bad, quite apart from subjective taste and personal feelings. He would soon acknowledge, in other words, a logic that permits us to speak about propositions we are obliged to respect, propositions whose validity is indifferent to the question of whether we agree with them or not.

As I have suggested, we can begin working our way out from under this collection of fallacies if we would simply notice in the first place that they render the meaning of morals itself incoherent. That is to say, we can make ourselves immune to the fallacies which beguile even some of our professional commentators on ethics if we begin with an awareness of the logic of morals itself. If we come to understand the difference between a moral proposition and a statement of personal taste, if we can give an account of truths which must be "necessary" and categorical, and if we can explain why the existence of morals stands as one of those necessary truths, then we can do far more than resist the fallacies of our conventional discourse. We would have the core of a discipline that must, perforce, endure. And so, if the commentators I have quoted manage to reproduce their kind, the fallacies offered by their progeny will be embarrassed fifty or one hundred years from now as they encounter, persistently, the implications which arise from the logic of morals and from the notion of a "rational creature," who has the freedom to choose between right and wrong.

I think I can offer, then, some final words of assurance to the readers who have followed me through these chapters. Generations from now, the person who insists that there is no truth—or who claims that he does not recognize the existence of space and time—will still suffer the embarrassment of self-contradiction. That luckless fellow who is thrown out the window of a tall building, and breaks an awning on his way down to earth, will still not be responsible for the damage which he did not intend and which he was powerless to avoid. Even if the cause of "animal liberation" should become more advanced than it has in our own day, people will still not be signing labor contracts with their cows or horses, and they will still not think it particularly informative or necessary to seek the consent of their resident dogs before they would presume to govern them. But those who continue to be aware of the differences in nature which separate human beings from animals will continue to understand that creatures who are capable of giving and understanding reasons deserve to be ruled only with their consent. At the same time, regimes which visit destruction on people because of their race or ethnicity, without making discriminations of innocence and guilt, will continue to mark themselves as despicable. The wrongness of their acts will be regarded, by men and women of understanding, as categorically, unconditionally wrong. That wrongness will not be lessened by the attenuations of circumstance; it will not be mitigated by matters of degree; and it will not be effaced by any claim to serve a larger "good." The willingness to inflict punishment without respecting the difference between innocence and guilt will be taken as the definitive and lasting mark of the corrupt, because its wrongness will continue to arise from the logic of morals itself, and it will continue to be wrong so long as the logic of morals itself endures.

Thus it is, and thus it shall ever be, for in the nature of things it cannot be otherwise.

426

Hadley Arkes is William Nelson Cromwell
Professor of Jurisprudence and Political Science
at Amherst College.

*Library of Congress
Cataloging-in-Publication Data*

Arkes, Hadley.
First things.

Includes index.
1. Social justice.   2. Ethics.   I. Title.
HM216.A65 1986   170   85-43267
ISBN 0-691-07702-9 (alk. paper)
ISBN 0-691-02247-X (pbk.)